Pricing

The New Frontier

Gábor REKETTYE

Jonathan LIU

To Heather

Enjoy.

Jonathan

In developing and fast moving economies like India, getting the pricing strategy right is a necessity for the short and long term future of the firm. The pricing decision will impact on the profitability and ultimately on the performance of the firm. Executives and managers responsible making pricing decisions will find this book useful and informative in shedding light on an area that is complicate and complex.

– **Dr M.K. Nandakumar**, Associate Professor of Strategic Management, Indian Institute of Management, Kozhikode, India.

Leading technological development across the world requires an in-depth understanding of the impact of the pricing decision and business strategy. This book will give its readers a clear understanding of impact of the pricing decision on the industry, the customer and its competitors. I fully recommend and endorse this book.

– **Jeff C.K. Lim**, BU Deputy CEO at ASM Pacific Technology Ltd. Singapore.

Pricing of goods and services is a critical decision that creates immediate competitive advantage. This book explains the principles of pricing clearly and concisely. It seamlessly knits concept and practice. It is a useful text book but also useful to practicing managers charged with challenging task of pricing goods and services. I strongly recommend the book to practitioners and students.

– **Professor Abby Ghobadian** FBAM, FAcSS, CCMI, Professor of Management, Henley Business School, United Kingdom.

At a time when almost continuous change is disrupting nearly all industries and the internet is putting ever more power in the hands of the customer, a book that treats pricing with substance and foresight is a welcome addition to the market.

– **Professor John R. Schermerhorn, Jr.**, O'Bleness Professor Emeritus, Ohio University, United States

In contemporary business pricing is much more than just the money equivalent of the product value. This book provides a high-quality review of different concepts and issues regarding pricing from different stakeholders' perspectives. It can be recommended both as students' textbook as well as a managers' toolkit for making strategic and tactical pricing decisions.

– **Professor Mirna Leko Šimić**, Professor of Marketing at Faculty of Economics at J.J. Strossmayer University of Osijek, Croatia

Price is the value that is attached to a product or service and is usually the result of complex set of calculations, research and risk analysis. This book provides comprehensive and understandable strategies and tactics that one may use to price a product or service in our current the multi-faceted operating environment. It is a great resource for both practitioners and academics.

– **Dr Dolores Rinke**, CPA, Professor Emerita, Purdue University, United States

In a fast-changing world with fierce competition, pricing has been increasingly the new frontier and battle field for business operations. Dynamic pricing needs to be deployed as the brand new strategy for global organizations to gain competitive advantages and sustainable profit growth. This book provides insightful knowledge of the dynamics of setting price in a networked global context, and enables academics and professionals to have a clear understanding of the principle and practice.

– **Dr Xinping Shi**, Associate Professor of Information and Operations Management, Hong Kong Baptist University, Hong Kong SAR China.

Getting the pricing of products and services right is challenging and difficult. It is more complicated in a globalized world and further challenging when it is across different types of economies. This book will offer guidance in setting and negotiating prices for trading across borders and on the digital platform, and will prove useful for practitioners and students. I highly recommend the book.

– **Professor Vincent XG Qi**, PhD, FRAI, Wolfson College, University of Cambridge; Marcel Mauss Chair Distinguished Professor of Global Supply Chain Management and Business Anthropology, Anshan Normal University in China.

Pricing

The New Frontier

Gábor REKETTYE

Jonathan LIU

TRANSNATIONAL PRESS LONDON
2018

Pricing - The New Frontier

By Gábor REKETTYE and Jonathan LIU

First Published in 2018 by TRANSNATIONAL PRESS LONDON in the United Kingdom, 12 Ridgeway Gardens, London, N6 5XR, UK.

www.tplondon.com

Paperback

ISBN: 978-1-910781-33-3

Cover Design: Gizem Çakır

Cover Image: Matthew Henry (https://burst.shopify.com/@matthew_henry)

www.tplondon.com

CONTENTS

ABOUT THE AUTHORS

Gábor REKETTYE, MSc, PhD, DSc, is Professor Emeritus at the Institute of Marketing and Tourism, University of Pécs, Faculty of Business & Economics. He is Honorary Professor at University of Szeged, Faculty of Business Administration. He received his master's degree at the Budapest University of Economics, and his PhD at the Hungarian Academy of Sciences, both in economics. Dr Rekettye is the author of several textbooks, which are taught at different Universities in Hungary. In addition, he has written over 300 publications in Hungary and abroad. In his carrier he was working in industry, in foreign trade and for five years he has served as commercial counsellor of Hungary in Tokyo, Japan. Between 1993 and 1996 he was the Dean of the Business School. For 16 years, between 1993 and 2009 he was heading the Marketing Department of the School. In 2003, Gábor Rekettye received the highest scientific title in Hungary, 'The Doctor of the Hungarian Academy of Sciences' (DSc). In 2005, he was elected to Chairman of the Committee of Marketing Science at the Hungarian Academy of Sciences. He served in this position till 2011. In 2013 he received the Hungarian Order of Merit Officer Cross from the President of Hungary.

Jonathan LIU is Professor of Global Business Management. He is the Lead on research and scholarship in the Faculty of Business and Management at Regent's University London. Jonathan teaches and researches in Entrepreneurship and Venture Management. He started his academic career as lecturer at Aston University and moved to Middlesex University as a senior lecturer. In 2002, he became Middlesex University's Professor of Chinese Management. He joined Newport University in 2006 as Professor of Management and was their Associate Dean for Research and Enterprise as well. Jonathan is the Editor-in-Chief of the *International Journal of Business Performance Management.* He is on the editorial board of the *Journal of Islamic Marketing*, and book review editor of the *Journal of Technology Management* in China. Jonathan publishes extensively and has over a hundred articles and ten books published in Business and Management. Jonathan is on the Council of the National Conference of Universities Professors, a Council member of the Universities China Committee in London, a Fellow of Higher Education Academy and a Chartered Fellow of the Chartered Management Institute. Jonathan is a trustee and Chairman of the board of the Directors of Ming-Ai (London) Institute.

PART 1. PRICING BASICS

CHAPTER 1. PRICING IN FOCUS

OBJECTIVE 1 To discuss the importance of 'pricing' as an operational and strategy tool in managing today's modern business in a global and turbulent environment.

OBJECTIVE 2 To explore the role that pricing plays in company functions, and explain the key goals of organization policies, which among market conditions can only be achieved with accurate pricing policies.

OBJECTIVE 3 To illustrate the challenges, sophistication and complex requirements of establishing a competitive pricing policy in the new economic and technology driven environments.

1.1. Introduction

Prices play an important role in all areas of the economy and society (Figure 1.1.). This role is present in all decisions made by people, families, communities, business ventures and non-profit organizations; what is more, the price of certain products can have a deep impact on the national economies or even the whole world market.

Figure 1.1. Prices, the economy and the society

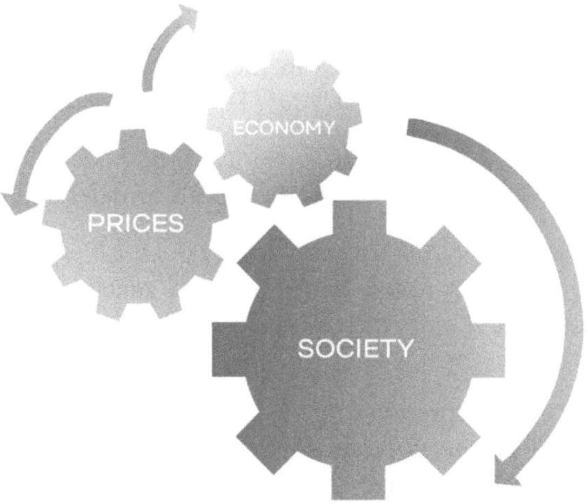

The relative balance between supply and demand is of critical importance for the functioning of national economies. In market economies, this equilibrium can be achieved through the *connecting role that prices play*. As far as the operation of businesses is concerned, there is another fact that should not be disregarded, namely: while money can flow out of the firms through a number of channels, there

is typically only one way available for the inflow: the sale of their products and/or services, i.e. through their prices.

EXHIBIT 1.1. AN EXPERIMENT WITH THE GOOGLE SEARCH ENGINE

If your search for a term produces a high number of results, you have reason to believe that the term in question is either widely used, or very important. Well, on September 2, 2017 the authors entered the term 'price' and its equivalents in major languages into the search engine and ended up with the following results (in about half a second for each term):

- English (price): 5 240 million results
- French (prix): 825 million results
- German (Preis): 415 million results
- Hungarian (ár): 160 million results
- Italian (Prezzo): 272 million results
- Polish (cena): 712 million results
- Spanish (precio) 1 040 million results

This leads us to the conclusion that price – whether we like it or not – is one of the most important phenomena that stay with us all our life.

Every manager is fully aware of the above-described situation, yet – surprisingly enough – they seem to know very little about prices or pricing. Most of the time prices are set either intuitively or by the rule of thumb. Even if well-founded methods and rules are available for price setting, they rarely go beyond the traditional method of costs + mark-ups in spite of the strong criticism, marketing experts have expressed for decades. This is also one of the dominant strategies companies use in the euro-zone. Commissioned by the European Central Bank in 2005, Fabiani and his research team conducted a survey involving 11,000 firms and found that 54% of all businesses in the euro-zone used the principle of cost + mark-up in their price-setting practice. (Fabiani et al. 2005, 14). There are basically two reasons that make this method so popular with company managers:

- it is relatively simple and easy to grasp, consequently the task of pricing can be delegated to lower levels of management, and
- this method helps them give the impression that they follow honest business practices since they do not make the buyers pay for more than the costs they incurred and a fair profit that is generally accepted by society.

In contrast with this, marketing teaches us that costs represent only one important group of considerations that businesses should bear in mind in the course of pricing. Parallel with the transformation of a sellers' market into a buyers' market, and expansion of global competition, an increasing number of CEOs is bound to learn - and often the hard way– that market criteria represent an equally important, if not more important, element of pricing. It is this recognition that serves as the philosophical basis for the market-oriented approach of this book to prices and pricing.

EXHIBIT 1.2. HISTORICAL CURIOSITIES

"Dealing with prices" has a considerably longer history than economics or even marketing. While the history of marketing is hardly a century old, and economics dates back a couple of centuries, writings related to prices appeared several thousand years ago. The Code of Babylon, issued by Hammurapi 4 000 years ago, contains a host of rules concerning prices.

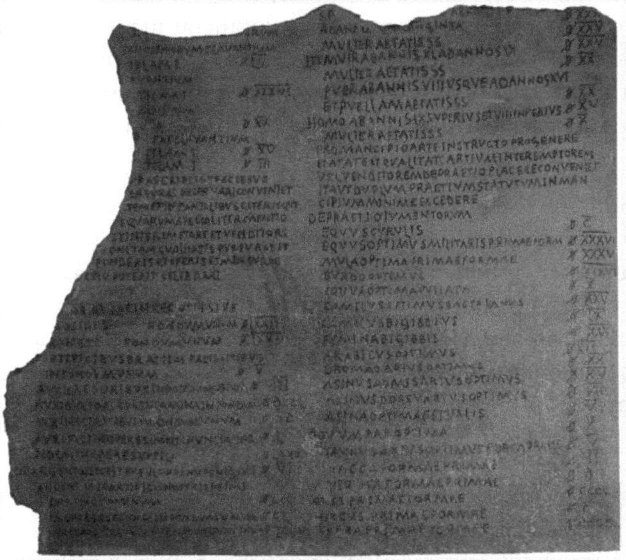

Another example is the decree on prices issued by Emperor Diocletian in 301 A.D. that can be read even in our days (titled in Latin: AEdictum De Pretiis Rerum Venalium). In this decree, the Emperor set maximum prices for the whole Roman Empire based on the principle that prices should be correct and fair. In the Middle Ages, the Catholic church also continued the policy of fair prices, thus protecting the poor and stipulating that merchants and craftsmen should not sell their products at prices that exceeded the value of the materials and labour used to produce them.

Picture: Edict on Maximum Prices Diocletian piece in Berlin.jpg MatthiasKabel CC BY-SA 3.0

1.2. Early 21st century: Increasing importance of prices

Price is the value expressed in money (or in some other item representing value) that buyers pay for products and services. Similar to the notion of product that is used in the broad meaning of the term, the notion of price also includes every item that is used for payment, although occasionally denoted by different terms. The following items can take the function of price:

- Charges (motorway toll, rent, tuition fee, expert fee, etc.)
- Fees (dentist's fee, expert's honorarium, etc.)
- Subscription (to papers/periodicals, TV programmes, etc.)
- Interest paid as price of credit received
- Commission, price of the activities performed by agent or consignee
- Tariff, expressing the price of gas or electricity
- Due paid for certain services provided by the state

A tip given in recognition of a good service also functions as price and similarly a salary can also be interpreted as price. We often say: the price of a good marketing expert is so-and-so today.

Management attitudes to the importance of prices have shown a cyclical nature in the period between WW2 and the present day. In the post-war years - i.e. at a time when the development of marketing practice enjoyed an international upswing – prices played an important or even dominant role in the

thinking of management and within marketing (Diller 1999, p. 39.). Contemporary authors devoted as much as 20-30 % of their works on marketing to the price function. The post-war period of reconstruction was characterized by quick recovery of the economy, the extension of markets and increase in consumption and living standards. From then on the price function seemed to be losing importance (perhaps the years of the oil crisis can be considered as an exception) compared to other marketing areas. The turn of the millennium was followed by a series of developments in international economy that – culminating in the economic depression starting in 2008 – led to a dramatic increase in the importance of prices and price management. This process was obviously triggered by the changes in consumer relationship to prices under pressure from the trends observed in the world economy.

A survey conducted in 1993-94 found that both the European and American managers expressed the opinion that - of all market related fields - prices caused the worst headache or exercised the strongest pressure on them (Simon 2009). Ten years later another study produced similar findings. The summary report on the McKinsey Global Survey of Business Executives dated November 2004 concluded that - of all the market related areas - pricing is the one they are mostly concerned with and where the impact of competition is felt to the highest degree. The reason is that a small change in the prices has a deeper impact on company profits than several other factors, like changes in costs.

EXHIBIT 1.3. THE IMPACT OF PRICE CHANGES ON PROFITS

Let us assume that prices set by the company contain 30% of fixed costs, 60% of variable costs and 10% goes for profit. If all other factors are taken to be constant, a 1% increase in the price improves the profit rate by 10%. A 1% improvement in variable costs will make the profit grow by 6 %, while a 1% decrease in fixed costs will result in a 3% growth in profit.

Marn and colleagues (Marn et al., 2004, 5) made this calculation using data of the year 2002, the so-called Global 1200 (the world's 1,200 biggest companies quoted at the stock exchange.) They also examined the impact of volume increase on the profit. Their results are shown in the diagram below.

Figure 1.2. The effects on profit in percentage

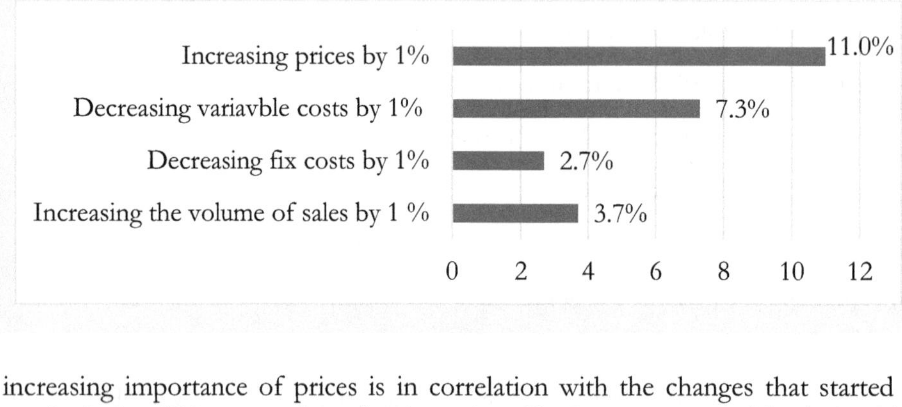

This increasing importance of prices is in correlation with the changes that started in the world economy in the late 20th century from the viewpoint of both consumers and businesses. The processes beginning at that time have become more and more decisive in the 21st century and we have reason to believe that their impact is going to stay with us, in all probability, in the coming decades as well. Let us see now what these impacts are.

1.2.1. The impact of global climate change, the emergence of the requirement of sustainable development.

Potential impacts of climate change have been the subject of discussion by scientists for a few decades already. However, in the first decade after 2000 we witnessed an acceleration of the extreme climatic events that have forced the actors of the economy and society to take the requirement of sustainability more and more seriously. The influence of a more socially responsible behaviour adopted by consumers and corporations on products and prices cannot be questioned. This impact can be detected in the gap between the costs or prices of developing and consuming or using environmentally friendly products, the emergence of consumer repulsion towards energy-wasting products, the demand for such products, the currently higher price of environmentally-friendly energy, the differences in the cost of operation of products using this kind of energy, etc...

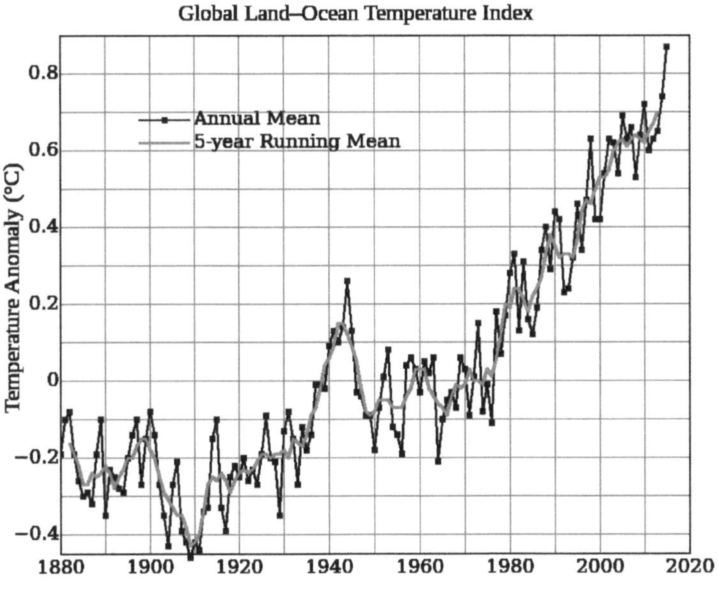

Photo: Public Domain File:Global Temperature Anomaly.svg, Created: 21 January 2016

1.2.2. The global crisis of 2008-2010 and its aftermath

By 2009, the recession that started in 2008 became global and affected the whole world economy - although it reached different levels of intensity in different countries or regions. Demand for several commodity categories diminished, turnover fell, and prices went down as a result.

Consumer behaviour changed in many respects: consumers became more price-sensitive and spent more time comparing the prices and the value offered by various products. Forecasts say that these changes in consumer behaviour may stay with us in the long run as well, even after the economy has gone back to normal. The after-effects of the crisis will be felt for a long time to come. The so-far unsolved problems of the victims of over-crediting, lack of trust in investments due to the excessive spending of certain countries and the unpredictable fluctuations in exchange rates could be mentioned as best examples to illustrate this point. This situation greatly influences the attitude of market actors to prices.

1.2.3. Economic power shift in the world

In the second decade of the 21st century we can witness the further rapid growth of large developing countries. Due to their lower wage level, the so-called emerging countries will become market and

cost leaders in the markets of a large number of products and consequently key factors in the price policy will apply. Their leading role is well illustrated by PriceWaterhouseCooper's' forecasts, which say that by 2014 the E7 countries (Brazil, China, India, Indonesia, Mexico, Russia, and Turkey) took over the lead in the world's GDP production and by 2050 it is expected to more than double that of the G7 (Canada, France, Germany, Italy, Japan, the UK, and the US) GDP (Figure 1.4.).

1.2.4. Acceleration of technological processes in the era of the fourth industrial revolution
We live now in the era of the fourth industrial revolution (called Industry 4.0). Its consequences are hard to foresee. The four industrial revolutions are illustrated in Figure 1.5.

EXHIBIT 1.4. IMPACT OF THE RECESSION ON HOUSEHOLD SPENDING IN THE US

In the fourth quarter of 2008 the total amount spent by households (in current prices) fell 2.0 per cent. This was the first fall in the value of household spending since 1968. Spending then fell for a further two quarters in the US.

The volume of goods and services purchased by households peaked in quarter four 2007, before falling by 0.7 per cent in the first quarter of 2008. This fall preceded the start of the recession period by one quarter and was the biggest single quarter reduction in the volume of goods and services bought by households since the 1990's recession. The reduction in volume of household spending continued for five more quarters, falling to the lowest level since 2005 (a fall of 6.5 per cent). By quarter three 2011, over two years after the recession's lowest point in 2009 quarter two, the volume of goods and services purchased by households had only recovered 1.0 per cent.

Figure 1.3. Household spending

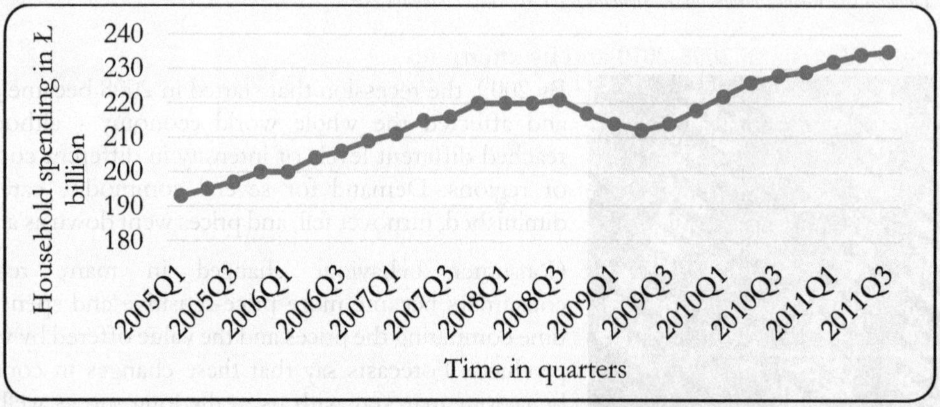

Source: Peter Gittins and Simon Luke: Impact of the recession on household spending, Office for National Statistics, 21 February 2012, http://webarchive.nationalarchives.gov.uk/20160105160709/http://www.ons.gov.uk/ons/dcp171766_256980.pdf

The Sogeti institution research group, named VINTlabs (Vision - Inspiration – Navigation – Trends) described in 2013, that the elements of a "smarter world" - social media, smart phones, analytics, the cloud, Internet of things - constitute such an interdependent and co-operating system (Figure 1.6.), that it is possible to create smarter things and make life easier.

From the point of view of pricing there will be certain consequences:

- There is a great probability the cyber era will change the value preferences of people - as Boem et al. coin it - "Smact is naturally the ongoing story of the automation that is intervening to an ever-increasing extent in life itself."

Figure 1.4. Expansion of the developing world

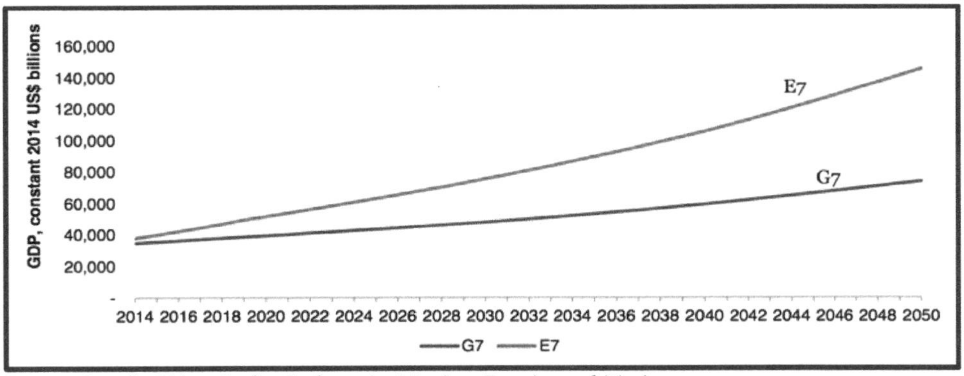

E7 = Brazil, China, India, Indonesia, Mexico, Russia, and Turkey
G7= Canada, France, Germany, Italy, Japan, the UK, and the US
Source: The World in 2050 Will the shift in global economic power continue? PWC 2015, February.

Figure 1.5. The four industrial revolutions of history

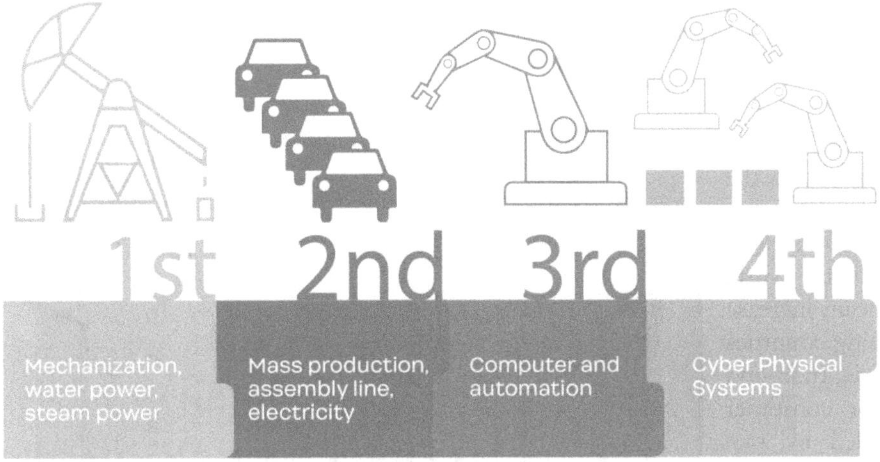

Adapted from Christoph Roser, at AllAboutLean.com [CC BY-SA 4.0]

- The rapidly changing manufacturing systems will result in lower costs - as the expert of the Boston Consulting Group wrote: "The value created by Industry 4.0 vastly exceeds the low-single-digit cost savings that many manufacturers pursue today". (Source: https://www.i-scoop.eu/industry-4-0/ Lower cost will affect the level of prices and the outcome of price competitions.

- The time to market, i.e. the period between the invention of a product and its launch to the market is being reduced, and products have a shorter life cycle. Consequently, new products

have a considerably shorter time to become profitable, and assets invested in research, development and launch onto the market are expected to have a quicker return.

- In the case of new products, a mistake in pricing or an error can lead to serious and often irreversible losses.

Figure 1.6. The elements of SMACT with the year of their creation

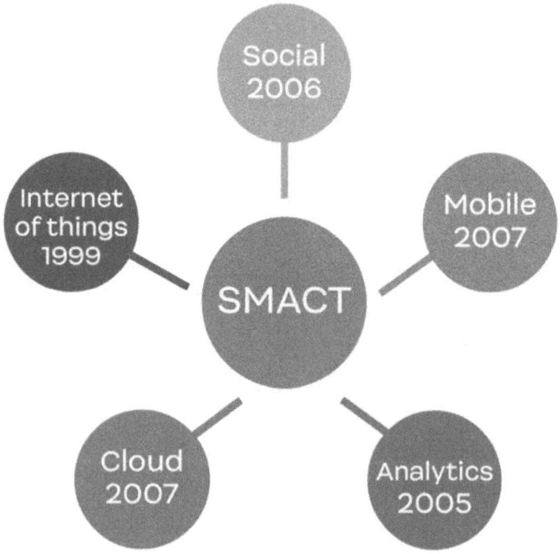

1.2.5. Changes in consumer behaviour on the advanced markets

By the turn of the millennium, the consumption of the population had reached rather high levels in the developed part of the world and started a significant increase in the largest emerging countries (BRIC – Brazil, Russia, India and China). Demand for consumer goods can be fuelled by two sources in the individual countries: additional consumption by the existing population or increased consumption induced by the growth of population.

Royal Galleries of Saint-Hubert, Brussels, Belgium
Source: Donaldytong - Own work CC BY-SA 3.0

By the end of the twenties both sources had lost their capacity to grow in the Western countries: population growth slowed and the increase in demand had also reached its physical and time limitations (You cannot drive more than one car at the same time, watch more than one television or use more than one computer.)

All entailed a change in consumer habits: those enjoying high living standards are not interested any longer in acquiring even more products or services but wish to generate as much benefit as possible from the ones they already have (This is the moment when smart shoppers enter the scene). The amount of needs left unsatisfied is on the decrease and the quality of supply becomes more important. This process goes together with an increase in the social awareness of consumers:

- Health protection becomes more important.
- Conservation and protection of the environment comes into focus.
- The use of products is expected to be economical and practical at the same time.
- Consumers have more price sensitivity and price awareness.

1.2.6. Competition expands and is globalized

The slowdown of consumption growth experienced in the developed countries goes hand in hand with the unprecedented expansion of competition. The expansion of competition can be interpreted from various aspects. The inner movement of the economy results in the continuous establishment of new businesses, which make efforts to gain their own market share and thereby mean a constant threat for existing businesses - especially under conditions of less rapidly increasing consumption. Competition now extends to sectors that used to be monopolies (the energy sector, public transport, utilities, etc.). Competition becomes characteristic in the non-business sectors of society as well (education, health services, etc.). A more and more typical dimension of increasing competition is its nearly total globalization. The greater freedom of the movement of capital, goods and services creates a situation in which the local market does not exist anymore, and whenever the process of meeting local needs starts taking place, international competition can be expected to appear without delay. These changes have, of course, an impact on pricing as well. Globalization of competition has the consequence that - parallel with the internationalization of the flow of information and the media – consumer habits and familiarity with prices also become globalized, and even in less developed countries the consumers' expectations concerning the value and price of products and services become similar to those that characterize the most highly developed countries. This means that, as soon as local competition ceases, local price policy also disappears. In our days, products and prices have to face the conditions of international competition practically everywhere.

1.3. The role of pricing among the managerial functions

1.3.1. The role of price in the marketing mix

Price is an important element of the marketing mix (Figure 1.7). Corporate price policy – like other marketing tools - is an important area of corporate activity, closely related to the other functions and influenced largely by the environment in which the company operates. Prices do not exist by themselves, only in conjunction with products (services) and can be interpreted in the context of their interactions with the other elements of the marketing mix.

Figure 1.7. Price in the marketing mix

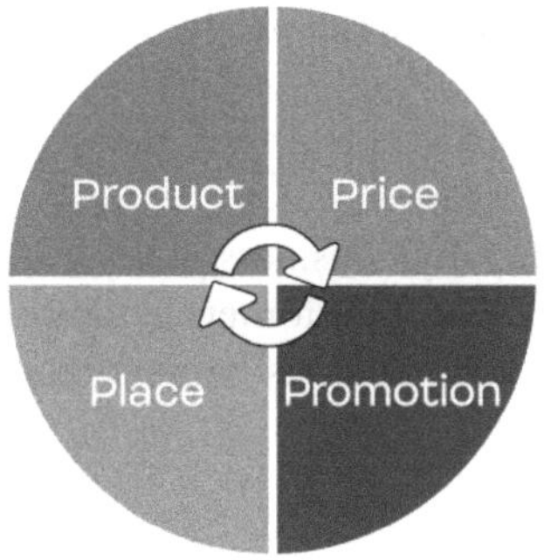

Interpreting the price function as a policy means that the company;

- defines its long-term objectives; and in order to achieve them
- outlines its strategy for the long run;
- defines principles for the application of prices in practice, and
- checks the practical implementation of the price strategy and price application.

The development of price policy presupposes the analysis and consideration of a number of factors both within and outside the company as shown in Figure 1.8.

Figure 1.8. Factors influencing price policy

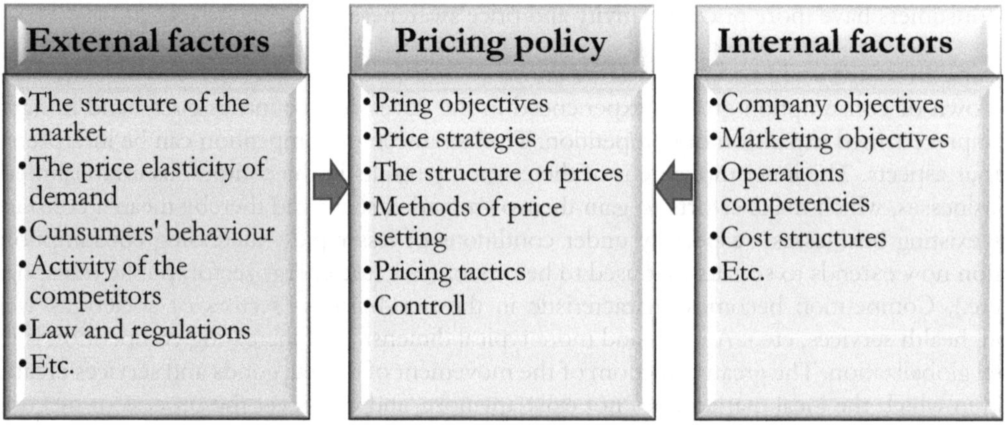

Figure 1.9. Magic triangle of price policy

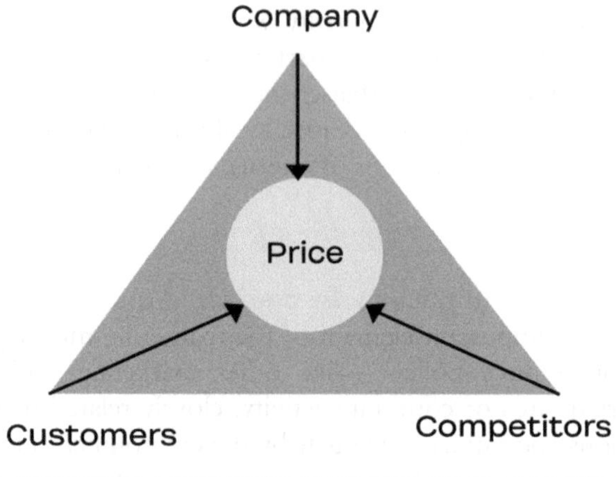

Viewing the inter-relationships in a simplified way, and highlighting their most important compo-nents we come to the conclusion that price setting is most strongly influenced by the 3Cs, i.e. the c*ompany* itself, the *customers* or *shoppers* and the *competitors.* These three factors constitute the magic triangle that should never be overlooked when price strategies are developed (Figure 1.9.)

This emphasis on the key internal and external factors of price policy should not lead us to forget that pricing is, at the same time, an expression of the company's business policy. "The company's price policy carries a message to the market – it is through prices that customers get important information about company philosophy", writes Dolan (1995, p. 4.), and, so do its competitors, we could add.

EXHIBIT 1.5. PRICING SWATCH WATCHES

The above statements are well illustrated by the price policy of Swatch watches. The message they convey is that this watch means a lot more than its basic function. It gives the buyer pleasure, a kind of pleasure that might induce him or her to buy more watches of this kind. The manufacturer has not changed the 40-dollar price of the basic model for more than 10 years. In an interview given to Harvard Business Review Franco Bossino, head of Swatch's designing laboratory, said that price has become the mirror of qualities they intended to communicate. Buying a Swatch watch is a kind of decision that buyers can make easily and even repeatedly. It is true that they are provocative, but they do not make buyers think hard.

Source: Message and muscle: An Interview with Swatch Titan Nicholas Hayek, Harvard Business Review, March-April, 1993; Photo: Edwardx - Own work, File:Swatch store, Oxford Street, London, March 2016 CC BY-SA 4.0

1.3.2. Pricing objectives

Pricing objectives, similarly to prices, cannot be interpreted as independent notions; they are always interrelated with the strategy of the company and its marketing objectives:

Profit-related pricing objectives:

- To maximize long-term profits.
- To maximize short-term profits.
- To achieve return on investments.
- To increase volume of sales in order to reduce unit costs and thereby increase profits.
- To realize quick return on R&D costs.

Market share - related pricing objectives:

- To increase market share.
- To keep market share.
- To increase sales.

Competitors - related pricing objectives:

- To build up the price leader role, or keep it.
- To prevent new competitors from entering the market.

- To push/squeeze competitors out of the market.
- To follow prices of bigger competitors.

Special marketing objectives:

- To represent a particular image through prices.
- To establish and maintain relations with customers/shoppers.
- To keep up intermediaries' loyalty.
- To maintain the appearance of being a fair actor in the market.

1.4. Second decade of the 21st century: new circumstances of reaching price objectives

The importance of pricing and price management is growing all over the world, primarily due to the turbulent economic situation, accelerating technological development, the saturation of markets and the globalization of competition – as has already been mentioned. All these trends affect the achievement of company objectives, place prices, pricing and price management in a context that differs greatly from what has been known before.

Let us first look at the main characteristics of the past. For many decades, pricing was dominated by the method of 'cost + mark-ups'. The rationale of this way of thinking was that, in the case of individual industries, costs provided firms with relatively correct information about potential prices. Costs, on the other hand, were easily identified, i.e. associated with the products manufactured and distributed by the firm, or with various activities. Before computers appeared, costs were allocated and prices calculated manually, which made it impossible to use those complex cost-accounting and pricing methods that are widespread these days. In the past few decades, we have witnessed significant changes. Let us first have a look at the changes in cost structures and value relations.

With the increase of globalized competition, companies with rather different cost structures have become direct competitors. In this situation, the market is obviously indifferent to the cost the company has to incur in order to produce its supply. When different price structures are fighting each other, the cost + profit method can only lead to wrong price decisions: either it will be higher than the one accepted by the buyers, consequently the company will lose market share, or it will be lower, which will lead to a loss of surplus profit.

Most of the time it is not by its physical or basic functions that buyers judge the values of a product. The concept of value has become broader by now: starting from basic benefits it has shifted in the direction of augmented product. In the opinion formed of a product sometimes priority is given to components surrounding the product – like brand image, related services, availability, etc. - whose costs cannot be allocated or only with difficulty. Quite frequently, these are fixed costs, and this fact contributes to making information less reliable about unit costs.

At the same time, a significant cost efficiency improvement could be observed all over the world in the manufacturing of products, particularly those based on physics, technology and knowledge. As a result of the economies of scale and the impact of the experience-learning curve, the unit costs of material, energy and labour spent directly on production can be significantly smaller. In addition to all this, the whole 20th century, and the 1990s in particular, were characterized by a considerable decrease in the prices of raw materials. (According to the raw material price index published by the

Economist, in the 1990s the price level of the basic raw materials was about 30% of the 1840-1850 price level, used as a base and expressed in real dollar value.) The first two decades of the 21st century have brought turbulent changes in this field as well: compared to 2000, the base year, we witnessed a significant increase in the prices of raw materials.

Parallel with the fall of direct costs per unit (measured in real value) there was a great improvement in the quality of products. Operation research and the development of production management have introduced methods like lean manufacturing, flexible manufacturing, just-in-time-method, kanban, total quality management, etc. which resulted not only in an improved average quality of products, but also made it possible to increasingly customize offers.

In later chapters we will explain in more detail that the elbow room firms have for price decisions is limited by two factors. From below it is the cost of production (in the short run the variable unit costs, and in the longer run the total unit costs) and from above the market (the willingness of buyers to accept the price) that represent the limits that close down the zone of pricing (ZoP) policy.

Summarizing the trends that have been outlined so far, we can conclude that the zone of pricing is widening (Figure 1.10.): the lower limit is shrinking thanks to better cost-efficiency, while the upper limit, customers' acceptance of value and price, is also on the increase due to improved quality and the better, more customized services offered. This broader zone makes it possible (or rather requires) that more priority should be given to the market-oriented methods in pricing. This widening of opportunities entails the appearance of new pricing alternatives and their more differentiated use. It must be noted, however, that the depression starting in 2008 temporarily restricted this elbow room, because its upper limit – the acceptance of prices – shifted downwards due to the customers' lower income.

Figure 1.10. The elbow room of pricing policy (ZoP – Zone of Pricing)

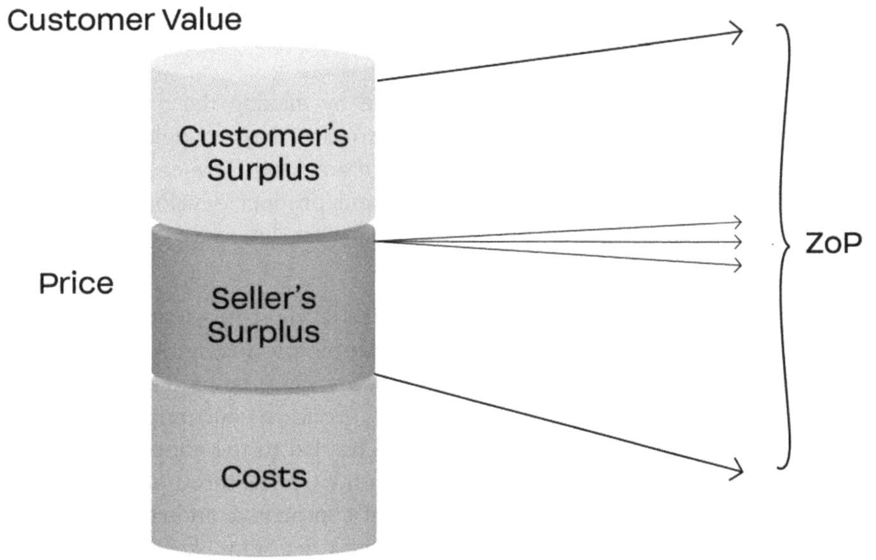

Note: The original idea ofthis figure is from Shapiro's work published in 1998

1.4.1. Conditions of sharing the growing surplus

Surplus value – generated by the gap between decreasing unit costs and increasing customer value – is shared according to the balance of power in the market. After WWII, and particularly in our time, we can observe an incredible strengthening of retail trade conglomerates in North America and especially in Western Europe. Mass retailing proves to be a very profitable business in 21st century Europe. Nine out of the world's ten largest food retailers are European (the American Wal-Mart is the largest). Europe's biggest retail companies, like the German Metro Group, Britain's Tesco, as well as Interspar, Cora, Auchan, Lidl, Aldi, etc. have established themselves in a large number of countries.

These huge companies are suitable for becoming price setters, both for manufacturers and consumers. They are in a position to force their prices and other conditions upon suppliers, to make them manufacture their own store brands and, what is more, make them pay various extra charges for the display of their products on the shelves. It seems that large food chains rip out an increasing share of the margin between production costs and consumer value and the manufacturer-driven channels that were dominant in the former decades are losing ground. It has, of course, an impact on the pricing policy of both manufacturers and retailers.

1.4.2. Composite product structure – complicated price structure

These days, the number of companies that manufacture or sell only one or just a few products is on the decrease. Most companies offer different kinds of products or services that are, more or less, closely related to one another. This increasingly composite product structure has two main characteristic features:

- The management of the ever-widening product structure focuses on product lines, i.e. the joint management of products that *presuppose identical competence.* When it comes to differentiate its products from those of the competitors, a company with up-to-date management will apply unique features, qualities, shapes and images to its product lines and not to its individual products. Product lines are becoming dominant not only in product design, but in product management as well.

- The last third of the previous century was characterized by making the product mix of companies more consistent, which put an end to the period of large conglomerates with profiles that at the level of products had no relationship of any kind. This change increased synergy which can be felt not only in product design and product development, but in manufacturing and marketing as well. This uniform product line image triggered the development of the single company image.

These changes obviously have their impact on pricing policy. Price levels (consistent with product quality) and price differences emerging between products lines or within product lines get a key role. Managing price differences and, at the same time, maintaining product variations and optional prices developed with a view to meeting the requirements of exquisite service to customers, cannot be implemented without sophisticated price management. This need has led to the appearance of new methods, like price segmentation – price differentiation, definition of price thresholds and price-difference thresholds, creating package prices and setting prices of competitive and complementary goods independently from one another, etc. Preparing price-related decisions, keeping record of prices and managing them would not be possible without up-to-date computers.

1.4.3. Services make headway – a new age of pricing

In most countries the share of services in GDP production exceeds by far the share of the extracting and processing industries. This has been the case for quite a long time now. The early years of the 21st century, however, brought some new developments, namely:

- The deregulation and liberalization of a host of formerly typically state-owned and therefore monopolistic services (banks, telecommunication, the energy sector, etc.) has been completed by our times and the former monopolies have gradually found themselves in conditions of market competition.
- The revolutionary development of information and communication technology (ICT), together with its rapid globalization has a decisive impact not only on certain national economies, but also on the world economy as a whole.

Both factors affect prices and pricing policy as well. Services adapted themselves to the competitive environment by introducing new price policies and pricing techniques that are extremely interesting in themselves but can also influence other services and even the price setting practice of physical products. Services are generally characterized by a low level of variable costs.

As a result we can witness a number of formerly hardly known or applied methods at a quick pace: the sophisticated methods of non-linear pricing: package prices, price bundling, subscription fees, tariffs charged in one or two parts, block-type tariffs, various allowances/discounts, bonus programmes, yield management, etc. Information and communication technology influences price policy not only by promoting the diffusion of our specific pricing practice in other sectors, but in at least two other ways:

- By virtue of the role they play in the transfer of information, they accelerate the wide spread of information on products and prices within the national economy and to other national economies. This leads not only to an uniformization of consumer habits but contributes to an equalization of prices both domestically and internationally.
- The Internet has opened up a formerly unknown distribution channel in B2C and B2B sectors. The pricing practice of on-line commerce differs from traditional methods in many respects.

1.4.4. Globalization – narrowing elbow room for price policy

Companies involved in international trade used to capitalize on the significant differences in the price levels of various countries. Full equalization has not been realized yet, but there can be no doubt that the price levels of the various countries are approaching one another. There are several reasons for that:

- One is the accelerated growth rate of international trade both as far as the volume and the nature of goods sold is concerned. Nowadays it is not only the goods that move in their physical form from one country to another, but services as well.
- The international movement of capital goes together with the international spread of managerial skills (including pricing).

EXHIBIT 1.6. PRICES IN EUROPE - AN OVERVIEW

In 2015, price levels for consumer goods and services differed widely across Europe. The highest price level among EU Member States was observed in Denmark, 37% above the EU average, while in Bulgaria the price level was 53% below the EU average (See table 1.1.) An understanding of the differences in price levels is important in the comparison of economic data, such as gross domestic product (GDP), because higher relative prices could make an economy look healthier than it really is.

Table 1.1. Price level index for 4 groups of goods and services

	HFCE	Food and non-alcoholic beverages	Alcoholic beverages and tobacco	Clothing	Footwear
Switzerland	163	173	129	134	116
Norway	137	159	221	130	131
Denmark	137	145	119	133	128
United Kimgdom	131	111	180	98	106
Iceland	125	130	173	152	153
Ireland	123	119	170	112	109
Sweden	121	124	126	129	125
Finland	120	119	132	120	120
Luxemburg	119	116	87	101	98
Netherlands	109	98	106	108	113
Belgium	107	108	95	108	108
France	105	109	103	101	96
Austria	105	120	89	99	100
Italy	101	110	95	101	99
Germany	100	103	92	100	98
EA19	100	104	95	100	99
Spain	90	92	85	88	93
Cyprus	87	107	90	97	97
Greece	83	103	89	100	105
Portugal	81	94	86	98	97
Malta	80	104	95	101	96
Slovenia	80	96	80	96	83
Estonia	75	88	81	106	104
Latvia	69	89	80	102	107
Slovakia	67	89	70	101	96
Croatia	65	91	70	95	92
Czech Republic	63	79	57	92	80
Lithuania	63	78	70	100	99
Turkey	61	90	79	53	67
Hungary	57	79	65	81	97
Montenegro	55	78	57	94	103
Poland	55	63	69	96	88
Romania	52	64	69	89	98
Bosnia and Herzegovina	51	74	48	102	101
Kosovo (1)	50	70	50	89	95
Serbia	49	69	47	93	94
Albania	47	68	51	93	86
Bulgaria	47	70	55	79	78
FYR of Macedonia	46	58	38	79	81
Variation coefficients:					
EA-19	19.5	11.6	23.6	6.4	7.8
EU-15	14.6	11.5	26.5	11.3	10.0
EU-28	28.6	19.1	30.9	11.6	11.7
All 38	36.2	26.4	43.0	16.5	15.7

(1) Kosovo under UNSCR 1244/99

Note: Household final consumption expenditure, abbreviated as HFCE, consists of the total outlay on individual goods and services by resident households, including those sold at below-market prices. HCFE includes imputed expenditures or transactions, which do not occur in monetary terms and can therefore not be measured directly.

Source: File: Price level index for 4 groups of goods and services,2015, EU-28=100C1.png http://ec.europa.eu/eurostat/ statistics-explained/index.php/ File:Price_level_index_for_4_groups_of_goods_and_services,_2015,_EU-28%3D100C1.png

- The expansion of international integrations (e.g. the European Union that directly affects our countries and, within that the Euro Zone) also contributes to the process of price equalization. It is well illustrated in Figure 1.11 which compares the price level differences of the household's expenditures in the original EU countries, in the Euro Zone, in EU and in Europe.

Figure 1.11. The variation coefficients for the differences of the price level of the household's' final consumption expenditures in Europe in 2015 in % (Calculation from Eurostat data)

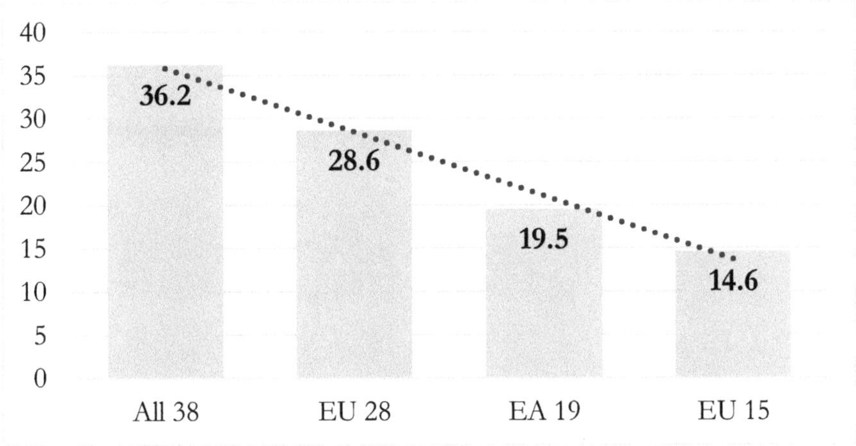

Note: EU 15 = EU before 2004; EA 19 = Euro Zone; EU 28 = All countries of EU; All 38 = All countries of Europe

While earlier the tendency was for the expansion of elbow room in the case of price policy, now it is more reasonable to forecast a decrease in price differences at international level. There is no contradiction between the two trends because price policy elbow room is still expanding for certain companies and products in the narrowing international price corridor, which means the increase of the margin between lower unit costs and higher value.

CHAPTER 2. THE ECONOMICS OF PRICING

OBJECTIVE 1: To inform the reader of the dynamic relationship of prices and demand.

OBJECTIVE 2: To explain the elasticities of demand, and discuss the role and different forms of the price elasticities, and its interrelationship with the income and cross elasticity.

OBJECTIVE 3: To illustrate the different forms of market structures including, perfect competition, monopoly, oligopoly and monopolistic competition and to explain the influence of these market forms on the way pricing can be managed.

2.1. Introduction

Market-based company policy can only be implemented if managers are familiar with the laws of the market and are able to understand and analyse market competition. Economics studies people's efforts to make the best possible use of their limited resources to meet their practically unlimited needs (McEachern, 1988; McConnan et al. 2008; Barancsuk, 2008). While doing so, it examines not only the economic behaviour of individual decision-makers (microeconomics) but that of the economy as a whole (macroeconomics) as well. The conclusions and methods of economic analysis – especially the demand and supply curves, the elasticity of demand and the forms of the market – provide valuable information that marketing managers can benefit from and foster the achievement of practical objectives, and the price objectives in particular.

2.2. The demand curve

Economics teaches that the demand curve represents the quantity of demand for a given product at various prices, assuming that all the other factors remain constant. It is a well-known fact that the demand curve has a tendency to slope downward, since higher prices usually mean lower demand, while demand increases if prices go down.

Figure 2.1 shows that a change in the price of a product modifies the quantity of demand for it. There is a different quantity demanded for every point of the curve, which means that demand moves along curve D. If the factors supposed so far to remain constant are also involved in the analysis, in addition to the move along the curve we can also observe the shift of the demand curve ($D \rightarrow D'$) (Figure 2.2). In addition to price, the shift of the demand curve can also be caused by any change of one of the following factors:

- incomes,
- taxes,
- number of consumers,
- consumer expectations,

- price of related products,
- consumer preferences.

Figure 2.1. The demand curve

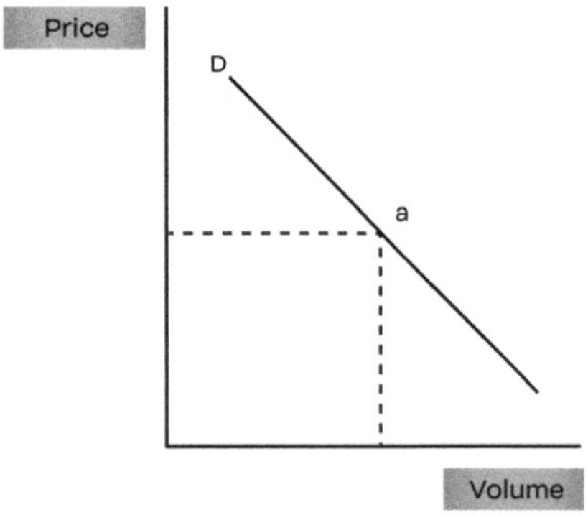

Figure 2.2. Increase in demand

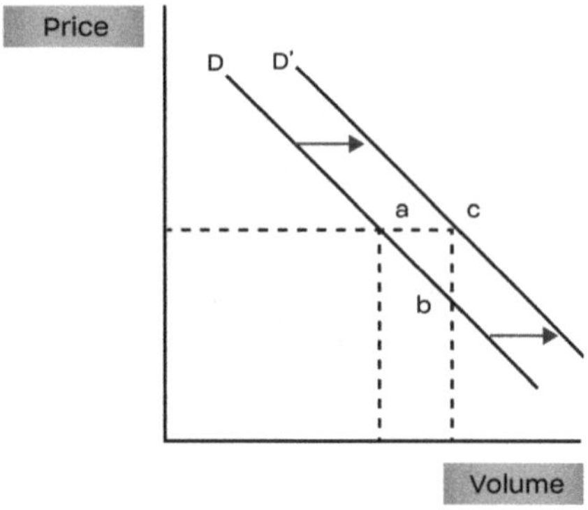

2.3. Demand elasticities

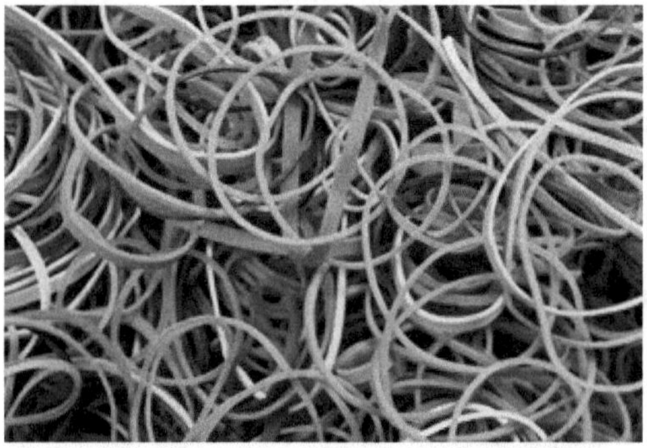

Photo: Bill Ebbesen - Own work, Rubber bands in different colors. Studio photo taken. CC BY-SA 3.0 File:Rubber bands - Colors - Studio photo 2011.jpg

2.2.1. Price elasticity of demand

The main concern of companies' product and price policies is the reaction of market demand (i.e. the demand of the total number of customers) to price changes. The relevant basic principle is usually discussed by economists under the heading *price elasticity of demand.* Changes in consumer demand are caused not only by price changes. Other types of elasticity will be discussed in a later chapter.

The following formula can be used to calculate price elasticity of demand:

$$\text{Price elasticity of the demand} = \frac{\text{Percentage change in the quantity sold}}{\text{Percentage change in price}}$$

Expressed in mathematical equation:

$$E_d = \frac{\frac{Q_1 - Q_2}{Q_1}}{\frac{P1 - P2}{P1}} = \frac{\frac{\Delta Q}{Q1}}{\frac{\Delta P}{P1}} = \frac{\Delta Q}{\Delta P} \cdot \frac{P1}{Q1}$$

where

E_d is price elasticity of demand,

ΔQ is the qualitative change in demand,

ΔP is price change and,

Q1 and P1 is the original demand and the original price.

EXHIBIT 2.1. DOES THE FORMULA WORK VICE VERSA?

Photo: Michiel1972 from nl goudkleurige, CD-Video disk, File: CDV2 .jpg, CC BY-SA 3.0, Created: 9 October 2004, Licensed under the GFDL by the author

The formula can be checked with the help of a practical example:

Let us suppose that the original price of a CD Video was $ 5. At this price retailers were able to sell 2000 pieces. An increase of $ 1 in the price caused a fall in the number sold to 1600. Price elasticity of demand for this CD can be calculated as follows:

$$E_d = \frac{\frac{2000-1600}{2000}}{\frac{500-600}{500}} = -1$$

Given the fact that demand and price move in opposite directions in most situations, the result of the calculation is usually negative. (Considering that the result is usually negative, the minus sign in front of the coefficient is usually dropped leaving only the absolute value to characterize price elasticity.) The above case could also have taken a different turn: A fall in the price from $ 6.00 to 5.00 could result in an increase in the number sold from 1600 to 2000 items. Using the same figures but calculating a shift in the opposite direction, we get the following result:

$$E_d = \frac{\frac{1600-2000}{1600}}{\frac{600-500}{500}} = -1.5$$

The result is surprising since the shift is of the same type. The two calculations will not produce the same result, unless the formula is changed as follows:

$$E_d = \frac{\Delta Q}{\Delta P} \cdot \frac{0.5(P1+P2)}{0.5(Q1-Q2)}$$

In this way the formula will have the result -1.22, i.e. |1,22| in both directions.

When discussing price elasticity of demand, economists usually distinguish three alternative cases between the two extremes (perfectly inelastic and perfectly elastic):

- the rise in the quantity demanded falls short of the change in price, i.e. Ed < 1 , demand is *inelastic,*
- the rise in quantity demanded exceeds price change, i.e. Ed > 1, demand is *elastic*
- and the measure of the two changes is identical, i.e. Ed = 1, than the demand has a *unit elasticity.*

It is important for companies to know elasticity of demand for their products, because as a result of elasticity, the consequence of price change will manifest itself in the quantities sold and eventually in their revenue from sales. The total revenue from sales is the product of the price and the quantities sold at the given price (PQ). Consequently, the various states of the price elasticity of demand have various impacts on the revenue (Figure 2.3).

Figure 2.3. Typical cases of price elasticity of demand

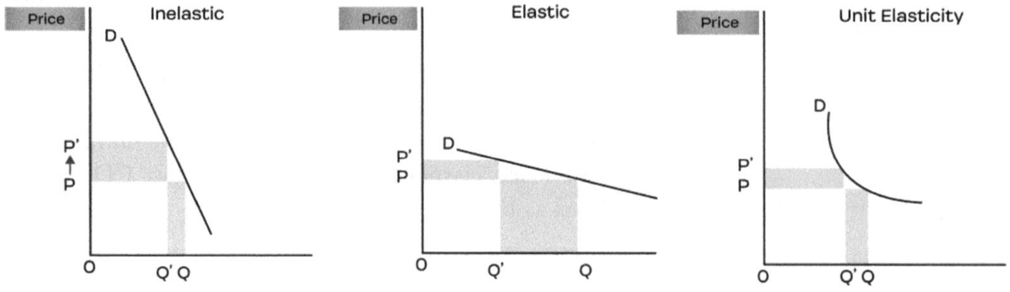

Elasticity is not easy to measure, because the price elasticity of demand for a certain product is never constant. Elasticity can change in function of price, for example.

Table 2.1. The impact of price rise on the various measures of elasticity

Value of E_d		Impact of price rise	
	Description	on the quantity demanded	on the revenue
$E_d = 0$	Absolutely inelastic	No change	Percentage increase equals price rise
$0 < E_d < 1$	Inelastic	Percentage decrease smaller than price rise	Percentage increase falls short of price rise
$E_d = 1$	Unit elasticity	Percentage decrease equals price rise	No change
$1 < E_d < \infty$	Elastic	Percentage decrease exceeds price rise	Decreases
$E_d < = \infty$	Absolutely elastic	Falls back to 0	Is reduced to 0

There are cases (typically the so-called high-prestige products) where changes in price elasticity of demand do not follow the pattern seen before; on the contrary, price rise reaching or exceeding a given level can actually lead to an increase in demand. The demand curve for these products will change as shown in Figure 2.4. Such demand can develop, for example, in the market of porcelain figurines. As long as a product fails to get into the category of treasure goods by virtue of its high quality and image value, demand for it *will be about the same quantity* as for the other products. However, once porcelain has become one of the reliable stores of value, a rise in its price can increase the quantity of demand for it.

In practice, price elasticity can occur in many different forms. Demand for the same product or service can be elastic in one period of the year and inelastic in another. The next exhibit presents variations in elasticity of demand for flight services by customers, destinations, and distances, based on a

Canadian survey. The data show that elasticity of private flights is greater than that of business trips (presumably, because they can be postponed more easily). It is also obvious that short-haul flights have greater elasticity than long-haul flights, owing to the higher number of alternatives.

Figure 2.4. Demand curve for high-prestige products

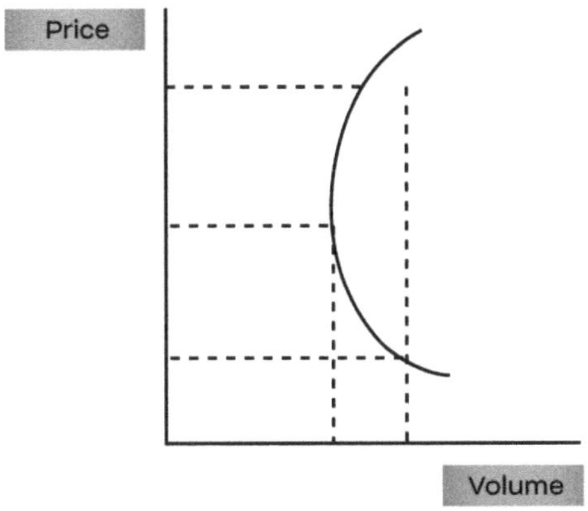

2.3.1. Factors influencing price elasticity of demand

Price elasticity of demand for various goods can be of quite different degrees. One of the main reasons is the existence of *substitute products.* If the substitute product available is so similar to the product in question that the utility it offers is identical or very similar to it, demand for this product will most probably be elastic. When the price of the product goes up, customers are most likely to turn to the substitute products. If, however, substitution of the product is realized only in part, or at a lower level, price elasticity of the demand for the substitute product will be relatively low. Electricity, for example, in our present consumption system can be substituted for to a limited measure only; therefore, demand for it has relatively limited price elasticity. Products of similar character include insulin, used for the treatment of diabetes, and many other goods.

When selecting potential substitutes for a given product, we have to face a definition problem that is similar to the one we have to solve when trying to define competing products. A broad range of substitutes can be misleading. Demand for food, for example, is considerably less elastic than demand for soft drinks, which also belong in the category of food stuffs, because we have no other product group to substitute for food. Soft drinks can be substituted with certain limitations; apple juice in this category can be substituted for several other soft drinks, therefore demand for it may have a significantly higher level of price elasticity. Within these groups, even more elastic demand can be observed for certain brands.

Consumers' judgement on the substitution potential is also determined by the *uniqueness* of the product. If its functions and specific qualities make a product rather differentiated, easy to distinguish from competing products, price will become less important for the consumers or, in other words, customers will be less inclined to accept the competing product as a substitute. This points to the conclusion that demand for products with unique qualities can be significantly less elastic than for goods that have no such unique qualities.

There are other factors as well that can influence the potential for substitution. One of them is the question whether consumers have sufficient *information* available on the substitutes that would enable

EXHIBIT 2.2. VARIATIONS IN THE PRICE ELASTICITY OF DEMAND FOR FLIGHT SERVICES

The homepage of the Canadian Department of Finance has published a detailed study based on a survey of price elasticity regarding flight services in 2006. The authors grouped passengers and flights according to the distance they covered and the nature of the trip in order to survey price elasticity of the various groups. The findings are shown in the next table.

Table 2.2. Price elasticity by segments

Segments	Median price elasticity values
Long-haul international business	-0,265
Long-haul international leisure	-1,04
Long-haul domestic business	-1,15
Long-haul domestic leisure	-1,104
Short-haul business	-0,7
Short-haul leisure	-1,52

Source: Gillen et al., 2006 (http://www.fin.gc.ca/consultresp/ Airtravel/ airtravStdy_1-eng.asp#1)

EXHIBIT 2.3. THE GIFFEN CASE AND VEBLEN'S CONSPICUOUS CONSUMPTION

Literature refers to the two typical extremes_that work against the rule as the Giffen Case and Veblen's conspicuous consumption. (Gabor, 1988: 251.) More than a hundred years ago, Sir Robert Giffen observed that whenever the price of the cheapest, basic food stuffs increased, the very poor people increased the consumption of these products. The explanation is that these products represented the majority of the poor people's consumption and, because of the price rise, they had so little money left that they could buy nothing else but these cheap products.

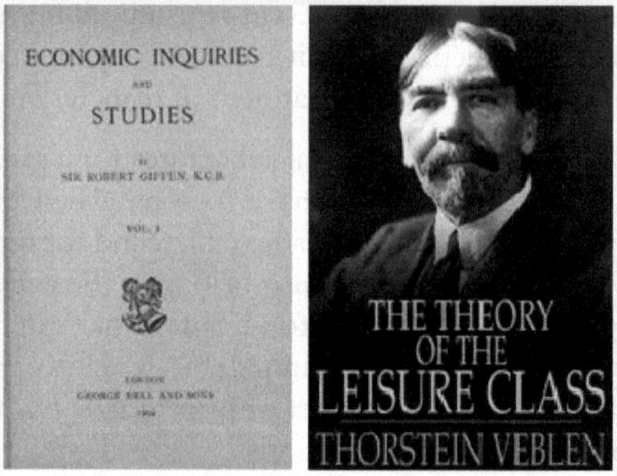

Photo: https://en.wikipedia.org/w/index.php?curid=31454876

Sometime later Thorstein Veblen, American economist and philosopher wrote that some of the products bought by the leisure class are not meant to meet their own needs, but 'to mimic each other in status hunting', consequently a rise in the price of these products can only increase the desire to buy them.

Many doubted the existence of the Giffen Case, since no real-world evidence was provided for it in literature for a long time. In 2007 two researchers, Robert Jensen and Nolan Miller, conducted an experiment in the province of Hunan, China that enabled them to prove the existence of Giffen behaviour. Poor families, selected at random, were given subsidies for the purchase of rice over a period of six months. In practice, it meant a cut in the price of rice. This cut led to a fall in the rice consumption of these families. The termination of the subsidy had just the opposite impact. To this very day this has been the first and only real-life evidence of Giffen behaviour.

them to compare the potential choices. Another decisive factor can be the cost involved in substituting one product for another. Shifting from one soft drink to another does not really involve any costs, but changing computers usually involves the use of new software or transforming one's heating system from electricity to gas can require a considerable investment and abandoning the nearby convenience shop for a cheaper supermarket can entail increased input of time and fuel.

The interrelationships between substitution and the costs of shifting throw light on the temporal aspect of the problem, i.e. *price elasticity of demand may also change over time.* Let us assume that the price of piped gas is raised dramatically and unexpectedly. What is going to happen to consumption? Consumption cannot be expected to fall significantly overnight or even within the next few weeks. What happens is that households continue to use their appliances but more economically, and thereby reduce their gas bill by a few percent. However, one or two years later they will have adapted themselves to the change and they will use a more efficient energy source for heating and cooking.

Price elasticity of demand also greatly depends on whether the product in question meets some *basic need* or not. The more basic the need, the less elastic the demand for the product that meets it. This distinction also applies within a group of products meeting a specific need. Let us consider the use of telephones, for example: Most of the conversations made during the day can be considered as basic need (initiated for business or other purposes), therefore the telephone companies do not hesitate to raise the daytime or peak-time rates and keep them high.

Demand for conversations that do not meet basic needs is considerably more elastic, therefore telephone companies offer significant dis-counts for conversations out of peak times.

The price sensitivity of consumers, i.e. the price elasticity of their demand also depends on *the magnitude that the purchase of a given product represents in the consumer's budget.* Literature has concluded that the larger the magnitude of the product in the consumer's budget, the more price sensitive the consumer becomes while the demand he represents becomes increasingly elastic.

The quality and brand image of the product also has an impact on the price elasticity of demand. In the case of products where customers presume *a close interrelationship between quality and price*, where high prices suggest good quality and high prestige, the quantity demanded may be rather inelastic. Factors affecting price elasticity of demand are summarized in Table 2.3.

2.3.2. Income elasticity of demand

Income elasticity of demand measures the extent to which changes in the consumers' income modify demand for a given product. Income elasticity of demand is calculated similarly to price elasticity, the only difference being that price (P) is replaced with income (I).

$$E_i = \frac{\frac{\Delta Q}{Q}}{\frac{\Delta I}{I}}$$ where

E_i is income elasticity of demand,

I is income,

Q is quantity demanded,

Δ Q is change in the quantity demanded,

Δ I is change in income.

We can distinguish goods demand for which reacts in an inelastic way to income changes, I.e. $0 < E_i < 1$ and goods where $E > 1$. Products with inelastic demand typically include those that meet basic needs. There are, however, goods for which demand decreases with the rise of income (i.e. E will turn negative): these are usually inferior goods that consumers gradually replace with higher quality goods. Table 2.4 shows data of income elasticity from a survey conducted in the USA in the 1980s.

Table 2.3. Factors influencing price elasticity of demand

Decisive factors	**Indicates elastic demand**	**Indicates inelastic demand**
Several substitute products are available	*	
Customers perceive product as a basic need		*
The product has unique qualities that are important for customers		*
Customers can easily compare the products and its competitors	*	
The price of the product is a significant item in the customer's budget	*	
The customer pays only a fraction of the whole price, e.g. medicines)		*
Shifting to other products costs relatively little	*	
Customers consider price to be an indicator of quality		*

Table 2.4. Elasticity of income

Product	**Income Elasticity**
Private tutoring	2.46
Car	2.45
Own flat	1.49
Furniture	1.48
Dental services	1.42
Restaurant bills	1.40
Shoes	1.10
Clothing	1.02
Beer	0.93
Medical	0.75
Cigarettes	0.50

In the autumn of 2009 Booz & Company conducted a survey to find out the areas where the income cuts caused by the depression forced consumers to economize the most (obviously the data also indicate the income elasticity of demand for the various product categories). The data of the survey are shown in Figure 2.5.

Figure 2.5. Areas of economizing

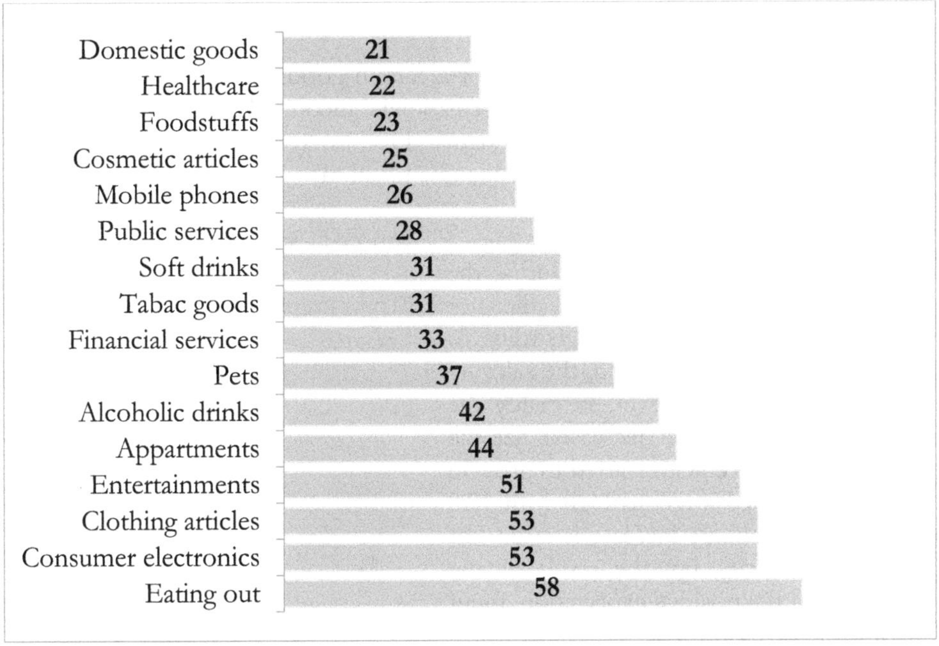

Note: Figures show the percentage of respondents who agreed with the statement: "In the past 12 months I cut my expenses related to these goods" The survey was conducted by Booz & Company in the USA in the autumn of 2009, using a sample of 2010.

2.3.3. Cross elasticity of demand

Cross-price elasticity measures the percentage change of quantity demanded of a certain product in response to change in the price of another product.

$$E_c = \frac{\Delta Q_a}{Q_a} \Big/ \frac{\Delta P_b}{P_b}$$

where

E_c is cross elasticity,

Q_a is change in demand for product a

P_b is change in the price of product b.

The cross elasticity index is usually positive in the case of the so-called substitute products, and negative in the case of products that complement each other. (Such complementary products are, for example, a printer and the ink cartridge, while substitute products are the various printers).

2.4. Market forms (market structures)

The elbow room available for corporate price policy is greatly determined by the market relations in which they operate. Economics describes the market forms characteristic of an industry (range of products) using the following criteria:

- number of companies operating in the market,
- limitations in the way of entering the market,
- possibility of differentiating the product and - closely related to this -

- the typical manifestation of the competition.

EXHIBIT 2.4. THE INTERRELATION OF THE DIFFERENT ELASTICITIES

In most cases, the actual change of the demand for a certain good depends not only on its price change but also on the modification of the customers' income. If the particular good plays an important part in the customers' budget, demand for it may also be influenced by the expectations of the customers about their future income position.

Let us examine two real examples!

The first is the US market of passenger cars. During the recession started in 2008, prices of cars did not increase; what is more they decreased. According to the theory of price elasticity of demand, the sales of cars should have increased. However, in reality the demand for passenger cars steeply decreased. See the chart! The sale of the light-vehicles started to grow in 2010 and in 2015 it reached a record high with 17.5 million cars sold. This dramatic increase is again not the result of price elasticity, but the result of the increase in income and the positive expectation about the future income of the customers.

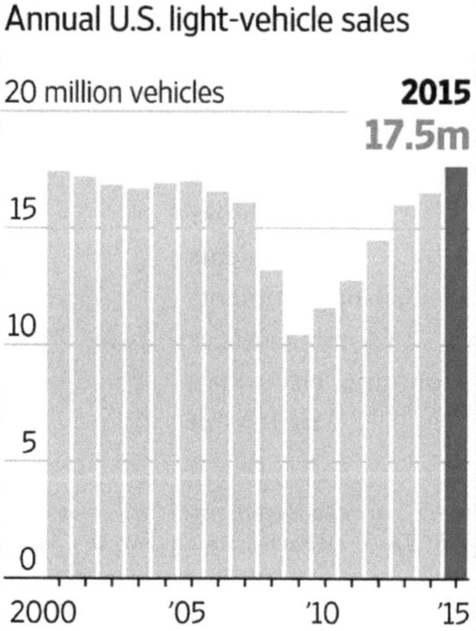

Source: Autodata
THE WALL STREET JOURNAL.

One more factor should be mentioned here. Beside price elasticity and income elasticity, cross-elasticity is also playing a role in this rapid increase. This relates to the price decrease of gasoline. The $2/gallon gasoline price in 2015 made customers optimistic about the future costs of having a new car.

The second example is gasoline consumption in Hungary. Professors teaching pricing used to say that gasoline belongs to the goods having a rather inelastic demand. The Hungarian case proved that it was true only to some extent. Experts from the Hungarian National Bank wrote in a study that the retail price of gasoline increased from HUF 270/litre level in April 2007 by 67% to mid of 2012, when it topped at HUF 451/litre.

The reason for the sharp increase was threefold: world market price increase of natural oil, tax increases (including consumption tax) levied on gasoline price and the weakening value of the local currency. At the same time, consumption of the gasoline decreased, as did the income level of the population. Using different statistical methods, they concluded that available money counts more than the price.

According to their calculation the price elasticity of gasoline in Hungary is -0.5 and income elasticity is 1.6. It means the one percent increase in price will decrease gasoline consumption by 0.5% while one percent decrease in income will cut consumption by 1.6%. Both figures are lower in the case of diesel fuel. The reason is that diesel is used by a larger number of companies (transport, etc.) and their demand is much more inelastic.

In 2015-2016, due to the movements on the world market of oil, gasoline prices lessened in Hungary parallel with the increase of the average income of the population. The elasticity of demand worked here as well. Hungary's car fuel sales recorded a 6.3% rise in the January-September period compared to the corresponding period of 2015, reaching more than 2.5 billion litres, the Hungarian Petroleum Association (MASZ) said, according to Hungarian news agency MTI.

Source: http://bbj.hu/economy/hungarian-car-fuel-sales-up-63-in-jan-sep_123343; Photo: http://bbj.hu/business/mol-aims-to-return-to-austrian-retail-market-_116239

2.4.1. Perfect competition

Perfect competition is an extreme case of market structure. This concept describes a market where competition prevails and where

- a large number of sellers and buyers are present, and none of them has a turnover large enough to dominate the market,
- the product is homogeneous, standardized, perceived by the buyers as identical or very similar,
- barriers of entry to the market are low, there are no legal or patent obligations that could be an obstacle to the entry, actors in the market have correct information about the prices, factors of production,
- product development and product differentiation does not take too much effort, and the marketing activities of individual companies are not decisive.

Firms participating in perfect competition take price for granted. Their small market share does not allow them to influence price, therefore the best they can do is accept it. (If they charge more than the prevailing price they will not be able to sell, if they offer to sell at a lower price, they will suffer a loss.)

Theoreticians say that in conditions of perfect com-petition and in the short run, manufacturers will increase their output as long as the price received for the additionally sold product exceeds the marginal cost of production (The term 'marginal cost' denotes the costs incurred during the manufacturing of an additional unit). At the same time, buyers will increase their purchase as long as the marginal utility provided by the additionally bought product exceeds the price paid for it. The so-called equilibrium price (and the equilibrium level of output) will occur when the marginal cost of manufacturing additional product equals the marginal utility that the purchase of an additional product offers to the buyer. According to the theory, equilibrium prices based on marginal costs can guarantee the most efficient allocation of re-sources, because buyers are not prepared to pay for a resource allocation that would result in higher prices.

In perfect competition every product is sold at equilibrium price, therefore both buyers and sellers realize a so-called surplus. For the buyers this is the difference between the price paid for the product

and the utility provided by the product, while in the case of sellers it means the difference between actual price received for the product and the marginal costs. The surplus realized by the sellers will cover the fix costs in-cured in the course of manufacturing and allows manufacturers to realize appropriate (usual) profits. Consequently, in the case of equilibrium output marginal costs equal per unit average cost.

Clear competition structure is rarely seen in reality and, when it is, certainly not in a perfect form. The only market that can be compared to it is perhaps the market of agricultural products and some minerals.

2.4.2. Monopoly

Besides perfect com-petition, monopoly is the other extreme market type. Monopoly is a term of Greek origin, meaning that there is only one seller present in the market. In the case of a monopoly, barriers to entry into the market are very high for outsiders, or entry to the market may hit legal, or perhaps natural obstacles. At the same time, the barrier can refer to the character of the monopoly:

- Legal barriers: state permits, licences or patents (good examples could be the wavelength licences allocated to mass communication companies.).
- Exclusive ownership of important natural and other resources. Individual companies may be in possession of resources, as happens in the oil, aluminium and diamond industries. Others have no chance of having access to these until research discovers new resources.
- Monopoly naturally growing out of economies of scale. It happens quite often that – thanks to its economical production - a company reaches dimensions that make it the exclusive manufacturer of a certain product. This kind of monopoly, that has developed from the competition is called natural monopoly, to distinguish it from monopolies created in an artificial way (e.g. with government measures).

Since the monopolist producer is alone in the market, his demand curve will coincide with the demand curve of the industry. It is also self-evident that, in this case, the monopolist producer - in contrast with the price follower companies in perfect competition – becomes a price setter. Many believe, that a monopolist can do with prices whatever he pleases, but this is not necessarily the case. There are other factors that also have an impact on the demand curve. The monopolist producer wants to maximize profit in the end, which is not synonymous with maximizing the price. Consequently, he should set a price that allows the quantity of demand to satisfy his monopolistic profit objectives.

Anyway, if the prices of the monopolist are not limited, he will most probably realize a much higher profit (extra profit) than the normally expected return simply by increasing his output only when and as long as the sales income from the additionally manufactured goods exceeds the marginal costs. It means that, in the case of a monopoly, prices are higher than the competitive prices. Although this price strategy may be favourable for the company, it is certainly unfavourable for the economy as a whole and customers because the allocation of resources is less efficient compared to the competitive market. This situation is particularly harmful when price elasticity of demand for the product is low. The monopolistic company is, of course, also prepared to increase its production if it can keep its prices above the level of marginal costs in such a way that demand does not diminish in the meantime. The way to achieve that is by differentiating prices. Customers with less elastic demand will be charged higher prices while customers with more elastic demand will be served lower prices.

A natural monopoly is not able to raise prices too much, because very high prices may attract potential competitors to the market and there is the threat of government intervention. A monopoly can be truly unfavourable for the consumer when it sells a product that has no substitute, yet meets important needs (e.g. public utilities).

EXHIBIT 2.5. PRIVATIZATION OF ELECTRICITY SUPPLY IN HUNGARY AND THE TRANSFORMATION OF PRICE CONTROL BY THE AUTHORITIES

The six electricity suppliers in Hungary were privatized in 1995. These companies enjoyed a monopolistic situation, because each of them had a separate region to supply. The government established the National Energy Office to supervise their price setting and business activities. Since there was very little competition, if any, the National Energy Office ordered them to have regular surveys of customer satisfaction with their activities both for household and non-household consumers from 1996 on. The findings of the surveys were used by the NEO in the evaluation of the companies' performance.

Act CX of 2001 on Electricity and related regulations opened up the opportunity for certain consumer groups to appear at the competitive market and make their own decisions whether to buy the electricity they needed from the producer of electricity, or the trader, i.e. not in the framework of a public utility contract. The liberalization of the Hungarian electricity market – advocated by the European Union as well – was implemented gradually, in several stages. First, on January 1. 2003, consumers whose annual consumption exceeded 6.5 GWh were authorized to buy electricity from the supplier of their choice. In addition, municipalities were also free to choose their provider up to the amount of electricity they consumed for street lighting. In the second stage, starting July 1 2004, all non-household consumers were given that right. In the third stage, i.e. from Jan. 1 2007 on, households too were allowed to choose freely among the suppliers and, at the same time, the authority ceased to control the price of electricity in Hungary. However, the consequences of liberalization were not favourable. The negative consequences became obvious for the Hungarian consumers in 1998, when the price of electricity in Hungary exceeded the level of German prices.

This is the reason why the Hungarian Parliament passed the amendments of the Act on Natural Gas and the Act on Electricity in June 2010. The new regulation stipulated that – similarly to the situation before 2007 - the minister in charge should approve prices offered to households and small consumers.

Source: Rekettye- Tersztyánszky, 1997, ELMÜ tájékoztató, VG 2010 Június 15.
Photo: By Yummifruitbat - Own work, CC BY-SA 2.5, https://commons.wikimedia.org/w/index.php?curid=1688551

In the case of a monopoly, government regulation is responsible for supervising, and limiting the freedom of pricing that is otherwise performed by the competition.

State regulation has several means at its disposal to limit the price policy of a company in a monopolistic position. The tool the government chooses to use depends partly on what politicians consider more important in the given situation: social efficiency in the utilization of resources, equal

opportunities to access products or perhaps the social justice of prices. If economic efficiency is given priority, the regulator will make efforts to approach P_{monop} to P_{comp}, and Q_{monop} to Q_{comp}. The pricing method of cost+profit, or pricing based on the target return seems to be the most suitable. The main problem with this kind of price regulation is that in most of the cases the authority is not capable of properly managing the huge amount of information on costs, profits and development projects. Consequently regulation loses its efficiency and the company in the monopolistic situation will be able to continue charging higher prices than justified by the competition, to generate higher profit and be satisfied with lower output. In this way, it is not possible to eliminate social loss. Strangely enough, the situation cannot be described as perfect even when supervision is efficient, i.e. the authority can cope with the amount of information. By using the cost+profits formula skilfully, the supervisor can avoid higher profits, but cannot make the company introduce internal rationalizations, or innovations in order to reduce its costs. On the other hand, the use of the prescribed rate of return can encourage the monopolist to realize extensive development projects at the expense of its labour and thereby increase profits.

Equal opportunity to access products or social justice can induce politics to disregard actual expenses and set lower prices in order to meet the needs of poorer population groups. There are countries, for example, where the poor do not have to pay a telephone base rate. In order to ensure social justice of prices, regulators often insist on keeping the same prices even when the costs of a service show considerable differences between groups of consumers. This is the case in Hungary with electricity: small consumers are charged the same rate per unit of electricity consumed as larger consumers (at present even less), whereas the unit costs of the service are obviously higher for small consumers. This kind of price regulation is based on cross funding and diminishes efficiency of resource allocation. This kind of pricing can even lead to situations when the customer who has been discriminated against (i.e. charged a higher price for the product) decides to shift to a substitute, whose marginal cost is higher and in this way damages the social efficiency of resource allocation.

EXHIBIT 2.6. WORLDWIDE SMARTPHONE SALES GREW 3.9 PERCENT IN THE FIRST QUARTER OF 2016

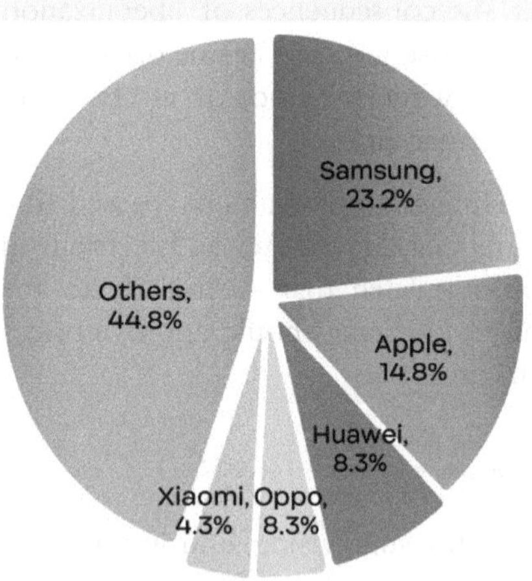

Global sales of smartphones to end users totalled 349 million units in the first quarter of 2016, a 3.9 percent increase over the same period in 2015 — according to Gartner Inc. "In a slowing smartphone market where large vendors are experiencing growth saturation, emerging brands are disrupting existing brands' models to increase their share" — said Anshul Gupta, research director at Gartner. "With such changing smartphone market dynamics, Chinese brands are emerging as the new top global brands. Two Chinese brands ranked within the top five worldwide smartphone vendors in the first quarter of 2015, and represented 11 percent of the market. In the first quarter of 2016, there were three Chinese brands – Huawei, Oppo and Xiaomi – and they achieved 17 percent of the market."

Source: http://www.gartner.com/newsroom/id/3323017

Several countries decided to use the so-called price cap method in order to eliminate the deficiencies of the method based on cost+profit or target return and to regulate natural monopolies. One example is the UK, where British Telecom was privatized in the mid-1980s. Hungary also used this method when regulation was developed for electricity suppliers. According to the method, the top level of prices is defined for the monopolist or his services and this is updated regularly, taking into consideration the levels of inflation and improved productivity.

The rates charged by British Telecom are updated annually with the percentage arrived at by the formula RPI-X. RPI means changes in the retail price index, while X means the level of productivity improvement established by the supervising body. Regardless of the regulation, however, one thing is certain: the monopolist is on his own in the market without competition pushing him to pioneer innovation or be consumer-oriented in all his activities. This is the reason why serious efforts were initiated to deregulate monopolies in the past few years.

2.4.3. Oligopoly

One decisive market form of our days is oligopoly, mainly characterized by the market being dominated by a few large companies. While in perfect competition it is the large number of market actors that exempts them from taking the activities of others into consideration, in monopoly the absence of competitors has the same effect. In oligopoly, however, the behaviour of actors at the market is affected largely by the activities of other actors. The conclusion is that oligopoly is the arena where some large participants in the market operate in interrelation with one another. The degree of mutual dependence is strongly influenced by the nature of their product. Where the product is nearly identical and cannot be differentiated as in the steel industry, mutual dependence is stronger. Just imagine the situation when the manufacturer of a non-differentiated mass product raises his price: even the smallest increase is enough immediately to send some of his customers to the competitors. Mutual dependence can also develop among oligopolistic companies manufacturing differentiated products. This type of oligopoly is often referred to as differentiated oligopoly. Here too, companies continuously keep an eye on the others and an action taken by one of them (e.g. a price change, an advertising campaign, the introduction of a new product, etc.), will immediately provoke a response from one of the others. Good examples of this behaviour can be found in the car, tobacco and soft drinks industries, as well as telecommunications, including smartphone business (Exhibit 2.6).

In the case of oligopolies, barriers to entry are rather big. It happened quite frequently that oligopolies developed simply because in some industries (steel, aluminium and car manufacturing, etc.) production could not be made economical without very large quantities that scared away newcomers with their sheer size. In other industries (e.g. soft drinks, consumer electronics), on the other hand, product differentiation increased costs to such a high level that the potential new participants cannot cope.

Considering that in an oligopoly the behaviour of businesses is interdependent, theoreticians also had difficulty creating a model that gives a good description of oligopoly companies' price behaviour. One of them is the so-called kinked demand curve model (Figure 2.6). Let us assume that E is the starting point, and curve DD is the demand curve for the oligopoly company. The company produces quantity Q, sells at price P and the competitors do not follow the price change initiated by the company. The situation when the competitors follow every price change can be described with the curve D'D'. If we start from the assumption that competitors follow price cuts but do not follow price rises, the oligopolies' curve will be DED' - which is the kinked demand curve.

Comparing the prices of oligopoly with those of perfect competition, we find that prices in oligopoly are higher. On the other hand, higher prices are characterized by a relative stability (because of fear of a price war). Firms often attempt to circumvent the regulations concerning prices and competition *and form cartels*. One possibility is to make one of the firms price leader, and the others follow suit. In oligopolies, similarly to monopolies, pricing is based on the costs+profit approach.

2.4.4. The monopolistic competition

Monopolistic competition includes some features of both the monopoly and perfect competition. Besides oligopoly, this is perhaps the most typical form of market in our day. In the monopolistic competition the number of participants is fewer than in perfect competition, but certainly big enough to prevent them from co-operating in the manner of oligopolies. At the same time, their number is sufficient to allow serious competition to develop in the market. In monopolistic competition none of the firms reaches the size required to become a decisive factor in the market.

Figure 2.6. The kinked demand curve

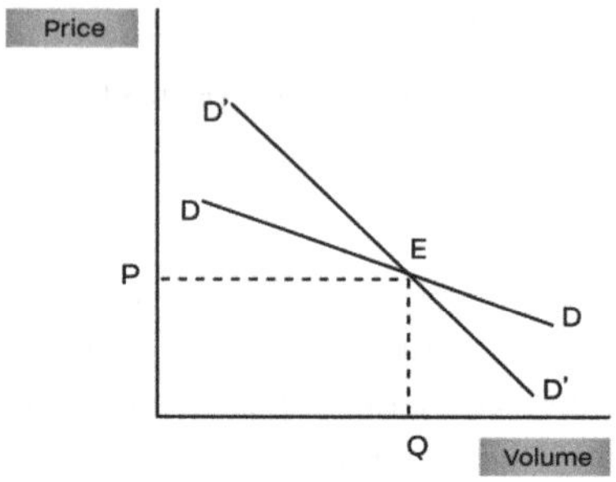

Products involved in the monopolistic competition are differentiated; i.e. although they are close substitutes, customers can tell them apart. As to the methods of differentiation, suffice to say that the differentiating feature can be added either to the physical or to the non-physical dimensions (related services, brand, image, etc.) of the product. To the extent the product concerned differs from other, substitute products, the firm marketing it enjoys privileges similar to a monopolistic situation of the same magnitude. Since customers do not consider the differences to be very big, they are easily copied, making the monopolistic situation quite relative. Companies therefore keep making efforts to modernize their products and serve their customers as well as possible. Monopolistic competition is the real arena of marketing. The characteristic features of the various market types are summarized in Table 2.5.

EXHIBIT 2.7. THE BIRTH OF THE TERM MONOPOLISTIC COMPETITION

The term monopolistic competition was coined by Edward Chamberlin, professor at Harvard University. In 1933 he published his work entitled: The Theory of Monopolistic Competition. It is interesting to note that in the same year Joan Robinson, professor at Britain's Cambridge University, wrote a work of quite similar conception, with the title: The Economics of Imperfect Competition.

Every time we have listed market types so far, we have taken the supply side as our starting point. However, the demand side can also have a significant influence on the market. By extending the morphological overview in this direction as well, we end up with the following list of combinations (Meffert, 1998:491; Pepels, 1998:36-37):

- Bilateral monopoly: one participant on both the supply and the demand side.
- Supply (side) monopoly: single seller, many participants on the demand side.
- Demand (side) monopoly: one consumer and many suppliers.
- Limited supply (side) monopoly: one supplier and some big consumers.

- Limited demand (side) monopoly: some big suppliers.
- Bilateral oligopoly: a few participants both on the supply and on the demand side.
- Supply side oligopoly: some big suppliers and many customers.
- Demand side oligopoly: a lot of suppliers and some big customers.
- Limited demand side oligopoly: some big suppliers and one customer.
- Limited supply side oligopoly: One big supplier and some big customers.
- Partial monopoly: one dominant and several smaller suppliers.
- Partial oligopoly: some dominant and several smaller suppliers.

Table 2.5. Characteristics of market types

Features	Monopoly	Oligopoly	Monopolistic competition	Perfect competition
Number of selling firms	One	Some	A lot	A large number
Size of firms	Big	Big	Medium	Small
Share of the specific market structure in the economy	Small	Big	Very big	Small
Barrier to entry	Big	Big	Medium	Small
Elbow room for independent price policy	Big	Smaller	Smaller	None
What is in the focus of attention?	The firm itself	Competitors	Consumers	Market price
Probability of possible state intervention	Big	Big	Small	Small
Typical feature of the product	Generally homogeneous	Homogeneous or differentiated	Differentiated	Homogeneous
Price elasticity of demand from the firm's viewpoint	Relatively inelastic	Elastic/inelastic (kinked curve)	Elastic	Perfectly elastic
Availability of substitute products	Not typical	To a small degree	Close substitutes	Yes
Efforts for product development	Not much	More	Very much	Not typical
Strong marketing activity	Not typical	To a small extent	To a great extent	Not typical

Let us mention a few examples from real life:

- One supplier/many customers: Post office, electricity-supplying companies.
- One supplier/some customers: Electricity Works, electricity-supplying companies.
- Some suppliers/many customers: sale of crude oil products, mobile phones.

- A lot of suppliers/some big customers: agricultural businesses supplying the sugar factories.
- Some suppliers/one customer: military equipment, planes.
- Some suppliers/some customers: TV programmes, TV channels.

EXHIBIT 2.8. MARKET STRUCTURE AND MARKET CONCENTRATION

In a specific industry concentration depends on the number of businesses operating in the market and the distribution of their output. Theoreticians say that high concentration tends to diminish competition in general and leads to an increase in prices. Various indices are available to measure concentration, but the Herfindhal index is the best known of all. The Herfindhal index (H) is the sum of squares of the market share (turnover) of the business units under examination. Its formula is the following:

$$H = \sum_{i=1}^{N} S_i^2$$

where S_i is the market share of the i-th business.

In order to determine whether - in terms of competition law - a market is concentrated or not, the following classification is used:

H > 1800: market concentration is high. The value: H =1800 corresponds approximately to the situation when the concentration rate (CR.4: market share of the first four largest businesses) is 80%.

If the values exceed H =1800, in terms of competition law, concentration is so high that it opens up the opportunity to abuse dominant position, therefore several countries have accepted this as their threshold value for intervention. (e.g. Sweden, the USA).

H < 1000: market concentration is low. H =1000 approximately equals CR=4 60%. Below this, competition authorities say it is not possible to abuse dominant position, consequently no intervention is necessary.

1000 < H < 1800: market concentration is medium. At this point competition law requires further investigation of the cases because neither the dominant position, nor its absence can be established beyond doubt.

The Herfindhal index can spread between 0 and 10 000. In terms of competition law 10 000 means perfect monopoly, and at 0 a market with perfect competition.

CHAPTER 3. CUSTOMERS' PRICE PERCEPTION

OBJECTIVE 1. To understand how customers, evaluate the value of products and services they buy and explore the processes used to establish price perception.

OBJECTIVE 2. To understand the importance of the role internal and external reference pricing plays in the evaluation process and to ascertain how customers arrive at the point of purchase.

OBJECTIVE 3. To understand price sensitivity and its different influencing factors and to gain a picture of the methods and techniques of price research.

3.1. Introduction

It is common knowledge that prices have a primary influence on the buying decisions of consumers. However, it is not always possible to explain clearly how. According to economic theory a decrease in prices increases the willingness of consumers to purchase and, vice versa, an increase in prices leads to a decrease in willingness. Reality cannot always be described with economic concepts or mathematical formulae. We can often encounter cases in a real market which contradict the laws of economics, or we can witness consumer behaviour which challenges the rationality principle.

The study of the relationship between prices and consumer behaviour is a relatively new field in marketing research. This chapter presents some of the areas which may be of interest to professionals and marketing researchers alike, and which may reveal - by bringing up problems - that everything we already know can contribute to our everyday pricing activity in a useful way, even if there is still a lot to learn about this area.

3.2. The value and price perception of the customers

Figure 3.1. Perceived value

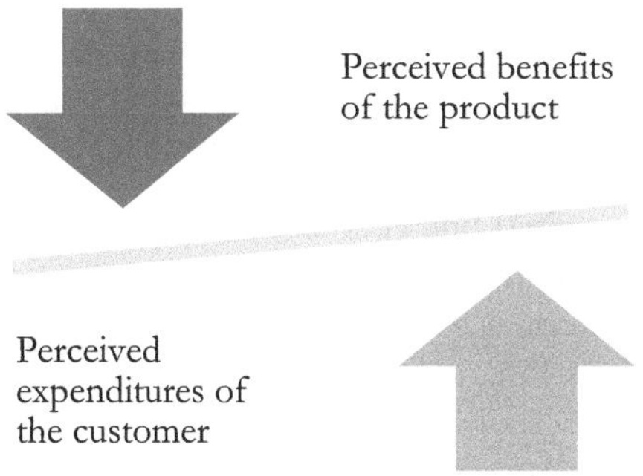

The book entitled *Creating Value in Marketing* (Rekettye, 1999) describes in detail that consumers' buying decisions are mainly affected by perceived value, making it the primary determinant of their willingness to purchase. Perceived value of a product or a service is illustrated in Figure 3.1.

If we are to approach and understand this relationship from the viewpoint of price, we can see that price is included in the denominator of the equation. The major part of consumers' expenditures consists

mainly of the price; there may, of course, be other consumer costs as well, such as the costs of using the product, the energy and psychological costs put into the purchasing process, and other costs etc. Price, therefore, will have a negative impact on the willingness to purchase and on the probability of purchase in this context.

EXHIBIT 3.1. THE WEBER (WEBER–FECHNER) LAW

Researchers usually refer to Weber's law when talking about the perception of price differentials or price change. According to Weber's law the small, equally detectable changes in response are proportionate to the changes in stimulus intensity:

$$K=\frac{\Delta S}{S}$$

where S is the intensity of the stimulus, ΔS is the change in stimulus triggering an equal response and K is a constant.

According to Weber's law, if a $30-increase is required to compel us to avoid buying a product costing $100, a 500$-price will have to be increased by $150 to obtain the same result. That is,

$$K=\frac{\$30}{\$100}=\frac{\$150}{\$500}=0.30$$

Weber's law was further developed by Fechner; so today it is called the Weber–Fechner Law:

$$R=k\log S+a$$

where R is the intensity of the response, S is the intensity of the stimulus, and K is a constant.

The law says that consumers' perception of price differentials and price changes depends on the magnitude of price differentials and price differences. There is a threshold value for perceiving these price differences, called differential price threshold. Any difference lower than the threshold value remains unperceived by the consumers, consequently their influence on the purchase decision is negligible.

Research studies also found that consumers, in general, reacted to the increase in prices in a more sensitive way than to the decrease in prices. Furthermore, it was proved that the threshold value of perception varied for different products that is, the K related to the threshold can have different magnitudes.

Several research findings support the opinion that price acts rather as a "complex, multidimensional stimulus" (Monroe, 2003: 105), and as such, will play not only a negative but also a positive role in the purchase decision. This positive role can be twofold (Lichtenstein et al. 1993):

- Price, for many consumers, can be the *indication of quality* (Ding et al. 2010), and as such can have an impact on the exponent of the equation. The evaluation of the perceived benefits of a product will also depend on the price (see, for example, the conclusions in the main work by the best-known researcher of price, Gabor André, 1998). As long as consumers consider price as the indicator of quality, price will affect their purchase decisions in a positive way. Research studies have also pointed out that the importance of the role price plays as indicator of quality depends largely on the type of the product, the purchase situation and the individual characteristics of consumers.

- The other positive role of price manifests itself in conspicuous consumption, a term coined by Veblen. Similarly to the price-quality pattern, the price of a product or a service purchased represents not only quality in the mind of a consumer, but conveys information about that particular consumer to other people as well. Therefore, the consumer may choose a higher priced product not only because the quality associated with it is better, but because they believe that the product chosen will reflect a higher social status to others. (Lichtenstein et al. 1993; Wheatly–Chiu, 1977; Gabor, 1975).

3.3. From price to willingness to purchase

In this part we review the cognitive process that consumers go through from the perception of the price to the decision to purchase. The previous part of this chapter focused on the comparison of perceived benefits and perceived costs (prices). Before being able to perceive the value of a product a potential buyer must know and perceive its price. Price perception has been the topic of several research studies on consumer behaviour in the past few years. These studies have mostly used the 'stimulus-response' model, where the price the consumer sees is the stimulus, which triggers the perception process. After seeing a given price, the potential buyer will try to understand, evaluate and store it, then integrate it with a set of other related prices and price-like information (Chernev, 2003).

3.3.1. Price perception as the process of numerical information processing

Prices are made up of *numbers*. People encounter numbers in almost all areas of life. Some of this numerical information is easy for them to process, some may prove more difficult. There is a complicated cognitive process underlying even the easiest calculation or comparison of numbers, called numerical information processing. The same is true for the understanding and comparison of prices. There is a vast literature on numerical processing, but the present book will focus mostly on the presentation of research results with regard to price relationships.

a) An important question arising in connection with prices is how people compare numbers (i.e. prices). Well, according to relevant literature there are

- *The holistic model* assumes that when people compare two or more multi-digit numerical data (for example, $452 and $684) they do not compare the individual digits, but first they develop a mental representation of the perceived analogue magnitude, and then they compare these magnitudes.
- *The digital model,* on the other hand, assumes that when we compare prices we typically proceed by digits. According to this model people compare two numbers by looking at the digit on the left and they immediately conclude that the second number is higher than the first (because 6 > 4.)

Using one or the other model will not produce the same result: with the digital model the difference between $299 and $400 will be the same as the difference between $200 and $400, but with the holistic model the difference will be the same as the difference between $300 and $400. The experiment carried out by Thomas and Morwitz showed that people typically apply the digital method when comparing numbers that fall nearer and the holistic model for numbers that fall more distant from each other.

b) The role of the difference between numbers and the magnitude of the digits is also important. Several research projects cited by Monroe (2003) observed that people needed more time to compare numbers with a small difference between them than those with a big difference (e.g. more time is needed to perceive the difference between 6 and 8 than to perceive the difference between 2 and 8). When the differences are similar, the so-called small numbers are perceived differently from larger numbers. In the decimal system 5 represents the neutral number; anything lower than that is

considered to be a small number and anything higher a large number. Research findings suggest that the difference perceived while the two numbers are being compared decreases depending on the size of the digits. People perceived the difference between smaller digits (1, 2, 3 and 4) to be bigger than the difference between larger (6, 7, 8 and 9) digits (Coulter–Coulter, 2007). Weber's Law seems to reverberate here as well.

c) Regarding price perception, another important question is how people can *remember* the prices seen earlier and how accurately they can *recall* them. Addressing this topic, Vanhuele *et* al. (2005) stated that there were several ways to memorize prices. People encode shorter sequences of digits verbally in their short-term memory, from which the authors concluded that people were more likely to remember wrongly or to round numbers which take longer to recall or which are made up of several syllables. Another way to encode price in memory is to evaluate it as a quantity. In this case, people are less likely to remember bigger numbers correctly, so they tend to round them instead. Remembrance and recall are therefore also influenced by the individual's speech rate and the differences in spoken languages.

d) How people notice, understand and compare prices also depend on *the way prices are presented.* By presentation we mean the form of the number, the letter fonts, the colour of the sign, the size of the letters and the way prices are displayed.

EXHIBIT 3.2. STARBUCKS PRICING - TAKING ADVANTAGE OF WEBER-FECHNER LAW

According to the blog of Tucker Dawson, Starbucks raised their beverage prices by an average of 1% across the US end of July 2013. Implementing such a specific and minor price increase when the bottom line is already in great shape might seem like a greedy tactic, but the Starbucks approach to pricing is one we can all use to improve our margins. One 1% increase in prices can raise profits by an average of 11%. According to Dawson Starbucks is a master of employing pricing to maximize profits, since they use research and customer analysis to formulate targeted price increases that capture the greatest amount consumers are willing to pay without driving them off.

Rather than trying to compete with cheaper chains like Dunkin, Starbucks uses price hikes to separate itself from the pack and reinforce the premium image of their brand and products. Since their loyal following is not especially price sensitive, Starbucks coffee maintains a fairly inelastic demand curve, and a small price increase can have a huge positive impact on their margins without decreasing demand for beverages.

Sources: http://www.priceintelligently.com/blog/all

e) Coming back to numbers, we can already conclude from the above that the digit found on the left hand side of the price has a special significance. Paradoxically, this effect appears in the case of number endings (9 ending pricing). It also implies that the right-end of the number also plays an important role. The very well-known practice in marketing of using odd numbers at the end of a price, and its further developed version: prices ending in 9 are all based on this idea. Psychology has found that for some reason people prefer odd numbers, even if they deal with even numbers more easily. This is how the odd number 9 before a round number comes into play. When most prices were below $10 in American retail shops, it turned out that people would concentrate more on the digit on the left and would overlook the amount in cents given after the dollar. If that is the case, clever

salesmen thought, why shouldn't prices end in 99? A survey conducted by the Marketing Bulletin in 1997 showed that about 60% of the prices ended in 9 and 30% ended in 5, the second most popular number. Prices ending in 0 represented 7%, and those ending in all other numbers 3%. Schindler (2007) cautions that prices ending in 99 could also give the impression of cheapness (inferior quality). This is why many companies try to improve the image of their products by using rounded numbers.

EXHIBIT 3.3. SENIOR CITIZENS IN THE SUPERMARKET

The proportion of elderly people in the total population is constantly increasing. (The share of people aged over 65 was 18.9% in the EU on 1st January 2015). These people also purchase, and prices may have more importance for them than for younger people. Let us consider the installations and the price labels in a supermarket. The first problem is how to locate a given product. (If a product is displayed on the lowest or on the top shelf elderly people might not even notice it, let alone find the way to take it off.) But where are the prices displayed? Well, on the shelves obviously, but are they at the bottom or on the top? It is a difficult decision for an elderly person to make and they may even postpone the purchase as a result. If the elderly want to buy clothes in the supermarket, its size is usually printed in 14-point size letters in a small box on the tag hidden in the garment.

Photo: https://infogr.am/Elderly-shopping-pablo_karrash_1372595336

Some retailers in the US have already recognised these anomalies and started the preparations for providing better service to the elderly. This includes changing the colours, and making price labels and product information more visible.

3.3.2. Price perception in the case of multidimensional prices

Discussions about price perception have generally assumed that prices are expressed as a single amount (number sequence) (e.g. $8,799). The last one or two decades, however have witnessed a surge in the number of products and services in particular, where the offer price is not expressed by one sequence, but in a more complicated way. The comprehension, processing and comparing of these multi-component, multi-dimensional prices requires a more complex cognitive process from people than a price expressed as a lump sum.

The term 'multi-dimensional price' is used when a supplier quotes the price of a product or service using several number sequences at the point of sale or in advertisements. The term was introduced by Hooman Estelami at the end of the 1990s (Estelami, 1999). In the case of multi-dimensional prices consumers have to perform different arithmetical operations to get to know the actual price. However, some consumers may not be willing or be able to perform these operations. Let us review some of the methods used for communicating prices that require arithmetic and other operations from potential consumers:

- Price discount:
    - Discount is expressed in $ (–$50 off the original price): the customer has to do the subtraction.

- Discount defined as a percentage (discount –15%): the customer has to perform several operations.
- Discount linked to a certain amount of purchase (e.g. 10% discount on purchases over 300$),
- Promotions like "Buy two and get the third one free", or "Get two for the price of one" etc.

- Complex prices:
  - The price of the product or service, and that of the accessories necessary for use are indicated separately (price of the flight ticket and the airport tax individually.)
  - Bulk packages (e.g. beer is often packaged in 6-pack, 12-pack or 24-pack: it is difficult for the consumer to decide which pack has the most favourable price).
  - Indication of delivery costs separately (e.g. ordering products from Amazon).
  - Indication of installation prices separately.
  - Package price (product bundle prices), where the individual items can be purchased separately, etc.
- Purchasing on consumer credit (leasing):
  - Indication of the monthly instalments and the number of payment periods.
  - Presentation of different rates of charge (exchange rate risk).
- Difficulty of understanding the multi-dimensional prices of public utility services:
  - Garbage collection fee: the basic fee comprises the price of bin collection, however the monthly fee is calculated on the basis of bin collection frequency, the size of the bin, and the billing cycle.
  - Electricity bill: it has a great number of components, and can be divided into three parts at least: the energy fee, the network fee and VAT.
- Subscription fees (some parts of which can be purchased separately).
- Tuition fees (for a month, for a semester or for the whole period of the training) can include all the additional services, but you might have to pay separately for them.
- Composite/Two-part tariffs (a basic fee/lump sum and usage fees/per unit rate) e.g. telephone and telecommunication services.

Research in the perception of multi-dimensional prices has found (Estelami, 2008: 64–66) that the majority of consumers do not take into account all the dimensions of price (i.e. do not make detailed calculations), preferring to focus instead on one of the components of price dimensions — for example, on the monthly payment in the case of car leasing. The more dimensions that are added, the larger the number of consumers likely to simplify the process. The time required for evaluating prices can be quadrupled by the necessity to perform multiplication. The complexity of the calculation can be further increased by prices ending in 99. Contrary to European regulation (where gross consumer prices must be shown on products) the price tags in the United States show the so-called sales tax-free prices. Calculating the actual price of a product with a price tag of $169.99 (assuming an 8% sales

tax) may prove to be a difficult task even for a teacher of mathematics: (169.99 x 0.08) + 169.99 = $183.59.

3.4. Perception of prices: summary

The first part of the process leading up to the purchase starts with the understanding of prices published using different marketing tools. The previous parts of this chapter dealt with this complicated cognitive process. What has been discussed so far can be summarized in Figure 3.2.

Figure 3.2. The model of price perception

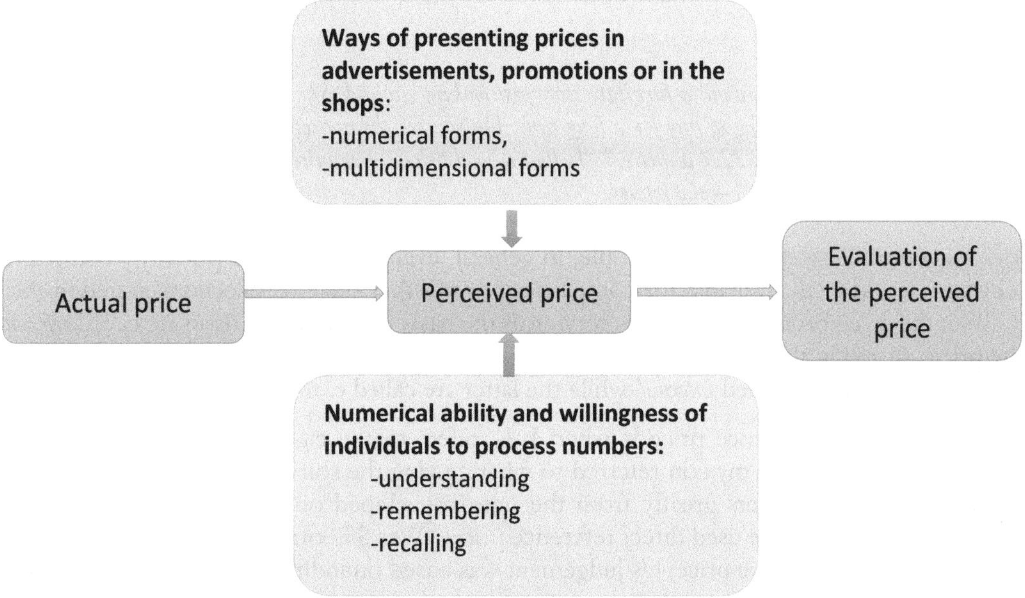

The next part will focus on the process of evaluating the perceived price.

3.5. Evaluation of perceived prices: reference prices

Once prices are understood, the purchasing process moves on to evaluation. Let us now examine how consumers evaluate and perceive the prices they have understood (perceived).

Purchase situations:

Situation 1:

> *My son came home the other day wearing a very smart, branded new shirt. "Look Dad, what a fantastic shirt I have just bought", he said. "How much did it cost?", I asked. "I paid $160 for it", – he replied. "Oh my Goodness!" was my reaction. "I could have bought four shirts for that price." "Come on Dad, what kind of world do you live in? This was the cheapest of the ones I liked", he replied.*

Situation 2:

> *B. O., associate professor in the Marketing Department visited the vegetable section of a new, beautifully furnished grocery store well-known for its exclusive products. After praising the decoration, he asked for a kilo of bananas, then suddenly said: "No, I don't want them after all, they are too expensive for me". The manager of the store, who had until then proudly believed that the store's prices were competitive, despite its luxurious*

appearance, asked, with disappointment in his voice: "Why, how much would they cost in other stores, Professor?". "I have no idea", came the reply.

Situation 3:

J. L. is a visiting professor from London at a Hungarian university. He smokes Benson and Hedges (a brand of cigarettes). We walk into a supermarket where this is the most expensive brand of cigarette costing HUF 1,000 a pack. J. L. asks for two cartons because, as he explains, "the price would be three times as much in London".

Situation 4:

My wife and I are strolling around a furniture store just looking around. She suddenly says: "Come, let's buy that curtain I've been planning to buy for a long time. Do you see the notice? It says that there is a sale, the price is reduced from $30 to $22.9 a metre." "Is that a good price?" I inquire. "I do not know the prices, but it is certainly better than $30", – she replies.

The above examples illustrate well that people, in general, evaluate the actual prices by comparing them to other prices directly available for comparison, or to other price recollections stored in their memory about the given product. The prices serving as the basis for the comparison are called *reference prices*. The prices stored in the memory should be distinguished from the prices directly available for comparison. The former are called *internal,* while the latter are called *external* reference prices.

An example for internal reference price is when J. L. refers to the cigarette prices in London in purchase Situation 3. The price my son referred to when buying the shirt is also a reference price; it is a reference price which differs greatly from the one I developed on the basis of my $40 shirt purchases (Situation 1). My wife used direct reference price: "Was $30 originally" (Situation 4). O. B. did not have an explicit reference price; his judgement was based on indirect information (the quality of the shop's interior (Situation 2).

The scientific background to research dealing with price sensitivity is provided by the adaptation-level theory known in psychology: according to this, the behaviour of an individual is determined by the individual's adaptation to three stimuli: focal, contextual and organic stimuli. Applying this theory to prices, the focal stimulus will be the offer (or the price) in question to which the consumer responds; the contextual stimuli include the internal reference prices, the funds available, the purpose of the purchase, the environment in which the purchase takes place, etc. The organic stimulus comes from the individual's psychological make-up.

Monroe has drawn the following important conclusions about the perception and acceptance of prices (2003: 132):

- The perception and acceptance of a price depends on other prices and the use of other products.
- Each level of quality distinguishable within a product category has its reference price which influences how other prices are judged.
- Reference prices have a so-called indifference scale, which means that a change in prices within certain limits has no impact on the way prices are perceived.
- The reference price is a kind of average of the prices of similar products and is not necessarily the same as the actual price or the price of the leading brand.

- Consumers do not judge prices solely on the basis of one factor, but they compare them with reference prices and with the prices which fall in the same price range.

EXHIBIT 3.4. IMPACT OF THE APPEARANCE OF A NEW PRODUCT PRICE ON THE LEVEL OF ADAPTATION

The adaptation level (in this context, the reference price) can change when a new product price appears. According to the theory this change will take place based on *assimilation or contrast.* If the new stimulus (the new price) is consistent with the level of assimilation (i.e. the discrepancy is not dramatic), the new price will be assimilated into the already developed value-system and will shift the reference level either upward or downward. This impact is called 'anchoring'. Let us illustrate this theory with a practical example. Let us assume that the reference price of a low category car is around 15K dollars (or between 12K and 18K). An article is published in one of the car magazines about a new small car which will be marketed at 20K dollars or more. It will trigger the individual's reference level to shift upward — perhaps to 17K (or between 15K and 19K). The individual who had considered the cars offered at 14K as average priced earlier could find the same price cheap as a result of the new adaptation level. The new price acts as an 'anchor' pulling the assimilation level downward, in our case.

If, however, the discrepancy between the new price and the reference price is too big, the contrast effect will occur, and the consumer will exclude the new stimulus from the existing value system and will evaluate it as a new or different category. Returning to our example, if the price of the new small car costs 30 K, our individual can perceive it as a new category (a different quality), and his original reference level will not change. An example can be Toyota IQ about which the famous Top Gear team wrote "Toyota rethinks the city car. Then charges too much for it." Its price was much higher than the other small city cars. Most probably, people thought about it as a new category.

Photo: By Matthias - A feltöltő saját munkája (own photo), Attribution, https://commons.wikimedia.org/w/index.php?curid=7092528

3.5.1. Internal reference prices, price awareness, price consciousness

With regard to reference prices a few questions arise about how well consumers know prices, how conscious they are in their price judgements and about differences in their familiarity with the prices of other products or among different consumer groups. Research in this field was carried out in the United States and in the United Kingdom. In the presentation of the research findings we will rely mainly on the work by Gabor (1988). He used the notion of price consciousness for describing price awareness. Vanhuele and Drèze (2002) used price knowledge, while Monroe (2003) adopted two other notions: (1) price awareness, i.e. people's ability to remember prices; and (2) price consciousness, which can be interpreted as price sensitivity. This indicates how sensitive consumers are to differences in prices. Price-conscious consumers will not be willing to pay a higher price for products of better quality or with different properties if the difference in the price is too big. Less price-conscious consumers, however, will be ready to pay more (e.g. in a more fashionable shop) for a product they like (or it may also be the case that they do not know the prices well enough to perceive the big difference). Price-consciousness expects customers to possess the appropriate information, and have high price awareness.

The level of price awareness is not constant, even in the case of price-sensitive consumers. When one intends to buy a durable consumer product of higher value, for example, one searches the Internet,

compares prices and knows exactly at what price the given product has been purchased. This is a case of high level price awareness, which will be practically reduced to zero by the next purchase: the purchase price is likely sink into oblivion by that time. (A long time can go by before a durable consumer item is purchased again, during which not only the product itself may change significantly but the comparability of the price as well.) Consumers' price awareness is assumed to be more reliable about regularly purchased convenience goods (food and other daily necessities). When determining the price of such products it is important for sellers to understand how well consumers know the prices. This information can have an impact not only on the pricing methods but on the other elements of marketing tools as well.

Gabor (1988: 237–247) used two methods for measuring price awareness:

- He measured price recall by asking consumers to state the actual price of certain products purchased within two weeks and tested how many of them could cite the actual price regardless of whether the price was correct or not. The results of the study encompassing 5,276 purchases are presented in Table 3.1. The list is topped by tea (the survey was carried out in the UK) and eggs, while people could least recall the price of cornflakes and flour. The findings confirmed what researchers had already suspected, that price awareness was inversely proportionate to income status, i.e. the poorer consumers are, the more attention they pay to prices.

- The other method measures how accurately consumers can recall prices. American studies have shown that the rate of accurate recall (within certain tolerances) was very low. The findings of the survey carried out by Vanhuele and Drèze on accuracy in 2001 using a sample of 1,186 are presented in table 3.2.

Table 3.1. Results of price recall by socio-economic classes

Socio-economic class	Distribution (%)	Number of purchases	% of price recall
Rich	2	120	63.3
Upper middle class	7	363	66.4
Lower middle class	27	1523	80.8
Working class	55	2895	85.5
Poor	9	375	80.3

Table 3.2. Accuracy of price recall

Accuracy level	In cumulative % of respondents
Accurate	2.1
within 5% margin of error	21.3
within 10% margin of error	37.3
within 20% margin of error	60.3

Source: Vanhuele– Drèze, 2002

The conclusion is that consumers do not always remember accurately the prices of regularly purchased products either. However, it is important to emphasize that these prices (not always accurate prices) reflect the price expectation of consumers about the given product. When prices are

set it is important to bear in mind how these price expectations relate to the actual prices; this relationship can imply how consumers will respond to possible price change.

3.5.2. Internal reference price as price scale

We have been talking about internal reference price (IRP) without clarifying if IRP is a fixed price or a relatively elastic range of prices. Experience shows, and it has also been confirmed by literature, that IRP is basically a price range which can be illustrated in the following way (Figure 3.3.).

Figure 3.3. Zones of reference prices

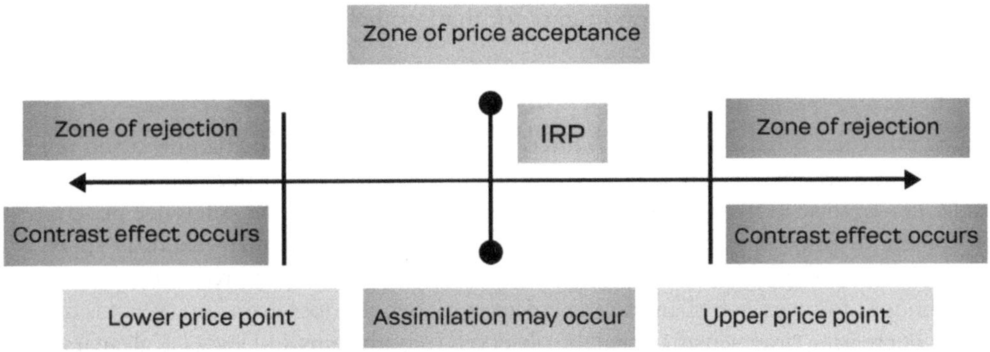

Source: Shinha–Prasad, 2004: 25

It means in addition to having a reference price, consumers also develop a range of prices they find acceptable. There is a lower and upper limit (price threshold), below or above which price they will not consider buying a certain product or service. The upper price threshold is clearly understandable for everybody; however the lower limit is not that obvious and cannot be explained by the demand curve theory of economics either. The findings of price research have proven the existence of the lower price threshold beyond doubt. What it comes down to is that each product price has a value, which can be expressed by a positive number higher than zero that consumers find too low for purchasing the product. It can be assumed that below a certain price level consumers are afraid that the quality of the product is inferior (or perhaps the seller has not acquired the product by lawful means).

The range of internal reference prices (i.e. of price acceptance) can be influenced by several variables. These include:

- Product category
- Brand loyalty
- Frequency of purchase
- Level of price awareness
- Purchased quantity
- Purchase location
- Individual factors

3.5.3. External reference prices

External reference prices usually come into focus when the supplier provides the reference price in addition to the actual price. Examples include advertisement comparing the prices of the competing

products (which is very popular in the United States, but Europe has banned some of its forms), or the very widely used promotional method which lists the 'original' or 'regular' price next to the reduced price on the leaflets, in the advertisements or even in the shop. Consumers encounter two prices: the original price and the reduced discount price. The question remains which price they will choose as a basis for judging the value of the product, and whether they will accept the promoted original price as the reference price. If they do, the discount price will obviously become attractive for them. If they don't find the implied reference price credible, they will replace it with a different price. They will probably rely on earlier price recollections, which means they will look for an internal reference price. If they cannot find one, they will continue to gather more information about the price (the price comparison websites provide excellent opportunity for that), to help them decide on the value of a product and also whether to purchase it or not.

EXHIBIT 3.5. IMPACT OF REFERENCE PRICES ON AGGREGATE DEMAND

Economic theories agree that reference prices have an influence on demand too and refer to it as *reference effect* (Popescu–Wu, 2006). According to this theory (prospect theory) consumers consider as *gain* (discount) any purchase made at a price lower than the reference price and as a *loss* (premium price) any purchase made at a price higher than that. There is an *internal asymmetry* between the evaluation of the gain obtained and the loss suffered in this way: loss is usually thought to be greater than the same degree of benefit (loss aversion). What is more, a gradually decreasing price sensitivity can be observed to both gains and losses. Kalyanaram and Winer (1995) processed and synthesized the impact of reference prices on aggregate demand and proved the broken S-shaped curve representing this impact on demand.

Empirical studies have shown that suppliers are very much aware of the professional recommendations on how to communicate prices. What we haven't yet touched upon in this book is how consumers perceive time-limited price promotions. Based on the research findings about the topic two American researchers Howard and Kerin (2006) have drawn the following conclusions:

- Communicating only the reference price will affect price perception positively only if the consumer concerned would like to purchase the type of product in question.
- Communicating both the reference price and the limited time will produce a more positive effect than communicating only one or the other of them.
- This positive effect will arise even if the consumer had no intention of purchasing such a product.

3.6. Extending the reference price: reference value

So far, we have presented the process that leads consumers to a decision on the extent to which the price of a product or service meets their price expectations. It has been concluded that they use both internal and external reference prices for making such decisions. Consumers, however, often find themselves in situations when they are to purchase a product, which is not fully identical with the products purchased earlier, therefore their price recollections can only be applied in an indirect way. In such cases consumers need to compare the value of the new product with the value of the internal (saved in their memories) or external (directly comparable in their physical forms) reference products (Nagle–Holden, 1995). Consumers adjust the value of the reference product with the difference value of the new product. According to Nagle and Holden the reference value represents the cost of the best alternative to the product considered for purchase, while the difference value represents the

difference (either positive or negative) between the value of the reference product and the product in question. (Figure 3.4).

Figure 3.4. Illustration of the reference value

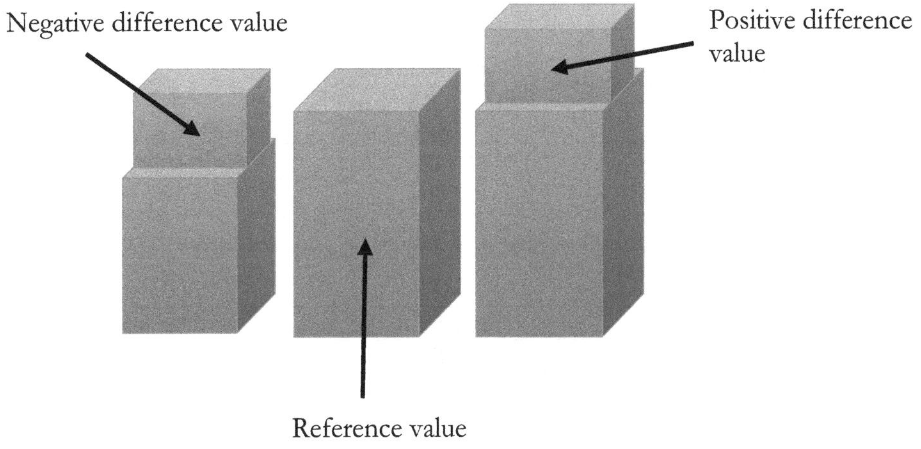

Source: Based on Nagel–Holden, 1995

EXHIBIT 3.6. CALCULATING THE CUSTOMER VALUE (LIFECYCLE COST) OF ELECTRIC VEHICLE VS. GAS VS. HYBRID CARS

As more and more people become environmentally conscious, eco-friendly vehicles have emerged as an attractive alternative to gas-powered cars. According to NerdWallet's analysis, electric-vehicle drivers in USA can save over $10,000 on car ownership costs over five years, compared with those driving gas automobiles. NerdWallet crunched the numbers on the costs of driving a gas, hybrid and electric car in some of the nation's largest cities. They compared:

- Toyota Camry, a gasoline powered-vehicle
- Toyota Prius, a hybrid that runs on gas and electricity
- Nissan Leaf, an all-electric car

From their analysis made in September 2015 the data for the city Boston were picked out and presented in the table and graph below. Driving an electric car can save money for buyers. Although all three car models are similarly priced, on average Nissan Leaf owners will spend $11,196 less than Camry drivers and $10,210 less than Prius owners over five years. The savings are mainly due to the $7,500 federal tax credit provided to Leaf and all electric car owners, but even without the credit, the Leaf is cheapest to own. The figure shows the savings of the drivers of Nissan Leaf.

The figure, which contains the prices and the five-year maintenance, repair and insurance costs (in dollars) of the three models shows that, although the price of the Nissan Leaf (without tax credit) is similar to the other two cars, calculating the life cycle costs (now the five year costs), buyers can save money with it because insurance and fuel costs are much lower.

Table. The five year costs in the Boston area of the three cars (in dollars)

	TOYOTA CAMRY a gasoline powered-vehicle	TOYOTA PRIUS a hybrid that runs on gas and electricity	NISSAN LEAF an all-electric car

Source	*By Ron Cogswell - Flickr: Toyota Camry -- Cockspur Island (GA) July 2012, CC BY 2.0, https://commons.wikimedia.org/w/index.php?curid=32336114*	*By OSX - Own work, Public Domain, https://commons.wikimedia.org/w/index.php?curid=15078302*	*By IFCAR - Own work, Public Domain, https://commons.wikimedia.org/w/index.php?curid=17238574*
MSRP*	22,335	23,459	23,444
Maintenance	2,584	2,849	2,347
Repair	560	560	601
Insurance	7,587	8,212	5,828
Fuel	7,000	4,000	2,750
Fed. tax credit**	0	0	7,500
Total	40,066	39,080	28,870

**MSRP = Manufacturers' Suggested Retail Price*

*** Federal tax credit is deductible from the person's income tax. If the income tax is lower, it can be deducted only to the actual value of the tax.*

Figure 3.5. Savings of drivers of Nissan Leaf

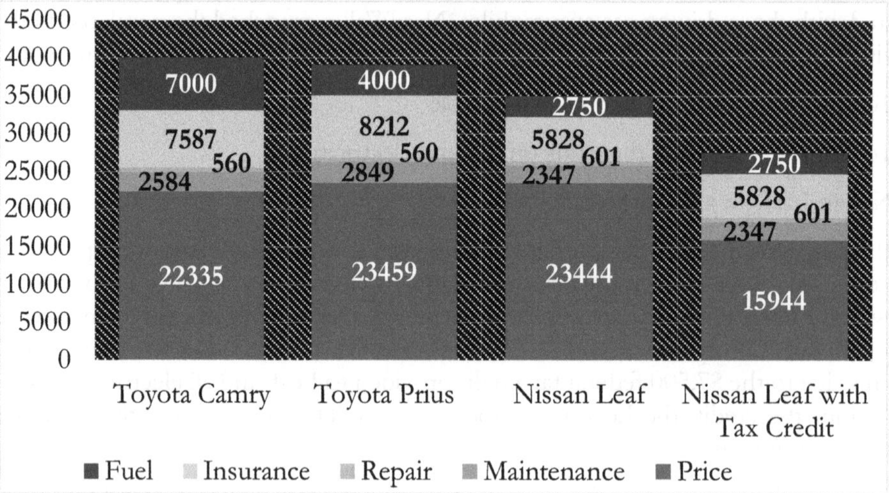

When high value products (and similarly high-value industrial goods) are purchased, the comparison of the reference price, or the reference value and the value of the new product is based not only on price. Reasonable consumers will take into account not only the price of the product but all the additional costs, which will arise during its use. Monroe (2003) refers these costs as *life-cycle costs.* This approach will prove especially useful in *customer value pricing method.*

3.7. Price sensitivity and its influencing factors

It is obvious from the above that price plays a pivotal role in consumers' purchase decisions (There are always exceptions: sometimes the price of a product does not make a difference, because it is either insignificant or the need inducing the purchase requires immediate satisfaction). The effect which describes the relationship of consumers to prices is called price sensitivity. The next part will focus on the factors that have an influence on the degree of price sensitivity. The factors affecting price sensitivity are similar to the theoretical factors influencing the price elasticity of demand. The only difference is that our discussion of the price elasticity of demand is intended to draw conclusions about the behaviour of the market as a whole, while the current discussion is more concerned with a company, product or service.

Being more aware of the factors that influence price sensitivity, business managers will be better able to form prices that meet the price expectations of consumers. It has already been concluded that consumers do not perceive prices per se, but in relation to the benefits offered by the product, the so-called customer value. Factors influencing price sensitivity are related to the perceived value of the product. Next, we will review the factors which have an impact on price acceptance by consumers.

3.7.1. The impact of price and quality relationship

Researchers argue whether there is a relationship between the price and the quality of the products, whether price can function as a determinant or indicator of quality (Gabor–Granger, 1966; Wheatley–Chiu, 1977; Koku, 1995; Yoon–Kijewski, 1997). According to classical economic theory such a relation does not exist, otherwise the downward sloping of the demand curve could not be explained. Yet, everyday experiences prove that consumers very often evaluate the quality of a product based on its price. Even common proverbs and sayings provide evidence for this; in the following sentences for example, "When you buy cheap, you get cheap", "I'm too poor to buy cheap", or "Those who buy cheap products pay the most" the word *cheap* refers to low quality.

In many cases all consumers can do is to rely on price when judging a product, because they are unable to evaluate and compare the real quality of products which are becoming more and more complex technically. The price-quality relationship is not always real, but it is definitely not linear. The perception map consumers develop about the level of prices and quality is referred to as a 'value map' in literature, as can be seen in Figure 3.6.

The horizontal axis of the value map represents the perceived price, while the vertical axis represents the perceived quality of the product or service. If the perceived quality and perceived price are in balance in the minds of the consumers (i.e. lying on or close to the value equivalence line, a vector drawn at a 45 degree angle), we talk about balance, and consumers can choose according to their needs between the different quality and price categories. If, however, the judgement about certain products deviates significantly from this balance, consumers will become suspicious. If the perceived price is much higher than the perceived quality, consumers will feel deceived and may decide to postpone the purchase or to give preference to other substitute products. In the reverse case, consumers may be suspicious and will not understand how the supplier can deviate from the balance,

and will question whether the product offered is faulty or its performance is poor. If these deviations persist for a long time, consumers will be compelled to modify their reference prices and redress the balance.

Figure 3.6. The relationship between price and quality

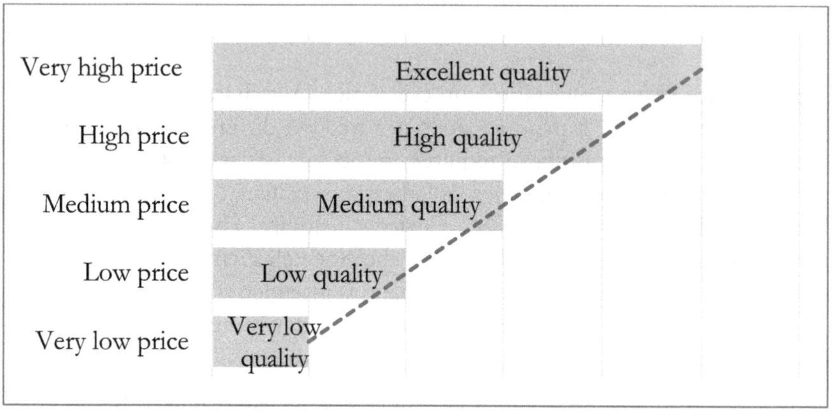

EXHIBIT 3.7. PERCEPTION MAP OF CARS

The authors (Rekettye – Liu, 2001) have prepared a so-called perception map of cars sold in large quantities in Hungary, with price (and the maintenance costs) shown on one axis, and the use value of the car (the quality in the broad sense) on the other. The perceptions of six different cars by Hungarian consumers in relation to the curve drawn at a 45-degree angle are illustrated in Figure 3.7.

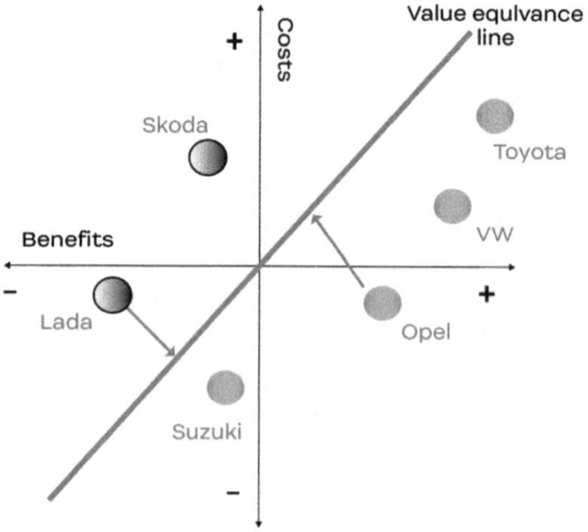

Figure 3.7. Perceptions by costs and benefits

The line drawn at a 45-degree angle at the intersection of price and the benefits of the product may ultimately be interpreted as the axis of balance between consumers' perception of the price and the benefits. As actual perceptions only fall on this line in ideal or random cases, the range of balance should be broadened. Pepels (1998: 63) for example determined a balance zone (Korridor für ausgewogene Preis-Leistung-Relation) which can be illustrated by Figure 3.8.

The relationship between price and quality (= benefits, performance) becomes increasingly evident in the longer term. Two components can be observed in this interaction:

- the reliability of the price-quality relationship,
- the significance of the role the price-quality relationship (i.e. price as the indicator of quality) plays in the purchase decisions. The role of these two components may vary across different consumer product categories (Figure 3.9).

On the whole, we can conclude using the words of Gabor (1998: 251) that price "can function as a strong indicator of quality and will remain an important attribute of the product even after the purchase".

Figure 3.8. The value equivalence corridor

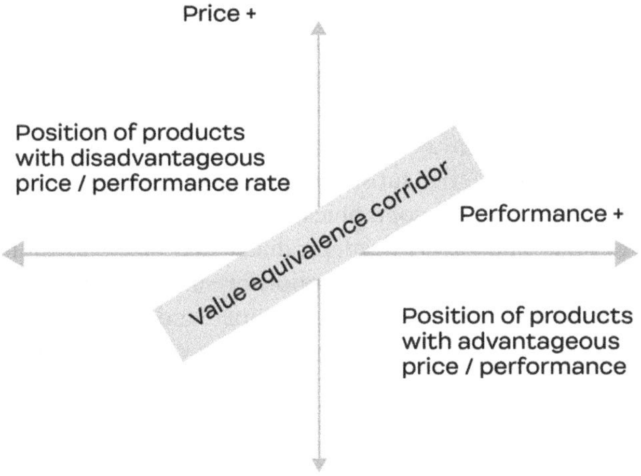

Figure 3.9. The intensity and reliability of price-quality relationships across different product groups

3.7.2. The impact of perceived substitute products

Research has found that the higher consumers consider the price of a given product or service compared to that of the substitute products or services, the more price sensitive they become. There are fewer substitute products for new products, therefore consumers are likely to be less sensitive to the price of a new product. That is why revolutionary new products are often launched at a high, so-called skimming price on the market.

Some consumer groups are less informed and some purchase situations make it more difficult to make this comparison. One of the best examples is tourism. A tourist visiting a given town for the first time does not know the choice of restaurants and is less sensitive to the high prices charged by the restaurants for their services in areas that are frequented by tourists (these are often called tourist

rip-off restaurants). Locals are more familiar with the supply and are therefore more sensitive to restaurant prices.

Companies can influence the perception of substitute products by using different marketing tools. One such tool is the positioning of the product in a better way. If the positioning is focused on the competitive product, consumers will be induced to take the product or service selected by the company as the basis for comparison. For example, a less expensive but centrally situated hotel can offer a cheaper alternative for guests than a five-star hotel. But the perception of substitute products can also be influenced by different distribution methods. In the case of products that are delivered to and sold in the homes of consumers (e.g. Avon and Amway), comparison with other substitute products becomes very difficult. How consumers perceive the substitute products can also depend on where these products are displayed in the shops or on the geographical location of the shop itself (A lower priced product placed among high value and high-priced products may become more attractive than if it were displayed among similar products). The perception of substitute products may also be affected by how the individual items of a product line are developed and priced (If the top model is overpriced, the cheaper model released later will become immediately very attractive).

3.7.3. The influence of difficulty in comparison

It is not easy to compare substitute products and to evaluate the price of a product or service if the prices of the products are hard to compare. There are many products the quality of which will be revealed only during use. As to other products or services, it is not always possible to compare their prices. Let's take the account management fees charged by banks or brokerage firms as an example. These fees (one-time account opening fee, annual and monthly account charges, transfer charges, commission depending on the amount, etc.) are so complicated in many cases, that a clear comparison becomes impossible. But this is the same with the different packages offered by insurance companies and mobile telephone service providers. Theorists claim that the more difficult it is to make a comparison, the more price sensitive consumers become. This is particularly true for industrial products and more specifically for capital goods. The real efficiency of equipment will be revealed only in use. That is why the purchasing company does not take the risk of making a decision purely on the basis of price. This is when the reliability and reputation of the supplier will come into play. In the case of consumer goods, the well-known brands will be given preference.

A company can facilitate comparison (or make it more difficult) even in this case. The company newly entering the market can facilitate this comparison by sending free product samples, organising tasting or testing events. Specialist publications (test magazines, Consumer Reports in the Unites States, different car magazines etc.) can also help with comparison.

3.7.4. The influence of distinctive value

The existence of substitute products can significantly increase price sensitivity. The most efficient tool companies can use to protect themselves against it is to market products that have distinctive, unique characteristics in contrast with the products of their competitors. The more unique and distinctive a product or service is, the lower the price sensitivity of its potential consumers will be. That's the essence of product differentiation. As price sensitivity will always depend on the *perceived* value of the given product and those of the available substitute products, it is not enough to make the product unique or different from the other competitive products, it is also imperative to make the potential consumers aware of this. Marketing communication plays an important role in raising awareness.

3.7.5. The impact of switching costs

The higher the costs of replacing a product (costs can be financial, but learning how to use the new product is also considered a cost), the less price-sensitive consumers become with regard to products they have used so far. The magnitude of the cost of switching a product will have a reverse impact on the price sensitivity about the new product. The higher the perceived switching costs appear, the more price sensitive consumers become. For example, if the urban transport company has been using a certain type of bus, switching to a new model will not only include the costs of replacing the buses, but also the costs of learning how to maintain the new vehicles and the costs of replacing a large amount of spare parts. A more typical situation occurs in the case of certain software; switching to new software requires training and compatibility with other software solutions used. Or let us consider the example of a company and the supplier responsible for providing accounting services for this company. The two companies develop personal relationships during their cooperation and they get to know each other's methods. Switching to a new accounting firm may prove to be a risky move, because the lower fees charged by the new company may lead to higher costs in other respects. All the three cases presented above prove that users become less sensitive to the price of products already in use, and more sensitive to the price of new products.

3.7.6. The impact of the size of the expenditure

Expenditure can be interpreted as the amount spent on purchasing the product or service, and also the share of the expenditure in household budgets. According to the theory, a higher expenditure, or a higher share in the budget will increase price sensitivity. This is true for both corporate and household purchases. It seems quite logical, as higher expenditure should be more carefully deliberated than lower expenditure. The share of an expenditure is, of course, related to the level of income. Price sensitivity to the same product decreases as the level of income improves.

Satisfaction with the price of electricity is a good example. Coordinated by the Marketing Department of the University of Pécs, a national survey of consumer satisfaction with electricity services was carried out for 10 years from 1996 on. One group of questions was related to price (the importance of and satisfaction with). Figure 3.10 provides evidence that satisfaction with price depends very much on the level of income. The figure summarizing the results of the analyses between 1996 and 1998 shows that the level of satisfaction improved significantly in 1998, when the general income level increased in the country.

3.7.7. The impact of the full benefit

Companies and households use many products, the benefits of which will manifest not by the product itself but as part of a process or a system. Let us take a few examples both from industrial and from household consumption. The steel sheets used in car manufacturing and the bulbs installed in brake lights contribute to the end benefit of the car. As the steel sheets represent a higher share, manufacturers are probably more sensitive to the price of the metal sheets than to that of the bulb. The example can be made even more explicit if we focus on the steel sheets alone. Steel sheets are purchased by leather bag manufacturers to reinforce parts of the bag. The car manufacturer's price sensitivity is higher than the bag producer's for whom the steel sheets only contribute to the end benefit to a small extent. The water softener (Calgon) used in households for washing and dishwasher machines achieves its end benefit by ensuring that the expensive appliance can run for a longer period without repair. Product positioning and communication with consumers can significantly increase the way the contribution to the end benefit is perceived (and lower the price sensitivity as a result). Just remember the advertisements in which manufacturers of car tyres attempt to emphasize the way tyres

contribute to the end benefit of the car by making travel safer for children. The same is true for oil and other additives used in cars. Products are positioned to show what a significant role they play in the end benefit of the main product despite their relatively low value. All this is done in an attempt to lower price sensitivity.

Figure 3.10. The importance of electricity and consumer satisfaction (%)

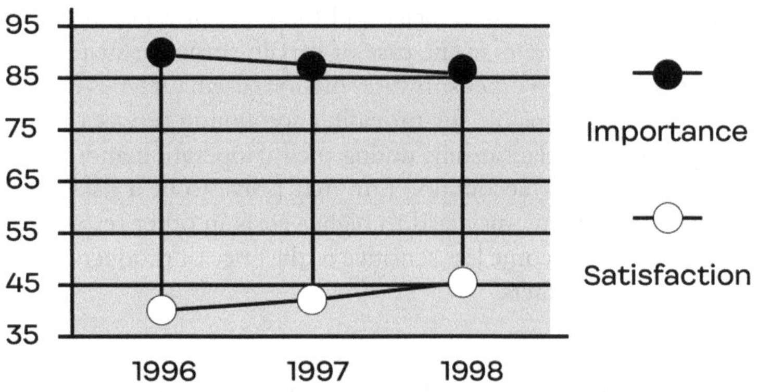

Source: Rekettye–Orosdy, 1999: 20

EXHIBIT 3.8. MICHELIN

One item from 2010: Michelin was the first to introduce 'Green X' marking for sports tyres: the 'Green X' mark found on the side wall of Michelin Pilot Sport 3 guarantees that the level of energy efficiency of the rubber tyre is among the highest in the market. With this marking Michelin assumes responsibility for decreasing the consumption of fuel and lowering the CO_2 emissions as a result.

One item from 2016: While many companies focus on programmed obsolescence – meaning an ever-shorter life span for products – MICHELIN has chosen to focus on the programmed longevity of its tyres, while also strengthening their safety performance. That's what we mean by sustainable performance and what is expected of MICHELIN's experts.

Source: http://www.michelin.hu/hu/front/affich.jsp?&codeRubrique= 50001003 0107560350 (2010.08.19.) Photo : By Source, Fair use, https://en.wikipedia. org/w/ index. php? curid= 14107414

3.7.8. The impact of shared costs

Price sensitivity for a certain product decreases if the financing of the product is not borne solely by the consumer. The best examples include medication or, if the costs of travel are covered by the company, a traveller may opt to travel first class and stay in exclusive hotels if the costs can be deducted from the taxes; the price sensitivity for the products decreases in these cases as well.

3.8. The model of price evaluation

Figure 3.3 shows how consumers perceive prices. Perception is followed by understanding which basically happens in the context of comparison with reference prices. If the price of a product falls within the price range developed by the individual based on reference prices for the given product or

service, the price will meet the expectations of the consumer. This process can be influenced by a set of objective and subjective factors, as discussed earlier. If the price (and other related costs) meet the individual's expectations, consumers will be willing to purchase by comparing the costs and the benefits provided by the product or the service. The assessment of the benefit is a complicated process and may occur differently with different types of products. The benefits provided by the product are discussed in the chapter dealing with product policy in marketing, so it is enough to mention that benefits can be grouped in two categories: functional and emotional. By comparing the perceived benefits with the perceived costs consumers make the decision whether the benefits provided meet their expectations or not, and will develop their willingness to purchase as a result. Figure 3.11 gives a summary of what has been discussed so far.

EXHIBIT 3.9. SHOPPING FOR OTHERS

A new business sector is emerging in developed societies, shopping with other people's money. Consumers delegate part of their decisions to professional purchasers. Hollander and Rassuli (1999) devote a whole study to the description of this new type of purchase situation. The delegation of decisions has become widespread in healthcare (dietetic programmes, medications, etc.), in the financial sector (insurance, financial advisors, fund managers, etc.), in real estate (real estate agents, real estate investors, etc.), in the construction sector (architects, interior designers, etc.), in tourism (flight agencies, travel agencies, etc.). The price sensitivity of consumers will change with the inclusion of these organisations. These situations are characterized by a more professional purchase behaviour (Hollander and Rassuli call it "Surrogate-Mediated Consumer Decision Making") than purchases by individuals.

The possibilities of making a profitable business for grocery shopping for others is discussed in the next citation: "If you have a dependable vehicle and a cell phone, you can start your own grocery shopping business. It is a simple business to start and operate, so you do not need much start up money. In fact, many have started this business with just a few hundred dollars.

You may be wondering "Why would anyone pay someone else to do their grocery shopping?" Here is why. There are two groups of people that need help with grocery shopping, those who are too busy to do their own grocery shopping, and those who have no choice, such as homebound seniors or those with health problems or handicaps that prevent even a simple trip to the grocery store. Both potential customer bases are quite large and growing every year."

Source: http://www.groceryshoppingbusiness.com/wp-content/uploads/2013/03/grocery_shopping_business_preview.pdf

Figure 3.11. Price evaluation model

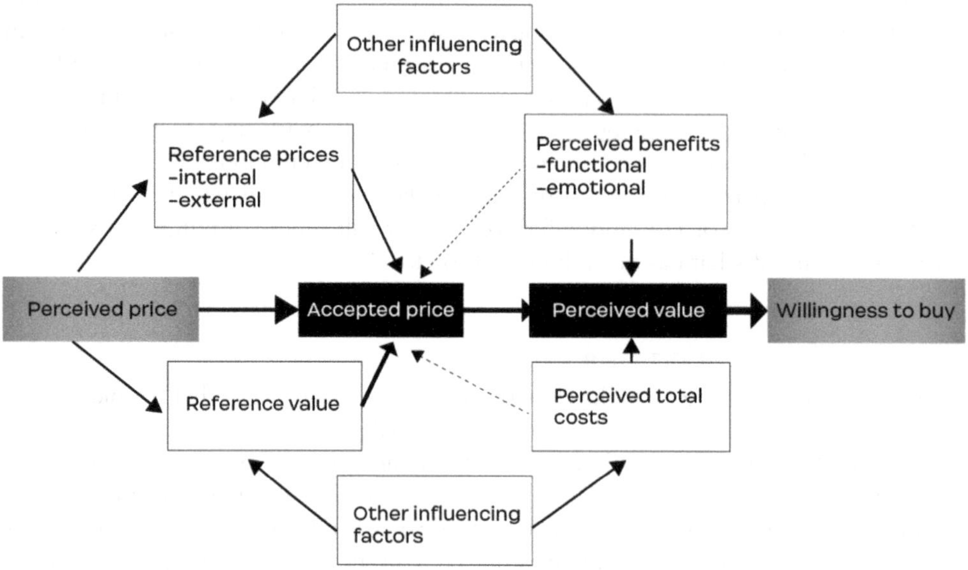

3.9. Methods of price research

In order for a company to make good price decisions, it should have internal and external knowledge. Internal knowledge includes the evolution of costs in the past, their expected changes, while external knowledge provides information about the response of actual and potential consumers to prices, as well as about the relationship of competitors to the prices of the company in question. Now we will take a look at the methods used in price research which measure the behaviour of consumers with regard to price.

Several methods are used in price research. Before choosing any of these methods we have to decide if:

- we want to test price sensitivity for a given product in isolation, or in comparison with other competing products,
- we want to use a direct or an indirect method, and
- we want to measure the acceptance of a given price or a range of prices.

3.9.1. Questionnaire surveys

The most frequently used method for measuring price sensitivity is the questionnaire survey (oral interviews, telephone interviews, or questionnaires sent by post). The use of questionnaires is a relatively simple and cheap method, but their efficiency largely depends on how professionally the questions are formulated and how the responses are evaluated. The evaluation of responses requires prudence, because experiences have shown that respondents tend to provide the socially accepted answers to questions about price. Another problem which may arise when using this method is, that those who do not seriously consider purchasing the given product will not give much thought to the answers, and the result of their willingness to accept the price is not always relevant. The Van Westendorp model described below presents a specific method based on questionnaire surveys.

EXHIBIT 3.10. Measuring price sensitivity: The van Westendorp Model

This model was conceived by the Dutch economist Peter Van Westendorp in the 1970s. The model intends to determine the range of prices for products and services that are acceptable for consumers. One end of the scale of acceptable prices is the point where the majority of consumers begin to question the quality of the product at the given price, and the other end of the scale is the point where the majority of the consumers consider the price to be too high. The expressions used in the model are the following:

- Point of marginal "cheapness" (PMC) is the price point where the sales lost are higher due to the questionable quality than the gains generated by the new consumers attracted by the low price.
- Point of marginal expensiveness (PME) is the price point above which consumers consider the price to be too high for the benefits offered by the product.
- Optimum price point (OPP) is the price at which the percentage of consumers who consider the price to be too high is the same as the percentage of those who consider it to be so low that the quality becomes questionable.
- Indifference price point (IDP) is the price point at which a higher percentage of consumers consider the price to be too high than the percentage of consumers who consider the price to be cheap (offering a great buy).

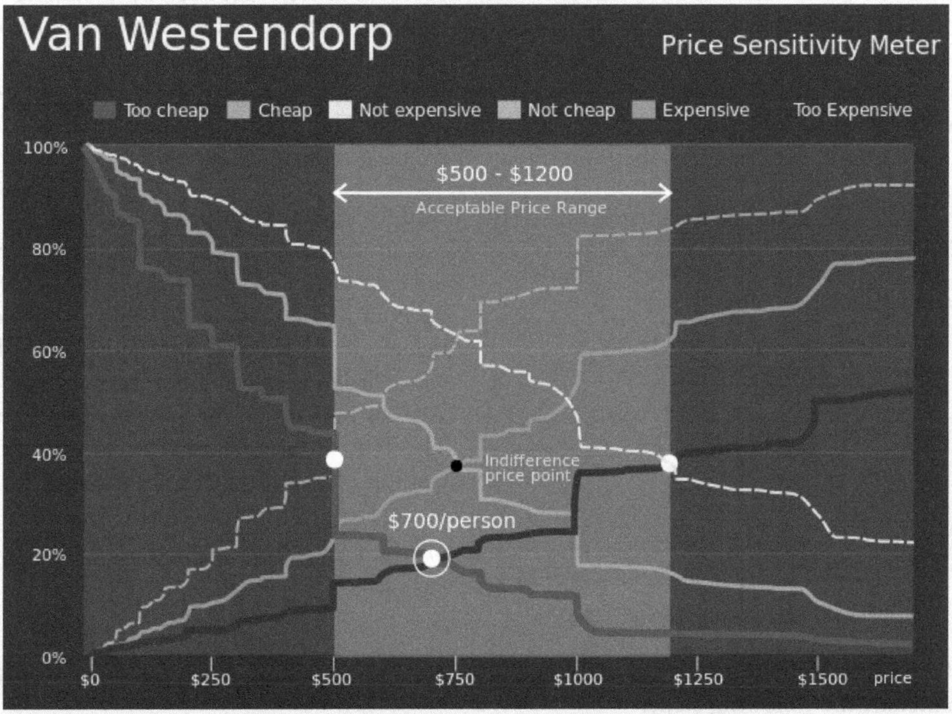

For the model, consumers should to be asked the following questions:

- At what price would you consider the product to be too expensive to buy?
- At what price would you consider that the quality of the product couldn't be acceptable?

- At what price would you consider the product to be too expensive to seriously think about buying it?
- At what price would you consider the product to be a good bargain?

The model analyses the frequency distribution of the answers. The analysis focuses on the intersection of the curves. The intersections of the frequency distributions determine the points (PMC, PME, OPP, IDP) based on which optimum decisions can be made. According to the model, the range of acceptable prices by the market lies between the points of marginal cheapness (PMC) and marginal expensiveness (PME). The points of optimum and indifference prices (OPP, IDP) fall between these two points, and mark the places of most preferred prices by the consumers on the scale of acceptable price.

Source: By Levasha - Own work, CC BY-SA 4.0, https://commons.wikimedia.org/w/index.php?curid=46126719

3.9.2. Simulation tests

In countries with highly developed marketing infrastructure a multitude of simulation techniques are available for companies wishing to launch new products in order to forecast the success of their products and the acceptance of the planned prices on the market. The techniques used by the big marketing research institutes are usually called 'simulation laboratories'. The services offered by simulation laboratories are typically requested by the manufacturers of fast moving packaged goods. The simulation laboratories always measure the success of a new product by assuming a pre-determined marketing strategy, which includes the price too. Other techniques complement the tests performed in simulation laboratories with mathematical modelling, which allows the analysis of the responses to a product at different prices (and different marketing strategies). Research institutes also offer to carry out personalized tests, so-called 'sales waves'. The latter can be performed relatively easily and fast, and have been designed to estimate the rate of repeat purchase (or repurchases) too.

EXHIBIT 3.11. Van Westendop Analysis of the Kennedy Space Centre's ticket prices

William M. Bailey (2001) carried out a Van Westendorp analysis for the setting of the entry ticket prices to the Kennedy Space Centre. The optimum price point (OPP) for all-inclusive tickets (including the film and the exhibition) was a little bit below 32 dollars – based on the analysis performed on a sample of 500 people. The IPP was 39.74 dollars. According to the test the 24-dollar ticket price used by the centre could prove attractive for visitors.

Photo: By Slammer111 at the English language Wikipedia, CC BY-SA 3.0, https://commons.wikimedia.org/w/index.php?curid=19988559

The different simulation tests use various techniques, but they have the same underlying features. All of them include the following steps:

- The selection of consumers taking part in the experiment and the understanding of their purchasing habits is done using questionnaires.

The advertisement and other market influencing tools related to the new product are presented (together with other advertisements) in such a way that the subjects of the experiment are not aware of which product is tested. 'Purchasing' opportunities are created in experimental or real shops where the consumer can decide which product to 'buy'. Those who have 'purchased' the product are asked about the use of the product and their willingness to repurchase it. This is also a good opportunity to measure further purchase willingness in the future.

3.9.3. Market testing using retail bar code scanners

The use of bar code scanning technologies in retail started in the early 1970s, and two forms became widespread in two forms: (1) the so-called UPC-code (universal product code) scanner and computerized data storage system, and (2) the OCR (optical character recognition) system. The former is typically used by supermarkets, while the latter is mostly used by department stores. In addition to enjoying the advantages of easier inventory, management of orders, and faster customer service, these retail scanning systems make it possible immediately to measure the efficiency of marketing actions locally. For example, how much the sale of the products offered at a discount has increased during the short period following the price promotion compared to previous periods. Marketing research institutions try to benefit from this possibility when they agree with some selected retailers who, upon the request of the institute, register special data as well, when the targeted consumers do their purchases.

3.9.4. Mathematical-statistical analyses

Several statistical-mathematical models have been developed for measuring the elasticity of demand. These so-called econometric models use mathematical equations to express how demand responds to different variables (price, income, location of the store, etc.). The data collected about independent and dependent variables are modelled by computers and provide estimates on how demand will respond to the changes in independent variables (among them prices in the first place).

CHAPTER 4. PRICES, COSTS AND PROFIT

OBJECTIVE 1 To understand that profit is dependent on the quantities of products sold and their prices; and to illustrate the limits of pricing at which products can be sold.

OBJECTIVE 2 To ascertain what type of costs influences price setting by companies and how costs can determine the elbow room of price making for forecasting costs and future prices.

OBJECTIVE 3 To understand the relationship between price policy and corporate leverage and how break even analysis can be used establish the price movement.

4.1. The elbow room of pricing decisions

In the case of profit-oriented companies, profit is the difference between the company's sales revenue and its costs:

Profit = PQ – C

where:

P is the unit price,

Q is the quantity sold and

C is the costs incurred by the company.

The equation makes it clear that prices have a direct impact on profit. Decisions about price are complicated by the fact that price also affects demand for the company's products (see Chapter 2) and, in this way, the quantity of products sold as well. It follows from this statement that, although information about costs is indispensable for making the right decisions about price, companies operating in real market conditions should never rely exclusively on costs in their pricing decisions. The reason is that costs - as we are going to discuss later in detail - depend on the quantity of products or services sold (which, in turn, depends significantly on price - as has been pointed out).

Customers in competitive markets do not care about the costs the company in question absorbed while manufacturing and marketing the product. Customers are interested in obtaining the value they have in mind at the lowest possible price, or obtaining the highest possible value for the price they pay. If the costs of a company and the prices it calculates on the basis of these costs exceed the level prevailing in the market of the product in question, customers won't buy its products and the company will fall behind the competition.

It is crucial for a company to have clear-cut information about expected costs at the time when decisions about the prices of its products are made. In other words (Figure 4.1): costs represent the

lower limit of the elbow room for price decisions, while the customers' willingness to accept the prices (in the terminology of economics: the reservation price) is the upper limit.

Figure 4.1. Elbowroom for decisions on prices

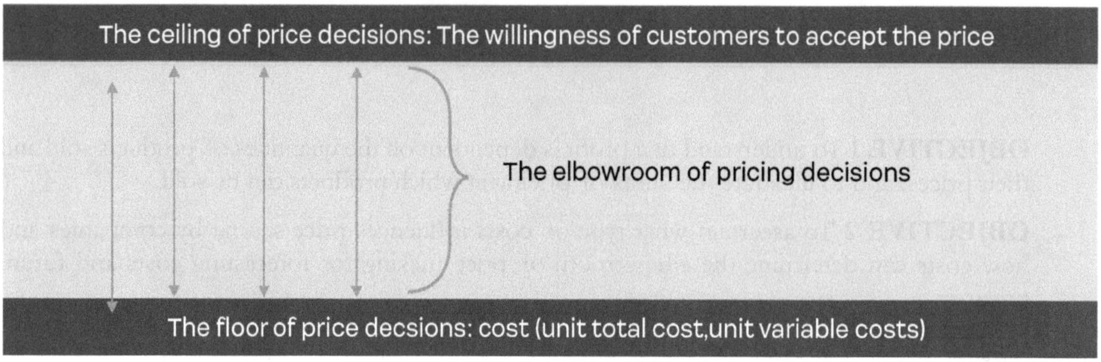

Note: After discussing the costs, we will return to the point: which group of costs (unit total or unit variable costs) can function as a lower limit for price decisions.

4.2. Costs

This section discusses various type of costs and their relationship to the quantity of output. Costs can be grouped by various criteria; however, as far as the setting and controlling of prices are concerned, two are of critical importance:

- The first is how costs should be divided into constant and changing components, i.e. how various costs correlate with changes in the company's output.
- The second is the allocation of costs. It is possible to determine which costs can be directly associated with a certain activity (product) and also to identify the costs that cannot be associated with any specific activity or product and are therefore considered to arise in relation to the company or business unit *in a general way*. Accordingly, literature distinguishes the cost groups listed below.

4.2.1. Direct costs

Direct costs arise when a product is manufactured, a service is provided or an activity is performed and they can be directly assigned to these. The value of basic materials (leather and lining first) used for making leather gloves, the piece wage that a glove seamster or cutter gets are all direct costs. Similarly, the wages paid to the assistants in the retail shop are also considered as direct cost. These two examples illustrate quite well that direct costs can be of both fixed and variable character. (The cost of material used in the manufacturing of gloves changes with the quantity produced, while the wages of assistants working in the shops are independent from turnover most of the time.)

4.2.2. Indirect costs

These costs can be assigned to a specific activity (or product) but the simple fact that they arise does not contribute directly to the performance of the activity. A classic example could be the cost of maintaining the plant.

4.2.3. Fixed costs

The group of fixed costs contains indirect costs that cannot be associated with a specific activity, product or service, not even indirectly. The costs contribute to the operation of the company as a whole, and therefore they are relatively constant: their amount does not change when the manufacturing of a product is abandoned, or that of another gets started.

The literature of economics uses the distinction of variable and fixed costs based on the correlation between the amount of costs and the quantities produced.

This group of fixed costs is typically independent from changes in output – in a definite period of output. To stay with the example of glove-making: if a manufacturer produces one million pairs of gloves in a specific period of time and his fixed costs amount to 20 million USD, then – assuming that all other factors remain constant - a 20,000 pair-increase in production (meaning a 2% increase) will most probably not change the amount of fixed costs. The restriction: 'definite period of time' refers to the eventuality that a certain level of production increase may raise fixed costs as well, requiring new work stations for cutters, renting or building of a new plant, or the employment of more managers.

EXHIBIT 4.1. YOUR IPHONE PROBABLY COSTS BETWEEN $12.50 TO $30 TO MAKE

The exact figure of how much it costs to manufacture an iPhone is not public; a rare peek inside Apple's factory in China granted to ABC News reporter Bill Weir provided significant clues to these numbers. Based on his figures industry analyst Horace H. Dediu concluded that these "costs are likely to range between $12.50 and $30 per unit. The iPhone manufacturing costs are likely to be twice or three times the average. Labour costs are still a small part of the overall cost structure between 2% and 5% of sales price."

According to another study made by Barua et al. the material cost of iPhone 4, which was sold at the beginning for $600 in the US, was $187.5, while the added value in China was $6.54. Distribution and miscellaneous cost added up to $136.58. It meant that the contribution at the price of $ 600 was $269.28.

Photo by Calerusnak at English Wikipedia, CC BY-SA 3.0, https://commons.wikimedia.org/w/index.php?curid=36930756; Sources: http://nextshark.com/real-cost-of-iphone/ Posted on March 3 2016. Akrur Barua, David Gruner, and Sunandan Bandyopadhyay: Global value chains: More a development strategy than a mere process, in: Global Economic Outlook 4th Quarter 2015, Deloitt University Press

4.2.4. Variable costs

Variable costs change in agreement with output (production, activity) changes. Some of them change in proportion with the change in the output (proportionate costs), while others have either a progressive or a digressive character compared with output, i.e. they grow faster or more slowly than the output. A typical variable cost is direct material cost: if a glove factory has used 30 dm^2 of leather for a pair of gloves so far, when the manufacturing of the same product type increases, the use of material will increase parallel with it, i.e. by 30 dm^2 per pair, and the cost of material will go up accordingly. Within the group of variable costs there are so-called semi-variable costs as well. These (e.g. the cost of auxiliary materials needed for manufacturing) contain fixed elements as well, but their amount changes basically in proportion with the amount of activity.

EXHIBIT 4.2. PRODUCT COSTS AT SONY

The cost system generally used by Sony distinguishes two cost types: direct and indirect costs. Direct costs are those that can be assigned to a specific product beyond doubt; and indirect costs are those that cannot be identified in this way. Direct costs include components purchased and direct wages. These are measured as exactly as possible. Those in charge, for example, regularly supervise material costs, they list the components bought and used for certain products, including and tracking the purchase price agreed with the suppliers and sub-contractors. Direct labour costs are also tracked very thoroughly. Each stage of the manufacturing process is analysed in detail and in this way it becomes possible to determine the length of time needed to fix four rubber stands for example. The former experiences are used to determine the work time and the technological time required for the actual production.

Indirect costs are divided in two groups: one contains the costs that can be assigned to a specific product, and the other contains those that cannot. Indirect cost, assignable to a product is, for example the cost of the welding and other large equipment used in the course of manufacturing, as well as the engineering work that can be assigned to the product beyond doubt. Assignable indirect costs are divided among the various products by dividing them with the number of products Sony plans to manufacture. The quantity planned is calculated on the basis of the sales experiences gained with former products, the improved qualities of the new product, the general market situation and the feedback received from the retailers. Considering the short life cycle of the products, the sales forecasts Sony's product designers make are quite reliable. Non-assignable indirect costs include, for example R&D costs, costs of design, services, paperwork, marketing and all the other costs that the company decides to charge on the audio division. The non-assignable indirect costs are charged on specific products in proportion of their material costs.

Source: Cooper, 1994, 8-9. old.; About the Japanese way of pricing and costing see the study of Robert Hsu published in Global Business & Economics Review (Hsu / GBER, V.1, #2,1999, pp 164-171); Photo: By Simone Urbinati - my shot, CC BY-SA 3.0, https://commons.wikimedia.org/w/index.php?curid=1895667

4.2.5. Marginal costs

Marginal cost is a frequently used concept in cost analysis. It shows how much it will cost the company to manufacture a new unit of its products.

We can analyse the various cost types taken either as a whole or in their specificity. Table 4.1, Figures 4.2 and 4.3 present a hypothetical cost structure. In the example, the specific variable costs are not identical: as the use of capacities improves, they tend to decrease for some time, and then they start going up (because employees need to be paid for extra work).

Using the figures given in Table 4.1 it is possible graphically to present the changes in sales revenue, profit, and the total costs (Figure 4.2) as well as the unit costs (Figure 4.3.).

4.3. Break-even analysis - with identical variable costs assumed

The simplest way to analyse the relationships between costs (variable and fixed), prices, the quantity sold and profit is to perform a break-even analysis. Let us first have an overview of the relationships between the product's price, costs and contribution. Figure 4.5 makes it clear that price can be defined as the sum total of unit variable costs and unit contribution. (In the terminology of economics: producer's surplus), while contribution includes the fixed costs per unit of production and unit profit.

Table 4.1. A hypothetical cost structure

Output (Q)	Total fixed costs	Total variable costs	Total costs	Unit fixed costs	Unit variable costs	Unit total costs	Unit price	Revenue	Profit
0	300000	0	300000		0		150	0	-300000
1000	300000	100000	400000	300.0	100	400.0	150	150000	-250000
2000	300000	180000	480000	150.0	90	240.0	150	300000	-180000
3000	300000	240000	540000	100.0	80	180.0	150	450000	-90000
4000	300000	280000	580000	75.0	70	145.0	150	600000	20000
5000	300000	325000	625000	60.0	65	125.0	150	750000	125000
6000	300000	420000	720000	50.0	70	120.0	150	900000	180000
7000	300000	525000	825000	42.9	75	117.9	150	1050000	225000
8000	300000	640000	940000	37.5	80	117.5	150	1200000	260000
9000	300000	810000	1110000	33.3	90	123.3	150	1350000	240000
10000	300000	1000000	1300000	30.0	100	130.0	150	1500000	200000

Figure 4.2. Graphic presentation of sales income, profit and total costs.

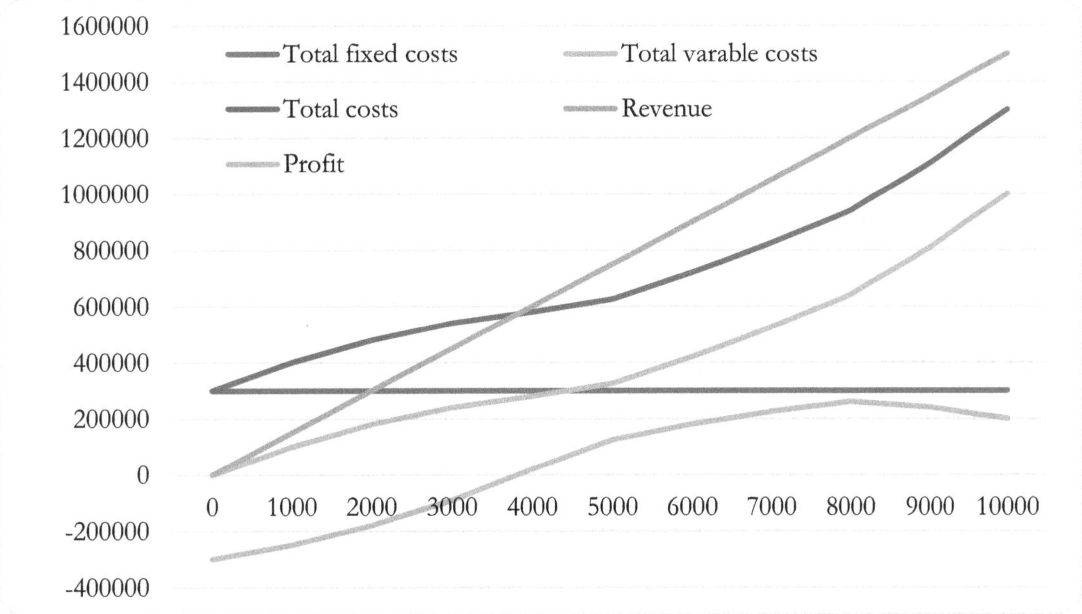

Figure 4.3. Graphic presentation of unit costs

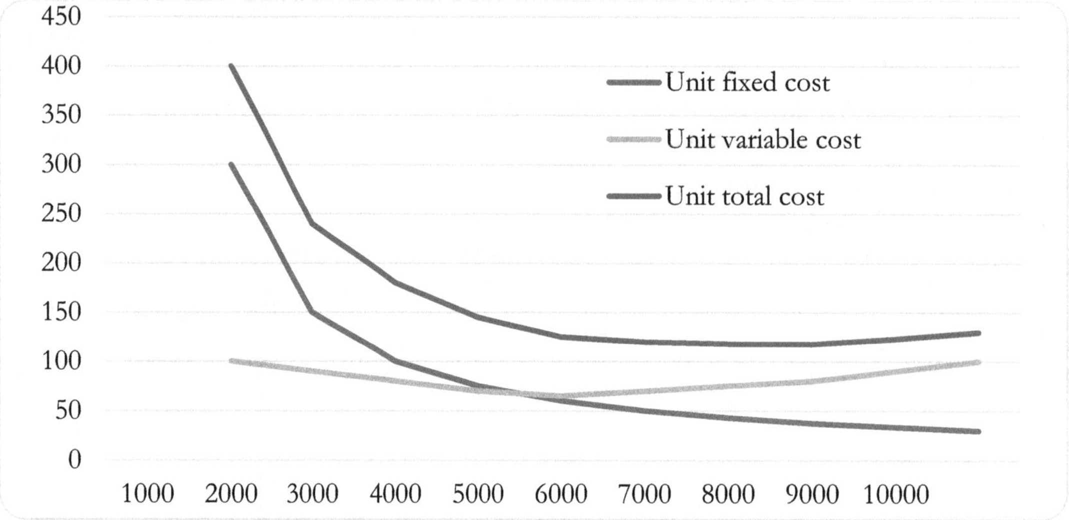

EXHIBIT 4.3. THE THEORETICAL EXAMPLE OF A WINE SHOP

Let us take a simple example to explain break-even analysis and assume that a wine shop sells only one kind of bottled wine. The shopkeeper buys a bottle of wine for $ 8 and sells it at $ 12. He has one employee working in the shop, whose monthly wages- including labour charges total $ 1,500. The rent for the premises costs $ 500 per month and the other fixed costs amount to $ 1,000. The shop usually sells 1,500 bottles of wine per month. The simplified monthly calculation the shopkeeper makes is the following (see Table 4.2.).

In literature the value of output measured in natural units which – when sold - makes fixed costs equal to contribution i.e. neither profit nor loss is made is called *break even point.* At this point, the revenue equals costs. Express it in an equation:

$P \times BEQ = \text{total fixed costs} + BEQ \times C_v,$

where

P is the price

BEQ or BEP is the break-even quantity or break-even point and

$\mathbf{C_v}$ is the unit variable cost.

Break-even point (BEP) can be computed from the following equation:

$$BEP = \frac{TC}{P - C_v} = \frac{\text{Total fixed costs}}{\text{Unit price} - \text{Unit variable costs}}$$

Applying this to our example, we get the monthly break-even quantity of the wine shop as follows:

$$BEP = \frac{\$\,3\,000}{\$\,12 - \$\,8} = 750 \text{ bottles}$$

Break-even quantity (point) for the wine shop is shown in the diagram of Figure 4.4

Table 4.2. Business data of the wine shop for a month

	Unit	Total
Sales per month (bottles)		1,500
Selling price per bottle	$ 12	
Revenue		$ 18,000
Fixed costs (1500+500+1000)	$ 2	$ 3,000
Variable cost (purchasing price)	$ 8	$ 12,000
Profit	$ 2	$ 3,000

Figure 4.4. Plotting the break-even point (the vertical axis is the value, the horizontal is the quantity).

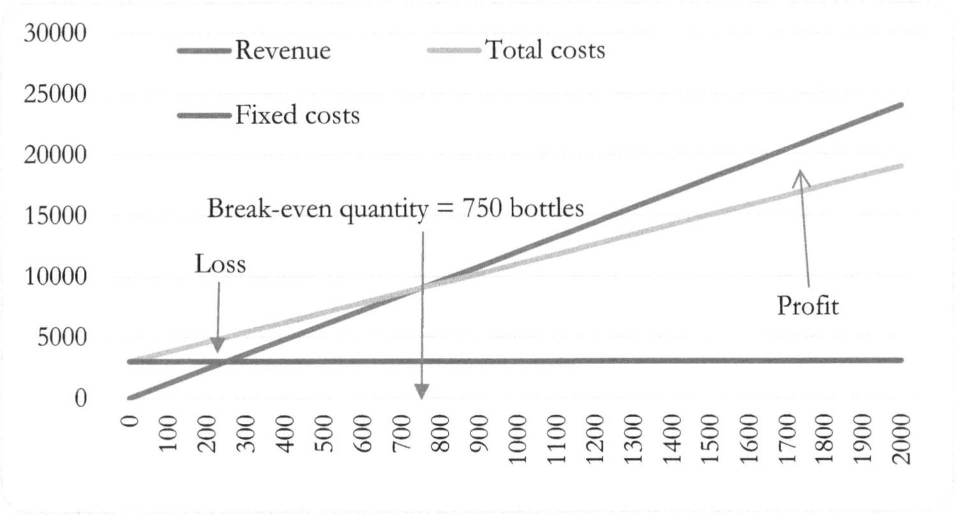

Figure 4.5. Price, unit costs unit profit and unit contribution

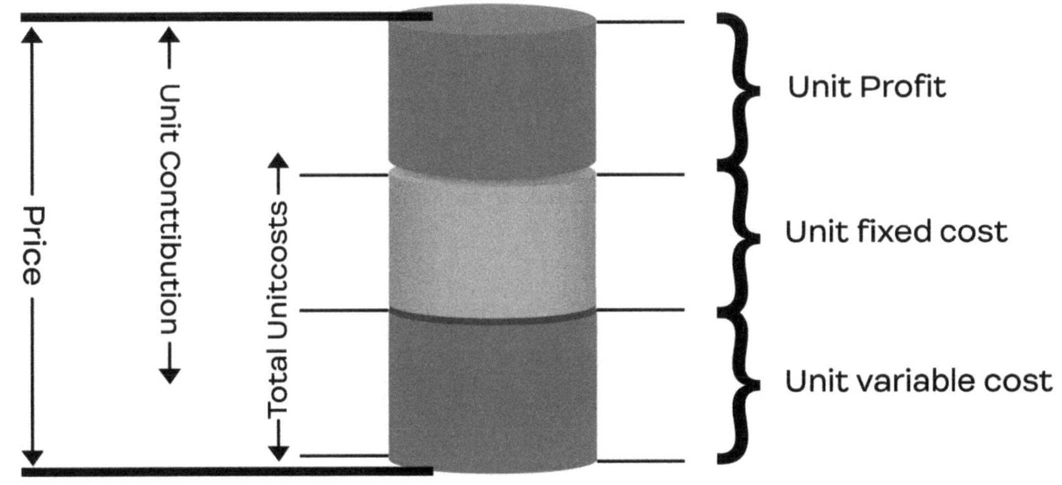

What has been seen so far is meant to prove that break-even analysis is a very simple, but at the same time extremely useful method for analysing the relationships between prices, quantities sold and profits. It follows from the logic of the analysis that break-even quantity can be calculated not only for a specific price, but also for all possible prices. Remaining with the example of the wine shop, Figure 4.6 shows the curves of break-even quantities belonging to various prices.

Figure 4.6. The break-even quantity curve (the vertical axis represents the break-even quantities, the horizontal axis represents the prices)

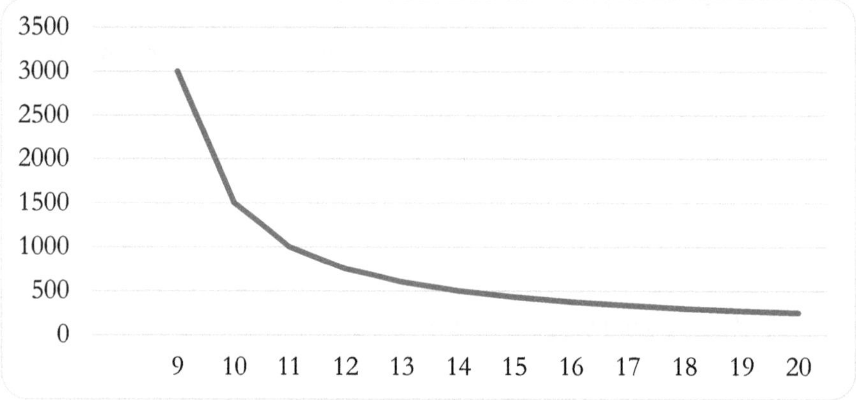

It is equally simple to compute the break-even curves that belong to the various profits: all you do is add the profits planned to the fixed costs. This kind of curve is also referred to as the isoprofit curve, which means that profit is the same on all points.

The formula is the following:

$$\text{The required quantity to achieve the planned profit} = \frac{\text{Total fixed costs + Planned profit}}{\text{Unit contribution}}$$

The feasibility of an investment or marketing action can be analysed in a similar way. Let us suppose that the wine-shop is contacted by a local marketing agency with the offer of an advertising campaign for $ 24,000 promising to increase the shop's turnover by at least 10% during the next 6 months. The owner of the shop makes the following quick calculation:

Total of fixed costs for 6 months = (6 x 3,000) = $18,000;

Cost of the action recommended: $24,000.

Quantities required for return of investment and making the so far achieved monthly profit of $3,000 = (18,000 + 18,000 + 24,000)/4 = 15,000 bottles,

for 1 month = 2,500 bottles,

which would need a 67% increase of the quantity sold. Consequently, the promised 10% increase is far from being sufficient. The offer must be refused!

Figure 4.7. Curves of break-even quantities for various profit values and prices

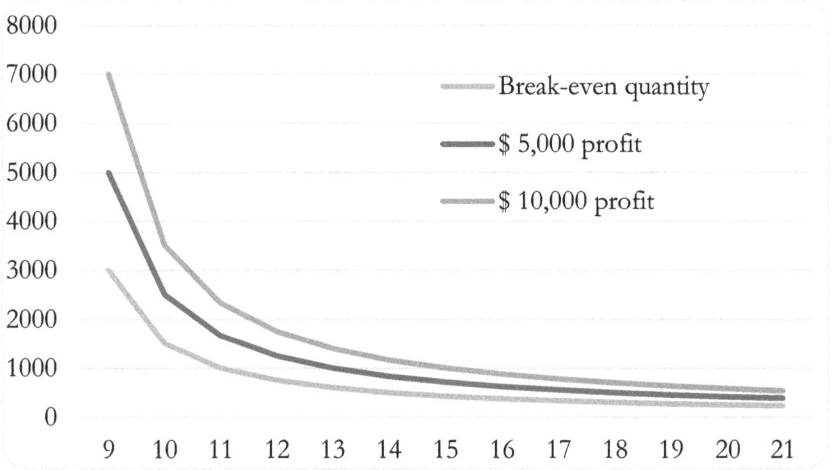

4.4. The role of profit-volume ratio (PV)

The break-even point can be defined not only in natural quantities, but in terms of value as well. In this case, the term break-even value is used instead of break-even quantity, i.e. the value of the company's sales that covers the fixed costs. Before calculating the contribution, we should familiarise ourselves with the concept of profit volume (PV) ratio, also frequently referred to as contribution ratio, or marginal income ratio (MIR) (Dolan, 1984; Hanna–Dodge, 1997).

The formula used for PV is the following:

$$PV = \frac{P - C_v}{P}$$

The formula of the break-even value (BEV) is:

$$BEV = \frac{\text{Total fixed costs}}{\text{Contribution ratio}} = \frac{TC_{fix}}{PV}$$

In the example of the wine shop PV= 0.333 ([12 – 8]/12) and break-even value is $9000 (3,000$/0.333). PV =0.333 means that 33 cents from each dollar of sales income goes to cover fixed costs and profit.

If PV is known, it is easy to define the impact that additional increase in sales over the quantities planned will have on profit. If monthly sales of wine can be increased by $1,000 over the value originally planned – keeping all other circumstances: sales price, procurement price, employees' wages, rents and all the other fixed costs unchanged, profit will increase by $330 (1000 x 0.33).

In the case of businesses operating within the same economic sector, the PV is usually of similar magnitude; there may, however, be significant differences among the sectors. Knowing the contribution ratio is very important, because it provides information on how quantity-sensitive a business type or an activity is. Quantity sensitivity, in turn can determine, among other factors, to what extent a business type is capable of taking part in a price war.

Let us consider now the example of two products that are sold at an identical price, but their contribution ratios (PVs) are very different:

- The first example could come from tourism, say from the *hotel business.*

Let us suppose that one night in a hotel in Columbus Ohio costs $100 per night for two adults. Variable costs are quite low in this type of business. Variable costs arise only from the laundry of bedding and breakfast if included in the price of the room. All other expenses belong to fixed costs, since the building should be maintained and kept in operation regardless of the number of guests; the cleaners and receptionists must also be paid. Let us suppose that variable costs with breakfast included amount to $20. For this service the PV ratio ([100 – 20]/100) is 80.0%.

Photo: Hotel Hotel room of the Renaissance Hotel in Columbus, Ohio, Derek Jensen (Tysto) - Public Domainv Own work (My own photo) Created: 26 Januari 2006 05.17

For the second example let us take a pair of leather shoes, at a producer price of say $100. The variable costs of the leather shoes consist of the materials used for making them (leather uppers, leather soles, lining, heels, glue, thread, etc.) and direct wages. Let us suppose that all this costs $50. In this case PV ([100-50]/100) is 50%. Now, how do these two industries, with strikingly different PVs behave in a price war? What happens if prices go up? Which is more quantity sensitive? Which can offer lower prices?

First, let us take the case of price cuts. In practice, we often find that hotels are ready to cut prices significantly in order to attract guests (discount prices for groups, special offers for weekends, conferences, honeymooners, etc.) It is quite a logical reaction, because if rooms remain unoccupied, they do not contribute to the high fixed costs. If, however, they accommodate guests and a guest pays more than 20$, the part over 20$ can contribute to the fixed costs. On the other hand, the shoe factory cannot cut its price below 50$ because, if it does, it will make a loss for the simple reason that the materials used and the wages would cost more than the income from the sale of the shoes.

All this points to the conclusion that companies with high PV have larger elbow room for price cuts than those with low PV. This is the economic background that allows hotels, air carriers, and many other, mainly service providing businesses temporarily to offer significant price cuts with a view of attracting customers. This ability is also closely interrelated with volume-sensitivity.

Speaking about price rises, let us suppose that both companies intend *to raise their prices by 10%.* Experience has shown that a price increase usually decreases the quantity that can be sold. However,

the question remains; how much is the decrease in quantity that the two businesses can tolerate without seeing their contribution diminished?

Since the total contribution generated equals the product of unit contribution (price minus variable costs) and the quantity sold, the total contribution generated will not diminish if

$$(P - C_v)X \leq (1.1P - C_v)Y$$

where X is the present quantity, and Y is the quantity following price rise, and 1.1 represents the 10% price increase.

After reordering the equation several times, we end up with the following result:

$$\frac{PV}{0{,}1 + PV} \leq \frac{Y}{X}$$

It means that in case of a 10% price increase the new quantity sold, and expressed as a percentage of the former quantity, is supposed to be more than the **PV/(0,1+PV)** ratio. In the case of the hotel a 10% price rise can be justified only if the quantity does not fall below 88,9%. In the case of shoe manufacturing this ratio is 83,3%. Our conclusion is that the higher the PV of an activity, the stronger its quantity sensitivity. This also explains why businesses with high PV are more inclined to implement various actions in order to keep their market share (quantity sold) or protect it. The degree of quantity increase or quantity decrease still allowed to go together with price rise or price cut is the following after the equation has been reordered:

if prices are raised **100×(X/[PV + X]),** if prices are cut **100×(X/[PV — X]).**

All this can be calculated in advance and presented in the form of a table to offer businesses practical assistance (Tables 4.3 and 4.4).

Table 4.3. The maximum allowed decrease in quantity when prices rise

Price rise				**PV ratio**			
%	**0.1**	**0.2**	**0.3**	**0.4**	**0.5**	**0.6**	**0.7**
1	9.09	4.76	3.23	2.44	1.96	1.64	1.41
2	16.67	9.09	6.25	4.76	3.85	3.23	2.78
3	23.08	13.04	9.09	6.98	5.66	4.76	4.11
4	28.57	16.67	11.76	9.09	7.41	6.25	5.41
5	33.33	20.00	14.29	11.11	9.09	7.69	6.67
6	37.50	23.08	16.67	13.04	10.71	9.09	7.89
7	41.18	25.93	18.92	14.89	12.28	10.45	9.09
8	44.44	28.57	21.05	16.67	13.79	11.76	10.26
9	47.37	31.03	23.08	18.37	15.25	13.04	11.39
10	50.00	33.33	25.00	20.00	16.67	14.29	12.50
15	60.00	42.86	33.33	27.27	23.08	20.00	17.65
20	66.67	50.00	40.00	33.33	28.57	25.00	22.22
25	71.43	55.56	45.45	38.46	33.33	29.41	26.32
30	75.00	60.00	50.00	42.86	37.50	33.33	30.00

Table 4.4. The minimum required increase in quantity when prices fall.

Price reduction	PV ratio						
%	0.1	0.2	0.3	0.4	0.5	0.6	0.7
1	11.11	5.26	3.45	2.56	2.04	1.69	1.45
2	25.00	11.11	7.14	5.26	4.17	3.45	2.94
3	42.86	17.65	11.11	8.11	6.38	5.26	4.48
4	66.67	25.00	15.38	11.11	8.70	7.14	6.06
5	100.00	33.33	20.00	14.29	11.11	9.09	7.69
6	150.00	42.86	25.00	17.65	13.64	11.11	9.38
7	233.33	53.85	30.43	21.21	16.28	13.21	11.11
8	400.00	66.67	36.36	25.00	19.05	15.38	12.90
9	900.00	81.82	42.86	29.03	21.95	17.65	14.75
10		100.00	50.00	33.33	25.00	20.00	16.67
15		300.00	100.00	60.00	42.86	33.33	27.27
20			200.00	100.00	66.67	50.00	40.00
25			500.00	166.67	100.00	71.43	55.56
30				300.00	150.00	100.00	75.00

4.5. Break-even analysis of several products

In textbooks, break-even analysis is usually discussed for just one product. It is, however quite rare for factories to manufacture and distribute only one product. Therefore, we must find a way to extend the analysis to companies with several products. Let us suppose that our imaginary company has three products and their prices and costs are the ones shown in Table 4.5.

Table 4.5. Financial data of the three products (in USD)

Data	Products		
	Product A	Product B	Product C
Selling price	800	600	600
Unit variable cost	300	400	500
Contribution/PV per unit	500	200	100
Total fixed costs		1,000,000	

Note: the example is a transformation of a calculation published in Mudie (1997: 93–97)

In such cases, the weighted versions of prices, costs and contribution data are used to calculate break-even point (break-even quantity). Weighting follows the proportions found in distribution. Let us take the case when the proportion of products A, B, and C in sales is 2 000: 4 000: and 3 000,- and the company does not intend to change that situation. The financial data should be multiplied with the weights of the three products (e.g. the weight for product A will be 22.2%: 100 x 2000 /9000). The results of weighting are shown in Table 4.6.:

Table 4.6. Weighted data

Data	Products			
	Product A	Product B	Product C	Total
Selling price	178	267	200	645
Unit variable cost	67	178	167	412
Unit Contribution	111	89	33	233

Now it is possible to calculate the break-even quantity:

$$\text{Break} - \text{even quantity} = \frac{\text{Total fixed costs}}{\text{Weighted unit contribution}}$$

BEP = 1,000,000/233 = 4,292 pieces

The beak-even value = break-even quantity x weighted selling price, i.e.

BEV = 4,292 × 645 = 2,768,340

Using the average PV, we get the same result:

$$\text{PV} = \frac{\text{Weighted price} - \text{weighted unit variable costs}}{\text{Weighted price}}$$

In our example: (645 – 412)/645 = 0.361

Consequently the break-even value = 1,000,000/0.361= 2,770,083 (Note: the difference between the two figures is only due to the rounding.)

Now we can plot the contribution diagram both by products and in summary form (Figure 4.8) for which data should be sorted according to Table 4.7.

Table 4.7. Sorting data

Products	Sales (pieces)	Revenue (USD)	Contribu-tion (USD)	PV ratio	Total sales (USD)	Profit (USD)
A	2000	1 600 000	1 000 000	62.50%	1 600 000	0
B	4000	2 400 000	800 000	33.34%	4 000 000	800 000
C	3000	1 800 000	300 000	16.67%	5 800 000	1 100 000

4.6. Lower limit of price decisions

At the beginning of this chapter we pointed out that being familiar with the costs is not sufficient for a company to make good price decisions. Therefore, costs were defined in Figure 4.1 as the lower limit of pricing decisions. However, we failed to define which cost elements can constitute the lower limit of this zone. Now, that we have discussed the costs and reviewed the relationship between the costs, price, quantity and profit, it is time to go back to this question and answer it.

Figure 4.8. The break-even chart

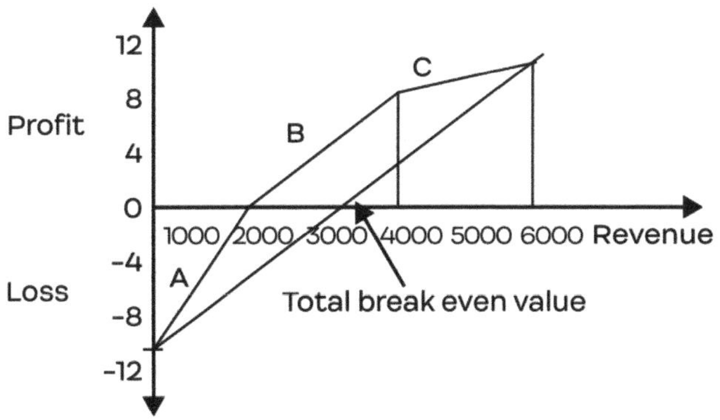

It will be practical, first, to distinguish between the short and long-term lower limit of pricing decisions. We can use the example of the hotel again: earlier we concluded that any price exceeding the 20$ variable cost contributed to the fixed costs. It means that in the short run, it is the unit variable costs that constitutes the lower limit of price decisions. Let us suppose that the total unit cost of a hotel (cost of a room per night) is $60 at 70% occupancy. If the hotel sold the rooms for less than $60 over a longer period it would be in the red. In the short run, it can do so and most hotels use the method of selling below total unit price (special weekend discounts, discount for groups, etc.). In the long run, however, a hotel can only be profitable if the price exceeds the total level of unit cost. In summary, it can be stated that the lower limit of price decisions is constituted by

- the product's unit variable cost in the short run and
- the total unit cost in the long run.

4.7. Leverage and corporate price policy

Management theory and physics have similar interpretation of the function of leverage: find a way to increase results/profit with the smallest possible input. Financial management distinguishes several types of leverage:

- operating leverage,
- financial leverage,
- combined leverage.

4.7.1. Operating leverage

The concept of operating leverage is related to the relation between all the variable and fixed costs. It examines how the increase in quantities sold affects the profits generated.

The formula used to describe operating leverage is the following:

$$\text{Operating leverage} = \frac{\text{Percentage change in operating profit}}{\text{Percentage change in sales volume}}$$

that is

$$DOL = \frac{\Delta OP}{OP} : \frac{\Delta Q}{Q}$$

where:

DOL is the degree of operating leverage,

ΔOP: is the change in the operating profit (OP = operating profit — it means earnings before interest and tax, i.e. EBIT),

OP: Operating profit in the previous period,

ΔQ: Changes in the quantities sold,

Q: Quantity sold in the previous period.

There is a difference in the way operating leverage helps to increase corporate performance depending on the company in question's PV. To illustrate this point we can take – on the basis of table 4.8., the example of two companies manufacturing similar products.

Operating leverage is 1.5 for company A and 2.0 for company B. It means that due to the difference in their PVs, a 10% increase in quantity will improve profitability by 15% for company A and by 20% for company B.

Table 4.8. Operating leverage

Data on operation	**Company A (base year)**	**Company A (current year)**	**Company B (base year)**	**Company B (current year)**
Unit price	100	100	100	100
Unit variable costs	70	70	60	60
Unit contribution	30	30	40	40
PV ratio	**0.30**	**0.30**	**0.40**	**0.40**
Total fixed costs	1 000 000	1 000 000	2 000 000	2 000 000
Quantity of sales	100 000	110 000	100 000	110 000
Revenue	10 000 000	11 000 000	10 000 000	11 000 000
Total variable costs	7 000 000	7 700 000	6 000 000	6 600 000
Total contribution	3 000 000	3 300 000	4 000 000	4 400 000
Operating profit	2 000 000	2 300 000	2 000 000	2 400 000
Operating leverage		**1.50**		**2.00**

4.7.2. Financial leverage

Financial leverage shows how the amount of credits raised affects profit. Its formula is the following:

where

□ OPBT is = change in earnings after interest and before taxation

OPBT is = profit after interest and before taxation

4.7.3. Combined leverage

The degree of combined leverage is the product of operating and financial leverages:

DCL = DOL × DFL,

where

DCL is the degree of combined leverage.

Let us get back now to our previous example and review the operation of the financial and combined leverage together with the data given in Table 4.9.

Our example continues with the assumption that a 10% increase in sales required additional capital input, to which Company A responded by raising equity, while Company B chose to raise additional credit. The example proves that the higher the amount of credit used, the greater the financial leverage, the greater the profit earned by equity as well as the amount of the dividend payable per share. Nowadays it is very important for businessmen to understand the way leverage works because leverage can affect price policy which appears in the company's financial indices through the impact of prices on quantity sold.

4.8. Forecasting costs

The firm's ability to forecast costs is important for its future profitability on the one hand and, on the other, for the definition of a price policy that will support this profitability in the future. Familiarity with the costs incurred in the past is crucial for a clear understanding of the situation. Familiarity with the present costs is even more important, but perhaps the most important of all is the ability to forecast future costs relatively reliably. The forecast of costs covers two interrelated areas:

- forecast of changes in the structure of costs and
- forecast of changes in the proportions of the various cost types.

Cost structure means the proportion of the various cost types to one another. The most important of these is the ratio of fixed and variable costs but the changes in the proportion of costs found in the various cost groups to one another also belong here. Let us consider the supposition that the company - expecting a significant increase in labour costs in the country where manufacturing is located – decides to relocate a part of the production to a cheaper place. This decision will change not only the ratio there has been so far among the direct costs, but will affect the company's structure of variable costs – and fixed costs as well.

Table 4.9. Overview of the operating, financial and combined leverages (in USD)

	Data on operation	**Company A (base year)**	**Company A (current year)**	**Company B (base year)**	**Company B (current year)**
1	Unit price	100.00	100.00	100.00	100.00
2	Unit variable costs	70.00	70.00	60.00	60.00
3	Unit contribution	30.00	30.00	40.00	40.00
4	**PV ratio**	**0.30**	**0.30**	**0.40**	**0.40**
5	Total fixed costs	1 000 000.00	1 000 000.00	2 000 000.00	2 000 000.00
	The financial structure of the firm				
6	Own capital	500 000.00	1 000 000.00	500 000.00	500 000.00
7	Credit	500 000.00	500 000.00	500 000.00	1 000 000.00
8	Number of shares	50	100	50	50
	Indices of profitability				
9	Quantity sold (pc)	100 000	110 000	100 000	110 000
10	Revenue (9 · 1)	10 000 000.00	11 000 000.00	10 000 000.00	11 000 000.00
11	Total variable costs (9 · 2)	7 000 000.00	7 700 000.00	6 000 000.00	6 600 000.00
12	Total contribution (10–11)	3 000 000.00	3 300 000.00	4 000 000.00	4 400 000.00
13	Operating profit (12–5)	2 000 000.00	2 300 000.00	2 000 000.00	2 400 000.00
14	Interest payable (20% · 7)	100 000.00	100 000.00	100 000.00	200 000.00
15	Profit before tax (13–14)	1 900 000.00	2 200 000.00	1 900 000.00	2 200 000.00
16	Tax (40%*15)	760 000.00	880 000.00	760 000.00	880 000.00
17	Profit after tax (15–16)	1 140 000.00	1 320 000.00	1 140 000.00	1 320 000.00
18	Dividend per share (17/8)	22 800.00	13 200.00	22 800.00	26 400.00
	Leverages				
	Operating leverage		**1.50**		**2.00**
	Financial leverage		**0.95**		**1.27**
	Combined leverage (15 · 16)		**1.43**		**2.53**

The forecast of cost changes is closely interrelated with the forecast of prices and demand, and as such, relies on the well-known methods of forecasting, namely:

- mathematical and statistical trend forecasts using data from the past;
- expert estimates;
- simulation models.

In the next part we are going to review those economic and business concepts that affect future cost trends and consequently also pricing in the future.

4.8.1. Economies of scale

The term 'economies of scale' refers to the situation when the average unit cost of manufacturing a product decreases because the quantity produced is larger. In the short run, the main reason for cost reduction is the fact that the manufacturing of extra quantities (within the limits of available capacities) does not increase fixed costs, (or some of them), consequently the total of fixed cost is divided for a larger number of products, i.e. the average cost of a unit is smaller. In the long run economies of scale can be the result of changes like increased production, allowing better trained or specialist workers to be employed for certain work processes or the larger quantity may lead to certain benefits in procurement, and even the existing equipment or machinery can be used more efficiently. The working of short-term economies of scale is presented in the simplified example of Table 4.10,

Table 4.10. Economies of scale illustrated

Item	Basic situation	Impact of economies of scale after manufacturing extra quantity
Unit variable costs ($)	100	100
Total fixed costs ($)	3,000,000	3,000,000
Quantity produced (pieces)	10,000	12,000
Average total unit costs ($) production	**400**	**350**

4.8.2. Economies of scope

While 'economies of scale' refers to the advantages manufacturing of additional quantities of the same product, economies of scope emphasizes variety. This approach can result in economies of specific costs due to the fact that certain capacities (equipment) can be used to manufacture various products combined.

4.8.3. The experience (learning) curve

Experience has shown that unit costs can be reduced considerably in line with the increase of the quantity of products manufactured and sold. This phenomenon is summarized in the concept of the so-called *experience or learning curve*. Although in daily practice the learning and the experience curves tend to share the same meaning, literature insists on differentiating the two concepts. The learning curve shows that manufacturing costs decrease parallel with the increase in quantity. The cost of labour input diminishes because workers can manufacture the product more quickly, simply and efficiently but the specific material cost can also be reduced, because more experience at work allows more economical use of materials. At the same time, the experience curve is a concept concerned with the decrease of all types of unit costs.

EXHIBIT 4.4. EFFECT OF ECONOMIES OF SCALE ON COMPANIES, FACTORIES, EMPLOYEES AND SHARES

Economies of scale can be blamed for closing factories, laying off employees and even for establishing new opportunities. Here are two examples:

Unilever moved the production of vegetable oil and margarine spreads from Baltimore to Kansas beginning at the end of May 2015, shutting its Baltimore plant and laying off 137 workers. The consumer goods giant shifted operations to Kansas, where it embarked on a $152.5 million expansion in 2013 to improve *the economies of scale.*

Source: Natalie Sherman, Unilever to close last Md. Factory, The Baltimore Sun, May 12, 2015, File:Unilever logo.png, public domain, created 15 June 2013

Investment firms, 3G capital and Berkshire Hathaway, have teamed up to create a new company through the merger of H.J. Heinz Co. and The Kraft Foods Group. The new company thus created is called The Kraft Heinz Company. In terms of annual sales, it is the fifth-largest food company in the world and the third-largest in the U.S. (The deal has been valued at around $45 billion.) To sweeten the deal for Kraft's shareholders, they have been provided a one-time cash dividend of $16.50 per share. The biggest synergy effects expected from the merger were international growth and improvement *of economies of scale.*

Source: Trefis Team, Analysis of the Kraft-Heinz Merger, The Forbes, Mar 30, 2015 File KraftHeinz.svg is a Public Domain Created: 30 July 2015

EXHIBIT 4.5. 50 YEARS OF MOORE'S LAW

On the website of Intel Corporation, we can read the following sentences about Gordon Moore their co-founder. "In 1965, Gordon Moore made a prediction that would set the pace for our modern digital revolution. From careful observation of an emerging trend, Moore extrapolated that computing would dramatically increase in power, and decrease in relative cost, at an exponential pace.

The insight, known as Moore's Law, became the golden rule for the electronics industry, and a springboard for innovation. As a co-founder, Gordon paved the path for Intel to make the ever faster, smaller, more affordable transistors that drive our modern tools and toys. Even 50 years later, the lasting impact and benefits are felt in many ways.

Moore's observation transformed computing from a rare and expensive venture into a pervasive and affordable necessity. All the modern computing technology we know and enjoy sprang from the foundation laid by Moore's Law. From the Internet itself, to social media and modern data analytics, all these innovations stem directly from Moore and his findings.

The inexpensive, ubiquitous computing rapidly expanding all around us is fundamentally changing the way we work, play and communicate. The foundational force of Moore's Law has driven breakthroughs in modern cities, transportation, healthcare, education, and energy production. In fact, it's quite difficult to envision what our modern world might be like without Moore's Law."

In the photo, we can see him sitting in his office at the Robert Noyce Building in Santa Clara, Calif., several years after he officially retired. Moore's office remains mostly intact today, complete with plaques, photos and awards he received over the years.

Curiosity: On April 11, 2005, Intel posted a $10,000 reward for an original, pristine copy of the Electronics Magazine where Moore's article was first published. Intel ultimately awarded the prize to David Clark, an engineerliving in Surrey, England who had decades of old issues of Electronics Magazine stored under his floorboards.

Source: http://www.intel.com/content/www/us/en/silicon-innovations/moores-law-technology.html; https://en.wikipedia.org/wiki/Electronics_(magazine); Photo: CC BY-SA 2.0 File:Former Intel CEO Gordon Moore in his cubicle.jpg; Intel: Public domain, https://commons.wikimedia.org/w/index.php?curid=18559295

The manufacturing and distribution of larger quantities may go together with the diminishing of other costs as well (marketing, selling, distribution costs, etc.). If the market grows, costs decrease at a quicker rate but, in the case of stagnating or diminishing sales, cost reduction will slow down or even stop. It must be emphasized that the decrease in unit costs measured in real value does not happen automatically. Company managers are supposed to make continuous efforts to introduce more and more efficient methods to cut costs incurred during the processes within the company. The Japanese approach proves that employee initiative has an important role in improving efficiency. However, the trend presented by the experience curve is not valid in all parts of the world. Some industries and activities are so specific that quantity increase cannot result in considerable reduction of costs.

Figure 4.9. Correlation between costs and experience (with a 75% experience curve presumed).

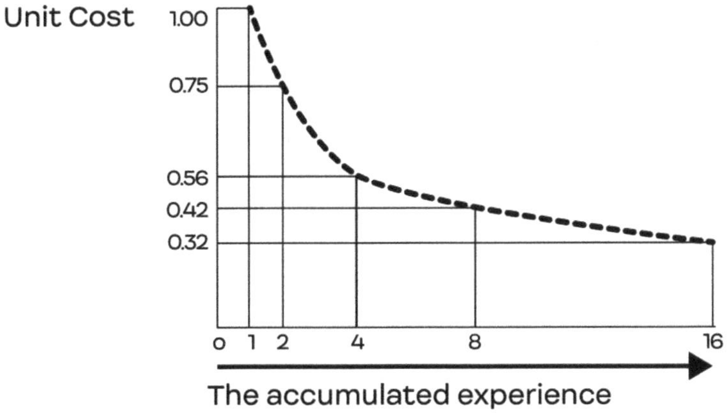

According to literature, whenever quantity is doubled, unit costs diminish by about 10-30%. The IT industry was particularly famous for the significant price cuts it implemented in the past. The price of video games went down to one fifth of the original price in three years, digital watches experienced a dramatic price cut to one hundredth of the initial price. In the background of these reductions we can find the dramatic increase in the production of electronic circuits (chips). When experience (quantity) was doubled in the production of chips, the result was a 30% diminishing of costs.

Figure 4.10. Correlation between unit cost, unit price and experience

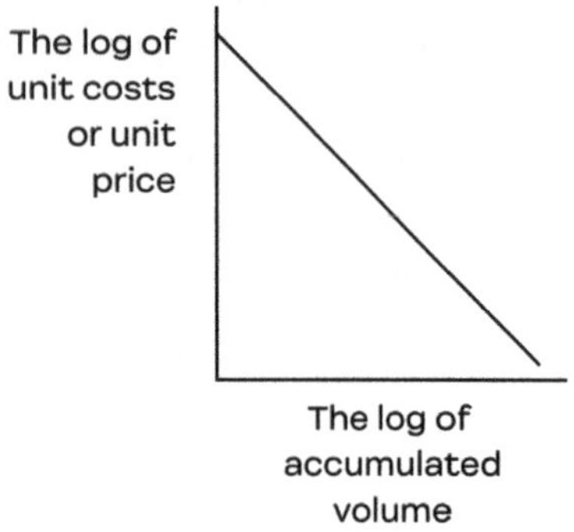

In case the cumulative quantity of the products manufactured increases by the same percentage annually (Monroe, 1990:256), it is reasonable to assume that its impact on costs will also be even. If this change is plotted as a logarithm, we get a straight line, which shows the relationship between the two factors quite clearly (Figure 4.10).

There are three points to clarify when we come to examine the correlation between costs, prices and increase in experience:

- when we speak about doubling the manufacturing or sales, we have in mind the doubling of the cumulative value of quantity between the two points in time. Let us see an example (Table 4.11)

Table 4.11. Doubling the experience

Year	Production	Growth (%)	Cumulative experience
1	100	-	1,00
2	110	10	2,10
3	121	10	3,31
4	133	10	4,64
5	146	10	6,10
6	161	10	7,71
7	177	10	9,48

The year in which experience will have doubled is in the shaded box. It means that unit costs will be reduced by the same degree by the 2nd , 4th and the 7th years.

- It must be emphasized, that all we have said so far is only true in real value. If the market is characterized by inflation, the cost data should be deflated with the rate of inflation.
- The impact of the experience curve is valid only for costs that are in one way or another, directly related to the products concerned.

The experience curve is easily applied to forecast the company's own costs and those of its competitors. This is illustrated with the method of forecasting cost reduction, based on the arguments of Monroe (1990: 265–268) and Karasiewicz (1998: 84–85). Cost reduction realized as a result of doubled quantity can be described with the following formula:

$$\mathbf{TC_x = KX^{1-b}}$$

where

$\mathbf{TC_x}$ is the cumulative total cost,

X is the number of units manufactured,

K is the estimated cost of the first product, and

b is the parameter computed from the efficiency improved as a result of doubled quantity.

The calculation of cumulative average cost:

$$\mathbf{AC_x = KX^{-b}}$$

The calculation of parameter b:

$$b = \frac{log100 - \log a}{log2}$$

Where "a" is the estimated percentage value of cost reduction.

It was stated earlier that doubling the quantity may lead to a cost reduction of as much as 30%. Let us have a look now at the values of parameter "b" that belong to values "a" in the table from 70 (30% cost reduction) to 100 (there is no cost reduction) (Table 4.12.).

Table 4.12. Computing parameter "b"

a	b	a	b	a	b
70	0.515	80	0.322	90	0.152
71	0.494	81	0.304	91	0.136
72	0.474	82	0.286	92	0.120
73	0.454	83	0.269	93	0.105
74	0.434	84	0.252	94	0.089
75	0.415	85	0.234	95	0.074
76	0.396	86	0.218	96	0.059
77	0.377	87	0.201	97	0.044
78	0.358	88	0.184	98	0.029
79	0.340	89	0.168	99	0.014
				100	0.000

Using parameter 'b' and with the formula:

$$\mathbf{AC_x = KX^{-b}}$$

We compute the values of the experience curve at different rates of quantity increase. Table 4.13. shows the degree of unit cost reduction that can be expected over a period of 10 years, supposing an even rate of quantity growth (5-10-15% per year) and values 90, 80 and 70% the experience curve.

The same method can be used to compute the decrease in the unit costs in conditions of uneven rates of quantity growth or rates that are different from the ones mentioned above.

4.8.4. Relationship between the experience curve and prices

The theory of the experience curve holds that as the experience accumulated is doubled, the unit costs measured in real value decrease continuously. The question that arises at this point is whether prices follow the decrease in unit prices and how. In literature, we can find the description of two price movement types:

- In conditions of strong competition and in industries that are characterized by rapid growth and fast technological development, prices typically move together with costs (except for the initial stage), i.e. the relationship between costs and price is stable. (Table4.11)

Table 4.13. Decrease in unit cost at various growth rates

Year	Output	Cumulative output	Values of the experience curve		
			90%	80%	70%
	5% annual growth			Changes in unit costs	
1	1.00	1.00	1.00	1.00	1.00
2	1.05	2.05	0.90	0.79	0.69
3	1.10	3.15	0.84	0.69	0.55
4	1.16	4.31	0.80	0.62	0.47
5	1.22	5.53	0.77	0.58	0.41
6	1.28	6.80	0.75	0.54	0.37
7	1.34	8.14	0.73	0.51	0.34
8	1.41	9.55	0.71	0.48	0.31
9	1.48	11.03	0.69	0.46	0.29
10	1.55	12.58	0.68	0.44	0.27
	10% annual growth			Changes in unit costs	
1	1.00	1.00	1.00	1.00	1.00
2	1.10	2.10	0.89	0.79	0.68
3	1.21	3.31	0.83	0.68	0.54
4	1.33	4.64	0.79	0.61	0.45
5	1.46	6.11	0.76	0.56	0.39
6	1.61	7.72	0.73	0.52	0.35
7	1.77	9.49	0.71	0.48	0.31
8	1.95	11.44	0.69	0.46	0.29
9	2.14	13.58	0.67	0.43	0.26
10	2.36	15.94	0.66	0.41	0.24
	15% annual growth			Changes in unit costs	
1	1.00	1.00	1.00	1.00	1.00
2	1.15	2.15	0.89	0.78	0.67
3	1.32	3.47	0.83	0.67	0.53
4	1.52	4.99	0.78	0.60	0.44
5	1.75	6.74	0.75	0.54	0.37
6	2.01	8.75	0.72	0.50	0.33
7	2.31	11.07	0.69	0.46	0.29
8	2.66	13.73	0.67	0.43	0.26
9	3.06	16.79	0.65	0.40	0.23
10	3.52	20.30	0.63	0.38	0.21

The figure below makes it clear that the relationship between costs and prices can be divided into two sections. In the first, when the product is just launched on the market, prices may be set below the costs to facilitate entry. Later, however, due to the strong competition of newly marketed products, prices tend to follow costs.

The other type of relationship between costs and prices is the so-called kinked curve (Figure 4.12). In the initial, introductory stage (I.) the innovator usually sets prices below cost to create a market for the product. Following market penetration and parallel with increase in quantities, costs will fall. In this second stage (II) the pioneer company and the firms that are newcomers to the market will maintain the initial price. They expect this relatively high price (at least compared to the costs) to bring them quick return on investment in development and marketing. High prices, however, make

the market attractive for further competitors. A fierce price war breaks out in the third stage and prices start decreasing at a quicker rate than unit costs. The fourth stage is characterized by a well-balanced movement of unit costs and prices.

Figure 4.11. The stable relationship between costs and prices

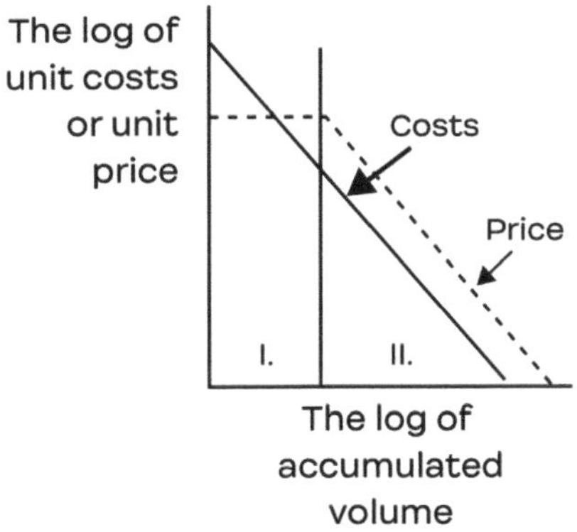

Figure 4.12. The kinked price curve

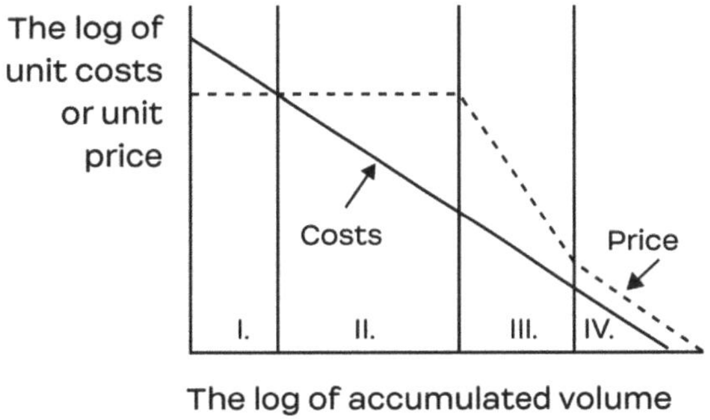

Literature studies the effect of the experience curve in relation to the manufacturing costs of individual products. The decrease of specific costs – as is has been pointed out earlier – appears sooner or later in the prices as well.

It must be emphasized, however that the impact of the experience curve is not present in all industries. It is obviously present in technological, especially electronic products and, to a lesser extent or not at all, in agriculture or strongly labour-intensive services.

EXHIBIT 4.6. BUILDING STRATEGY ON THE EXPERIENCE CURVE

"Experience curve strategies are particularly appropriate when a company's product is very sensitive to price changes. Cutting prices in such industries leads to huge jumps in demand. This additional demand accelerates the company's progress down the experience curve by permitting rapid increases in cumulated output. The lower costs that result provide leeway for the next round of price cuts and the process repeats itself.

The classic example of such a product is the hand-held calculator. Advances in C-MOS (complementary metal-oxide semiconductor) technology and enormous price-sensitive demand provided fertile ground for the calculator market. When Texas Instruments decided to enter it with an experience curve strategy in 1972, unit costs tumbled from thousands of dollars to single figures in less than a decade, while sales skyrocketed. Since prices were going to come down anyway because of the steep experience curve and the price sensitivity of the demand, TI did well in this market by choosing the role of an experience-based cost leader rather than a follower."

Source: Pankaj Ghemawat, Building Strategy on the Experience Curve, HBR From the March 1985 Issue; Photo: By Texas Instruments - Texas Instruments, CC BY 3.0, https://commons.wikimedia.org/w/index.php?curid=25394569.

CHAPTER 5. METHODS OF PRICE SETTING

OBJECTIVE 1 To understand how prices are established and set.

OBJECTIVE 2 To ascertain how cost based pricing is built up and identify the factors that influence price setting. To show the advantages and disadvantages of different pricing mechanisms and its impact on allocation of the fixed costs on the product items.

OBJECTIVE 3 To show how market conditions set important precondition of smart pricing and discuss how market driven pricing and value based pricing methods impact on the pricing policy of modern companies.

5.1. Introduction

Price setting means any method and technique used by product manufacturers and service providers to determine the price of the goods supplied. Companies can use two approaches to set their prices:

- pricing technique can be based on costs, or
- on the willingness of the market or consumers to accept the price.

According to these two approaches, we distinguish between the traditional, cost-based pricing method and the market-based pricing method. We should always bear in mind that neither method can exist without the other. Costs should be considered as the lower limits of price decisions, while the market (the demand, the price acceptance by consumers, the prices of the competitors, etc.) should constitute the upper limit.

5.2. Cost-based pricing

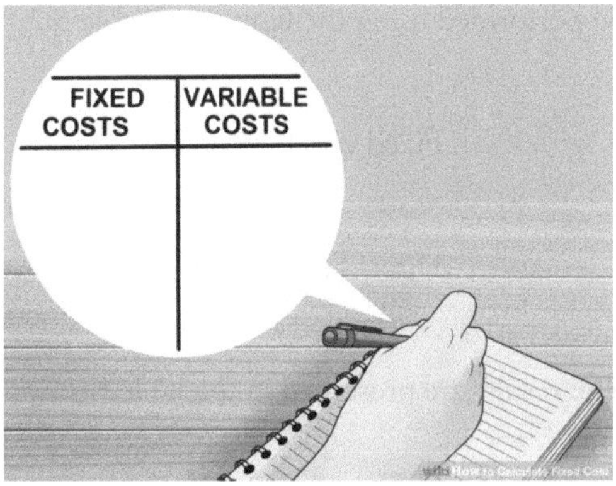

5.2.1. Traditional technique of pricing: 'total cost + profit margin'

The traditional, cost-based technique of pricing has remained very popular in business life to this very day. The details of the cost-based pricing method are presented through the example of a manufacturing company. The first step is to determine the value of the materials and labour used directly in manufacturing the product, and then – after adding the part of the fixed costs calculated in one way or the other that has been allocated to it - we can arrive at the total cost per product. The selling price can be set by adding the projected profit margin to the total cost as shown in Table 5.1.

The materials and labour used directly in the making of the product can be measured with relative accuracy; problems usually arise with the allocation of fixed costs. Using the example we had in Table 5.2 let us examine now how the allocation of fix costs with different methods leads to different results.

Table 5.1. The logic of the cost based pricing

Direct material content	xx
Direct labour content	xx
Fix costs	xx
Total cost	xxx
+ Profit margin	xx
Selling price	xxx

Note: The reasoning of Marshall (1979) was used to present the traditional method of pricing

Table 5.2. Annual cost and production figures (USD)

Materials costs	1,800 000
Labour costs	1,200 000
Fixed costs	2,400 000
Number of direct working hours	50, 000
Number of machine hours	40, 000
Materials used for product A	90
Materials used for product B	90
Working hours required for making product A	3 hours
Working hours required for making product B	1.5 hours
Machine hours required for making product A	1.5 hours
Machine hours required for making product B	2.25 hours
Number produced	20, 000
Hourly wages (including social charges)	24

Let us suppose that the allocation of fixed costs depends on the number of direct labour costs (based on the assumption that fixed costs arise in proportion to direct wages). The following calculation can be performed using the figures in Table 5.2.

$$\frac{\text{Fixed costs}}{\text{Direct labour costs}} = \frac{24\ 00000}{12\ 00000} \times 100 = 200\%$$

The results are presented in the table below.

Table 5.3. Allocation of fix costs based on direct labour costs ($)

	Product A	Product B
Materials	90	90
Labour	72	36
Fixed costs (200% of direct labour costs)	144	72
Total costs	306	198

Fixed costs can also be allocated on the basis of *labour hours*:

$$\frac{\text{Fixed costs}}{\text{Direct labour costs}} = \frac{2\ 400\ 000}{50\ 000} = \$48/\text{hour}$$

The latter calculation will produce the same result as the formula (a) as long as the planned hourly costs remain unchanged.

Table 5.4 Allocation of fixed costs on the basis of direct labour hours

	Product A	Product B
Materials	90	90
Labour	72	36
Fixed costs (Product A = 3 hours x $ 48; Product B = 1.5 hours x $48)	144	72
Total costs	306	198

The weakness of the method of allocating fixed costs on the basis of labour costs is found in the underlying assumption, as it is unimaginable that fixed costs will change according to direct labour costs. Fixed costs include elements, like depreciation, lease fees and others, which are nearly independent from direct labour costs. The problem with the method is that it under-prices the less labour-intensive products and overprices the more labour-intensive ones.

Fixed costs can be **allocated/distributed/assigned** according to *the quantity produced* as well:

$$\frac{\text{Fixed costs}}{\text{Number produced}} = \frac{2\ 400\ 000}{20\ 000} = \$120/\text{unit}$$

Table 5.5. Allocation of fixed costs on the basis of quantity produced

	Product A	Product B
Materials	90	90
Labour	72	36
Fixed costs ($120/unit)	120	120
Total costs	282	246

The flaws of the method include the following:

- It can only be applied for products which are very similar (a $1,000 and a $100 000 product obviously cannot have the same fixed cost bearing capacity).
- The level of fixed costs assigned to a unit largely depends on the number of pieces forecast to be sold. If the forecast is pessimistic and 30,000 pieces could be sold due to the favourable market conditions instead of the 20,000 pieces planned, the method will overprice the products, which, in turn, will increase the risk that the company loses some of its market share because of the high prices. In the opposite case, if the company sells only 15, 000 pieces, the calculated price cannot cover the fixed costs due to low sales volume.

It is also possible to allocate the fixed costs across products on the basis of *direct material plus direct labour costs*:

$$\frac{\text{Fixed costs}}{\text{Direct material and labour costs}} = \frac{2\,400\,000}{1800\,000+1200000} = \text{x}100= 80\%$$

Table 5.6. Allocation of fixed costs on the basis of direct material and labour costs ($)

	Product A	Product B
Materials	90	90
Labour	72	36
Fixed costs (80% of direct material and labour costs)	129.6	100.8
Total cost	291.6	226.8

The risk involved in the method is that the rate of fixed costs allocated largely depends on the price level of the materials used. If materials that are more expensive are used, the rate of allocated fixed costs will increase, even though the use of more expensive materials increases the level of fixed costs only with the amount of additional interest charges payable after the extra funds raised because of the higher material prices.

Fixed costs can also be assigned according to the number of machine hours used during production:

$$\frac{\text{Fixed costs}}{\text{Machine hours}} = \frac{2\,400\,000}{40\,000} = \$60/\text{unit}$$

The method has certain disadvantages as well, e.g. without any changes in the number of machine hours, certain elements of the fixed costs which are not closely related to it can increase significantly, although the sales revenues generated by the product do not cover this change.

Table 5.7. Allocation of fixed costs to machines hours

	Product A	Product B
Materials	90	90
Labour	72	36
Fixed costs (Product A = 1.5 machine hours x \$60; Product B = 2.25 machine hours x \$60)	90	135
Total costs	252	261

In conclusion, let us review the total cost levels obtained with the different calculation methods (Table 5.8.) and the selling prices we obtain with a 25% profit calculated on the costs.

Table 5.8. The impact of using different methods for the allocation of fixed costs (\$)

Calculation method	Total cost	
(allocation of fixed costs)	Product A	Product B
As % of direct labour	306	198
By direct machine hours	306	198
By units	282	246
By material and labour costs	291.6	226.8
By direct machine hours	252	261
Biggest difference in USD	54	63

It is clear that applying a different method for the allocation of fixed costs can lead to even higher price differences.

The disadvantages of the total cost + profit pricing method include the following:

- There is no real cause-effect relationship between the incurrence of the fixed costs and the basis of their allocation.
- The prices determined in this way do not provide information on the lower and upper thresholds of the prices and, as a result, do not allow the company to react to the price changes made by the competitors in a flexible way.
- It disregards the prices of competitors and those of competitive products, as well as the changes in demand.
- The total cost + profit pricing method leads to the overpricing of the product when the market conditions are unfavourable and to the under-pricing of the products when the market conditions are favourable (i.e. demand is on the increase.).
- It creates the illusion that prices are accurate and fair, even though the different methods can lead to a price difference as high as 30%.

EXHIBIT 5.1. PRICE CALCULATION BY FÉG CONVECTOR MANUFACTURING LTD IN THE 1990s

FÉG Convector Manufacturing Ltd became a successful and profitable company very soon after its privatization in the second half of the 1990s. It had a market share of 70–80% in the Hungarian market of gas convectors at the time. Since the company was practically the largest manufacturer in Europe, it had considerable cost advantages over its smaller competitors. The company had a good reputation for the reliable quality of its products, which was recognized by the market. In these circumstances the company could calculate its prices on the basis of the costs incurred. Even the prices calculated in this way ensured the company a serious competitive advantage.

Let us examine how the price calculation of a product was done.

Table 5.9. Cost accounting of the convector type ACHÁT LUX F8.50

Item	Amount (HUF)	As % of the selling price
Direct material costs	9,651	45.8
Direct labour costs	482	2.3
Social charges on direct labour	366	1.7
Special costs of manufacturing	100	0.5
Total of direct costs	10,599	50.4
Factory overhead costs (379% of direct labour costs)	1,828	8.7
Manufacturing costs	12,427	59.1
Company overhead costs (35% of direct costs)	3715	17.6
Total unit costs	16 142	76.7
Profit (22.6%	4 908	23.3
List price	21 700	103.1
3% discount	650	3.1
Selling price	21 050	100.0

Source: Rekettye–Vörös (1997, 6. Appendix)

5.2.2. Target return pricing

The technique of target return pricing is also based on costs, but its purpose is to set a price which can ensure a return on the investment with regard to the product. Target return pricing uses the following equation (or a similar one) to determine the prices:

$$P = C_v + \frac{TC_{fix}}{Qs} + \frac{rI}{Qs}$$

where P is the price to be set,

C_v is the unit variable cost,

TC_{fix} is the total of fixed costs,

Qs is the quantity planned,

r is the planned rate of return (profit),

I is the capital invested.

The method is based on the sales volume forecast for the given period. This is followed by estimates of the variable costs (materials, wages etc.) necessary for making the product, and the estimates of the fixed costs of manufacturing and selling the products. The return on investment realized during the given period is added to the fixed costs, and this is how we reach the price which guarantees the target return on investment. The above calculation is shown in Table 5.10.

Table 5.10. Calculation of the price based on target return

Item	Product A	Product B
Planned volume (units/year)	10, 000	20, 000
Variable cost per unit:		
Direct materials	$3, 000	$5, 000
Direct labour	$1, 500	$2, 000
Total unit variable costs	$4, 500	$7, 000
Fixed costs:		
Factory overhead costs	$2, 500 000	$5, 000, 000
Part of the allocated company overhead costs (e.g. 50% of factory costs)	$1, 250,000	$2, 500, 000
Total fixed costs	$3,750, 000	$7, 500 ,000
Planned rate of return (annual)	25%	25%
Investment	$15,000 000	$25,000, 000
Price	$5,250	$7,686

The weaknesses of the target return pricing method are very similar to those of the total cost + profit margin method. Its starting point itself can be questioned. The method is based on the volume; however, the quantities that can be sold depend largely on the price. The contradiction is obvious. If, for example, the demand (the quantity which can be sold) is lower than planned, the price has to be increased in order to reach the target return. Coming back to our example, let us assume that the demand for product B is only 15,000 compared to the budgeted 20,000. If the price remains unchanged, the return on assets will decrease to 11%. If we want to ensure the 25% rate of return as originally planned, the price should be increased to $7,917, e.g. by 3%. However, the price increase will result in further decrease in the demand (if the demand for the product is elastic). Consequently, the method can only be applied safely in markets characterized by shortage or monopoly.

5.2.3. The relationship of prices, costs, profit and rate of return indicators

Figure 5.1 reflects the relationship between prices, costs, profit and the volume of sales. The price multiplied by the units sold results in the sales revenues, from which the total margin can be obtained by deducting the total variable cost. Profit is obtained by deducting the fixed costs from the margin. By dividing the profit with the sales revenues we obtain the profit margin (profit ratio).

Assets can be divided into:

- fixed assets (intangible assets, tangible assets and invested financial assets) and
- current assets (inventory, accounts receivable, securities and other financial assets).

By dividing the total assets with the sales revenues we get the turnover rate which, multiplied by the profit margin, gives return on assets.

Figure 5.1. The interrelationships of the indicators

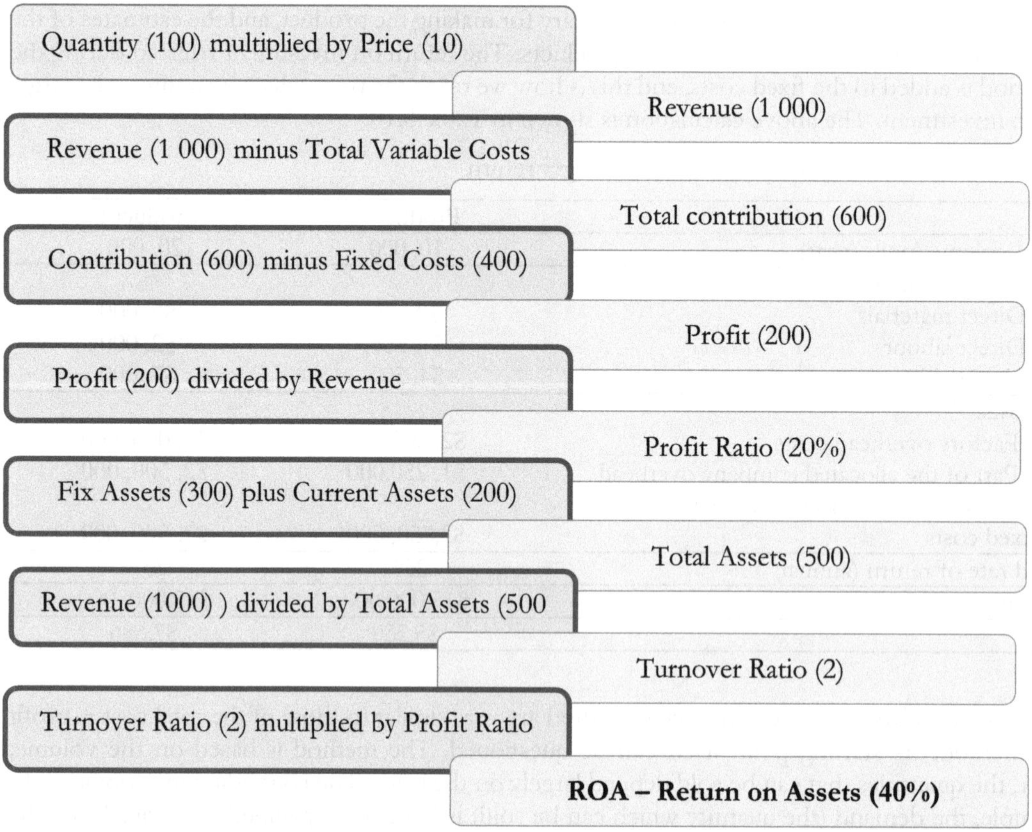

EXHIBIT 5.2. PRICING PRACTICES OF HUNGARIAN AND WESTERN-EUROPEAN COMPANIES

There is very little information available about the pricing practices and methods that companies apply. In Hungary, for example, only one survey has been known to be conducted on this topic; it was carried out by two researchers working for the Hungarian National Bank in 1998, involving companies from the processing, construction and trading industries (Tóth–Vincze, 1998). Below is one of the tables (with small modifications) published in their report (op. cit, p. 19) about the ranking of the methods applied. The researchers used a 5-point semantic differential scale to find out the importance attached to the different methods. The average value of the responses is shown in the third column of Table 5.11.

Table 5.11. Setting prices

Ranking	Description of the method	Average value
1.	Price of the main product is determined by the competitors' prices	3.54
2.	Price of the main product is calculated from the unit production costs plus a fixed, constant percent mark-up, but the percent mark-up varies (it can increase or decrease) to increase the contribution margin per unit.	3.47
3.	Price of the main product is made up of the unit production costs plus a fixed, constant percent mark-up. The percent mark-up is determined to include the target contribution margin per unit.	3.35
4.	Price of the main product is determined by the prices of the external markets and the exchange rate	2.68
5.	The main customer determines price of the main product.	2.29
6.	Price of the main product is determined in a different way.	1.39
7.	Price of the main product is determined at legislative level.	1.08
8.	The price authorities determine price of the main product.	1.08

In second and third places we can see two versions of the cost + profit margin pricing method. The methods ranked first, fourth, fifth and sixth refer to the market-based pricing method. The fact that the methods ranked in seventh and eighth place received a value just above 1 indicates that the pricing method based on regulation by the authority has been losing importance.

It is interesting that the only similar survey in Western Europe was also commissioned by a bank, namely the European Central Bank. Fabiani et al. conducted a survey in 2005 about the pricing practices of companies in the Eurozone. The findings of their research were published in a nearly 50–page report. Their main conclusions about the pricing methods are the following:

- More than half (54%) of the companies in the Eurozone determined their prices based on the cost + profit margin method. Germany is in the lead (73%), while the method is least frequently used in France (40%).
- Competition-based pricing with a 27% rate follows this method.
- Smaller companies more often use the cost plus profit margin method.
- There is a negative correlation between the intensity of the competition and the use of the cost plus profit margin method.

5.3. Market-based pricing

The logical process of cost-based pricing is illustrated by figure 5.2. Knowing the costs is indispensable for corporate decisions about pricing. Consumers in a competitive market, however, have no regard for the specific costs incurred by market players; their purchase decisions are not

affected by production costs. Consequently, the cost-based pricing method may lead to market failures.

Figure 5.2. The logical flowchart of cost-based pricing

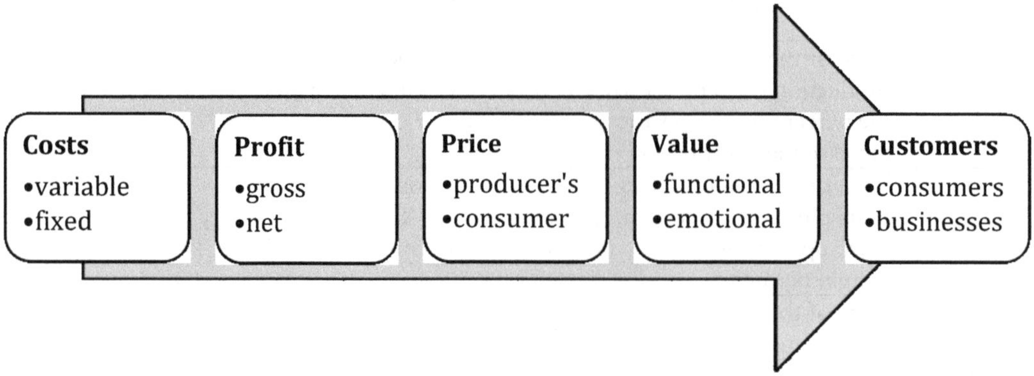

Customers usually give priority to the benefits (value) they expect from, or have already perceived in a product, often comparing them with the prices of similar ones (reference products, reference prices) also available in the market with similar functions before making buying decisions that sometimes escape rational justification. That is precisely the reason why market-based pricing uses an inverse logic, with the market or the consumer as the starting point.

From the prices developed in the market or from the values required by consumers, it gradually arrives at the prices and creates a profit margin by adjusting costs to available prices. (Figure 5.3) However, prices cannot be calculated in such a simple way with the use of the market-based pricing method, as with the cost-based method. In most product categories, the market abounds in products of different prices. The questions we have to answer are the following: how does our product fit into the range of competitive products and: will the targeted customers accept our prices or not? Literature recommends several methods for answering these questions.

Figure 5.3. The logical flowchart of market-based pricing

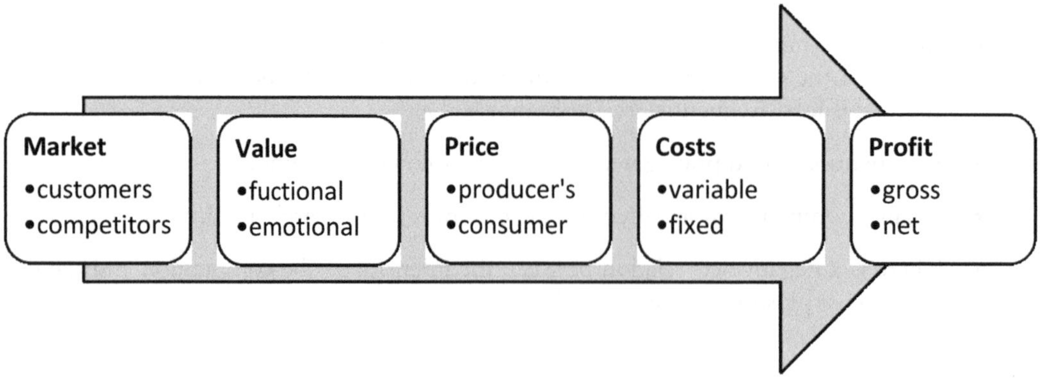

There is a multitude of products (companies) competing for consumers' wallets in most areas of the economy. This competition leads to the development of a market price, which is characteristic of the given product. The complexity and structure of this market price depends on market forms.

In perfectly competitive markets (many sellers, homogeneous products) price is seen by the sellers as a characteristic feature that they must adjust to when setting their prices. In the case of completely homogeneous products (which may include commodities as well) producers can mostly react to the changes in prices with the volume of their production.

Nobody, not even those who supply the competitive market with differentiated products can ignore the prices of the competitive products available there; rate pricing requires a lot more consideration in such cases. There is a need to

- determine the position of the product or service on the market (whether it belongs to the lower, middle or upper segment of the market);
- get to know the value preferences of consumers in the given segment;.
- get to know the competitors present in the segment;
- compare the value elements of the company's own products and those of the competitive products;
- identify the value differences, value advantages and disadvantages etc.

No price capable of leading the company to success in a market competition can be set without taking all of the above into account.

5.3.1. Going Rate Pricing

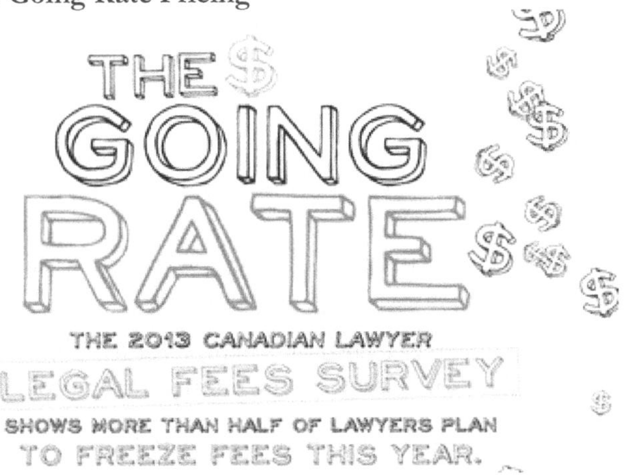

http://www.canadianlawyermag.com/4678/The-going-rate.html

The products of certain economic sectors are fairly similar, which means that consumers do not perceive the differences in the offers of the market suppliers to be significant. One example is air travel: if someone would like to travel from a European capital to New York, they have a choice of suppliers (SAS, KLM, Air France, British Airways, Lufthansa, etc.). Although there are differences in the services offered by the airlines, the difference for the one-time traveller is not significant compared to the service as a whole. That is why price will be the decisive factor in purchasing the ticket. None of the airlines can therefore ignore the prices of their competitors.

Monitoring the prices of competitors is very important in every business sector and for every company. Some companies even adopt a price following strategy, which means that they always adjust their prices to those of their competitor(s).

The first step in going rate pricing is to decide who the company considers their main competitor(s). It is relatively easy when there is one big (dominant) and several smaller companies on the market. The smaller companies consider the dominant one to be the price leader in most cases, and they

adjust the prices of their products accordingly. This type of pricing does not necessarily mean that each company works with the same price. Product quality, the level of the related services offered by the follower company (which may apply a niche strategy) may be better or worse than that of the dominant company. Knowing this difference, the follower company can set its own prices at a higher or lower level. Competitive pricing means that the follower company maintains the relative price difference. If the dominant company increases its prices, the follower company will do the same while keeping the relative price difference.

Competitive pricing is a very popular method, because it does not require the follower company to conduct expensive research related to market demand or costs. It simply follows the price movements of the dominant company and trusts that the so-called market price reflects the judgement of the consumers and the wisdom of the sector as well. It is also true that the follower company cannot do other than that in many cases.

5.3.2. Perceived value based pricing

The guiding principle of perceived value based pricing is to set prices in the region of their perceived value. Value is one of the most frequently used notions nowadays both in marketing and in price policy. Value pricing is often mistaken for lower prices or for bundle prices. However, the real meaning of value is the balance between the benefits offered by the product to the consumer and the price paid for it.

Market suppliers typically commit two mistakes. They spend very little on getting to know and determining the market position of their products in comparison with the products of their competitors. In addition, even if they do know this position, they have no energy left to deal with the dynamics of positioning their product. The most important lesson is that one should not rely on one's own value judgement as a basis, but build on the perceptions of consumers, and the factors they believe to represent value for them (Leszinsky – Marn, 1997).

EXHIBIT 5.3. CONSUMER-ORIENTED APPROACH TO PRICING FOR INDUSTRIAL PRODUCTS

- "A commitment to the philosophy that the customer chooses products by measuring benefits against costs.
- An understanding that benefits involve a great deal more than physical attributes and that in many industrial situations it is the "soft" services which differentiate products.
- A realization that cost involves more negative aspects of the purchase than price alone.
- The perspective of benefits and costs in terms of a complete usage system, not in terms of an isolated part of that system.
- Cognizance of the fact that difference customers view benefits and costs in difference ways, thus necessitating careful market segmentation.
- The application of graphic techniques to understanding the position of products and product lines in terms of customer needs and competitive offerings." (Shapiro–Jackson, 1978: 7).

The main difficulty is how to quantify perceived value. The following methods try to evaluate the product (or its benefits, properties) from the viewpoint of consumers and to compare it with the substitute (competitive) products

5.3.3. The EVC model

The pricing method calculated on the basis of customer value was introduced into the marketing literature as the EVC model (Economic Value to the Customer) after Forbis and Mehta (1981). The logic of the method is summarized in Figure 5.4.

The total life cycle cost (LCC) of the reference product (Y) is 1,000 units in our example. The total life cycle cost means the purchase price ($P_y = 300$), the start-up costs ($STC_y = 200$) as well as the post purchase costs arising from the use of the product ($PPC_y = 500$). Post purchase costs include, for example, the fuel necessary for the operation, the cost of maintenance, etc. The diagram illustrates the total life cycle cost of a new product. This new product (X) has a 100-unit higher incremental value (differentiation value) than product Y. The incremental value is marked as IV_x. The increased performances of the product, the higher degree of related services, the form, the image, etc. all contribute to incremental value. We assume that the seller's cost (SC) amounts to 300 units.

Figure 5.4. The illustration of value based pricing

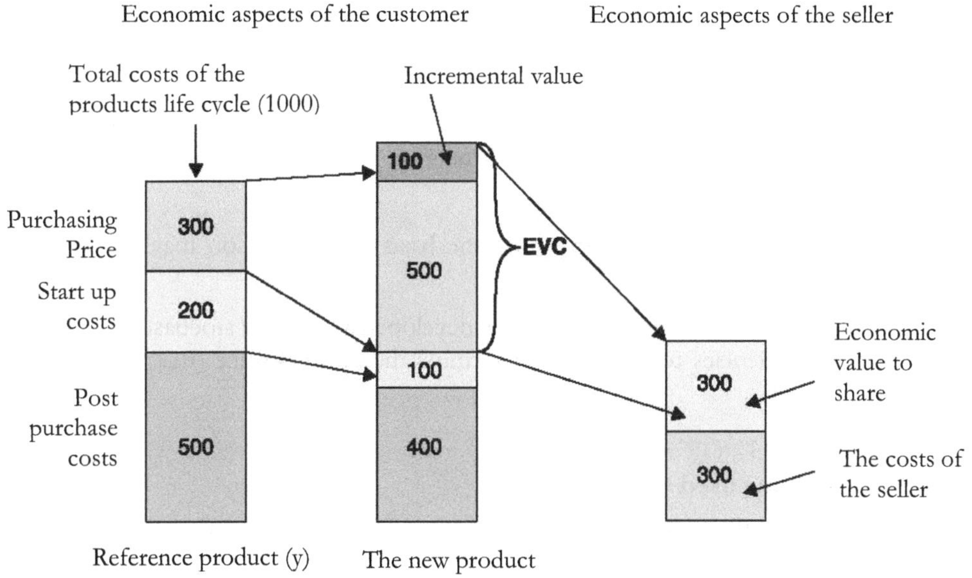

The seller's cost represents the lowest limit of price. It can correspond to the direct variable costs in the short term, and to the total average cost per unit in the long term.

The following equations can be established based on the above:

Total life cycle costs:

$$LCC_y = STC_y + PPC_y + P_y$$

Maximum achievable price:

$$P_{max_x} = LCC_y - STC_x - PPC_X + IV_X$$

Minimum calculable price

$$P_{min_x} = SC + TM \quad :$$

where TM represents the target margin (profit).

The actual price should be somewhere between the maximum and the minimum calculable price. In this way, the seller shares the incremental value of the product with the consumers and interests them in purchasing the product.

The limits of the EVC-model:

- The value outlined above does not necessarily reflect the consumers' evaluation of values, but rather the desired values of the seller. To turn this into an accepted value by the consumers the seller should spend a lot on communication, informing and persuading the consumers.
- The method can be best used when the seller negotiates with one consumer at a time and it is the least reliable in the cases of mass production and mass marketing (due to the different preferences and value perception of consumers).
- The method does not give an exact price, but rather a range of prices within which the sellers have to select the final price according to their intuition.
- The basis of comparison can be very uncertain: regarding both the reference product (a lot of substitute products with different benefits may be available) and the estimation of the non-price consumer costs.
- The value of the elements which constitute the basis of comparison may change fast in market and price conditions.

To eliminate part of the deficiencies, Thomson and Coe developed a so-called stochastic EVA-model, which uses distribution frequencies to be able to determine the optimal price ($P_{optimal}$) (Thomson–Coe, 1997).

EXHIBIT 5.4. EXAMPLES FOR EVC PRICING

The pricing technique used by Du Pont

When the company Du Pont introduced its new synthetic carpet fibre with a set of incremental values, it managed to prove to its customers with success that they would reach the same profit at the price of \$1.40 per pound as they did with the significantly cheaper material used earlier. Later Du Pont sold its product at lower than its \$ 1.40 per pound price allowing its customers to gain extra profits as well.

Source: Bush–Houston, 1985: 596

The pricing technique used by the company Caterpillar

One of the competitors of Caterpillar sold a piece of construction equipment for $ 90k. A similar product sold by Caterpillar at a price of $ 100k offers incremental value to its consumers in the following way:

90,000 dollars, the same as the competitors,

7,000 dollars incremental value due to longer durability,

6,000 dollars incremental value due to higher reliability,

5,000 dollars incremental value for more extended servicing network,

2,000 dollars incremental value due to longer warranty period,

110,000 dollars total value,

–10,000 dollars discount,

100,000 dollars final price.

CATERPILLAR

Source: Kotler–Keller, 2006: 446

EXHIBIT 5.5. PRICING OF CARS BASED ON PERCEIVED VALUE

Let us examine a different method of perceived price-based pricing by looking at the research about the perception of cars (Rekettye-Liu, 2001). By using focus groups the researchers first determined which properties of a medium category potential buyers consider to be the most important (on a scale of 1 to 10). These values of importance can be converted into relative weights.

Table 5.12. The relative weight of the properties

Factors	Importance	Relative weight
Safety of the car	9.35	17.0
Design	6.945	12.6
Costs of maintenance	9.19	16.7
Performance of the car	6.535	11.9
Image of the brand	5.875	10.7
Low rate of failure	9.19	16.7
Comfort offered by the car	7.95	14.4
Total	55.035	100.0

As part of the research respondents assessed one by one the properties of the 6 car brands included in the study. The following table presents the results of the assessment in percentage (the brand names of the cars are marked only by letters.)

Table 5.13. The judgement of potential buyers of the brands' different properties

Properties/Brands	A	B	C	D	E	F	Total
Safety of the car	14%	18%	13%	19%	20%	17%	100%
Design	15%	18%	11%	18%	20%	18%	100%

Costs of maintenance	15%	17%	15%	17%	19%	17%	100%
Performance of the car	14%	18%	13%	19%	20%	17%	100%
Image of the brand	15%	18%	12%	20%	20%	16%	100%
Low rate of failure	16%	18%	13%	19%	19%	16%	100%
Comfort offered by car	14%	18%	12%	18%	20%	18%	100%

To calculate the perceived value, the perceived value of the properties should be multiplied by their relative weight, which gives a relative value to each brand as shown in the table below:

Table 5.14. Relative value of the brands

Properties/Brands	A	B	C	D	E	F	Weight
Safety of the car	2.40	3.06	2.14	3.22	3.33	2.84	16.99
Design	1.87	2.26	1.37	2.33	2.54	2.25	12.62
Costs of maintenance	2.46	2.77	2.53	2.91	3.13	2.89	16.70
Performance of the car	1.66	2.12	1.52	2.25	2.35	1.98	11.87
Image of the brand	1.58	1.95	1.23	2.08	2.12	1.71	10.68
Low rate of failure	2.65	2.92	2.10	3.10	3.18	2.74	16.70
Comfort offered by car	2.01	2.59	1.80	2.62	2.88	2.54	14.45
Total	14.63	17.67	12.69	18.51	19.55	16.95	100.00

In the next step the perceived value of the given brand is divided by the average of perceived value, then multiplied by the average market price of the products in question:

$$\text{Perceived value based price} = \frac{\text{Perceived value of the given brand}}{\text{Average perceived value}} \times \text{Average selling price}$$

Assuming that the average selling price of these cars is 20 thousand dollars, the calculation will result in the following prices for the different brands as shown in the table below:

Table 5.15. Calculation of the price adjusted by perceived value

Item/Brands	A	B	C	D	E	F
Perceived value	14.63	17.67	12.69	18.51	19.55	16.95
Average value	16.67	16.67	16.67	16.67	16.67	16.67
Perceived value/average	0.88	1.06	0.76	1.11	1.17	1.02
Average price ($)	20000	20000	20000	20000	20000	20000
Price adjusted by perceived value in $	17600	21200	15200	22200	23400	20400

5.3.4. Activity-based pricing

The relationship between supplier and buyer, as well as the nature of the product or service in question allow, in many cases, the use of so-called activity-based pricing instead of fixed pricing. Activity-based pricing means that the supplier is paid the counter-value on the basis of their performance. One of

the certified forms of activity-based pricing is, for example, commission systems used by sales agents, or any other type of commission structure. The trader does not buy the product, but participates in selling it, and receives a commission in return. Their remuneration depends on the performance. Activity-based pricing is often used for customized projects and advisory contracts.

Financial consulting companies very often sign activity-based pricing contracts similar to the one concluded between Ford and ABB. These companies can benefit from the extra profit obtained during due diligence and the reorganisation of the company owing to the measures taken by the company.

One of the advantages of activity-based pricing is that both the buyer and the supplier can feel safe, because they provide and will receive as much of the services as the existing value of the services. This pricing technique however, is not simple and cannot be applied widely. It relies on cooperation between the seller and the buyer to have a full review of the objectives of the project and its possible outcomes, and to determine clearly the methods for measuring the result.

5.3.5. The tender

It is standard procedure to invite tenders in the market of industrial products and in the case of larger purchase orders, as well as for procurement by the government or other public organizations. For example, the European Commission's web pages state: "The Commission uses public contracts to buy goods and services - studies, technical assistance and training; consultancy, conference and publicity services; books and IT equipment etc. The providers are selected via calls for tender which are issued by the Commission departments, offices and agencies around Europe."

The main objective of the bidder in this form of purchase is to set the price, in most cases, without negotiating with the buyer. One of the most well-known definitions of tender is the following: "A written proposal naming the fee or the price sent by one party to another (usually a public body) to supply certain goods or to carry out certain work (activity) in accordance with the conditions published by the other party publicly, including in the press." Tendering is not a new-fangled form of large-scale commercial transactions: Simpson and Weiner describe that the English launched tenders as early as 1666, the time of Captain Cook.

EXHIBIT 5.6. ABB AND FORD: CREATING VALUE THROUGH COOPERATION

Ford was looking for a reliable and high quality enterprise to design and build its car painting plant in Oakville (Canada) as part of a turnkey project. Ford and ABB agreed that they would cooperate right from the preparatory phase and avoid the traditional tendering process where the bids are always submitted based on insufficient information. The two companies exchanged a huge amount of information during the cooperation in the preparatory phase and got to know each other's ideas. All this led to a new type of cooperation.

ABB became willing to build the plant at a lower price than usual, and according to the agreement they would receive a pre-determined percentage of any further savings achieved compared to the original price. This novel performance-based pricing proved more favourable for both parties than the price they would have reached in a conventional tender or a bilateral negotiation. Ford obtained its plant at a lower cost, while ABB managed to implement a range of modifications in the design, which allowed them to save some of the costs.

Source: Shapiro (1998) quoting the work by Frey and Schlosser: "ABB and Ford: Creating Vale Through Cooperation" (Sloan Management Review, Fall, 1993: 65–72)

EXHIBIT 5.7. ACTIVITY BASED COSTING — ABC

Activity-based pricing relies on the activity-based costing (ABC) method. It started to spread in the middle of the 80s and has reached its peak: the simple cost accounting method turned into an efficient profit analysing method.

According to Peter B. B. Turney, the CEO of Cost Technology: "ABC has shown a great improvement over the last decades. From a cost accounting experiment, it has become a performance-based management system (ABM), which is widely applied in many sectors in the planning of resources, capacities and the supply chain. ABC is a multifaceted algorithm and financial database which contributes to increasing the efficiency of performance management."

The following figure illustrates the 4 generations in the development of ABC.

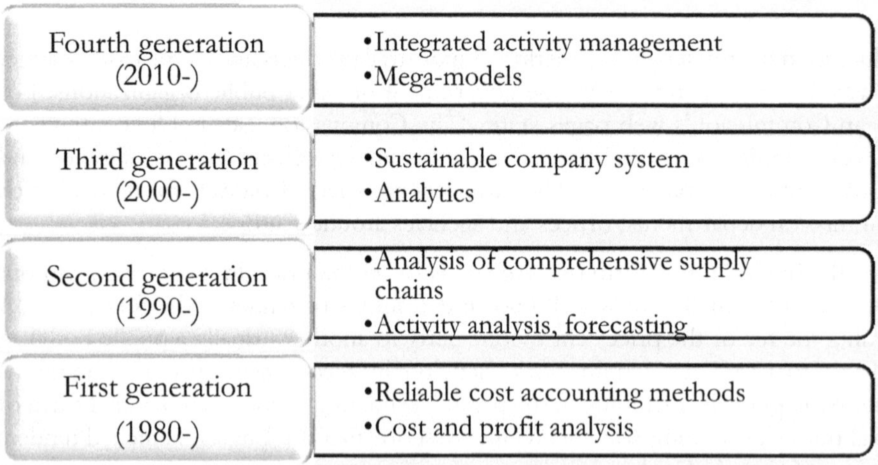

Source: Peter B. B. Turney: Activity-Based Costing, http://www.sas.com/resources/whitepaper/wp_5073.pdf (22 September, 2010

Tenders can take various forms:

- sometimes a selected number of suppliers are invited to make a bid, or
- the number of bidders is not restricted;
- at other times the best bid submitted in writing wins, or
- the bidders are short-listed based on their written offers, which is followed by bilateral negotiations between the bidder and the tenderer.

Tender is a special form, because companies first need to decide under uncertain conditions whether to submit a bid at all. The preparations for a tender can be very costly depending on the size of the project. Knowledge about the market, the estimates of experts, planning, scientific methods and statistical analysis all play a vital role in the preparation for a tender. This decision requires a detailed analysis of the three factors that are of key importance in every price decision (Figure 5.5.)

Figure 5.5. The most important elements of the tender process

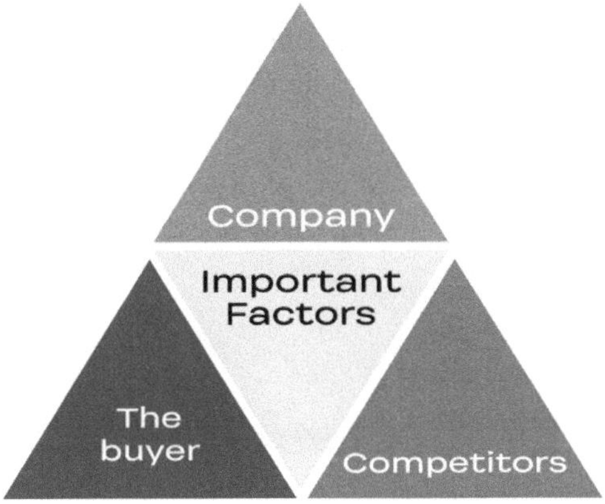

The company itself. When the terms of the tender come to be known, the company must decide whether it is able to meet its conditions profitably or not. In making this decision the company can rely on several screening and evaluating methods which allow it to assess the company's competence by weighing it against the priorities set out by the tender. The evaluation criteria may include the following: are there enough capacities available, is the company able to do high quality design work, are the human resources available, can it purchase the necessary materials, does the company have the necessary financial tools, etc. The company can decide whether it is suitable at all to submit a tender bid/proposal by using the assessment method (or a scoring system) developed for weighing according to the priorities of the tender. In addition to considering its suitability, the company should also decide whether taking part in the tendering process is in line with the company's market policy objectives or not. (If, for example, the publisher of the tender makes its decision purely on the basis of the price, the suppliers providing higher quality and therefore charging higher fees will most certainly not meet the requirements. In this case the best strategy for a company is to stay away from the tender.)

The buyer. The decision to bid or not also depends on how well the company knows the buyer. The priorities of the buyer can be inferred from the tender specification, but past relationships and former experiences, as well as further knowledge about the buyer other than the tender documentation can help the company decide whether to take part in the tender or not, and determine the conditions of the bid/proposal. The importance of the buyer and the potential purchase order should be assessed. The need to provide good service to the buyer or to retain the buyer can influence how the conditions of the proposal to be submitted are established.

The competitors. The company intending to submit a proposal to a tender should know who its competitors are. (It may sound difficult at first, but in reality companies working in the same profession usually know their competitors very well.) It should also estimate which competitors will submit a proposal. If a competitor against whom the company is unlikely to win is believed to make a bid, the company can be spared a lot of costs by not entering into the tender. The tendering method presented a challenge to the scientific community as well: several models were developed to facilitate decision-making. The following issues were individually addressed:

- what price should be offered when the number and the identity of the competitors is known;
- what price should be offered when the identity and number of potential competitors is not known;
- how many tenders should the company enter into at the same time, if its capacities are not sufficient to fulfil each.

Government to ensure the transparency of transaction made by official bodies also uses tender. Exhibit 5.8 deals with such a case.

EXHIBIT 5.8. THE SRI LANKA AIR FORCE INTENDS TO PROCURE 8-12 NEW COMBAT AIRCRAFT REPLACING ITS OBSOLETE FLEET OF AGING FIGHTER JETS.

The Sri Lankan government has publicly announced that it intends to purchase eight to 12 new multirole combat aircraft for the Sri Lanka Air Force (SLAF), according to local media reports.

In a bid to purchase eight state-of-the-art fighter jets for Sri Lanka Air Force (SLAF), the Cabinet of Ministers opted for *international competitive bidding* (ICB) ensuring both transparency and best possible financing method for the government, *The Sunday Leader* learns.

One of the possible candidates: The **PACJ F-17 Thunder** or **CAC FC-1** ***Xiaolong*** (*Fierce Dragon)* is a lightweight, single-engine, multi-role combat aircraft developed jointly by the Pakistan Aeronautical Complex (PAC) and the Chengdu Aircraft Corporation (CAC) of China.

Photo: By Peng Chen - Flickr: Pakistan Airforce FC-1 Xiao Long, CC BY-SA 2.0, https://commons.wikimedia.org/w/index.php?curid=12614771

"The Cabinet gave green light to SLAF to go ahead with open tender or ICB process in order to gain the ideal aircraft at the best financial package. So China, India, Pakistan, United Kingdom or any other country could submit EoI (Expression of Interest) outlining their respective financing method, be it credit lines or soft loans," said Defence Secretary Karunasena Hettiarachchi speaking to *The Sunday Leader.*

Sources: Nadira Gunatilleke, Cabinet nod to purchase multirole fighters, Thursday, August 11, 2016 - 01:00, Daily News; Franz-Stefan Gady, Sri Lanka Mulls Purchase of New Fighter Aircraft August 14, 2016, The Diplomat (http://thediplomat.com/2016/08/sri-lanka-mulls-purchase-of-new-fighter-aircraft/); Wiraj Silva Govt. Mulls International Fighter Jet Tender, May 1, 2016, Sunday Leader (http://www.thesundayleader.lk/2016/05/01/govt-mulls-international-fighter-jet-tender/)

The next part will give a brief overview of the most well-known procedures for preparing a bid.

A generally known method is when different prices are assigned to the calculated costs of a given project, which is then combined with the probability of winning to arrive at the price that will potentially generate the highest profit (margin). Let us illustrate it with an imaginary example using the data from table 5.16.

Table 5.16. Evaluation of the bids/proposals submitted to the tender

Project costs	Bid prices	Profit	Probability of winning	Expected profit
A	B	B-A	P	P*(B-A)
500 000	400 000	-100 000	1.00	-100 000
500 000	450 000	-50 000	0.95	-47 500
500 000	500 000	0	0.90	0
500 000	550 000	50 000	0.85	42 500
500 000	600 000	100 000	0.80	80 000
500 000	650 000	150 000	0.70	105 000
500 000	700 000	200 000	0.60	120 000
500 000	750 000	250 000	0.50	125 000
500 000	800 000	300 000	0.40	120 000
500 000	850 000	350 000	0.30	105 000
500 000	900 000	400 000	0.20	80 000
500 000	950 000	450 000	0.10	45 000
500 000	1 000 000	500 000	0.00	0

The table shows what price the company should offer in a tender bid in order to maximize the profitability of the given business deal. It can be seen that the price of 750K generates the highest potential gain (The two neighbouring prices of 700K and 800K would also generate a relatively high potential gain). The above analysis looks professional and convincing, however it has one very critical point, notably how to estimate the probability of winning, and how to obtain the information necessary for this estimation. The experiences gained from previous tenders and expert estimation can help to assess the probabilities. The theory related to the subject mentions three ways to determine the probabilities:

- The method built on the analysis of earlier winning bids/proposals.
- The so-called *"average competitor approach"*, which is applied when the company does not know who its competitors are.
- The application of the so-called *"specific competitor approach"* is recommended when the company has information about the potential competitor(s).

All three methods rely on the analysis of the winning bids/proposals submitted earlier to tenders issued on similar topics in order to determine the bid price. Using these methods, the company estimates how much its own direct costs would have been, regarding the supply of products specified in the earlier tenders (or, if the company was the winner, how much the direct costs actually were). Then the company examines how the earlier winning bids compared to the direct costs and how often the competitors had submitted a higher or lower bid than that. The probability of winning can be estimated on the basis of all this information as presented in Figure 5.5.

The specific competitor approach is based on the analysis of the bids submitted by the opponent earlier, while the general competitor approach is based on the analysis of all the winning and non-winning bids accessible in the given field. According to theory, the probability of winning decreases

in parallel with the increase in the number of bidders. For more details please consult, for example, Monroe's work (1990: 417–427).

Figure 5.5. Probability based on former successful tenders

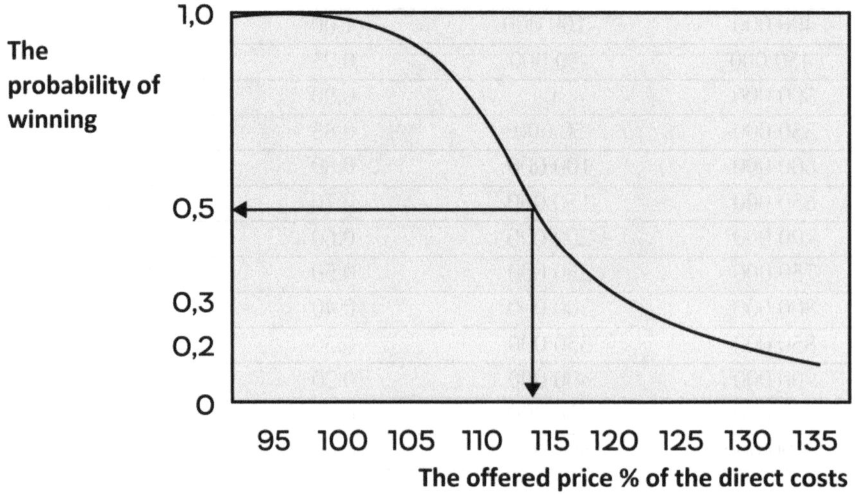

Mathematical models can also help with the preparation of tender bids. However, they cannot replace human creativity and cannot free the company from gathering information.

Although tendering is a useful method, which can ensure the transparency of business transactions and the comparability of offers, it cannot be regarded as a panacea, especially when its central element is the price. It is up to the buyer (with the exception of the public buyer whose activity is governed by law) to decide which method to use during the procurement: the tender or continuous cooperation with a reliable supplier, procurements by way of negotiation. Holmes examined in detail (1995: 7–17) in which cases tenders and in which cases other methods were recommended. Let us enjoy an anecdote concerning the doubts about tendering.

EXHIBIT 5.9. THE CASE OF AN ASTRONAUT

When reporters asked Commander Alan B. Shepard Jr., America's first man into space, what he thought about as he sat atop the Redstone rocket, waiting for lift off, he replied: "The fact that every part of this ship was built by the low bidder."

Source: Gene Kranz, "Failure Is Not an Option: Mission Control From Mercury to Apollo 13 and Beyond" Simon & Schuster, Paperbacks, New York 2000

PART 2. STRATEGIES AND TACTICS OF PRICING

CHAPTER 6. PRICING STRATEGY

OBJECTIVE 1 To explore how companies make important pricing decision by positioning its offering to the market by deciding the price level it wants to achieve. The price positioning then determines the nature of competitive rivalry that the company is faced with.

OBJECTIVE 2 To show the range of pricing strategies available when a company intends to launch new products or product lines and to illustrate the possible consequences, advantages and disadvantages of those strategies.

OBJECTIVE 3 To explain that the pricing decision is dependent on the market segment which the company targets.

6.1. Introduction

In principle, there are only two occasions in the life of a company when it must make price-related decisions. Firstly, when it enters the market with a new offer (or a new component for an existing product mix) and has to face the problem of determining the initial price of this new product or service. The second time is when it intends to change the price of its existing supply or some of its components. Of course, a pricing decision of this kind cannot be regarded as a strategy. Strategy means a series of similar pricing decisions made in support of one of the corporate policies (and within that the marketing policy) with a view of creating or improving the competitiveness of the firm. Price, as it is, does not exist in a vacuum. Only products or services offered for sale have a price. Therefore, pricing decisions should be in agreement with the considerations and deliberations concerning all other areas related to the company. Let us examine now which are the areas that require strategical deliberation:

- Deciding the price and quality level of the company.
- Deciding the marketing and pricing strategies used while launching new products.
- How to manage prices during the product life cycle.
- Deciding the appropriate structure of prices.
- Deciding how the firm manages its prices through the various levels of the distribution channels.
- Deciding to choose one price policy or price discrimination.
- Deciding the method of price setting and price adaptation.

6.2. Deciding the price level of the company's offer

Price level is the position of the company's products and services in the market among its competitors' offerings. Therefore, deciding the price levels of the products, product lines (and practically of the whole range the company offers) is more than merely a pricing policy issue. It is a decision involving company policy, market choice and product strategy; one in which price is only one element of the problem. Defining the price level means choosing the quality level at the same time. The price-quality correlation will determine which parts of the market the firm can target and which competitors it will have to fight for its share of the market. Decision on the price level has an impact on real prices, the quantities that can be sold, the costs arising during the course of manufacturing and sales and eventually on the profits that can be generated.

The structure of the market can be interpreted as an architecture of product clusters defined by their differences in quality and price, competing in the market. Kotler and Keller (2003) studied the relationship between price and quality in the market for passenger cars and ended up distinguishing eight price levels. They are the following (with a model mentioned as an illustration):

(1) Ultimate	Rolls Royce
(2) Gold Standard	Mercedes-Benz
(3) Luxury	Audi
(4) Meeting special needs	Volvo
(5) Middle	Buick
(6) Convenience	Ford Escort
(7) Me Too but Cheaper	Hyundai
(8) Price Alone	Kia

One of the authors of this book studied the Canadian leather gloves market for a former project focusing on price (quality) and the quantity that could be sold. He concluded that market structure is similar to a pyramid, because lower prices go together with larger quantities and vice versa. In the case of this typically labour-intensive industry newcomers - mainly developing countries with cheap labour - try to penetrate the lower segments. This bottom-up offensive pushes the whole structure upwards, forcing countries or producers with higher manufacturing costs to produce better quality, improve their marketing activities and move towards the upper segments. If they fail to do so, they will drop out (Figure 6.1).

In the context of perceived value most authors divide the market into three parts and present it as a three-tier structure (Figure 6.2). The three levels have been named in several ways: no frill, value, economy, budget-medium, middle-high, premium, etc.). The use of terms can also depend on the product: in railway transport we find third class (slowly disappearing), second class and first class. On air transport economy class, business (sometimes-called executive) class and first class are used. For passenger cars the American terms: sub-compact, compact and luxury have become generally accepted. Credit cards come in categories like normal, gold and platinum. In European hotels price level and quality are expressed with the number of stars (three, four or five). It is, however, not unusual to see the market divided into only two levels: branded and unbranded products.

Figure 6.1. The price structure of the Canadian leather glove market

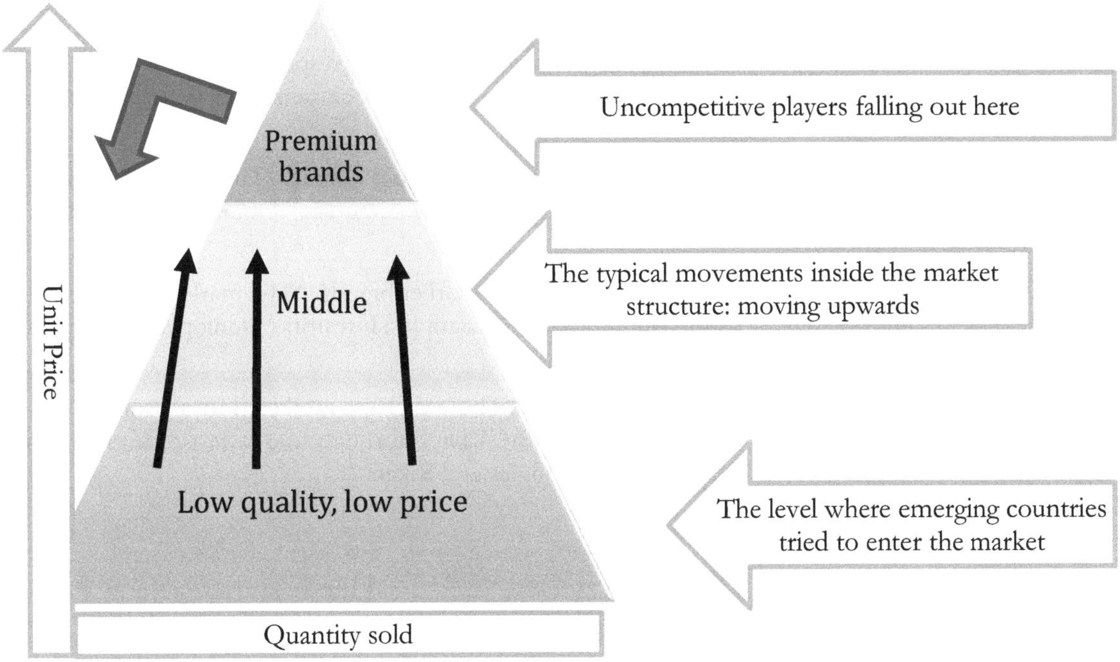

Figure 6.2. Market tiers on the matrix of perceived value and price

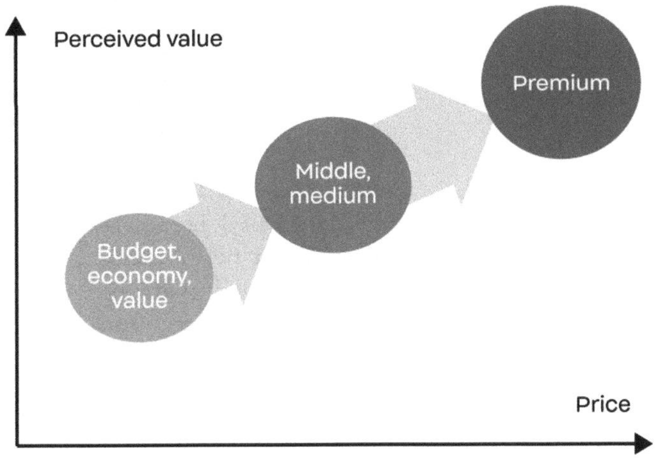

Categories do not always mean identical quality or identical price: it happens quite frequently that the levels are further subdivided. Let us take, for example, the levels of tire brands in the United States (See Exhibit 6.1).

EXHIBIT 6.1. THE US MARKET OF TIRES

The three-tier structure of tire brands (see next) was made as a response to a petition sent to the International Trade Commission asking for quotas on Chinese consumer tire imports. The American Coalition for Free Trade in Tires said tiers do not correspond to performance, but to price and profit margin. The coalition said there were three tiers, and defined them as follows.

1. Tier One is made up of the major tire companies' premium brands. "They carry the highest price tags and have the highest profit margins for the manufacturers." Examples: Bridgestone, Goodyear and Michelin.

2. Tier Two is made up of the tire companies' mid-market brands. "The marketing effort for these tires is not as extensive as for Tier One tires." Examples: Firestone, Dunlop, BFGoodrich, Continental, Yokohama and Toyo.

3. Tier Three is made up of "value" brand tires. "These tires are marketed to consumers who are more concerned with price than a brand name." They also have the lowest profit margins. Examples: GT Radial, Runway, Primewell, Douglas and Riken.

Tier 1
- Michelin
- Bridgestone
- Goodyear

Tier 2
- Firestone,
- Dunlop,
- BFGoodrich,
- Continental,
- Yokohama
- Toyo.

Tier 3
- GT Radial,
- Runway,
- Primewell,
- Douglas
- Riken,
- all private brands

Michelin says the new Pilot Sport 4S UHP tire solves the pleasure and safety equation for performance enthusiasts, offering unprecedented driving pleasure, exceptional steering precision and tremendous directional stability, while also providing maximum grip on wet or dry roads.

In his blog, the tire expert Bob Ulrich expressed his doubts with this system and suggested that a grouping based on *price points* would give a better picture about the tire markets. He said: "It is also hard to determine how many tiers there are. When a tire company places its brand "in the middle of Tier Two," *isn't it really creating tiers within tiers*? Maybe tiers should be determined by price point alone. Personally, I see tire marketing in the real world as more of a four-, maybe even five-tier system based on price points. For example, where would you put low-cost Chinese imports? The bottom of Tier Three? In their own tier? There are just too many markets within markets to define tiers in a hard and fast way."

Source: http://www.moderntiredealer.com/article/312245/what-is-a-tier-two-tire-tier-three (accesed January 10, 2017)

EXHIBIT 6.2. THE STRUCTURE OF THE HUNGARIAN HOTEL INDUSTRY

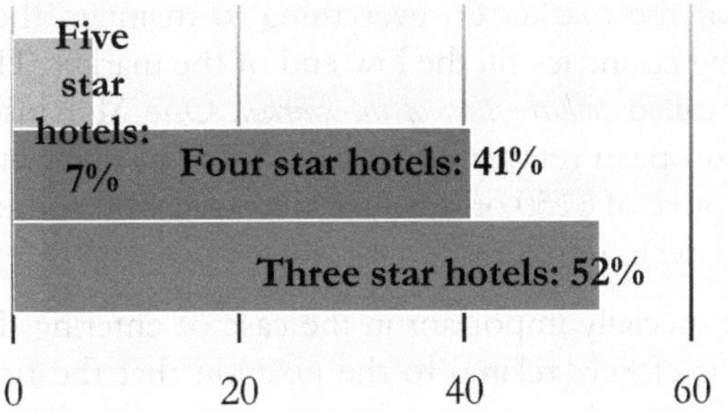

Stars separate the quality levels of the hotels in many countries – including Hungary - (three, four and five – in exceptional cases six or seven). According to this system, the greater number of stars indicate greater luxury. Forbes Travel Guide, formerly Mobil Travel Guide, launched its star rating system in 1958. The AAA (American Automobile Association) recommends using diamonds instead of stars to represent the quality level of a hotel.

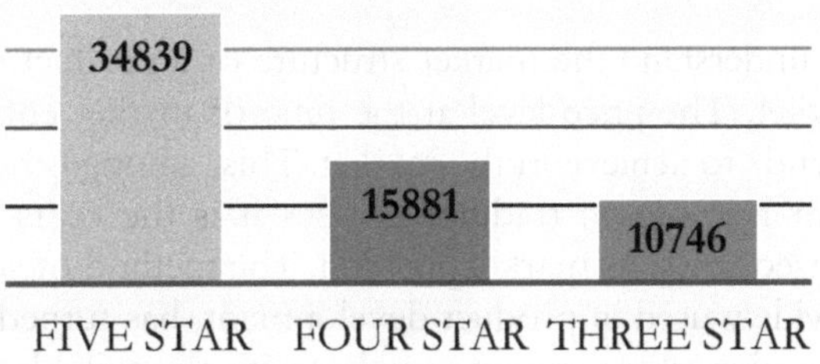

The hotel industry in Hungary shows a rather pyramid-type structure. The levels clearly represent not only better quality but also higher prices. The following figures show quality structure of the Hungarian hotels and price differences of the levels. The first figure shows the distribution of the hotels in Hungary in 2014, while the other figure displays the average room price of the three, four and five-star hotels in Hungarian Forints.

It is worthwhile to mention that the market structure of the different products and services in terms of quality and price may show different forms. Besides the prevailing pyramid structure, we can find markets showing an upside-down pyramid or even barrel or hourglass structures (Figure 6.3.)

Figure 6.3. Different market structures

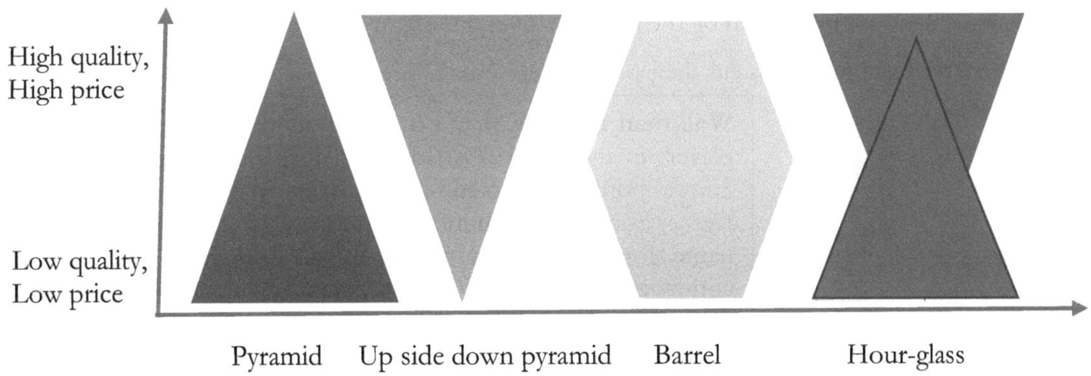

In this century, with the rapid development of emerging countries, the hourglass type is gaining in importance: the traditional brands at the high end of the market do everything to maintain their position while the newly emerging offers of developing countries fill the low end of the market. The middle is on the way to a decrease. This process is called *polarization of the market.* One McKinsey survey showed, for example, that in the case of the European refrigerator market, the high end (with a unit price of $900 or more) and the low end (with a price of $150 or less) has increased while others that featured prices between these two points showed declining sales.

To understand the market structure of a product is especially important in the case of entering the market. The price level at the time of market entry is closely related to the position that the firm intends to achieve in the market. This, among other factors, has an impact on the costs as well and, what is more, in traditional cases it is the costs that define the price level of the company and consequently its market position. The method of so-called target-costing, which started in Japan and is widely used in product development, has turned traditional logic upside down: it first defines the desired market position together with the suitable price. From this it draws conclusions concerning the price level that will allow the firm to sell the product at a profit. In this way, the development department will be charged not only with the desirable parameters of the product but target costing as well. The process of target costing is shown in Figure 6.4 and its application by Sony is presented in the next exhibit.

EXHIBIT 6.3. TARGET COSTING APPLIED ON THE SONY WALKMAN PRODUCT LINE.

Sony introduced the system of target costing to be able to define the allowed cost level well before starting product design. Target cost is developed as the result of a two-stage process: firstly they define the planned price of the product by subtracting the retailer's and wholesaler's margin plus 10% from the price the product will have according to the plans. This is followed by the definition of the target costs, which means subtracting the planned profit from the planned price.

The recommended retail price is planned by Sony in such a way that it should not exceed the so-called *magic price point* even after the discounts allowed. Prices are, therefore, set a little lower than the round numbers; for example, Sony's most popular model costs 19,800 yen in the domestic market, just a little less than 20,000 yen. Experience has shown that prices right under the magic price points significantly increase the quantities sold. Sony's recommended retail price is exactly at the magic point – after the proper discounts. The selling prices of Sony's Walkman are not influenced by the prices of competitors or similar products.

Whenever its competitors cut their prices, Sony usually prefers to accelerate the launching of

Walkman is a Sony brand originally used for portable cassette players in the late 1970s. In the 2010s, it was used to market Sony's portable audio and video players as well as a line of former Sony Ericsson mobile phones. After the "Discman" name for CD players was terminated in early 2000, Sony continues to use the "Walkman" brand name for most of their portable audio devices.

Source: By Marc Zimmermann at the English language Wikipedia, CC BY-SA 3.0, https://commons.wikimedia.org/w/index.php?curid=2863032

a new model with improved functions instead of following the trend of price cuts. In the case of other, alternative products Walkman is regarded as the so-called benchmark product to which the prices of the other products, e.g. CD players or cameras are compared. In order to keep this favourable benchmark position, and maintain maximum consumer satisfaction, Sony sets Walkman prices with regard to the consumers' perceived value. It defines the targeted margin adopted to the individual products in the course of a reiterative process, that has one goal: to support the realization of the division's long-term profit targets.

The division's profit target is the starting point. The target profit is developed by the firm's planning department during negotiations with the audio team. Once the plan has been agreed and accepted, the group becomes responsible for its own profitability. To calculate the first version of the new product's cost target they subtract the planned margin from the planned selling price. This sum is then compared with estimated costs of the new product. Should the target cost be deemed too low, it is possible to reduce the profit margin. (In this case, however, the other products must compensate for the profit lost.) When the decision has been made for all products, a simulation is run for the whole group to check if the profit target can be realized. If the simulation indicates that it cannot, all the decisions are reviewed.

This revision can take three stages: in the first the engineers examine if and how manufacturing costs can be reduced. In the second stage actions that could possibly increase profit are examined, e.g. in co-operation with the marketing department the possibility of reducing the share of low-profit products is examined. In the third stage the audio team and the marketing department together decide on decreasing the profitability target if the product is important for the company.

Source: Cooper, 1994

EXHIBIT 6.4. WHAT DOES LITERATURE HAVE TO SAY ABOUT ASYMMETRIC PRICE COMPETITION AND BRAND SWITCHING?

An experiment conducted by two American researchers, Sivakumar and Raj about some foodstuffs proved the asymmetric character of brand switching. They published their findings in the Journal of Marketing in 1977. Aggarwal and Cha reported similar findings at the end of their study of the competition between large national brands and commercial brands. They published evidence proving the asymmetric character of competition in 1998 under the title: Asymmetric Price Competition and Store vs National Brand Choice. Allenby and Rossi (1991) created the mathematical model of asymmetric brand switching.

Studies of quality and price levels (Dolan-Simon, 1996; Sivakumar-Raj, 1995; Blattberg-Wisniewski, 1989; Ross 1984) have revealed that the price competition takes quite specific forms between the various tiers, and within the tiers.

- Competition is stronger within the quality tiers than between them. This leads to the conclusion that the brands grouped into the same quality class by consumer perception (premium quality products, for example) compete with one another in the first place. Competition within the quality level means very little stimulation for mobility between levels. Competition within the level is targeted mainly for increased market share within the quality class and we do not often witness reshuffles between individual levels.

- The inter-tier competition has an *asymmetric* character because the transfer between levels is not necessarily a two-way street. A price cut implemented in the higher level, for example, is more likely to attract buyers from the lower levels to the top, than the other way around.

Figure 6.3. The process of target costing

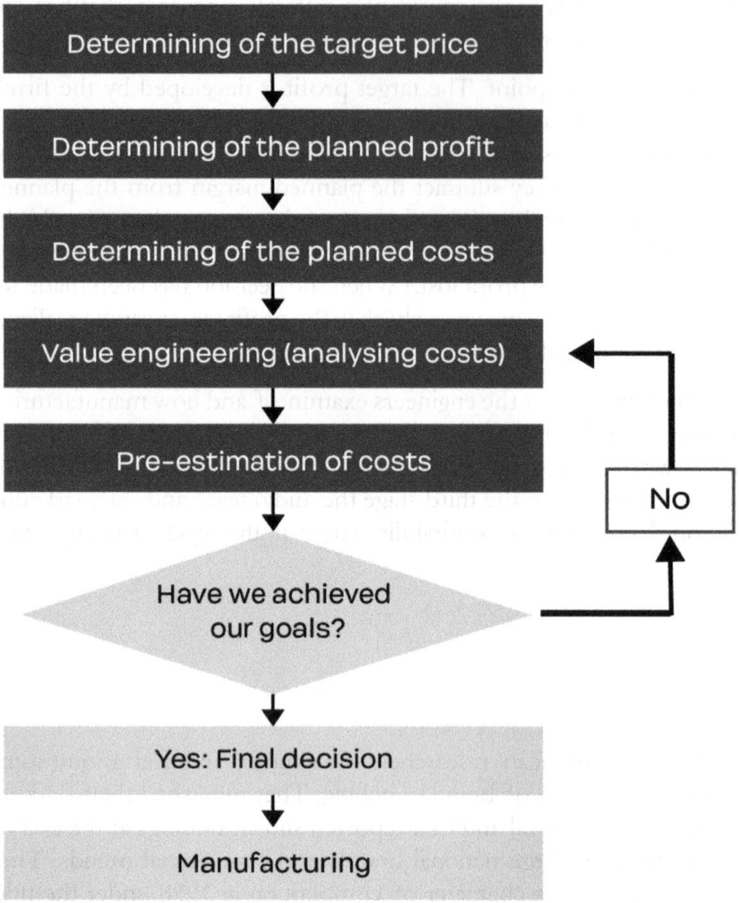

Analysis revealed the perceived quality-price tiers are separated from each other by a rather strong borderline (we might as well call it a psychological barrier). These barriers are, however, easier to cross in an upward direction than downwards. This aspect of competition is shown in Figure 6.4.

In our example taken earlier from the Canadian glove market this impact was described as the upward movement of the market structure. This upward movement is closely related to the general economic situation and – in the case of consumer goods – with changes in the population's income. In a situation when the economy is on the way of recovery and consumer income is growing, this upward movement can be quite significant, while even a small deterioration can induce downward movement. The global economic depression which started in 2008 has probably turned the trend, replacing the psychological barrier of downward migration with the income barrier of upward movement (Figure 6.5). If this consumer behaviour proves to be lasting - as forecast by several estimates – a large number of firms will have to rewrite the price policy they have applied so far.

Figure 6.4. The asymmetric nature of migration among quality tiers

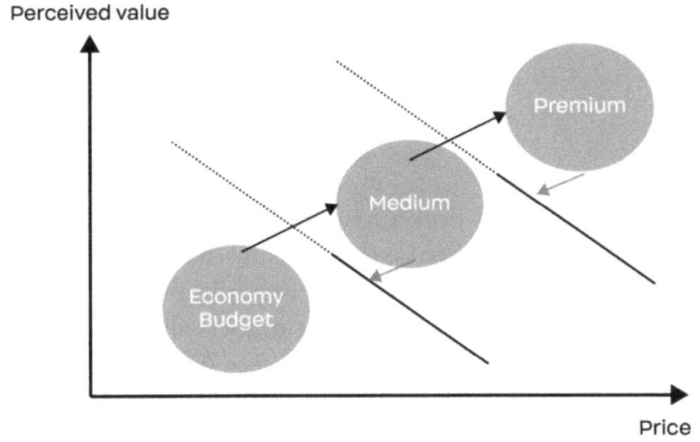

Figure 6.5. Transformation of the asymmetric character of price competition under the influence of global depression.

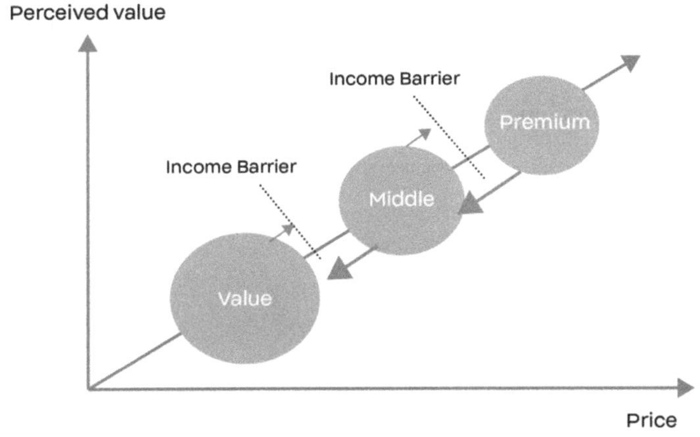

Before a decision is made on price and quality levels the firm has to study the market structure of the product line concerned and, within this structure, the competition typical of the various quality-price levels, the expected changes in the structure, as well as its own competencies, opportunities and limitations. The decision it makes will have an impact on the specific prices, their eventual changes and the use of other marketing tools too.

6.3. Pricing strategies for launching new products or services

Another important decision the company must make concerns the relative price level within the quality-price framework at which the new product or service should be marketed. The conditions in which the decision is made are completely different if the product to be launched is a revolutionary innovation without precedent from those that a product with only relative novelty meets and therefore its price will have to be adjusted to the structure that is inevitably present in the market.

The methods of pricing strategy that can be used for the new products also became widely known and extremely popular in marketing literature thanks to the works of Dean. He first published his views in 1951 in book form (Managerial Economics, Prentice Hall), but he owes his popularity to an

article published in Harvard Business Review, in 1976. Dean and his followers recommend three possible strategies to choose from:

- strategy of skimming (high) prices;
- strategy of penetration (low) prices
- strategy of (medium) neutral prices.

The amount of the price, its ranking as high, low or middle is only a matter of benchmarking based on perceived value. If a product is revolutionary, its novelty cannot be compared with other products. Even if there is a benchmark, it does not mean that high prices are necessarily higher or that penetration prices are necessarily lower than the prices of other, competing products already present on the market. The only reason why it is brought up at all is that one wants to see if the initial price is high or low, compared to the perceived value of the product.

The firm can choose to launch the product in the luxury/premium segment or in the economy segment. In either case, there is a chance of applying the skimming, penetrating or neutral pricing strategy. Let us consider the case of the Mercedes S Class and Lexus. Both products target the high quality price segment, yet the Mercedes uses high, skimming prices, while Lexus has chosen the strategy of low, penetration prices. This relation to the perceived value is shown in Figure 6.6., which builds on the VEL (Value Equivalence Line) the zone of neural or equilibrium prices.

Figure 6.6. The possible pricing strategies for launching a new product

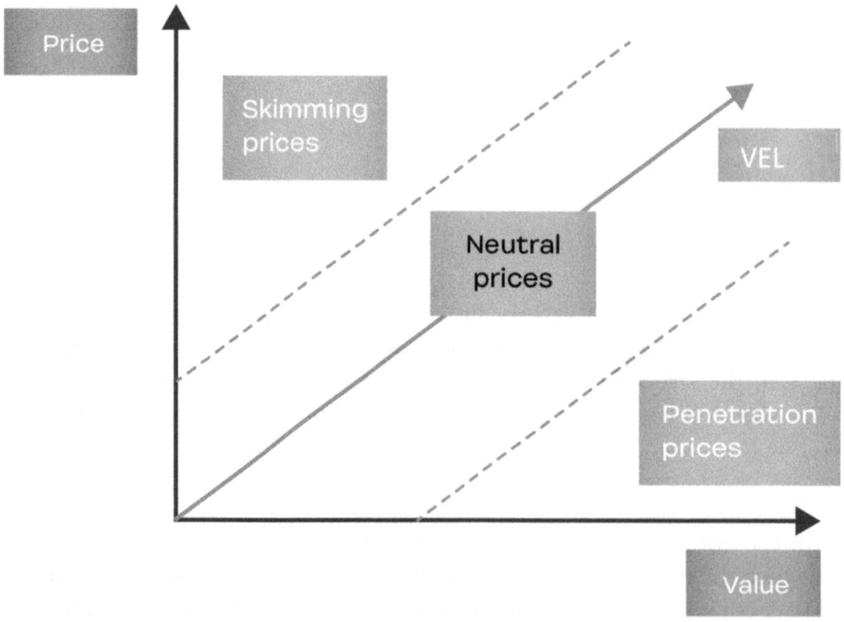

The prices adjusted to the market (neutral, middle) prices are located near the VEL, within the equilibrium price zone. Prices above these are skimming prices, and below we find the penetration prices. In the next part, we will review the conditions in which these three strategies can be applied, together with their advantages and drawbacks.

6.3.1. Price strategy of skimming

The price strategy of skimming is based on the observation that the market of the product concerned has a part with less price sensitivity still capable of appreciating the positive differential value of the product representing, at the same time, a large enough demand that can ensure sales of the expected quantity despite the relatively high price for the firm. Marketing literature differentiates fast and slow skimming strategies. Fast skimming means promoting sales of the product introduced at a high price with a high budget for promotion, in this way fostering the rapid development of the market. Products in the category of slow skimming do not enjoy the same expensive promotion, therefore their market takes a relatively long time to take shape.

Skimming price strategy has several advantages and disadvantages/drawbacks.

Advantages:

- High price can result in a relatively high profit and a relatively quick return on invested assets.
- Customers tend to believe that high price also means better quality; consequently, price in itself is capable of strengthening the prestige of the product.
- The bigger contribution generated by the higher initial price makes it possible for the firm to provide the product with intensive marketing support.
- Higher price creates elbow room for future price cuts or price differentiations.
- Higher price ensures a relatively large margin for the distributors, and makes it attractive for them to distribute the product

Disadvantages:

- A high price may delay the spread of the new product therefore the market takes a longer time to develop, than with a lower initial price.
- A higher price may appear attractive for potential competitors, which is why rival firms and products may appear in the early stage of the life cycle.

Conditions:

- There should be a market segment with a relative low price elasticity of demand. This relative inelasticity is maintained due to the individual qualities of the product, its incomparability and a lot of other features that have been discussed together with the factors influencing price elasticity.
- Applying the strategy of high price is less risky if the company has some kind of protection against its competitors. Such protection can be the patent of the product, possession of some limited resource, available only for the company, etc. The strong marketing positions of the company also represent a high barrier to entry for its rivals (strong brand image, support from the distribution channels, service network, etc.).

The strategy of skimming means high initial prices. Later the company may choose to keep, (or, very rarely), further raise, or reduce prices (in one go, gradually, perhaps step-by-step) (Figure 6.7.).

Figure 6.7. The graphical illustration of the skimming strategy

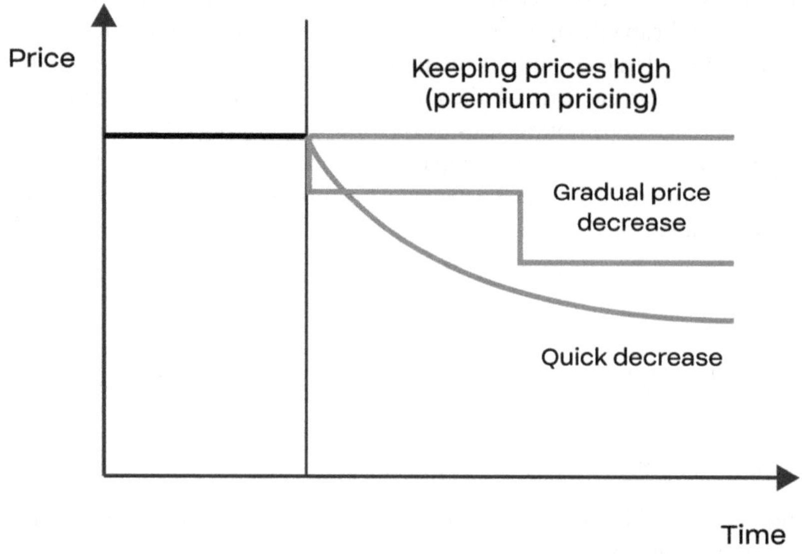

6.3.2. Keeping prices high

There are several products or services with high initial prices which were not reduced later on. Some of these are monopolistic products (with restricted opportunities for others to enter the market), the others belong in the category of prestige consumer goods or services. In this latter group it is actually the high price that motivates the purchase. By buying a piece of famous *haute couture* clothing, a top category car, a wristwatch, porcelain or using the services of a fashionable restaurant or hotel, people meet their need not so much through the usefulness of the product but rather through the pride they take in possessing something expensive and showing it off. Reducing the price of these products would mean the elimination of this original function. Due to the very special role of pricing this group is dubbed 'prestige price' to distinguish it from skimming price and to describe this pricing method the term *prestige price setting* is used.

> Form 2013 the company's webpage (www.herend.com) reports:
>
> Hungary presents a Herend porcelain set as official gift to the newborn British Crown Prince George.

In most cases the strategy using prestige prices is applied to the kind of products or services where unit costs are relatively stable, i.e. they are not characterized by the phenomenon of cost reduction expressed by the learning curve. These products are rendered exquisite by the high share of manual work and human services, the opposite of mass production. What makes the porcelain of Herend so valuable is the fact that it is hand-made. Going to the Waterside Inn gives one prestige because the building, the atmosphere of the interior, the dishes and traditions all combine to impress guests,

suggesting the high ratio of services, the use of the most valuable ingredients, the high costs and consequently high prices that only a few can afford.

Waterside Inn, the first restaurant outside France to hold three Michelin stars for 25 years.

Source: By Nancy - Own work, CC BY-SA 3.0, https://commons.wikimedia.org/w/index.php?curid=4295720

6.3.3. Decreasing prices

Companies using the strategy of high initial price will have to face - sooner or later - the eventuality that the relative monopoly of the new product ceases, competitors launch products of identical or similar value often at lower prices, so the only thing to do is reduce prices. If the product enjoys some kind of protection from competition, this period can be prolonged. Protection can take the form of a patent. In the pharmaceutical industry, for example, a patent means excellent protection, but when it expires the manufacturer should count on its competitors to appear with their cheaper supply. In this situation all the firm can do is apply price reduction as a last resort. If it fails to do so, it can quickly lose some of its market share or even drop out of the market. It can also mean that the manufacturer of the product still under protection takes the initiative for the price reduction because the demand represented by the segment that is willing to accept higher prices is lower than what is required for the firm's development. On the other hand, price reduction opens up new markets, increases the quantities that can be sold and consequently generates more profit on the whole. As far as costs are concerned, increased quantities lead to a significant decrease in costs (experience curves), which also has a favourable impact on the company's profits. Skimming can continue at lower prices as well. When - with the initial high prices - the firm has exploited the capacities of the market segment insensitive to these prices, the firm will reduce its prices and set the next target: to meet the needs of the next segment in line regarding price sensitivity. The continuous or step-by-step reduction of prices is an acceptable solution as long as the product's protection is valid. The method and the measure of price reduction depends on the product, e.g. a different approach is used in the case of frequently bought consumer products or in the case of durable consumer goods.

- In the case of durable goods, continuous price reduction can involve two main risks:
- If price reductions follow each other quickly and regularly, the price-conscious consumers will count on it and defer their purchase until the next price cut.

Calculations can prove that meeting the needs of the whole market (with a one-time bigger price cut) may produce more profit than the gradual price reduction.

Nagle and Holden (1995:154) used the term 'sequential price cut' to describe the implementation of the skimming strategy with a series of price cuts and used the prices of Polaroid cameras as their example: the price of the black-and-white camera was reduced in six steps from 200 to 15 dollars between 1948 and 1977. The price of the colour camera was also reduced in six steps between 1963 and 1977 from 290 to 25 dollars.

EXHIBIT 6.5. THE IPHONE PRICE DROP

On September 5th 2007, just 10 weeks after launching iPhone at a price of $599, Apple cut the price of it by a third - from $599 to $399.

Steve Jobs with iPhone 4.
Source: By Matthew Yohe, CC BY-SA 3.0, https://commons.wikimedia.org/w/index.php?curid=10584359

The same day USA Today asked Steve Jobs: "What do you say to customers who just bought a new iPhone for $599? Sorry?"

Steve Jobs answered: "That's technology. If they bought it this morning, they should go back to where they bought it and talk to them. If they bought it a month ago, well, that's what happens in technology."

The New York Times reported next day that if you bought an iPhone within the last 10 days, you can get a $200 refund (minus a restocking fee) by taking it back to the store. Otherwise, you're in the same boat as anyone who's ever bought something a couple weeks before a price drop: out of luck.

But Apple felt a little bit guilty so later they decided to compensate and Steve Jobs posted an open letter that offered a $100 store credit for those early purchasers. With luck, that should ease the sting – at least by half.

Source: NYT: https://pogue.blogs.nytimes.com/2007/09/06/the-iphone-price-drop/comment-page-3/

6.3.4. Strategy of penetration prices

In the strategy of penetration, the new products are priced low (below customer value), in order to penetrate the largest possible market in a short time. Here, again, we can make a distinction between strategies of quick penetration (low prices+ high marketing costs) and slow penetration (low prices + low market marketing costs).

Advantages:

- A low initial price allows the firm to sell large quantities in a short time, which – despite the relatively small amount of unit contribution - may lead to the accumulation of the total contribution.
- Thanks to the accumulation of the contribution it becomes possible to give the new product or service appropriate marketing support.
- The strategy of low prices can result in the fast diffusion of the new product leading to the growth of the firm's market share.
- The quick increase in quantities makes the exploitation of the economies of scales and the experience curve-effect possible to the maximum.
- Low prices and the firm's quickly growing market share can discourage potential competitors from entering the market.

- The possibility of raising prices is inherent in the low initial prices, especially after these have already strengthened the firm's presence in the market.

Disadvantages:

- Penetration prices are not suitable for exploiting the relative price insensitivity of innovator consumers, and generate extra profit in the first period.
- The per unit profit generated in this way is rather low, therefore the firm may have a low ROI (return on investment).
- Lower prices may evoke the idea of poorer quality in customers, therefore it is not always possible to reach quality-oriented prospects with this price strategy.
- The rapid increase in quantity may require additional and immediate increase in capacity, which may not necessarily be justified by the lower rate of ROI.

Conditions:

- The strategy of low (penetration) prices can only be successful if demand for the product or service in question has great price elasticity, and lower prices lead to quick increase in turnover.
- It is important to make the economies of scale and the experience curve have an impact on the production of the goods or services, i.e. have the increase in quantities reduce unit costs significantly.

In the case of low initial prices, the company has three directions to choose from when it wants to change its prices, as shown in Figure 6.8.

EXHIBIT 6.6. THE JAPANESE PRICING STRATEGY ON THE WORLD MARKET OF CONSUMER ELECTRONICS

The difference between the two pricing strategies (skimming and penetration) is well illustrated in the classic example of the world market of consumer electronics. While the original Western European or North-American inventors of certain consumer electronic products started with very high prices and could penetrate only an extremely narrow part of the market, the Japanese companies (among them Panasonic) used low penetration prices and could realize rapid increase in quantities sold, high export and market share, even in the markets of the original inventors. Turning the manufacturing process into mass production in a short time, they not only managed to exploit the economies of mass production but constantly improved quality at the same time. After some time, the original market leaders were practically squeezed out of the market.

Panasonic's current and historic brands
Source: By Melvinx44 rules - Own work, CC BY-SA 4.0, https://commons.wikimedia.org/w/index.php?curid=39064622

The classic strategy of penetration follows the upper line of three possible price developments illustrated on the graph. The company which chose to follow this strategy used the low initial price to obtain a market share of its own and gain a foothold in the market. As soon as this had been achieved, the gradual increase of the prices could start. However, this classical strategy can only be successful if the product or market enjoys protection from the competition.

In the case of patented products there is no threat of competitors appearing on the market soon, so nothing stands in the way of price increases. In the absence of such protection, however, it is not infrequent that the growing market becomes attractive to competitors, in spite of the low price level; their appearance at the market may persuade the original seller at least to hold price levels or - if worse comes to worst - reduce them.

Literature distinguishes further varieties of the strategy of low prices:

Figure 6.8. Strategy of penetration prices

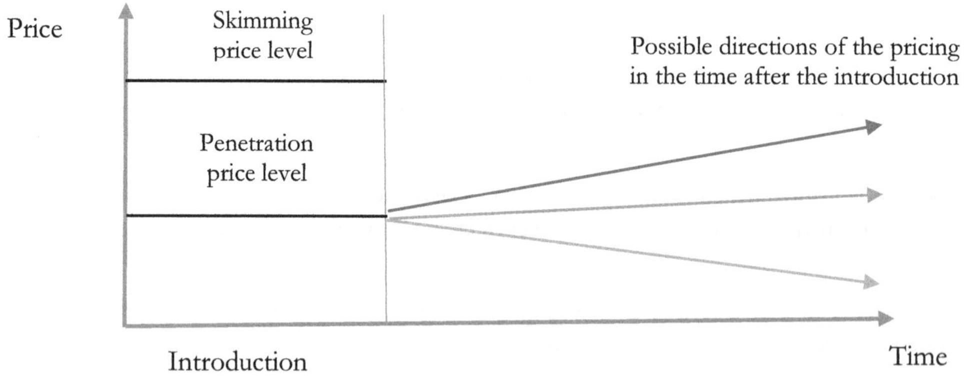

6.3.5. Strategy of expansion prices

This strategy uses an initial price level that is even lower than that of the penetration prices. The purpose of using such low prices is to underpin the company's extremely quick market expansion. Hanna and Dodge (1997: 85) illustrate the use of this strategy with the entry of Toyota and Honda to the American market. The two firms managed to secure their share of the American market with two standard, low-cost, extremely cheap models, namely the Toyota Corolla and the Honda Civic. As soon as their market position stabilized they started the gradual introduction of more expensive varieties and highly priced models. In international practice extremely low prices always imply the charge of dumping claims. Dumping price means export at a price that is below cost. The rules of international trade allow the target countries to use sanctions against countries using dumping prices, on the ground that dumping prices can squeeze domestic manufacturers out of the market.

The use of prices lower than expansion prices is often referred to as predatory or aggressive pricing, occasionally 'undercutting' strategy. In this case the company in a strong financial position uses prices lower than costs or, in extreme cases, prices that do not even cover variable costs. The competitors present in the market are usually not able to follow it at all and, as a consequence, they abandon their business activities, or perhaps become bankrupt. At this point, the seller firm buys up the bankrupt companies or their remains and later, with no competition in sight, does not hesitate to raise prices. The dumping charge applies, of course to these prices as well.

The possible outcomes of this strategy are summarized in Table 6.1.

Table 6.1. Possible outcomes of aggressive pricing

	Competitors' power to fight back	**Injuries suffered by competitors**	**Response expected to be taken by competitors**	**Possible consequences**
Aggressive price cut	No power to fight back	serious	Lower the quantity of production Leave the market	Super low prices Shorter assortment of goods
	Medium power to fight back	significant	They start to co-operate, adjust prices and marketing Decrease fix costs Decrease variable cost	Lower investment in R & D Poorer customer service Lower product quality Shorter assortment
	Significant power to fight back	small	They ignore the price cut They also cut their prices	No consequences Low prices

Source: Adapted from Guiltanan és Gundlach (1996).

6.3.6. Strategy of medium initial prices adjusting to the market

When initial prices of new products and services are to be defined, price setters consider not only the skimming and penetration strategies but also make attempts to adjust the price level to comparable products and services already present in the market. This is called the neutral price strategy. Neutral, because here prices play a less important part in market and business policy that in the previous two. While both in skimming and penetration strategies prices play a decisive role in the achievement of a given purpose (profit increase, increasing market share) the strategy of neutral prices transfers this role to the other tools of business and marketing policy. If price is medium, the increase of market share becomes the task of other marketing tools (intensive distribution, efficient promotion, improved efficiency of personal selling, etc.).

The reason for applying the strategy of medium adjusting prices can be found in the company's price structure, or the need to ensure the consistence or unity of the product line concerned. If the product range of the company or the individual product line is characterized by a well-defined price level to which the customers have already become accustomed, the introduction of a significantly different new price may cause confusion and uncertainty in the market. It must be noted, however, that confusion of this kind can be avoided with the proper branding policy.

The term 'medium prices adjusting to the market' does not necessarily mean that the prices are the same as the prices of products or services already present at the market. Medium prices are proportional with the benefits they provide or, with reference to Figure 6.6., they are positioned in the equilibrium zone.

EXHIBIT 6.7. PREDATORY PRICING — ACCORDING TO OECD AND THE EUROPEAN UNION

OECD:

The traditional theory of predatory pricing is straightforward. The predator, already a dominant firm, sets its prices so low for a sufficient period that its competitors leave the market and others are deterred from entering. Assuming that the predator and its victims are equally efficient firms, this implies that the predator as well as its victims has incurred losses and that these losses are significant. For the predation to be rational, there must be some expectation that these present losses (or foregone profits), like any investment, will be made up by future gains. This in turn implies that the firm has some reasonable expectation of gaining exploitable market power following the predatory episode, and that profits of this later period will be sufficiently great to warrant incurring present losses or foregoing present profits. The theory also implies that some method exists for the predator to outlast its victim(s), whether through greater cash reserves, better financing or cross-subsidisation from other markets or other products.

Source: Predatory Pricing, OECD 1989, http://www.oecd.org/competition/abuse/2375661.pdf

EU:

Holding a dominant position is not itself unlawful. However, dominant undertakings have a special responsibility to behave in a way that does not damage or hinder the development of competition. Where a company has a dominant position, it will be in breach of the EU competition rules if it "abuses" that position.

Examples of unilateral conduct or behaviour that may be considered abusive include:

- predatory pricing: This term is used to describe pricing at unfair low levels (e.g. below average avoidable costs), particularly if there is evidence of intent to drive competitor out of the market;
- excessive pricing: High prices may be found to be abusive if thesebear no reasonable relationship to the economic value of the goods….

Source: Slaughter and May: An overview of the EU competition rules, June 2010

6.4. Market segmentation based on price and perceived value

One of the most important strategic decisions that a company has to make is to decide at what quality or price level it intends to enter the market. If it wants the decision to be well-founded, it must have information about the market, the customers' habits and buying behaviour. Some of the buyers are more sensitive to prices, preferring cheaper products, while others are willing to pay a higher price for better quality products, appreciating the differential values of the product concerned, However, instead of making some vague remarks about the market situation, we had better analyse the composition of potential buyers. Let us recall the features listed earlier among the factors influencing price-sensitivity:

- Impact of the interrelationship between price and quality;
- impact of the perceived substitute products;
- impact of the difficulty in comparison;

- impact of the unique (differential) value;
- impact of the switching costs;
- impact of the amount of expenditure, it requires;
- impact of cost sharing.

EXHIBIT 6.8. INTRODUCTION OF UNICUM NEXT: WHAT IS THE NOVELTY OF THE NEW PRODUCT?

The logo is the most striking and noticeable difference. Unicum has a logo reminiscent of a red cross, in. a slightly different colour. Next has the same figure turned at an angle of 45° and as part of the name 'Next'. After opening the bottle we discover different flavours. The bitterish flavour of Unicum ensured by herbs has given way to a fresher flavour, more strongly dominated by citrus fruits. There is also a difference in the age of the two drinks. The original was presented by Dr Zwack as early as 1790, Next, on the other hand can be considered an innovation of our modern age, with a history of hardly 10 years. As far as alcohol content is concerned it has become 5% less. In the category of premium drinks Unicum has more than a quarter of the market, while the younger Next has not more than 4.5%.

Source:www.unicum.hu).

Flavour	Bitter, herbal taste	Citrus fruits
Year of introduction	1790	2004
Alcohol content	40%	35%
Price	HUF 2 733/0.5 l	HUF 2 755/0.5l

Next is recommended mainly to consumers who do not like the traditional Unicum flavour very much, or simply feel like having something new, something different. (www.zwackwebshop.hu). While working on the renewal of the product, the firm followed the European and Hungarian trends, which meant the development of a branded product, mainly characterized by lower alcohol content and a cooler but sweeter taste. Unicum Next not only

gives a new experience to its consumers, but has received a new design as well. It still comes in the well-known bulbous bottle but where colours are concerned, red has become dominant, conjuring up the atmosphere of youthful, passionate party-nights. (www.napi.hu)

The success of Unicum Next is proved by the fact that during the one year that has elapsed since its introduction it has gained nearly 5% market share. The communication strategy of the new drink is not targeted at the traditional Unicum drinker, but at those who have never tasted the drink before.

In this way the danger of product cannibalization does not arise, because the new target group represents a completely different social group. The classic Unicum is consumed by a quite well off intellectual of about 55, living in the countryside while Next is mainly the drink of urban youth, aged between 25-30. In spite of the different target groups, the two products have mutually beneficial effect on each other. After all the rejuvenation of Unicum and the introduction of Next coincided, allowing them to project their success on each other.

Source: Project work by Júlia Arany-Tóth, Zsuzsa Ádám, Andrea Csovcsics, Katalin Kóródi and Szabolcs Pap, MSc students, University of Szeged.

Richard Harmer, professor at Boston University, created a specific segmentation model. In his view, the perceived differential value of a product and the perceived consumer expenditures (price + others) allow the distinction of four buyer segments (Figure 6.9.):

- price segment
- convenience segment
- value segment
- loyal segment.

Figure 6.9. Harmer's price segmentation model

		Low	High
Perceived pain of expenditure	high	Price segment	Value segment
	Low	Convenience segment	Loyal segment

Perceived pain of differentiation

Cited by Siguaw, J A and Bojanic, D C Hospitality Sales – Selling smarter, Thomson, Delmar learning, 2004

6.4.1. The price segment

This group includes people whose buying decisions are primarily motivated by low prices. They are not willing to pay for extra services provided by the product, they are not concerned with the image of the product and are not loyal to any brand. They consider price to be the most important therefore they are less sensitive to quality or performance.

6.4.2. The loyal segment

The behaviour of buyers in this group is just the opposite of those in the price segment. Loyal customers greatly appreciate the specific values of services and products, and have a strong preference for certain brands. Customers belonging in this group are not sensitive to prices, because they are willing to pay more for their preferred brand. Price elasticity of demand of loyal customers is lower than that of those in other groups.

6.4.3. The convenience segment

In this group we find people who are not particularly sensitive to prices or the differences inherent in products (brands). They like to do their shopping with the least psychological input possible and most of the time buy the goods that are most readily available.

EXHIBIT 6.9. PRICE ELASTICITY IN THE LOYAL SEGMENT OF BUYERS

Two Spanish researchers performed empirical studies in Barcelona focusing on the category of washing powders. The summary of their findings is given in the next Figure

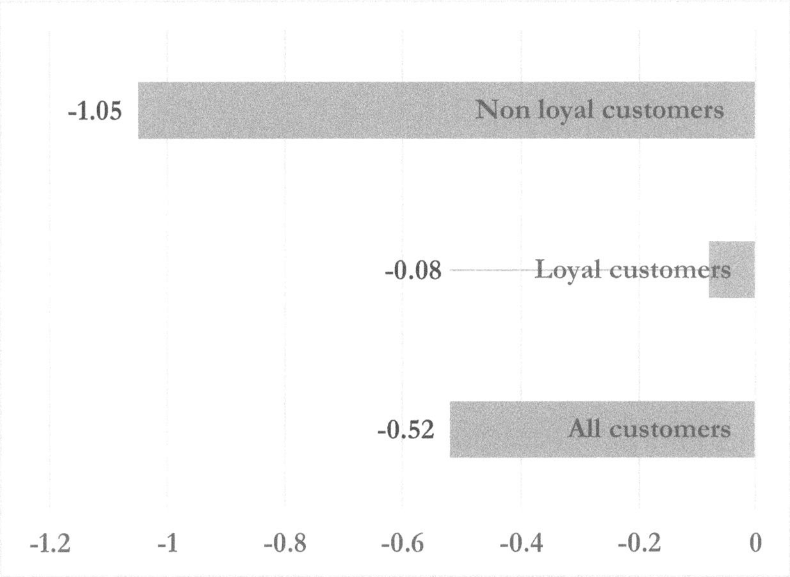

The figure shows that loyal customers have the lowest price elasticity of demand. It means that whenever there is a price rise, they are the ones who are least inclined to switch to a cheaper brand.

Source: Cavero-Cabollada, 1999

6.4.4. The value segment

This group contains all those who are equally sensitive to price, the quality of products and their individual features. Value-oriented customers carefully analyse the usefulness of the product, compare it with consumer expenditures and decide on the purchase according to the conclusion of this analysis.

Every segment can be large enough to make it worth for some firms to specialize in meeting the needs of customers belonging to a certain segment. The best examples are found in commerce. Discount shops target the price segment while brand outlets count on shoppers from the loyal segment.

Specialist shops with a wide range of supply are popular with value-oriented buyers. Convenience seekers shop typically in general stores or perhaps in convenience shops open around the clock.

For companies, however, the favourite segment is that of loyal shoppers. They keep coming back to buy the firm's products and use its services, are not very price sensitive and are prepared to pay more for anything extraordinary the firm offers. Firms, on their part, make efforts to strengthen this brand loyalty, or belong to the segment with various programmes meant to promote stable seller-buyer relations, such as membership cards, regular newsletters on latest programmes and developments, frequent buyer cards or programmes.

CHAPTER 7. PRODUCT LIFE CYCLE PRICING

OBJECTIVE 1 To understand the concept of product life cycle and learn how all product goes through the stages of the product life cycle and to establish the impact to marketers and price specialists of products at different stages of their cycles.

OBJECTIVE 2 To establish how companies can lapse into price wars from sudden price cuts and how price wars may hurt the participating entities.

OBJECTIVE 3 To explore how different pricing strategies and tactics may be used in the different stages of the life cycle.

7.1. Introduction

When launching a new product on the market the company has three options to choose from to determine the initial price, depending on the novelty of the product, the planned marketing strategy, as well as market conditions:

- Skimming price strategy with high initial prices;
- Market penetration pricing with low initial prices;
- Competition pricing strategy with medium level (neutral) prices.

7.2. The life cycle of products on the market

When a new product (or service) is launched onto the market, it begins its path on the market that literature dubs 'product life cycle'. The concept of market life cycle is a generalized model of the sales trends for a given product or product group, which can provide useful recommendations for the marketing strategy of a company by dividing the market path into different stages and grasping the effects of competition in each of these. The main shortcoming of using the product life cycle approach is that products do not follow the same path of life. There are products (see the exhibit) which have been on the market for decades, or even centuries and which have not gone through the stages of life cycle described in literature.

The type of life cycle curve presented in Figure 7.1 is mostly typical of technology and research-intensive products. After the product development stage the product starts its market life and usually passes through four stages until reaching its natural end. The sales trend of these products is not always the same, and the determination of the life cycle will largely depend on which aggregate of the product or service is studied. Despite all its limitations, analysis of the life cycle of products is an indispensable element of today's marketing activities.

Figure 7.1. The stages of product life cycle

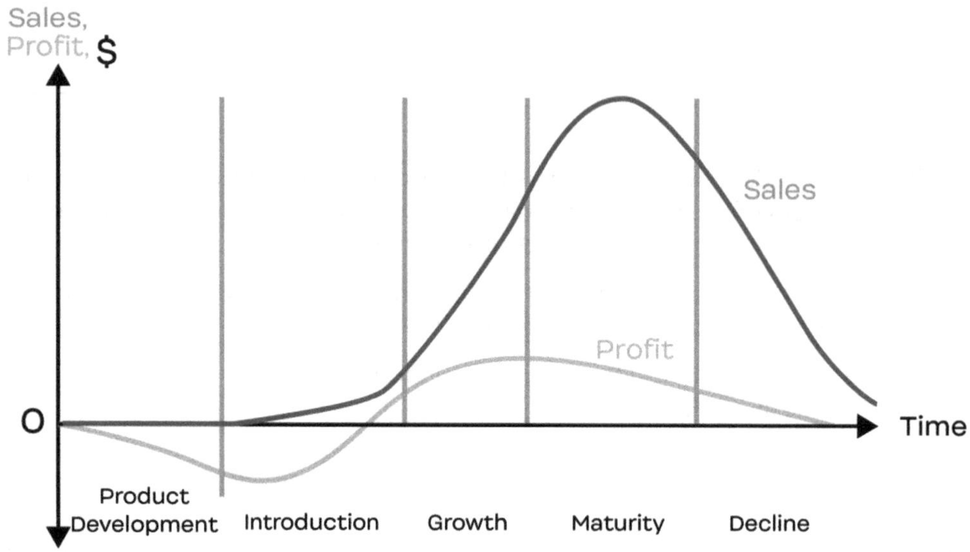

7.2.1. The Introduction Stage

The first stage for many newly launched products is characterised by a slow increase in sales. This is due to the resistance of the market on the one hand, and to the inflexibility of production capacity increase on the other. The company introducing the new product enjoys a monopolistic position for a temporary period at this stage. This monopolistic position comes from the product's differentiating character and its duration depends on the level of novelty, the possibilities of legal protection, the difficulty of imitation and other factors. The marketing to revenue ratio will be the highest during this stage. Promotion is mainly aimed at informing potential consumers about the launch of the new product and the relative benefits it has to offer, as well as its possible uses. The effort required to persuade traders to include the product in their portfolios is also important. The company first markets a limited quantity of the product and focuses on correcting its initial faults if it has any. The distribution of the product is often selective.

7.2.2. The Growth Stage

Sales of a successfully launched product experience a sudden surge after the initial slow increase. The expansion of the market and production is reflected in the increase in profit margins. The favourable conditions attract competitors to the market of the product. The appearance of competition will have an impact on prices, and may result in the relative decline of profit margins in the second half of this stage, or rather in the stage of maturity. Promotion will gradually shift from building awareness about the product to emphasizing its relative benefits compared to those of the competition.

7.2.3. The Maturity Stage (Saturation)

Maturity is the longest stage in the life cycle; this is the stage where most products can be found. The sales increase – when sales volumes almost reach the absorption capacity of the market (market potential) – slows down and becomes stable. The competing producers can only increase their sales to the detriment of the other, so the competition will shift to the field of product and pricing policies.

The market, which has been regarded as more or less unified, becomes segmented and competing companies will try to gain stable market shares by introducing product varieties which match the special requirements of these segments (product differentiation).

EXHIBIT 7.1. THE WORLD'S TEN OLDEST BRANDS AND THEIR POSITIONING STATEMENTS (According to the British Unum Company)

The companies listed below are characterised by careful and committed brand management: the products bearing the brand name have been continuously updated, modified and adjusted to the changing requirements of the market. No matter how old these brands may be, they do not look obsolete at all.

LOGO	ESTABLISHED IN YEAR	POSITIONING STATEMENT
CAMBRIDGE UNIVERSITY PRESS	1534	REPUTATION IS EVERYTHING
BUSHMILLS	1608	BE THE BEST
BARCLAYS	1690	CHANGING WITH THE TIMES
Coutts	1692	TRADITIONAL VALUES AND PROFESSIONALISM
TWININGS	1706	QUALITY CONTROL
FONDÉ EN 1743 MOËT & CHANDON CHAMPAGNE	1743	PIONEERING SPIRIT
Sotheby's	1744	DON'T BE AFRAID TO EXPAND
CASWELL-MASSEY	1752	HAVE INTEGRITY
JIM BEAM	1795	STAY FOCUSED
citibank	1812	CREATE TRUST

Source: http://www.unum.co.uk/hr/the-worlds-oldest-brands-and-the-secrets-to-their-longlives (accessed 12.12.2016)

The aim of promotion changes from educating people about the product to emphasizing the differences of competing product varieties and to boost awareness of product differentiation. Expenses related to facilitating sales stabilise compared to sales revenues.

While the stages of introduction and growth are very similar for most products, the stage of maturity (saturation) shows different types of life curves. The length of the maturity phase and the marketing trends can both vary across different products. We can distinguish between the relatively stable mature products, where sales continue to increase for longer periods at the same pace or a little slower than the increase in population and purchasing power. (This is usually the case of products which satisfy basic needs and are less sensitive to innovation.) Products that are more sensitive to innovation and other changes (e.g. fashion) typically have a shorter maturity period, which is characterised by the increase in innovation. It mainly depends on the modernizing and innovative developments of manufacturing companies through which new product features and uses are created. These modernizing innovations usually have periodic impact; the products can go through several maturity stages as a result. (A typical example is the so-called 'two-humped' life curve.)

7.2.4. The Decline Stage

The maturity stage can last a long time, but every product enters the stage of decline after a while. Decline is characterised by falling sales and their ultimate stop, the companies' attempt to get rid of their inventory and their continually reduced advertising activity.

EXHIBIT 7.2. THE KODAK STORY

Kodak film is a good example of the death of an old updated product. Innovation is the moving force of business. Some innovations, like the invention of the digital camera, are named by literature as "disruptive innovation" i.e. it can and will destroy whole industries built on old values.

The most tragic aspect of Kodak's decline was that *they had invented the digital camera in 1975.* According to the Kodak engineer who developed it, management's reaction was "that's cute - but don't tell anyone about it." This is what literature calls "marketing myopia". Kodak, the fourth biggest company in the USA in 1996, did not realize that the new technology would eventually make their traditional product obsolete. They had nearly ten years to prepare for the change but they failed to do that. So, not only the traditional product but the whole company went bankrupt. "For industries where technology is changing how business has been always been done, that change can be frightening. But for those companies that learn to incorporate technology as a way to *enhance* their business are the ones that continue to grow," writes Lucas Einstein in his blog.

Kodak remains a sad story of potential lost. The American icon had the talent, the money, and even the foresight to make the transition. Instead, it ended up the victim of the aftershocks of a disruptive change.

Sources: Post by Lucas Einstein on Jan 26, 2017 (http://blog.devicemagic.com/kodak-moment)
Scott Anthony, Kodak's Downfall Wasn't About Technology, July 15, 2016, HBR
(https://hbr.org/2016/07/kodaks-downfall-wasnt-about-technology)
Photos: By Work-Order Studio - http://www.kodak.com/ Transferred from en.wikipedia to Commons., Public Domain, https://commons.wikimedia.org/w/index.php?curid=52387539

7.3. Price competition in the different stages of the life cycle

Only companies that introduce substantial novelty into the market can expect to have their own price policies or to reach a price leading position. Competition usually does not occur when the novelty is introduced into the market. This phase without competition typically lasts until the turnover of the product reaches the threshold (see Figure 7.1.) indicating that the market has developed and the product has become profitable. If the market for a new product has developed and become attractive, it will attract competitors to the market. The appearance of competitors will make the life of companies more complicated and product and price policy decisions more difficult. Nothing is simple, even without competitors: attention must be paid to the price sensitivity of the consumers, and the price must be determined in such a way as to ensure a sales volume which can guarantee the return on investment. With the appearance of competitors, companies are required to review their product and price policy related strategies and to match their marketing tools (including their prices) to those of the competitors. A potential change in prices will change:

- the company's vision about the market and
- its previously established marketing strategy;
- provoke a response from the competitors; and
- elicit a response from consumers as well.

7.3.1. Price competition or 'price war'

From a decision theory point of view three types of competition (rivalry, fight) can be distinguished.

- There are positive-sum games, where everybody wins in the long term and in the broad sense. One example is a sports race: although there are winners, each participant wins by having a good a time, training and making new friends.
- There are zero-sum games, where one party wins and the other one loses. This is the case of the stock exchange situation where the gains or losses of the bulls are offset by the gains or losses of the bears.
- There are also negative-sum situations, where neither party wins, and the gain of the winning party is less than the loss of the other. Wars typically lead to negative sums. If the price competition turns into a price war (i.e. the so-called price reduction spiral is activated) it will result in a negative sum. During the price war, part of the competition is forced out of the market - its loss is evident, but the winner of the price war can suffer losses as well, e.g. the margins can drop and may eventually turn to loss. Company profit margins react to price reductions in a very sensitive way. (The relationship between prices and profit margins has been discussed in detail in Chapter 4 and it has been concluded that, depending on the cost structure of the company, it can be determined how much volume increase can compensate for a given level of price decrease. Figure 7.2 shows that a decrease in price has an unfavourable impact on the profit margin if the company cannot offset it by increasing the volume of production: a 2% decrease in price can lead to a 20% drop in profits assuming that other factors remain unchanged.).

Consequently, the 'armed conflict' must be prevented by every possible means, that is, the company must try to do its best to stay out of the price war.

Price wars carry big risks. The level of the risk depends on several factors. These are summarized in table 7.1 based on the work by Garda and Marn (1993).

EXHIBIT 7.3. A SMALL STEP FROM PRICE COMPETITION TO PRICE WAR - AS DISCUSSED BY KRÄMER, JUNG AND BURGARTZ

An often cited example of a price war: in 1992, Peter Pan Trailways initiated a fierce price war on bus services between New York City and Washington D. C. after acquiring a Washington D. C. terminal. Peter Pan lowered their initial fare of $25 to $9.95, to "turn some heads". Their main rival, Greyhound, responded by cutting their fare to $7, whereupon Peter Pan lowered its fare to $6.95. Greyhound pushed its fare to $5 (which was less than Greyhound had charged 40 years before). Peter Pan immediately matched, resulting in both firms operating below cost price.

Several major factors motivate a competitor to start and likely win a price war:

(1) Excess capacities raise the question of whether there are ways to increase sales significantly. A dominant company owning more than 50 percent market share in a profitable industry is a prominent indicator for a highly probable price war, since it carries more risks for a dominant company to initiate or respond to price decreases.

(2) Managers increasingly face the risk of commoditization. As a recent study of Roland Berger (2014) shows, 60 % of managers believe they are caught in a "commodity trap" (a situation where even complex products and services are downgraded to "commodities", with limited differentiation and a competition that is primarily price-based).

(3) In many new markets, lowering prices makes the market grow more quickly. The flat-screen TV market is a recent example where the prices started at a high level and, as prices fell, more and more people demanded and purchased flat-screen TVs, so the market grew.

(4) Lower costs might play a role: If a company can dramatically lower its costs by increasing volume, then it is more likely to start a price war. Ryanair is a good example. The airline is attacking traditional full-service airlines by offering lower fares (low costs per passenger seat are a precondition).

After carefully studying the practice and the literature, the definition of price war was coined. 'A scenario when (1) market players try to win market share by utilizing aggressive pricing taking into account potential losses in the short term, (2) prices are undercut to fall below the level of industry profitability (at least for main players in the market) and (3) actions are driven by suppliers rather than consumers.' Even if the step between price competition and price war should be small, it can be clearly explained on the basis of this definition.

Source: Andreas Krämer, Martin Jung & Thomas Burgartz: A Small Step from Price Competition to Price War: Understanding Causes, Effects and Possible Countermeasures, International Business Research; Vol. 9, No. 3; 2016, pp. 1-13

The nature of the competition that develops during the growth or maturity phase largely depends on the competitors' mentality, on how well they are informed and on their strategy. That is why it is very important for the companies involved in the competition to know their rivals well, to find ways to be in control of the competition, and to turn confrontation into cooperation if necessary. Cooperation here does not refer to price agreements which limit competition and are banned by price regulations, but to methods (e.g. publicity and many other tools) which help maintain 'diplomatic relations' between the competitors.

Firstly, the direct competitors must be known. The company must understand clearly at what level of the market structure it is in competition (premium, medium price, and low end), who the main competitors are at that level, and what motivation they may have. It is difficult to avoid price competition if the primary motivation of the main rivals is to increase their share in the market by all means, rather than to reach a sufficient level of profit. Dolan and Simon (1995: 102) consider the IQ (intelligence quotient) of the competitors very important. There are markets where the intelligence quotient of the players is higher; the competitors are not striving to eliminate each other, but to expand their share by increasing the general level of profit that can be reached on the market. The amount of the market price developing as a result of the competition has a fundamental effect on the value of the percentage point of the market share. In such a case the price competition will not turn into a negative-sum situation for the market players.

Figure 7.2. The impact of 2% price reduction on the margin

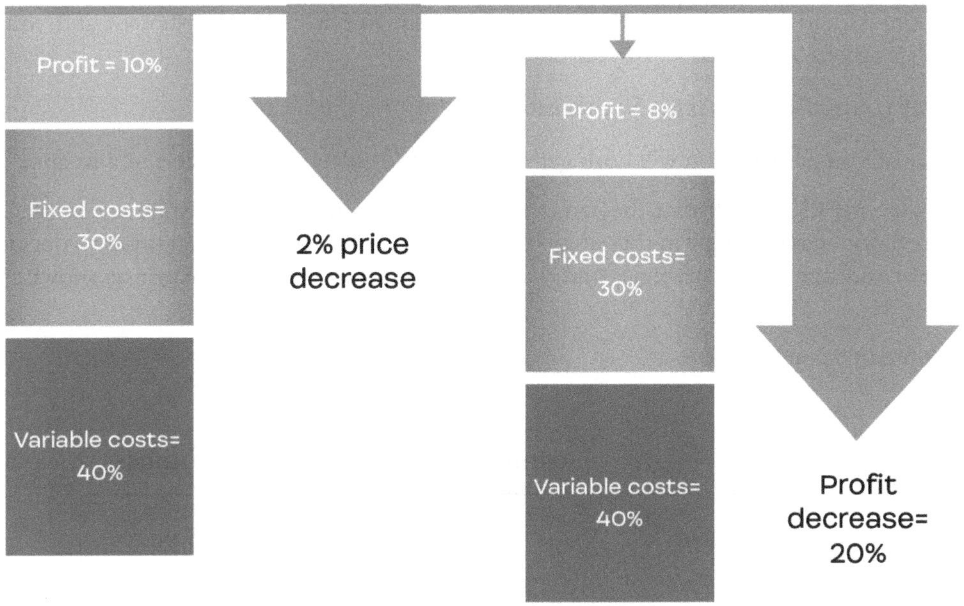

Table 7.1. Risk factors of price competition

	Lower risks	Higher risks
Product features	differentiated	homogeneous
Capacity utilization	high	low
Market growth	high	low/stagnating
Customer concentration	low	high
Transparency of price	low	high
Cost of product switch	high	low
Price sensitivity of consumers	low	high
Cost structure	low PV ratio	high PV ratio

Decisions about prices must usually be made in situations where the reaction of the competitors is hard to assess with certainty. The decision always means a choice of certain options (Barakonyi, 1998: 175). "The critical point, or we could say the climax of each decision process is the selection of the most suitable alternative," writes Barakonyi. He argues that there is always an emerging dominant alternative, which is best in every respect. The strategy which is dominant for one competitor can be different for another, and both strategies can differ from the alternative which offers the optimal solution for both parties. This type of problem is referred to as "the prisoner's dilemma" in the literature (quoted from Rapaport by Barakonyi, 1998: 165).

7.3.2. The prisoner's dilemma

The story concerns two prisoners who have robbed a bank and are awaiting their fate on remand. The prosecutor needs a confession from them, so he makes the following proposition to the two delinquents separately:

- If you confess and the other one doesn't, you'll be set free without punishment and your accomplice will be sentenced to 10 years;
- If both of you confess, you'll get 5 years each;
- If neither of you confess, you will both get 1 year for the unlawful possession of a weapon.

The prosecutor informs them both that the same proposition has been made to their accomplice. Question: is there a dominant strategy in this situation and, if so, what might it be? In order to decide it is best to present and analyse the strategies and the resulting consequences in a matrix as shown in Table 7.3.

Figure 7.3. The prisoner's dilemma

		Prisoner 2: confesses	Prisoner 2: does not confess
Prisoner 1	confesses	5 years or 5 years	0 year or 10 years
	Does not confess	10 years or 0 year	1 year or 1 year

Let us look at the case of the first prisoner. He has a choice between two alternatives: he either confesses or not. The consequences will depend on the confession of his accomplice:

- If his accomplice has confessed, he is better off confessing himself, because he would be sentenced only for 5 years instead of 10;
- If his accomplice has not confessed, he would be in an even better situation if he confessed, because he would be set free, otherwise he would be sentenced for 1 year.

So there is a dominant strategy: the best strategy for both of them is to make a confession[1]. Their dilemma is the following: if they both choose the dominant strategy (which is the best strategy in the individual's interest), both of them will be jailed for 5 years, but if they opt for the non-dominant strategy (neither of them confesses), then both of them will be in the bin for 1 year.

Price competition involves two market players rather than two prisoners. The possible decisions comprise: decrease the prices (confess), or maintain the prices (don't confess). The consequences will depend on the decisions of the competitors here as well:

- being set free would correspond to high profit margins;
- a 1-year sentence would mean medium level gains;
- a 5-year sentence would mean low level gains;
- a 10-year sentence would equal losses.

The possible solutions are presented in a matrix shown in Figure 7.4.

Similarly to the two prisoners, if the two market players do not communicate with each other and do not obtain information about the strategic ideas of the other, the dominant strategy for both of them is to decrease the prices. This will result in low gains for both parties. However, according to the matrix, the optimal strategy for both would be to maintain pricing levels, which would offer medium-level gains for both parties.

Figure 7.4. The dilemma of the two market players

		Market player 2	
		decreases prices	**keeps prices**
Market player 1	**decreases prices**	Low profit or low profit	**high profit or loss**
	keeps prices	**loss or high profit**	medium profit or medium loss

The theoretical solution of the prisoner's dilemma is for both parties to act honourably. An 'honourable' decision in economic life means that parties should attempt to have consideration for the interest of their competitors when making their decisions. The cornerstone of the 'prisoner's dilemma' is that there is no communication between the two arrested people. It is, however, not the case in economic life: even though the parties cannot make a price agreement (at least legally), they have the option to communicate. There exist many ways to put forward or obtain information mutually.

---

[1] According to theory, the strategy "confess" is a strictly dominant strategy: the choice of Prisoner B does not change the way Prisoner A will act, and vice versa. The "confess/confess" scenario is also the only Nash equilibrium in this problem. (See for details – among others – the "Prisoner's dilemma section" in http://rationalwiki.org/wiki/Prisoner's_dilemma.

Companies can obtain information about the strategy, prices and plans of others. For example:

- Through the press. Larger companies regularly publish their intentions to modify prices in the press, long before their prices are increased or decreased. This time could be long enough to assess the expected responses of their competitors (and of the customers as well).
- Price lists published by companies also carry information. Price lists can contain information about the price policy of the company, potential discounts and any other price influencing factors.
- Company reports and balance sheets can also prove useful sources of information for competitors.
- Information can also be obtained from consumers and sales personnel.
- Participation in professional organizations, professional conferences and meetings is also a good source of information exchange (and perhaps of direct communication too).

EXHIBIT 7.4. PRICE WAR BETWEEN APPLE AND SAMSUNG IN INDIA

By Kevin Bostic (Tuesday, April 16, 2013)

Apple and Samsung started a price war in India in 2013, with both offering discounts on smartphones to attract customers in one of the world's largest developing smartphone markets.

The pricing fight between them started with Apple's decision in April 2013 to offer discounts to customers trading older smartphones for Apple's iPhone 4. Trade-in customers received a cash discount of around $128 to purchase of an iPhone 4, the basic model available in India.

Samsung soon followed Apple's action, offering 15 percent cash back to consumers buying a Galaxy Note II, Galaxy S III, Galaxy Grand, or Galaxy tablet. That offer was in connection with a prior offer allowing customers to buy those devices on a 12-month, interest-free instalment plan. These models were all part of Samsung's high-end products in India.

As India represents a tremendous market opportunity for both companies Apple's premium pricing, though, has presented some obstacles to wider adoption of the company's wares. To address the issue, Apple also recently introduced payment plans for Indian consumers, a decision that led to a threefold increase in the company's sales in the country.

Since mobile providers in India do not subsidize the cost of smartphones, Apple is faced with a difficult situation in the country. The company's flagship iPhone 5 was sold for 45,500 rupees, while Samsung's Galaxy Grand was available for 21,500 rupees.

Industry observers expect that Apple would have to address the issue further by introducing a lower-cost iPhone in the near future. The current low-cost iPhone 4, they say, is just a stopgap measure that allows Apple to build a presence while clearing the inventory of older models.

http://appleinsider.com/articles/13/04/16/price-war-breaks-out-between-apple-and-samsung-in-india; By Rwxrwxrwx - Own work, based on File:GalaxyLOGO.Png, Public Domain, https://commons.wikimedia.org/w/ index.php? curid= 45593374; By Apple Inc. (Transfered by NerdyScienceDude/Original uploaded by Scott Bywater)/SVG created by antiuser - Apple - iPhone (Original uploaded on en.wikipedia), Public Domain, https://commons.wikimedia.org/w/index.php?curid=10763343

Price wars can break out despite all communication. Companies should prepare themselves for this, or they could be caught in the 'price trap' illustrated in Figure 7.5.

EXHIBIT 7.5. A FEW WELL-KNOWN SPORTS BRANDS AND PRICE COMPETITION

Let's take for example Adidas, Nike and the other famous global sportswear and fashion brand manufacturing and distribution companies. These companies suffer continuous (price) attacks from companies using cheaper labour for manufacturing, mostly in Asian and South-American countries. They, however, never engage in a price war. On the contrary, they continue to rise on the quality - price ladder by continuously improving quality, product design, brand image and the service provided to their consumers, and they manage to protect their stable market positions. They are fighting but they do not want to destroy each other. They fight, for example, for the biggest market, the US.

"Nike's growth has come from great products, careful, thoughtful distribution and excellent marketing," footwear expert Matt Powell of industry analysis group NPD told us. "In the sneaker business product always comes first. Great marketing can never lift bad product." While Nike's marketing prowess is renowned – the brand spends $8 million per day on so-called "demand creation" – the fact of the matter is their products are instant hits all over the world.

In the USA – which accounts for 40% of all sportswear sales globally – Nike gear is lapped up on a huge scale, whether it's next-level running gear (where it owns roughly 60% share of the market) or must-have basketball sneakers (a staggering 90%) or high-performance skate shoes (roughly 20%).

"Adidas has made a lot of right moves and, if patient, can gain back some of its lost share," Powell summed up for us, adding "but no one is a threat to Nike right now." Both Skechers and Under Armour have made huge gains in recent years – Adidas is now the *third* biggest footwear brand in the States after UA – but none of them can, it seems, realistically topple Nike at the top of the sportswear game".

"By 2016 Adidas had hit an important milestone: The German athletic wear maker recaptured the No. 2 sports brand position in the U.S. from rival Under Armour," writes John Kell in Fortune Magazine.

Source: John Kell, Adidas Is Once Again No. 2 in America, Oct 25, 2016, The Fortune (http://fortune.com/2016/10/25/adidas-under-armour-nike/)
UA: By Unknown(Vector graphics logo by Kalel2007) - http://www.underarmour.com/, Public Domain, https://commons.wikimedia.org/w/index.php?curid=23363618
By Adidas - http://www.adidas.com/, Public Domain, https://commons.wikimedia.org/w/index.php?curid=7565931
By Carolyn Davidson - SVG based on the "swoosh" logo [1], Public Domain, https://commons.wikimedia.org/w/index.php?curid=10696486

EXHIBIT 7.6. SUPERMARKET PRICE WARS: ARE THEY REAL OR PHONEY?

Nowadays with the high concentration of mass retailing, the big players are watching each other very carefully. With the appearance of the big discounters Aldi and Lidl the others are forced to compare their prices as customers do and make some corrections. There are big announcements about a fierce price war – in Britain, for example – and consumers will be the beneficiaries of these wars. Not always – as it turns out from the analyses of the Telegraph reporter Harry Wallop.

The price war started with the announcement by Morrisons that it is "investing" £1 billion over the next three years into cutting prices and improving its own range of food, in an attempt to reverse a drastic fall in fortunes and woo back all those customers who started shopping at Aldi and Lidl.

The move by Morrisons came just a few days after Tesco said it was cutting prices by £200 million, not least the price of milk and cucumbers, which it said it would cut from 65p to 49p.

The problem is, that we have had so many phoney supermarket price wars in recent years, it is hard to know whether this one will actually deliver real savings to families wanting to cut the cost of their weekly shop.

Most people would agree that they spend more on a trolley of goods than they have ever done. The run up to Christmas 2010, a season when we were assured - backed up by expensive adverts on the television - that all the supermarkets were launching price wars, is one example where promises and reality didn't quite match.

It turned out that Asda had cut nearly 800 prices between December 16 and 23 that year, with two thirds of the cuts being just 1p and 80 per cent of the total number being less than 10p. In the same period Tesco cut about 930 prices, with 70 per cent of them being just one penny.

Edward Garner, a retail analyst at Kantar, says: "It is so difficult to tell if price wars are genuine or phoney. It may be that that Morrisons really has gone nuclear, though I don't think it makes much sense to go head to head on price with Aldi and Lidl.

"But so many price wars involve smoke and mirrors, that many customers just don't believe it when their supermarket says they are cheaper."

Source: Supermarket price wars: are they real or phoney? Harry Wallop 14 Mar 2014 The Daily Telegraph http://www.telegraph.co.uk/finance/newsbysector/retailandconsumer/10698008/Supermarket-price-wars-are-they-real-or-phoney.html

There are quite a few things companies should know if they are to maintain a good position in the price war:

Firstly, they must know and understand the competition characteristic of their industry, its nature and the other factors influencing that competition. These include:

- The typical market structure in the given industry, the size of the companies which take part in the competition, their relationship, their market positions, etc. (for a more detailed description see the chapter discussing the theoretical principles).

- The typical cost structure in the given industry. The competition is different if the sector is characterised by high or low PV ratio. The ratio of direct variable costs and fixed costs can provide information about degree of the so-called volume sensitivity in the given industry (for details see the chapter discussing costs and profits).
- How high the entry and exit barriers are in the given sector.
- What is the typical level of capacity utilization in the sector during the given period?
- The nature of the product or service. How homogeneous the product is and to what extent it can be differentiated; what role brand policy plays in the marketing of the product, etc.
- What are the demand trends: is demand increasing, stagnating or decreasing?
- What is the price elasticity of demand?
- How concentrated are consumers?
- How price sensitive are consumers?
- What substitute products are available?

They must also know the prices of their direct competitors, the strategy they follow, the sales conditions applied when serving the different market segments. In order for companies to make efficient use of the data and information collected from multiple sources for their price decisions, they must collect, process and spread this information within the company in a systematic way. The knowledge related to the competitors should form an integral part of the marketing information system.

Table 7.2 shows one of the possible ways to consolidate information about the price policies of the competitors. Updating this information should not be a problem for companies with today's computers. The system can be expanded; each company can build and modify it according to their own needs.

Figure 7.5. The price trap (based on Bradley, 1995: 601)

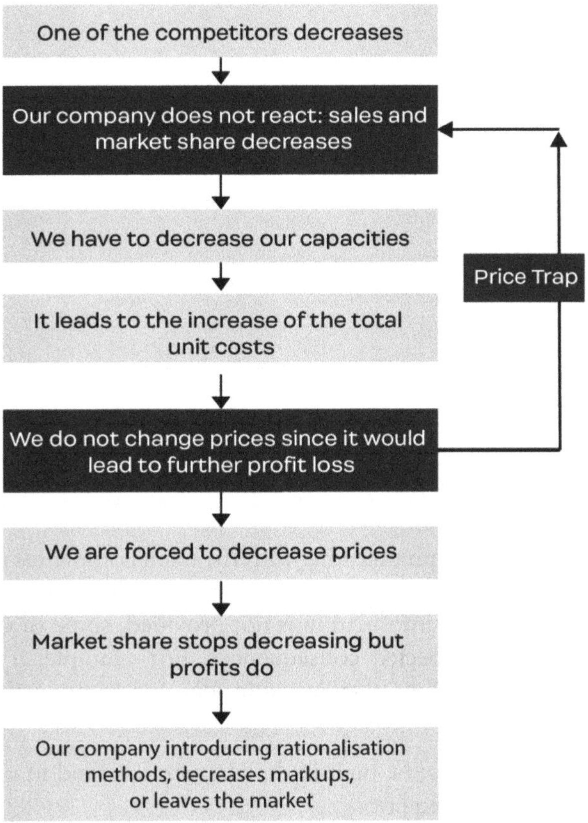

Table 7.2. The consolidation of information (an example from the food industry)

Competitors/ channels		Wholesalers	Multinational and domestic commercial chains	HORECA	Local retailers	Description of the price and marketing strategies generally used by the competitor
Competitor no. 1	Estimated market share					
	Price level (own = 100)					
	Terms of payment					
	Other					
Competitor no. 2	Estimated market share					
	Price level (own = 100)					
	Terms of payment					
	Other					
Competitor no. 3	Estimated market share					
	Price level (own = 100)					
	Terms of payment					
	Other					

Note: The abbreviation HORECA indicates the sales channels of products not consumed at home (Hotel, Restaurant, and Catering)

The channels for communicating with the main competitors must be developed. Many believe that it is best if the competitor knows as little as possible about our company. It is not necessarily true. If the required level of information is not provided, some of our actions may be misinterpreted which could lead to unexpected consequences. For example, if we provide no information about the objectives of our actions, they may consider, for example, the discounting of a closeout product as a frontal attack.

Strong positions must be built in the competition (and in the price competition as well) in order to be successful. This requires:

- An attempt to build a strong market position. The most common marketing tools for achieving this include: segmentation of the market, selection of the target market, differentiation of the products and related services according to the special requirements of the target market, product positioning, increasing the visibility and acceptance of the product or service, use of brand policy tools (building brand awareness, brand consciousness, brand preference, brand loyalty) etc. If the company possesses strong market positions, it will be able to respond to the price reduction carried out by its competitors using the above tools instead of reducing its own prices; it will be able to respond by increasing the value offered and will not be forced to turn to the extremely dangerous weapon of price reduction.

EXHIBIT 7.7. PRICE COMPETITION CAUSED BY MISUNDERSTANDING

One of the tyre manufacturers invoiced one of its products to the retailer for 35 dollars. By the end of the year the cumulated quantity discount ($2) and the marketing discount ($1.50) decreased the net price to $31.50. The company found out that one their competitors invoiced $32 to the retailer for the same product. Afraid to lose market share the company decreased its invoice price from $35 to $32. It turned out later that the competitor had not offered any volume or marketing discount to the retailer. As the company was unable to compare the prices well, it decreased its prices by 3 dollars, even though they had already been 50 cent lower than those of its competitor. Unfortunately, the realization came too late: the price war had already broken out.

Source: Garda–Marn, 1993

EXHIBIT 7.8. THE MEANS OF DECREASING PRODUCT COSTS

Based on his research in the electro technical sector Jürgen Kluge (1997: 212–215) concluded that there were three means to decrease the costs of products:

- Product simplification: material costs can be significantly reduced by decreasing the number of parts used for the manufacturing of the product.
- Product redesign: redesigning a product in order to save costs can result in new products that will not decrease consumer value, but may even increase it.

Successful companies achieve substantial cost savings by outsourcing production. The more competitive the environment the company operates in, the more important it becomes to outsource the production that cannot be undertaken efficiently inside the company. The company can obtain further results by cooperating with the suppliers and contributing to improving the efficiency of their planning and operational activities. (A so-called virtual vertical integration is created: where the buyer enjoys the advantages of the integration without the disadvantages of high capital investment.) The so-called world class producers work with world class suppliers.

Flexibility can also mean that, if a company cannot participate in price competition effectively, it should be able to withdraw from it, or even change its profile. It is the ability of foreseeing the change that makes certain companies and company executives ‘great’ and that distinguishes them from the others. Most companies and company executives cling to the habitual ways till the end, and carry on as if nothing has changed, even when it has been obvious for a long time that they would only emerge from this situation with losses.

- Besides the market position, a solid cost basis must be established as well. It has been proven that high quality does not necessarily go hand in hand with cost increase. Economies of scale, the effects of the learning and experience curves confirm the economic phenomenon that unit costs can be decreased while maintaining, or moreover increasing the quality level. Preparations for the price war are required on the cost side too. Such a technology or operational system must be applied which allows more room for price movements including the possibility of price decrease.

7.4. Typical price decisions in the different stages of the life cycle

It is not easy to make price decisions that are typical in different stages of the life cycle. The task becomes complicated as the given market, demand, technological, marketing and environmental conditions may require different price strategies.

7.4.1. Maintaining the price level - price reduction

It has already been mentioned several times that companies launching a new product have a choice of three strategies (high, medium and low initial price). The level of the initial price can clearly influence the price behaviour at a later time. While the target may be to maintain price levels in case of high or medium initial prices, with low initial prices it may be to increase prices if conditions are favourable.

It is also true, however, that as production reaches mass-scale, the unit costs of production decrease in most cases. This allows for price decrease. The strengthening competition transforms this opportunity into a necessity during the stages of growth and maturity. As the product life cycle progresses, the price decrease becomes a requirement (at real price levels). Companies usually follow three strategies compared to this general tendency:

- They try to avoid decreasing the price and focus their activities on continually enhancing the quality and the performance of their products, modernising their product support marketing activities, and improving their customer service. These competing companies try to divert attention from prices to the other value elements, and put quality and progress to the fore on the price determined 'ladder'. If they can do this successfully, the top segment of the market structure will develop from their offers.

- A different group of companies – typically the ones that manufacture so-called 'me too' products or ones that have very strong cost positions – decrease their prices significantly as the life cycle progresses, and try to gain market share with their relatively favourable price positions. These companies spend less on product development, on modernisation and product support marketing activities. Companies competing only with their prices will make up the lower third of the market structure.

- There is usually room between the two extreme positions for companies that have a middle, neutral marketing and price policy. Their activities are characterised by prices and marketing support that vary between the two extreme values.

7.4.2. Product differentiation - price differentiation in the middle stages of product life cycle

When launching a new product the product or service is often introduced in different versions. The supplier who is still enjoying a monopolistic situation can adopt the methods of price differentiation to boost demand, but the growth and maturity stages remain the periods for price differentiation. The basic form of the product becomes dominant by this time and the differentiation begins according to

the requirements of the different market segments. Product differentiation does not typically concern the basic benefits of the product, but is rather aimed at enriching and expanding the objectified form of the product. Product lines develop for a shorter or longer period leaving room for different methods of pricing. Companies use complicated price differentiating methods during the maturity stage, including non-linear pricing, different types of price differentiation and bundle prices. These will be presented in more detail in a separate chapter. The importance of these forms of pricing increases as soon as the product and service on the market reaches its maturity stage. In the market of FMCG (fast moving consumer goods) private labels pose a competitive threat to big-name brands gaining higher and higher market share with their lower prices.

7.4.3. Withdrawal from the market, significant price reduction

Most products and services enter the stage of decline sooner or later. This stage is characterized by a fast decrease in demand and the withdrawal of suppliers from the market. A few companies may specialize in trying to satisfy the remaining small level of demand (or may be involved in the after-care of the products still in consumption, e.g. provision of spare parts); such companies may even increase their prices. Most manufacturing and trading companies, however, will seek to get rid of their stocks. Product prices suffer a significant decrease during this time.

CHAPTER 8. DYNAMIC PRICING

OBJECTIVE 1 To understand the concept and dynamic nature of price discrimination and its relationship with theory and practice.

OBJECTIVE 2 To learn to use different methods and bases of price discrimination such as place, time, intensity of use, terms and time of payment, and characteristics of customer segments in order to understand the workings of different forms of non-linear and two-tier tariffs pricing systems.

OBJECTIVE 3 To understand the advantages of and disadvantages of yield management to debate the correctness and fairness of its use and to discuss how the methods and techniques perceived fairness of this method can be improved.

8.1. Introduction

Notions related to the discrimination of prices are often presented in literature in contradictory or confusing ways. By price discrimination we mean corporate price policy decisions allowing sellers to set different prices on the same product with or without making small changes on it, or when the same product is sold under different conditions but at different prices - even though these price differences are not justified by differences in costs.

Sellers have a right to do so but this right must not lead them to abusing their dominant position (see next Exhibit!).

EXHIBIT 8.1. PUBLIC OPINION OF PRICE DISCRIMINATION AND ABUSE OF ECONOMIC DOMINANCE IN THE EUROPEAN UNION

In case there is a difference in the conditions of selling, the seller has the right to sell products at a lower price to customers who are willing to buy under conditions more favourable to him/her. However, if the seller, who enjoys a position of economic dominance, fails to make it clear to all his customers under what conditions they can shop more favourably, this behaviour is considered an offence against the prohibition of abusing economic dominance.

The European Commission has published guidance on its enforcement priorities in applying EC Treaty rules on abuse of a dominant market position (Article 82) to abusive exclusionary conduct by dominant undertakings. Such conduct aims to exclude actual competitors from expanding or would-be competitors from entering a market, thereby potentially depriving customers of more choice, more innovative goods and services at lower prices. The guidance sets out the Commission's determination to prioritise those cases where the exclusionary conduct of a dominant undertaking is liable to have harmful effects on consumers.

(Source: http://europa.eu/rapid/press-release_IP-08-1877_en.htm?locale=en)

EXHIBIT 8.2. PRICE DISCRIMINATION IN THE USA: ROBINSON-PATMAN VIOLATIONS

A seller charging competing buyers different prices for the same 'commodity' or discriminating in the provision of 'allowances' - compensation for advertising and other services - may be violating the Robinson-Patman Act. This kind of price discrimination may give favoured customers an edge in the market that has nothing to do with their superior efficiency. Price discriminations are generally lawful, particularly if they reflect the different costs of dealing with different buyers or are the result of a seller's attempts to meet a competitor's offering.

The Supreme Court has ruled that price discrimination claims under the Robinson-Patman Act should be evaluated consistent with broader antitrust policies. In practice, Robinson-Patman claims must meet several specific legal tests:

The Act applies to commodities, but not to services, and to purchases, but not to leases.

The goods must be of "like grade and quality."

There must be likely injury to competition (that is, a private plaintiff must also show actual harm to his or her business).

Normally, the sales must be "in" interstate commerce (that is, the sale must be across a state line).

Competitive injury may occur in one of two ways. "Primary line" injury occurs when one manufacturer reduces its prices in a specific geographic market and causes injury to its competitors in the same market. For example, it may be illegal for a manufacturer to sell below cost in a local market over a sustained period. Businesses may also be concerned about "secondary line" violations, which occur when favoured customers of a supplier are given a price advantage over competing customers. Here, the injury is at the buyer's level.

Source: Federal Trade Commission website
https://www.ftc.gov/tips-advice/competition-guidance/guide-antitrust-laws/price-discrimination-robinson-patman

The notion of price discrimination is often used in literature in the meaning of *price customization*. The notion is very similar to the one used in product policy or management literature to denote customization of products or sometimes the whole marketing activity. In marketing literature, we can also find a concept that describes the differentiation of prices simply as *price segmentation*. To speak about the use of different prices new terms were coined in literature like *dynamic pricing* or *flexible pricing*. Representatives of quantitative sciences prefer to speak about issues related to different prices using the term *non-linear pricing* and devote lengthy studies or books to elaborating a methodological background to the concept (Wilson, 1993).

8.2. Economic approach to price discrimination

The literature of economics exclusively uses the term 'price discrimination' to describe situations in which the seller attaches different prices to the same product. Actually the notion of 'price differentiation' sometimes befits the terminology of marketing better. In reality both carry the same meaning: the term 'discrimination' itself has a double meaning, namely differentiation and exclusion. A buyer who is sold the same product in the same circumstances at a higher price, has reason to feel discriminated against, and to consider this kind of behaviour unethical. It should be noted here that such discrimination is against the law in several countries (in the US, e.g.). In practice, however, we

find that the current economy tends to favour price discrimination as the dominant attitude to prices. In order to meet the requirements sellers must learn to distinguish between the products offered, consumer groups or any other circumstance in which the deal was realized.

After this introduction, let us examine the forms of price discrimination described by economics.

In economics, three degrees of price discrimination are distinguished:

1. *First degree or perfect price discrimination*: In this case the seller sets for each buyer a price that is as high as the buyer's reservation price, i.e. the maximum a buyer is willing to pay for the product. In this case the seller would skim - at least in principle - all consumer surplus. In order to achieve that the seller should know the reservation price of every buyer. In practice, however, it is not feasible.

2. *Second degree price discrimination.* In this case the seller sets prices according to the quantity of goods sold. The main criterion for the distinction is the fact that the various consumer groups buy different quantities (which means that in all probability they also differ in the price elasticity of their demand). For this price discrimination, the seller does not need to know any other distinguishing factors like demographics.

3. *Third degree price discrimination.* Here sellers offer their products to consumer groups at various prices, which are easy to identify with well distinguishable criteria. Such criteria can be domicile, age, time of consumption, etc. This third-degree price discrimination is extremely widespread in today's economy. The groups that have been differentiated by the various criteria also have different price elasticity of demand. For example, the price elasticity of those who use the telephone at weekends is obviously much higher than of those who use it on weekdays.

According to microeconomics, at least three conditions should be fulfilled for price discrimination to occur:

- Price setting capacity. In order to practise price differentiation, a firm should exercise a certain degree of control over prices. This is why the price differentiation of a firm operating in perfect competition cannot be efficient.
- Sellers should be able to identify *those consumer groups* who have different price elasticity of demand and their reservation prices are different as well.
- The different consumer groups should be properly separated, i.e. they should have no opportunity to resell the products.

8.3. The theory of price discrimination

In order to develop a well-founded theoretical background to price discrimination, we must go back to the demand curve already discussed in Chapter 2. The demand curve shows that various prices go together with differing demand, which means that buyer groups of different sizes are willing to buy the product at different prices.

Let us take – for the sake of illustration – the case of the Metropolitan Opera House (MET) in Lincoln Center, New York, which happened to celebrate the 50th anniversary of its construction in 2016. On December 27, 2016, a production of Verdi's Nabucco was staged there. The opera house can seat, say, 3,800 people and the costs related to the performance of Nabucco (the variable costs: fees paid to the singers, musicians, director etc.) amounted to USD 380,000 this meant an average of USD100 per available seat. We can also assume that at a ticket price of USD 100 (and in this case, the income

would cover exactly the variable costs) the opera has a full house. On the other hand, nobody is willing to book tickets at USD 1,000. The demand curve of the Nabucco performance is like the line A-C on in Figures 8.1.

The MET building (left of the photo)

Source of the photo: By Nils Olander from Panoramio - Own work, GFDL, https://commons.wikimedia.org/w/index.php?curid=4061295

Figure 8.1 Demand curve for the MET

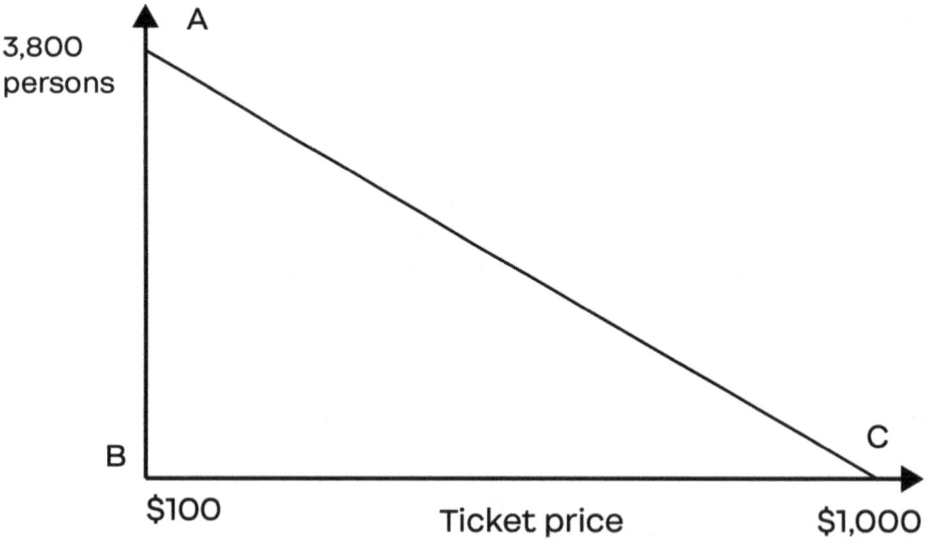

The ABC triangle shows the potential revenue generating capacity of the opera. This would produce the following result: ½ x 3,800 (height of the triangle), x (1,000 – 100) (the base of the triangle) = USD1,710,000. This amount does not exist in reality, because the MET's management is not able to produce 3,800 different prices.

If only *one price were used*, it should be defined in such a way as to yield the highest possible revenue. The price of the ticket could vary between USD 100 and 1,000 because at USD 100 only the variable costs could be covered, while over USD 1,000 nobody would buy tickets. If the demand curve is linear, it is easy to define the optimal price. All we have to do is calculate the average between the two extreme points, which is USD 450 ([1,000 – 100]/2). At this price the opera house will be only half full and generate a revenue of USD 855,000. Deducting the variable costs ($ 380 thousand) it would result in a contribution amounting to USD 475,000 (Figure 8.2).

This one-price policy would allow the MET to be filled up to 50%, because the tickets are still very expensive for some of the buyers. The buyers lost in this way are responsible for 25% of the contribution (AB1D triangle). The other 25% (B2DC triangle) was lost because some ticket buyers would have been willing to pay a higher price.

This is the moment when the discrimination of prices comes in. MET has the liberty to decide setting, say, four price categories (Figure 8.3).

Figure 8.2 Maximum revenue if there is only one price.

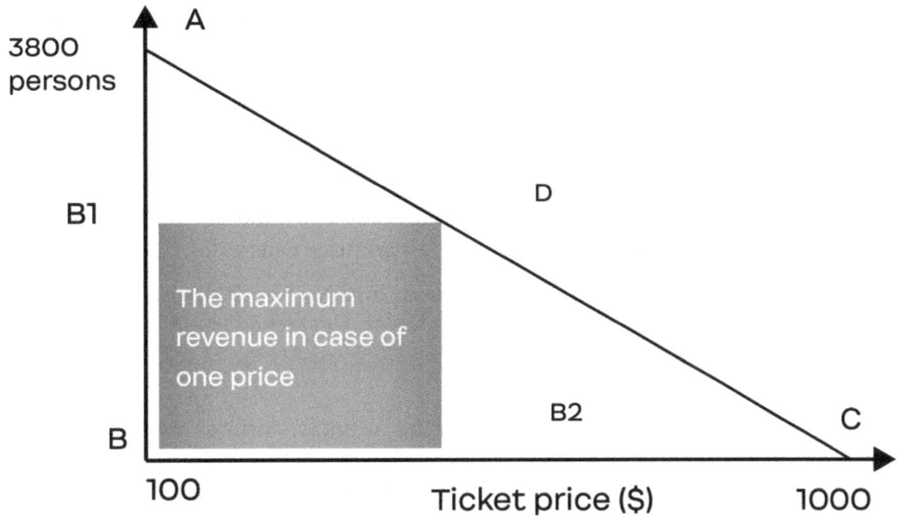

Figure 8.3. The effect of the differentiated price policy.

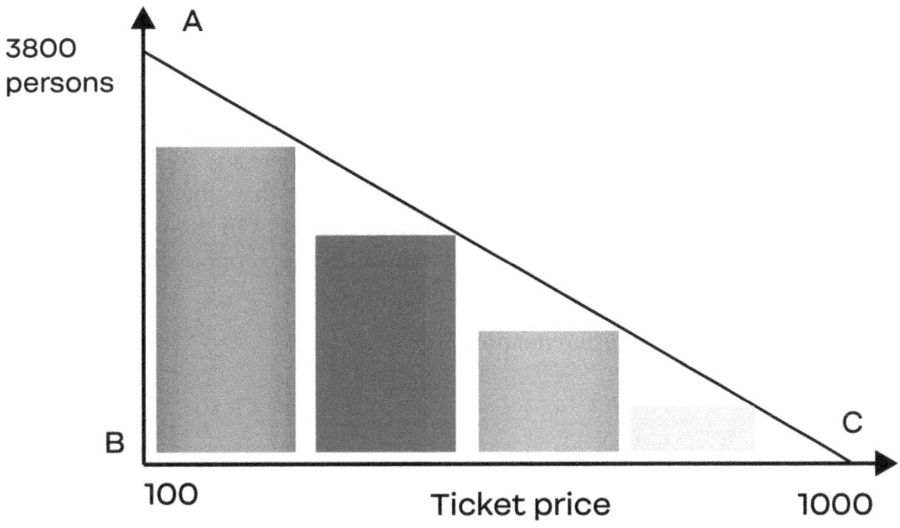

This situation is illustrated in Figure 8.3. It can be seen that there is no doubt that the number of unbooked seats is much smaller than with the one-price policy.

What can be the justification for or the condition of the MET applying more than one price - or four, as in our example? The answer is obvious: the audience can see much better from the more expensive seats, which are also nearer the stage. The tickets belonging to different price categories are distinguished by other criteria as well, e.g. the most expensive seats can also be more comfortable, there may be a separate, buffet or programmes may be distributed.

If the organizers wish to charge different prices they must work out the separation of different seat categories, otherwise the differentiation is not feasible. The rules are the same for the other service providers as well.

Note: in reality, ticket prices for the Nabucco performance on 27th of December 2016 in the MET ranged from $125 to $659 and the management used about twenty-two price categories.

Photo: the auditorium of the New York Metropolitan Opera house
Photo: Andreas Praefcke - Own work (own photograph), CC BY 3.0, https://commons.wikimedia.org/w/index.php?curid=2243009

A classic example of the use of price discrimination is the airline business. Airfares are usually sold in three price tiers: first, business and economy classes. Fares on business class can cost two, three or even four times as much as in economy class, although the products are identical: you will certainly get safely from point A to B by plane. Seats in business class are more comfortable and the service offered is better too. The two classes are separated by a fence, although this is usually represented merely by a curtain. A higher class involves other advantages, such as a separate waiting lounge at the airports (another fence), easier flight changes, higher bonus points in the frequent flier programme, separate check-in desks or a combination of such fences.

However, price differentiation means additional costs. In a sports arena, seat categories must be separated (more fences to build), additional attendants need to be hired and other additions to comfort also entail extra costs. The situation is the same for all the air carriers and for any product or service which features price differentiation. Experience has shown that the costs of price differentiation increase at a faster rate than the number of prices applied. On the other hand, the benefit of price differentiation increases more slowly. It is reasonable to suppose that there is an optimal number for the price categories applied, as shown in Figure 8.4.

Figure 8.4. Cost- benefit analysis of price differentiation.

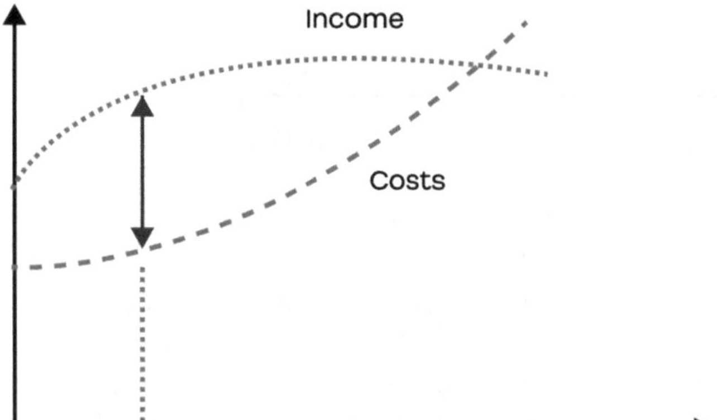

Source: Simon, 2009: 115.

8.4. Modes of price discrimination

Price discrimination recommended for the MET Opera House depended on where the seats were. Airlines follow a similar pattern when they divide tickets into classes. The conditions, which allow companies to change the price or the rating of their products or services, can be classified as follows:

8.4.1. Price discrimination by place of consumption

Price discrimination by place of consumption can be interpreted in several ways:

- Prices can be discriminated according to the actual location within the unit where consumption takes place (e.g. on sports grounds, in theatres, or lecture halls). The basis for differentiation is typically the nearness to the event, how well it can be seen. Similarly, we can speak of price discrimination when a hotel charges more for its rooms with a particularly nice view. Travel brochures frequently advertise rooms with the same facilities but overlooking the sea in a higher category.

- In the second case of price discrimination a firm has several points of consumption each with the same function and facilities but geographically at various distances from each other and this is the basis for differentiation. Good examples could be members of a restaurant chain: the one located in the town centre will no doubt charge higher prices than the one in a less popular part of the town. We could also mention the price of the parking lots within the same district of a town (see parking fees in Westminster in Table 8.1.)

Table 8.1. Parking prices in the Westminster district of London

Zone	Location	Sub-zones	Price per hour
A	Knightsbridge, Belgravia and Pimlico	A1, A2, A3, A4	£3.70
B	Bayswater and Maida Vale (Sth)	BC1, B2, B3, B4, B5, B6, B7, B10, B11	£2.70
C	Harrow Rd, Queen's Park and Maida Vale (Nth)	CB1, C1, C2	£1.70
D	Victoria, Westminster and Millbank	D1, D4	£2.50
E	Mayfair and St James	E1	£4.90
F	Hyde Park, Marylebone and Fitzrovia	F1, F2, F3, F4, F5, F6	£4.90
G	Soho, West End and Covent Garden	G1, G2	£4.50
H	Terminus Place and Allington Street (6 streets only)	H1	£2.40

https://www.westminster.gov.uk/parking-zones-and-prices (22.12.2016)

- The third case of price discrimination by place occurs when a firm charges different fees or prices for the same service or product in different regions (or towns) of the country. A well-known example for regional price discrimination in Hungary is the insurance of cars: in the capital, nearly all insurance companies charge more for the same service (Casco) than in other parts of the country.

- It seems quite natural that some firms set different prices for their products region by region or country by country. The different prices applied in the markets of various foreign countries are also part of price discrimination. For the customers this can be a problem only if, for example, buyers log in from different countries to the same homepage and can download a software at different prices (see Exhibit on iTunes).

- The situation is similar to the international variation when sellers attempt to justify geographically different prices with the difference in freight costs. This point will be discussed later under the heading 'geographical pricing'.

EXHIBIT 8.3. DISCRIMINATIVE ITUNES PRICES

Britain's Office of Fair Trade has long objected to the behaviour of iTunes and has now turned to the EU Commission with its complaints that the iTunes music store illegally discriminates against customers on the basis of their country and thereby restricts consumers' free choice.

British consumers complained that iTunes' homepage treats them differently from consumers coming from other countries. Identified with their credit card numbers British music fans have discovered that they have to face a completely different supply and tariff. iTunes sent them much higher bills and they had no access to pages with cheaper offers. It became visible when the Canadian iTune store was opened. The Canadian store's bills were 16% cheaper than the iTunes page that has operated in the US for a long time.

Apple charged customers from the United Kingdom 90 pence (USD1.53) for a song while Americans were charged only USD1.33. Canadian credit cards attracted the best deals, only being charged USD 0.83 per song. Apple kept referring to the local situation of the music market and the differences in taxation, which resulted in varying prices in different countries.

Since OFT's complaint iTunes has used fixed prices (i.e. $0.99, $1.29 etc.) but – according to G. Spencer – for stores outside the US these price levels were converted using a very conservative prediction of the future value of a particular currency. The price levels in non-US stores seemed not to have been updated in a long time, yet the value of the non-US currencies have mostly appreciated since then. As a result, in 2011 people purchasing from most of the non-US iTunes Stores were paying *more* than US customers and Apple was earning more from those customers. (See table below.)

When the value of the dollar went up Apple started to update their prices more frequently. "Apple raising the price of apps in 7 countries within 72 hours due to exchange rates," wrote Owen Williams in 2016.

Country	Store Price	Price in $US	Difference	Inflation
Mexico	15 pesos	$1.24	-$0.05	-4%
USA	$1.29	$1.29	N/A	0%
Canada	$1.29	$1.30	$0.01	1%
UK	£0.99	$1.56	$0.27	21%
Norway	10KR	$1.71	$0.42	32%
Eurozone	€1.29	$1.72	$0.43	33%
Denmark	10KR	$1.79	$0.50	39%
Japan	¥150	$1.81	$0.52	41%
New Zealand	$2.39	$1.83	$0.54	42%
Australia	$2.19	$2.18	$0.89	69%
Switzerland	2.2 francs	$2.30	$1.01	78%

Value in USD calculated using average of January 2011 exchange rates

Sources: http://pcworld.hu/diszkriminativ-itunes-arak-20070404.html)
https://www.macstories.net/stories/the-great-disparity-in-global-itunes-prices/
http://thenextweb.com/apple/2016/01/18/apple-raising-the-price-of-apps-in-7-countries-within-72-hours-due-to-exchange-rages/
https://www.apple.com/itunes/

8.4.2. Price discrimination by time of consumption

Discrimination by time of consumption means that the firm charges different prices for the same offer depending on the time (season, week, day, hour) of consumption. This type of price differentiation is important mainly for services. The argument service providers use to justify differentiation is that without it consumption is not even, the use of capacities would deteriorate (and, in the case of physical products costs of stocks, or storage would increase). The following groups are found here:

- *Seasonal price discrimination.* There are products and services we typically consume or use seasonally. In order to reduce seasonality, sellers apply higher prices for the peak season, and lower ones out of season. Good examples are holidays and related services. Among physical products we can find quite a few that are consumed seasonally, like agricultural produce, fuels and building materials.

- *Discrimination by days of the week.* A lot of products and services experience great differences between workdays and weekends as far as their consumption is concerned (hotel industry, public transport, the use of telephones, etc.). For a better use of capacities, sellers may set lower prices for the least busy days (this is why you can book cheaper flight tickets if your trip includes a weekend).

- *Discrimination within the day.* There may be significant fluctuations in consumption within the day too. If the supplier has the capacity for continuous production, they will be interested in promoting consumption in quieter periods as well, with special, favourable prices. This is also the reason why we have cheaper rates for electricity and telephone during the night. On the other hand, the use of tennis courts can be made cheaper during working hours. Some restaurants and bars hope to maintain attendance or consumption and make the place more popular by introducing happy hours in the afternoons when business is quiet and offer drinks at considerably lower prices.

- *Price discrimination at the time of some important event.* Demand can suddenly grow at the time of certain events (celebrations, programmes) to which sellers respond by increasing prices. Most restaurants, hotels, buffets in Budapest set exorbitant prices during the Formula 1 events.

8.4.3. Price discrimination by intensity of consumption

Another frequent method of price *discrimination* is that some service providers charge different prices for those consumers who use their services more often than the average. These prices can take the form of a season ticket (to the theatre, a spa, etc.) or, in public transport, the day, weekly or monthly ticket. The fee we pay for using the Internet also belongs here: service providers usually offer it in packages.

Some forms of membership - frequent buyer programmes - offer their participants or card holders more favourable prices if they buy their products or services.

8.4.4. Price discrimination by time of order

This method is frequently applied to make the use of capacities easier to plan and more evenly and safely distributed; therefore, clients who place their orders - for the delivery of a product or service - on a specific date are charged less than others. Airlines are good examples again, as are participation fees for conferences (early bird registration).

8.4.5. Price discrimination by features of consumer groups

Price segmentation by consumer type means that consumers belonging to (usually demographically) different groups are charged different prices for the same product or service. The differences often express the social assistance that society offers to certain groups (pensioners, soldiers, students, public servants), but sometimes other considerations of corporate policy are found in the background. Children typically enjoy preferential treatment when they buy certain services (flight tickets, admission to programmes, etc.) even if the service is the same as for the adults. The cost of life insurance often varies not only by age, but by health condition as well. There are countries where smokers are charged different prices for life insurance than non-smokers., or banks grant loans with more favourable conditions to clients deemed to be more reliable, etc. The ultimate case of discrimination by buyers is the situation when the supplier sets a different price for every single buyer after estimating their willingness to pay. This falls within the category of *first degree price discrimination,* but it is not easy to find good examples for it. One could be the *flea market*, the pricing of a private dentist, or the so-called Dutch auction.

EXHIBIT 8.4. DUTCH AUCTION

Dutch auction is a form of bidding at auctions (for selling cheese, and cut flowers, sometimes fruits, or fishes) practised mainly in the Netherlands (this explains the origin of the name). The auctioneer starts at a high price, which is gradually lowered until somebody is willing to buy the product. An advantage of the Dutch auction is that it takes a shorter time.

A 1957 Dutch auction in Germany to sell fruit
Source: By Bundesarchiv, B 145 Bild-F004491-0002 / Unterberg, Rolf / CC-BY-SA 3.0, CC BY-SA 3.0 de, https://commons.wikimedia.org/w/index.php?curid=5448709)

EXHIBIT 8.5. PRICE DISCRIMINATION FOR THE TENNIS-COURT FEES AT THE MAKÁR-TANYA SPORT CENTRE

MAKÁR-TANYA INDOOR

TENNIS COURTS

WINTER SEASON 2016/2017

26 Weeks between 15th October and 15th April

PRICES FOR AD HOC TENANTS				
Time zone (day-hours) HUF/hour	M - F 08-13 3 000	M - F 13 - 18 4 000	M - F 18 - 20 4 500	S - S 8 - 22 4 000
Full Seasons' prices				
Indicating colours				
Hour prices for regular tenants	2 800	3 500	3 800	
Season price/hour/court	72 800	91 000	98 800	

HOURS	MON.	TUE.	WED.	THU.	FRI.	SAT.	SUN.
08-09							
09-10							
10-11							
11-12							
12-13							
13-14							
14-15							
15-16							
16-17							
17-18							
18-19							
19-20							
20-21							
21-22							

Note: One Dollar was approximately 280 Hungarian Forints in January 2017.

The price list makes it clear that the tennis courts' prices are differentiated:

- by the time of day (the period after working hours is the most expensive, followed by the hours before work, and the cheapest times are between 10.a.m.and 3 p.m.)
- by days of the week (workdays and weekends)
- regular and non-regular tenants.

EXHIBIT 8.6. ZONE PRICES ON THE LONDON UNDERGROUND

The extensive London underground network applies several methods of price discrimination:

- zone prices
- single line or,
- day tickets - weekly-- and monthly tickets
- Credit (Oyster) card system, which is cheaper than the methods using cash and passengers pay just as much as their travel costs
- pay as you go
- student tickets
- peak-time, outside peak time, etc.

The next table shows the zone prices valid in 2016.

London Underground Fares 2016 *(From January 2nd)*

Zones Travelled	Single Journey Ticket		Oyster / Contactless Payment Card~	
	Adult	Child†	Peak*	Off Peak
Zone 1	£4.90	£2.40	£2.40	£2.40
Zone 1 & 2	£4.90	£2.40	£2.90	£2.40
Zone 1 To 3	£4.90	£2.40	£3.30	£2.80
Zone 1 To 4	£5.90	£2.90	£3.90	£2.80
Zone 1 To 5	£5.90	£2.90	£4.70	£3.10
Zone 1 To 6	£6.00	£3.00	£5.10	£3.10
Zone 2 To 6	£5.90	£2.90	£2.80	£1.50

No return fares.

† Children travel free if under 11 years old or between 11 and 15 years with an Oyster 11-15 Photocard
~ Children's fares (11-15 yrs old) on Oyster for any trip within zones 1 to 6 are £0.75 off peak, £0.80 peak
** Peak fares apply Monday to Friday between 6:30 a.m. and 9:30 a.m. and 4 p.m. to 7 p.m. except public holidays*

8.4.6. Relationships between geographical distances and pricing

There are commodities - primarily capital goods, but occasionally consumer goods as well - whose freight costs are rather high compared with manufacturing costs. Commodities of this kind include raw and semi-processed materials (iron, steel, etc. or products of the construction industry). Geographical pricing is known to incorporate the following modes:

- Seller calculates the prices without including freight costs. (International terminology calls this Ex Works, while Americans use the acronym FOB.) In terms of this calculation, the buyer will be responsible for the transportation of the product and will pay the costs and bear the risks. This form of pricing can harm the competitiveness of the seller, especially in remote areas, because competitors operating at shorter distances definitely have an advantage.

- In their attempt to avoid such disadvantages sellers introduced new forms of pricing which already include a part or all the transportation costs. They are the following:
    - *Uniform prices* include freight costs regardless of the geographical position of the buyers within the same market. Typically, sellers calculate an average freight. The disadvantage of this solution is that the price buyers near the producers pay is out of proportion, while far-away buyers are charged less than is strictly fair. Only buyers at average distance pay a price proportionate to the costs.
    - *Zone price,* which means that the seller divides his market into clearly outlined zones and sets a different price for each zone. This price already includes the freight to the buyer within the zone. (This system is similar to telephone zone rates) When defining the zones the seller should take care not to cause any negative discrimination to his large customers.
    - *Base points:* when base points are used the manufacturer, calculating his prices, includes transportation costs to a certain place (base point). This calculation can be regarded as averaging the actual freight because a manufacturer can have several sites. Buyers are charged the price calculated to the base point plus freight from the base point. A firm has the right to use one or more base points. In the case of multiple base points, the one nearest the buyer's premises are taken as valid. Pricing with base points is shown in Figure 8.5

Figure 8.5. Base point pricing

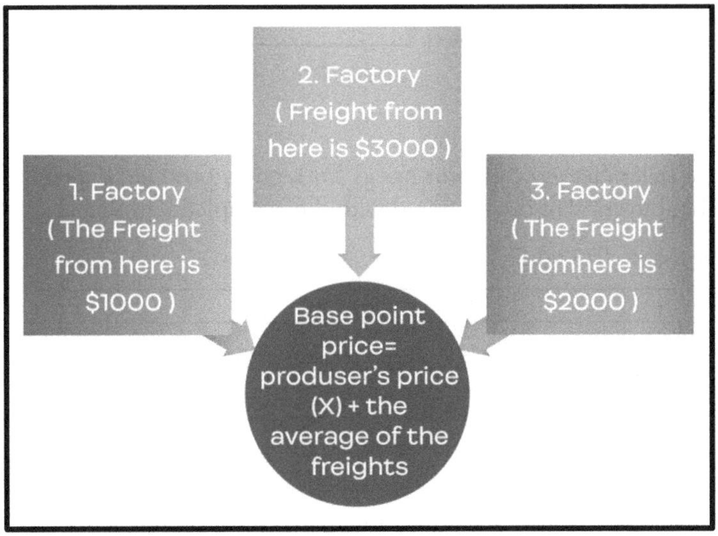

8.5. Non-linear pricing (price discrimination based on quantity)

The second degree of price discrimination is a frequently used method, when the price buyers have to pay depends on the quantity bought. In this case, price discrimination can take either of the following two forms:

- The firm sets the base price (list price) and during the process of selling – if all the pre-determined conditions are met – the firm offers a previously announced (or occasionally ad hoc) discount. The special offers, expressed in percentages, are discussed in special literature under the heading of *price allowances.*

- The other mode of differentiation is linked to different quantities bought; the firm states different prices for the different magnitudes from the start. Although the outcome of the two operations is the same, for teaching purposes it is practical to distinguish between price differentiation (when prices are different from the start) and discounts (when a price is reduced from the list price).

Figure 8.6 presents the difference between linear and non-linear pricing, highlighting the difference between the price and the total value paid by the consumer.

Figure 8.6. Linear and non-linear pricing

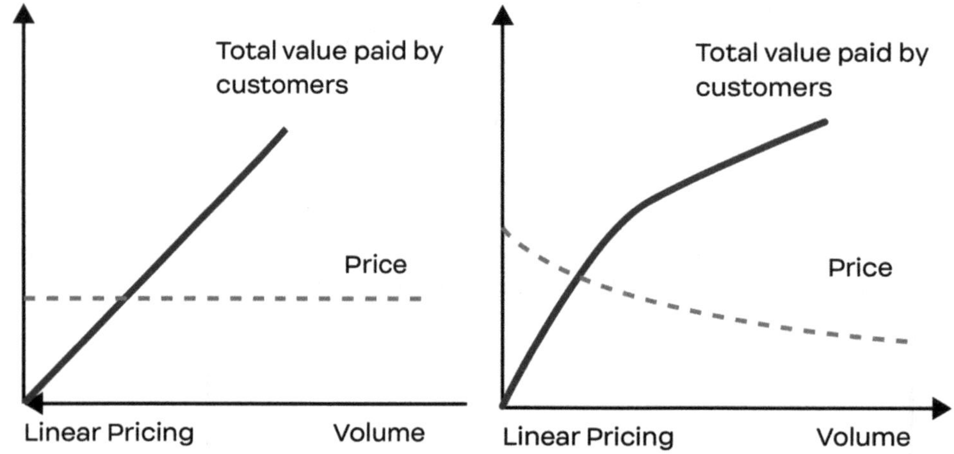

8.5.1. Unit prices depending on quantity

In its basic form, the seller charges different prices for a given product, depending on the quantity, giving reference to big buyers. This is illustrated with the example in Table 8,2.

Table 8.2. Price quotation depending on quantity

Product	Quantity bought	Price
XYZ product packed in paper boxes	1 — 5 boxes	$20/box
	6 — 10 boxes	$17box
	11 — 20 boxes	$14/box
	over 21 boxes	$11/box

- The lower price has a retroactive effect: Once the transaction reaches the given quantity, the lower price will hold for all. In our example: if somebody buys, say, 30 boxes, every one of the boxes will cost $11.

- If the lower price does not have a retroactive effect. It is valid only for the quantity over the price defined. If somebody buys 30 boxes of the product he will be charged $20 for each of the first 5 boxes, $17 for each of the second 5 boxes, and so on.

The price will be similar in both cases (Figure 8.7) but sales revenue is different (Figures 8.8 and 8.9. The figure shows that there are so-called inefficient areas in price revenues when prices go down. 10 boxes cost the buyer $170 and 11 cost only $154. The contradiction is even bigger when the reduction

allowed at 21 boxes is reached. In this case the buyer will obviously 'skip' and buy 21boxes, because it costs less than 19 boxes.

Figure 8.7. The quantity dependent prices

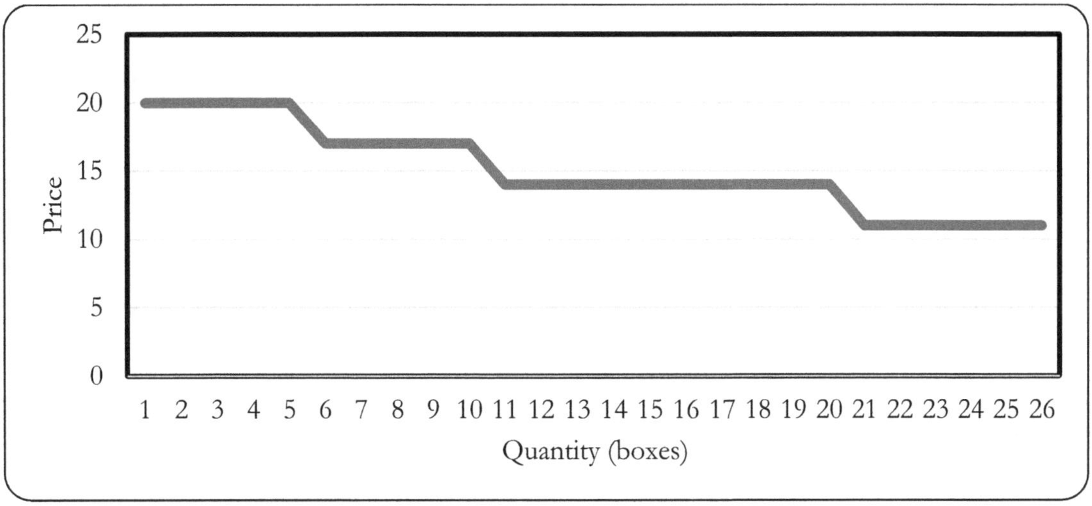

Figure 8.8. The impact of sales revenues when price reductions haven't got a retroactive effect.

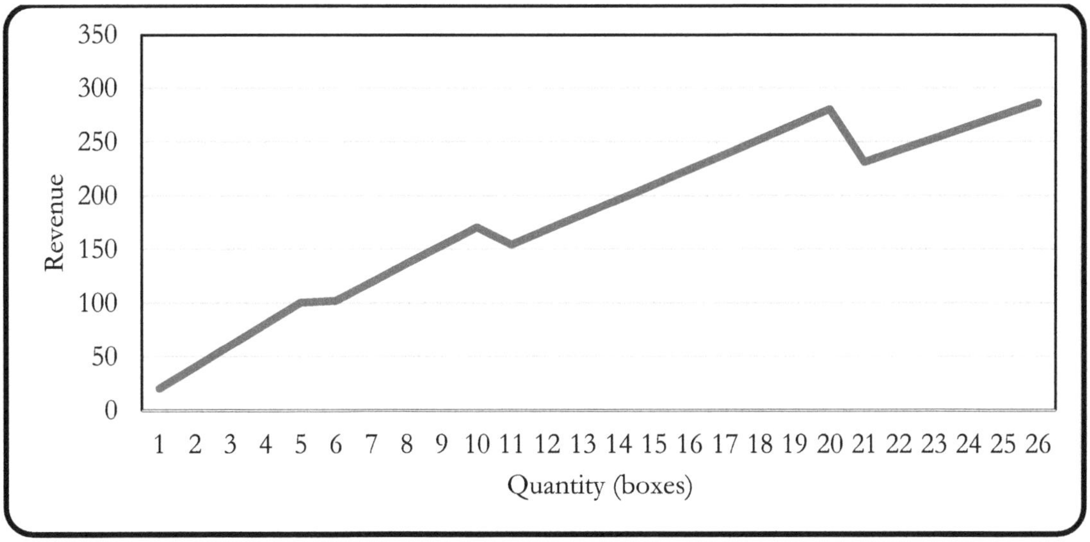

The situation is completely different with price reduction without retroactive effect. As shown in Figure 8.9, there is no decrease in sales revenue, consequently customers have no constraint to buy more than they actually need.

Figure 8.9 Changes in sales revenue if price reduction has retroactive effect

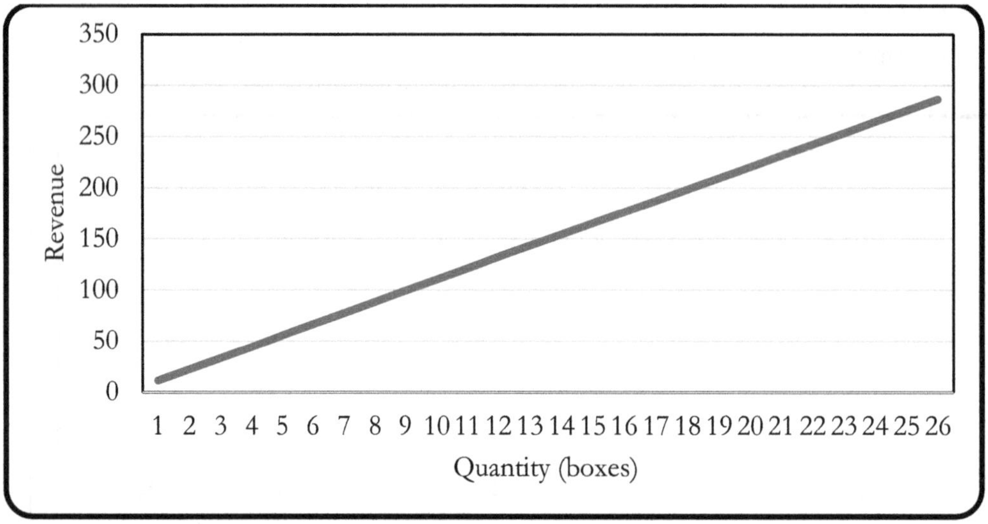

8.5.2. Two-part pricing in linear and non-linear combination

Two-part pricing is especially frequent in the case of services: the buyer pays first (a base price) for having access to the service and, secondly, secondly, pays in proportion to the service used (linear) or depending on the quantity of service used a lower (for more service), sometimes higher (non-linear) price. Typical examples are the rates of telephone use, electricity, and gas supply or car rental. If you rent a car, you are charged a fee per day or week, and also for the distance covered, calculated in km. Two-part pricing prefers higher levels of consumption, because unit prices – including the base fee as fixed cost - diminish with higher consumption. A person, who makes just a few phone calls a month pays a much higher unit price than someone who calls frequently. (Connection charge works differently: it prefers long conversations, since the rate per unit (minute) is lower, because one-time connection fee is divided for several time units. Two-part pricing is visualised in Figure 8.10:

Figure 8.10 Two-part pricing

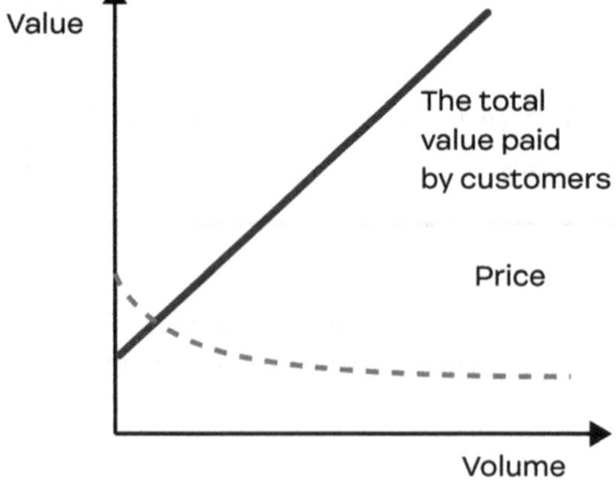

The philosophy underlying two-part pricing is the requirement that the fixed part of the fee should contribute to the costs of system construction. However, this method - if the prices are not chosen adequately – can be dangerous too. There are always potential buyers who cannot afford (or are not willing) to pay for the connection or the fixed price of telephone use.

EXHIBIT 8.7. HOW DO CONSUMERS CHOOSE BETWEEN FIXED PRICED SUBSCRIPTION AND FEE DEPENDING ON USE?

There is plenty of evidence that consumers prefer a flat rate to paying for individual calls. Some of the evidence is better considered as anecdotal, but there are factual surveys as well, proving that the majority of consumers prefer a flat rate. Most examples are related to telephone services. In the 1970s the American Bell System offered its subscribers a choice between the traditional, subscription fee of USD 7.50 allowing unlimited local calls and the new billing system based on calls, with a fix part of USD 5 per month, allowing 50 calls and a price of USD 0.05 per conversation. Those who had fewer than 100 calls per day had a better deal, nonetheless more than 50% of the consumers chose the flat rate. Other telephone companies had similar experiences.

Literature says that there are three main reasons why consumers prefer lump-sum subscriptions: (1) Safety: the so-called 'flat rate' protects from unexpected, large bills. (What, if my son comes home from the university and talks to his girlfriend 24 hours a day?) (2) Overestimation of telephone use: Consumers typically overestimate the length of time during which they use the service. (3) The uncertainty factor: if consumption is measured, the consumer starts to worry whether the call is worth the money that is charged for it. With a flat rate there is no worry whether calling the relatives is worth 5 cents.

All three factors are parts of the general consumer preference which gives absolute priority to simple and predictable charges.

Besides consumer preferences, there are other factors that make flat rates attractive for suppliers too; in areas like software, where network compatibility is important, many prefer these. Since the measurement of usage encourages consumers to be economical, this solution is not popular with suppliers, who would like to see users fall in love with their product, become familiar with the way it should be operated, and the commands, so that they would have difficulty exchanging it for another product.

Their ambition is to attract more and more people to test their products and thereby conquer more and more buyers. Flat rate subscriptions help them achieve this goal. Flat rate subscriptions even make it possible for the manufacturer to build a close relationship with the buyers. If payment is based strictly on calls, the supplier is not interested in collecting information about the buyer. On the other hand, subscription packages motivate them to get to know the customers' needs and customize their offer.

Source: Fishburn-Odlyzko-Siders, 1999.

8.6. Yield management

Yield management is a special case of price discrimination. Acting as a go-between the consumer segments' willingness to accept prices and the capacities available to suppliers and usually fixed (i.e. cannot or cannot easily be changed) it seeks a price structure that will generate the highest possible profit. This endeavour can be interpreted as a part of revenue management. The term was first used to describe the American practice of pricing introduced in the wake of the deregulation of American air traffic in 1978. The possibility of price discrimination developed in parallel with the computerized distribution system and the technology of yield management. (Isler, 2009).

Isler (2009) describes in detail the development of the global distribution system (GDS) used by the airline companies, how it was changed by the appearance of the Internet and the so-called e-agencies

and how yield management or revenue management became more efficient as a result. With the help of high capacity computers airlines can change their prices on a daily basis, depending on the demand between the two destinations in a specific part of the day, or on the given day, and on the seating capacity available. In 1989 United Airlines used 3000 different prices a day (Monroe, 1990:326). The system works on condition that the demand can be measured and checked immediately and in all parts of the service. (If the airline can see on the computers that a flight will not be full at the previously defined prices or the preliminary registrations, it can immediately decide to offer further price cuts.)

Figure 8.11 is an excellent illustration of yield management.

Figure 8.11. Yield management

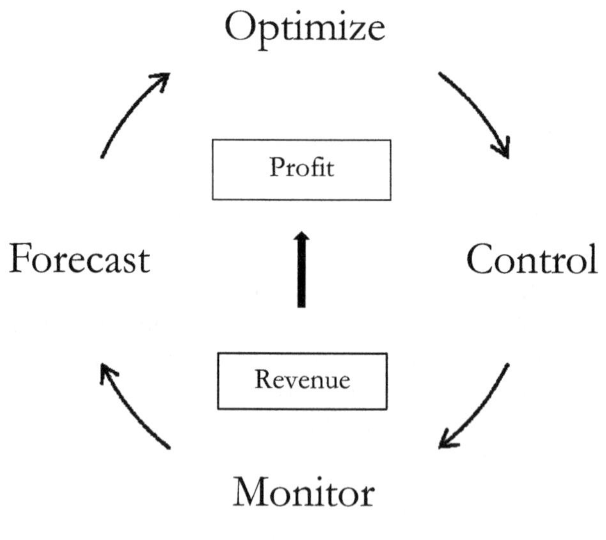

Yield management is successfully applied in the hotel industry (Marriott, International Hotels) car rentals (Herz) and cruising (Royal Caribbean Cruise Lines). However, in literature we can find examples for situations when the introduction of the method was far from successful, and the firms suffered serious losses.

Yield management can be applied with success in services where demand and the conditions of operation meet the following requirements:

- Capacities are relatively stable (the number of rooms in a hotel, or the number of seats on a plane) and cannot be stored,
- It is relatively easy to segment the market – especially from the viewpoint of price sensitivity.
- The service can be ordered in advance
- The fixed costs of the offer are relatively high, i.e. the role of operational leverage is quite important.

- There is great fluctuation in demand
- Demand is relatively easy to predict
- The information system available is sufficiently efficient

EXHIBIT 8.8. HOW TO OBTAIN GOOD FLIGHT TICKETS

(CNN)Travellers probably find the price of flight tickets the most mysterious. One minute they are soaring, then suddenly become affordable but by the time you are ready to book your ticket, prices are up again. They can make you feel dizzier than afternoon traffic Friday afternoon at Chicago's O'Hare airport.

In the hope of getting to know the system better, we have talked to one of the designers, Dr Richard Larson, professor at MIT, and also expert of revenue management. He is engaged in the study of models, which examine the profitability of services similar to air traffic. Larson used to work for American Airlines and the Sabre group as well.

He has some ideas about how to obtain the best possible flight tickets: "This is like gambling" he says. In operation research it is called 'action-timing problem'. There is a certain time when you get the opportunity to make a decision and once you have committed yourself, there is no way back.

It means that you had better book your seat as soon as possible, taking advantage of the cheap tickets offered to early bookers. However, it is important not to commit ourselves, because we might find a better offer later on, therefore - besides early booking - Larson recommends that we should choose a ticket, which can be returned with a refund.

"With a ticket like that in my hand it is easier to make phone calls: perhaps you can end up with an even cheaper, not refundable offer."

Not refundable? Well, it is not true. Well, you have bought that non-refundable ticket to Timbuktu, and two weeks later prices fell? No problem. Larson says, it is not impossible that in case you find a cheaper ticket, you are still on the winning side even if you pay the 50 or 75 dollar fine, that is the usual fine for cancelling

In the case of yield management, it is important to measure the correlation between the capacities available and their maximum exploitation. In literature, this ratio is called the I*ndex of Asset Revenue Generating Efficiency* (ARGE)

Let us see, as an example, how this index is calculated for a hotel. The basic assumption is that the list price of the hotel's 60 rooms out of the 100 is \$100 per night and the remaining 40 rooms cost \$80 each. On a certain day 50 rooms were sold for \$90, and 35 rooms for \$75. The I*ndex of Asset Revenue Generating Efficiency (ARGE) is:*

$$\text{ARGE} = \frac{(50 \times 90) + (35 \times 75)}{(60 \times 100) + (40 \times 80)} = 0.7745 \text{ i.e. } 77.45\%$$

This index is not the same as the simple index of capacity exploitation that hotels normally calculate from the rooms booked or available (the latter being 85/100 in this case, or 85%).

The purpose of yield management or the application of the ARGE index is to help the service provider find the optimum between the exploitation of the capacities and maximizing the revenues. As Kimes writes (1989:348):

"Yield management is a method which assists the firm to

sell the right goods in stock

to the right buyer

at the right time

at the right price.

EXHIBIT 8.9. AN EXAMPLE FOR THE ADVANTAGE OF YIELD MANAGEMENT

Let us check the above statements with a simple example quoted by Isler (2009: 256). We can assume that it costs a two-seater plane USD 1,400 to fly from point A to point B. There are two potential passengers, one willing to pay USD1,100 and the other only USD 600 for the trip.

It is easy to calculate that there is no single price that would meet this need. If the price were set at USD 600, both could travel, but there would be no return on the costs; if the price were USD 1,100 USD, only one passenger would fly and there would be no return on the costs in this case either.

The conclusion is that the plane cannot take off (or, if it does, it will make a loss).

Now let us suppose that prices can be discriminated, and one passenger pays USD 1,100, while the other only US 500. As a result, the revenue from the tickets will be USD 1,500, (which is USD 100 more than the costs of the flight). Both passengers can fly and, what is more, both of them pay USD 100 less than the reservation price. Everybody can be satisfied with the happy ending: the aeroplane has a producer surplus of USD 100 while the passenger's consumption surplus is USD 200.

Yet, there is something fishy about the example. The passenger who paid twice as much as the other feels he was taken in. And this outcome is found not only in this story. In today's world of YM or RM we may very well have people sitting next to one another on the plane, or staying in hotel rooms with the same level of comfort and service who have paid significantly different prices. Don't they feel this kind of 'supplier' behaviour is unethical? Well, certainly there are opinions like that. Some authors have also had a serious discussion about this issue (Kimes-Wirtz, 2003; Odlyzko, 2003; Armstrong, 2006; Wirtz – Kimes2007; Gerardi-Shapiro, 2009, Heo-Lee, 2010).

8.6.1. Price discrimination, yield or revenue management - ethical considerations

What price discrimination and yield management have in common is that both want to sell the same product to different buyers or different buyer groups at different prices without having any justification for such price differences in terms of costs. A lot of economists agree that price

discrimination leads to greater efficiency - in the case of sellers there is no doubt about it and often, in the case of buyers as well - than a one-price policy and, as such, contributes to the growth of general welfare.

If customers do not consider the practice followed by the firm fair and honest, they may turn their backs on it and, as a result, the firm loses clients. (It is of course, the customers who pay more that consider the practice to be discriminatory and the positive attitude of those who pay less can compensate for this effect. It is in the fundamental interest of companies to make efforts to have fewer and fewer people considering price discrimination immoral, This, however, requires a deeper insight into customers' opinion of or attitude to correctness in price setting of this kind.

Wirtz and Kimes (2007) studied in detail the way consumers perceive the fairness, honesty and justice of discriminated prices applied in revenue management. Using their ideas and extending them over other modes of price discrimination we can conclude that the perception of different prices (that cannot be justified with the costs) is influenced by two things:

(1) the unambiguity of the 'fence' separating the prices and

(2) the way the different prices are presented.

The perception of correctness or incorrectness is, of course, motivated by the way and degree in which the customer is involved, i.e. which side they take and whether they are beneficiaries or victims of the discrimination. Another motivating factor of correctness is whether the customers know the practice that has developed and been followed so far.

All that has been said so far is summarized in the model shown in Figure 8.12.

Figure 8.12. Model of perceived correctness and fairness in price discriminations

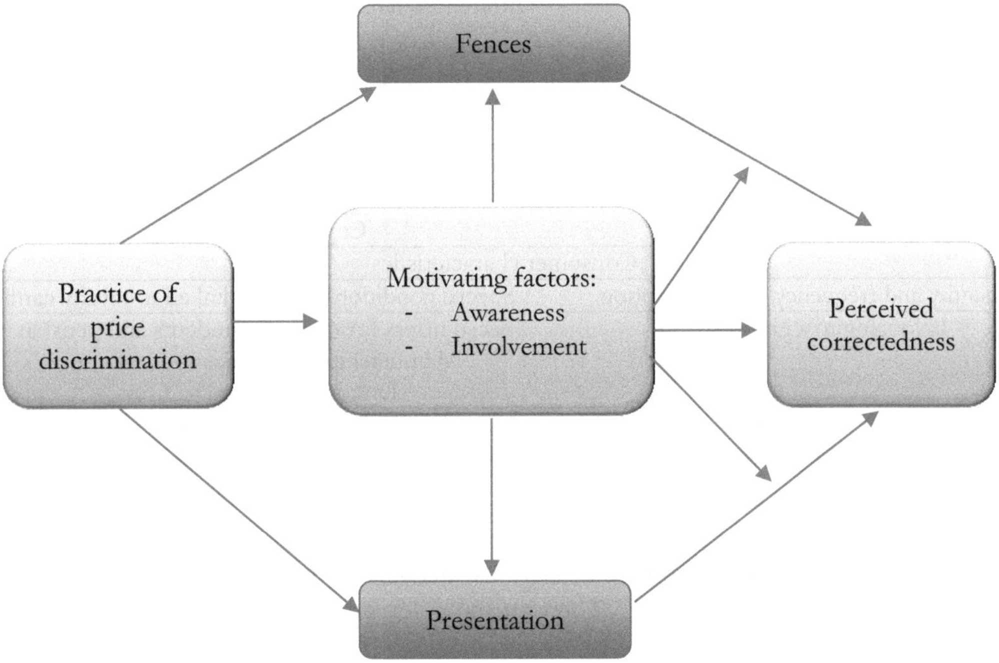

Based on the model by Wirtz- Kimes (2007:233) adapted by the author

8.6.2. Justification of the separation, "the fence"

Let us review first the issue of the fence that separates the prices. Speaking about the sports arena we mentioned that a multiple-price solution can only be introduced if the sectors are *physically separated.* The basis of the separation in this case was the distance from the stage or how well the stage could be seen. Those who want to see the play more closely are charged more for seats in a sector closer to the stage and physically separated as well. This practice is well known and accepted. It is time now to see what kind of 'fences" we can find: Lovelock and Wirtz (2007:140) grouped the possible fences as shown in Table 8.3.

Table 8.3. Fences used in price discrimination

Fences	Examples
Physical (commodity linked) fences	
Linked to the basic product	Flight classes (business/economy) Size and model of the rented car Size and furniture of the hotel room Location of the seat in the theatre.
Complementary services	Breakfast is included in the price of the hotel room Parking Free car on golf links
Level of service	Priority on waiting list, separate waiting room/lounge Higher level service (food and drinks) Personal(ized) service
Non-physical fences	
Linked to transaction	
Time of ordering or booking	Special offer linked to advance booking
Place of ordering or booking	Different airfare for plane tickets booked in different countries Cheaper prices for on-line booking
Linked to consumption	
Time and length of consumption	In the restaurant before 6.00pm. At least 5 days' stay Weekends
Place of consumption	City centre, outskirts
Consumer characteristics	
Quantity and frequency of consumption	Special conditions/actions linked to loyalty cards
Belonging to a group	Special offers for children, students and pensioners Membership in organizations (alumni) Discounts offered to firms
Size of the group	Discounts for groups
Geographical position	Special offers for domestic passengers in contrast with foreigners

Source: Lovelock-Wirtz, 2007: 140

Most people know the special prices offered to students and pensioners and accept them, consequently this fence is rated as "fair". There are, however, other fences that are not considered as fair by everybody.

8.6.3. The way price discrimination is presented

There are several ways in which different prices of the same product or service can be presented to various consumer groups distinguished and separated by various 'fences':

- It is possible to mark the different prices simply with the sum itself in the price list. For example, in the 2016 price list of the London Eye you can just find the prices: adults (16+) £24.95; children: (3-15): £19.50 (See: http://www.londoneye.com/tickets-and-prices/saver-tickets/) with the remark that in case of online booking a 15% discount is offered.

- The different ticket prices can be presented in another way as well, e.g. in the form of a *special offer*. 'Between September 10, 2016 and October 31 every student, teacher and employee of the Hungarian higher education service is eligible to a 10% discount on the list price of every MacBook13" 2.4 Ghz and MacBook Pro 13" 2.4 GHz model bought in our store; this advertisement appeared on the home page of one of the Hungarian chains.

- Similarly, *extra charges* can also be part of the presentation. On the cover of the price list of Halfen GmbH the following warning can be read: "A note concerning the present price list. You are charged the material and alloying charges valid on the day of delivery."

It is self-evident that most people prefer to belong to the beneficiaries, rather than to those who suffer a loss, therefore it benefits sellers to emphasize the 'allowance' side of the prices. If a hairdresser applies higher prices on Fridays and Saturdays, she can present it in two ways: either by announcing the extra charge, or by offering a discount for the other days of the week. Research in this topic has found that people are happier with the second version.

8.6.4. Ways of increasing perception of correctness

Firms are interested in letting fewer and fewer customers consider their price discrimination methods incorrect or unfair. Reports of research in this field recommend that in order to achieve this firms should:

- emphasize -whenever possible – the benefit side and

- improve – by all means – spreading information about the 'fence' (leaflets, information given by front office staff, internet, etc.)

EXHIBIT 8.10. PRICE DISCRIMINATION - INFORMATION TECHNOLOGY - VULNERABILITY OF PRIVACY

The unprecedented development of IT supports the application of increasingly sophisticated price discrimination. A few decades ago it would have been unimaginable for Coca Cola to experiment with a vending machine – as happened in 2000 – that would automatically increase prices on hot days, and vice-versa (this experiment was later prohibited – as indicated by Odlyzko, 2003). It would also have been unheard of that, while searching for a book on Amazon, we would be informed what other books were purchased by those who bought the one we are considering and, what is more, be recommended a package featuring books we are interested in, a package cheaper than the total of the individual books.

Well this development might be welcomed with pleasure, but whether we like it or not it can harm our privacy. With on-line purchases, questionnaires, frequent buyer programmes etc. firms acquire a lot of information that allows them to make fully customized offers and prices for the customers (Odlyzko, 2003).

In summary we can fully agree with Andrew Odlyzko, Director of the Digital Technology Centre at the University of Minnesota, who said the following in an interview to Business Week: "More and more information about the customer, less and less privacy: modern technology is leading us to an unprecedented measure of price discrimination."

Source: Jane Black: Sharper Tools for Discriminatory Pricing, July31, 2003, Business Week

CHAPTER 9. PRODUCT LINES PRICING

OBJECTIVE 1 To establish the strategy of pricing product lines and product items belonging to the line and learning the methods and techniques used in calculating prices in order to express perceived differences in their customer value.

OBJECTIVE 2 To discuss what methods can be used in pricing complementary products.

OBJECTIVE 3 To understand the relationship between the positioning of products, product lines, branding policy and price and how prices can be used to promote products and product lines.

9.1 Introduction

There are very few companies which produce or distribute only one or just a few products. The offerings of companies include a wide variety of more or less related products. If the management of a company has a marketing perspective, it should make sure that prices are also established in a market-oriented way, and this market-oriented corporate and marketing policy should be reflected by the product structure, by product prices and the pricing structure as well. The management of company offerings can be examined at three levels (Figure 9.1). The price strategy must be established and the prices must be determined for each level.

Figure 9.1 The three levels of managing company offerings

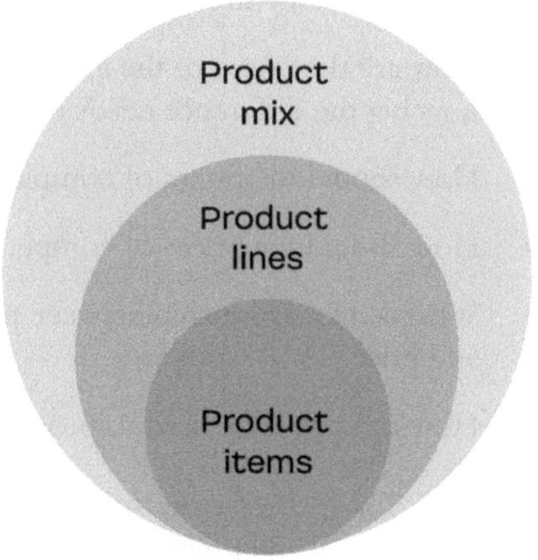

The central category of product management is the product line, and the same applies to price policy too. Figure 9.2 presents a hypothetical company which produces and distributes 3 product lines: product lines A, B and C. A product line includes a group of products, items that are related on the basis of certain criteria. The notion of product line has spread in company practice, so this category can be treated in a flexible way from a grouping criteria point of view: in some cases it is the similarity of the needs that link all the products, in others it is the similarity of the consumers, the materials used or the technology applied.

The concepts characterising product structure (and the offering) are the following:

- the length of the product line (the number of products belonging to the product line),
- the width of the product mix (the number of product lines offered),

- the depth of product line (the number of varieties offered from a product item), and
- the consistency of the product structure, in other words the expression of the extent of similarity between product lines, the consistency and the coherence of their structure.

Figure 9.2 The structure of the product mix

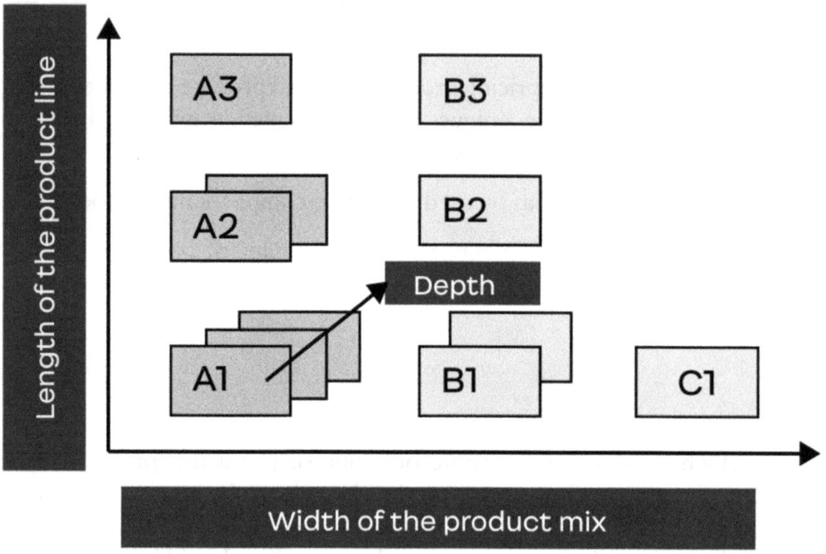

Pricing decisions concern the product items and the product lines. Pricing policy, similarly to the whole of product management, is closely related to branding policy as well. The frameworks of product and price management and their room for manoeuvre are determined by the company's policy decision about which part the market it wants to operate in (low end, middle, high end), as discussed in the chapter dealing with price strategies. The strategic questions of price structure within the main framework are the following:

- How are the prices of the individual product items in a product line related, in other words: how big the difference needs to be between the prices of the different products?
- How should the prices of complementary products be determined?
- How should the prices of competitive products be determined?
- What is the relationship between product, the positioning of the product line, branding policy and price?
- How can prices be used to promote products and product lines?

9.2. Establishing the price of product items belonging to a product line

There are theoretical and practical considerations which play an important role in setting the price of the individual product items of a product line. Let us assume that the general price level of the product line has already been determined by the corporate strategy (high prices, high quality, medium prices, medium quality, etc.). The next important decision is to determine the size of the price difference between the individual product items. This decision is influenced by several factors:

- When setting the price, the company should know how the different product items of the same product line are linked to each other in serving customers' needs. There are two basic cases:
    - The different product items in the product line are *complementary*, if they have to be used together. This means that the demand (sales) for one product results in the need for the other. (For example, the sale of men's suits in a clothes shop may typically induce the need for men's shirts and ties which match the suit.) This issue will be discussed under "The pricing of complementary products".
    - The second basic case is when the products belonging to a product line can substitute for or compete with each other. Focus, Escort and Mondeo, belonging to the Ford product line of passenger cars, not only compete with similar products of other manufacturers but, to a certain extent, with each other as well and price plays a special role in this competition.
- The branding policy companies pursue can also be very important. From a product line pricing point of view there can be two cases with different impacts:
    - The items of a product line are interconnected by their brands (umbrella brand: e.g. *Ford Focus*, *Ford Escort* etc.); this obviously requires the harmonisation of not only the products but their prices as well.
    - Each member of the product line is distributed under a separate brand name, and they are seen as independent products in customers' minds. (Good examples include the branding policies of Procter & Gamble or Unilever.) This type of branding policy allows more room for independent price setting.

Let's take as an example a product line where the individual product items can substitute for each other and are sold under an umbrella brand. The chapter on the relationship between prices and consumer behaviour described how consumers of the target market develop a scale of acceptable prices for themselves. Acceptable prices have an upper and a lower limit. These limits should be taken into account when planning the prices of a product line. It must be emphasized, however, that consumers differ from each other individually and across consumer segments as well when it comes to price thresholds. It is therefore very important to conduct a thorough market analysis before planning a product line and its prices.

Product lines incorporate a range of products which serve a similar need. This product range can be set in ascending or descending order depending on the benefits the products can offer. Planning the prices of product lines always starts by determining the limit values (the lower, upper or both). It is followed by determining the price difference between the products following each other in the ranking. *It must be clear, however, that only those products should be differentiated by prices the benefits of which are perceived differently by the consumers.*

To provide a theoretical support to this method let us recall the Weber–Fechner law.

$$R = k (\log S) + a$$

where **R** is the intensity of response,

S is the intensity of the stimulus,

k and **a** are constants.

According to this law consumers' perception of the price differences depend on the magnitude of the said price differences. The perception of difference has a threshold, which is called *differential price threshold.* Any differences lower than the threshold value are not perceived by the consumers, and their influence on the purchasing decision is therefore negligible.

The first task is to determine the price (**P_{min}**) of the lowest ranked product item (the one with the fewest benefits, the cheapest). The price of the next product in the rank can be determined with the help of component **k**. This method allows us to obtain a price structure which reflects the differences perceivable by consumers.

It follows from the formula that it is not the absolute value of these differences that matters, but the relative difference which reflects the threshold value of consumer perception. If consumers consider $2,000 as differentiating for a price of $10,000, then the perception threshold for a price of $20,000 will be $4,000.

Staying at theoretical level we can conclude that once we have determined the lowest price (**P_{min}**), the price of the product ranked **j** (Monroe, 2003: 403) can be calculated using the formula

$$P_j = (P_{min})k^{j-1}$$

where **k** is a constant number with a value higher than one. To perform this calculation we must know the value of **k**, the differential price threshold which is still perceived by consumers.

Let's check this calculation using a hypothetical example. Let's assume that the lowest ranked member of a passenger car product line is priced for $20,000, and the differential price threshold is $2,000 (that is $k = 1.1$). The price of the product ranked 4 is the following according to the formula:

$$P_4 = \$20000 \times 1.1^{4-1} = \$26620$$

When planning the product line, not only is the setting of the minimum price (Pmin) important, but the setting of the maximum price (Pmax) as well.

The price of the other items in the product line can be determined within the two limit values according to the following formula:

$$\log k = \frac{1}{n-1}(\log P_{max} - \log P_{min})$$

We have tested this calculation method through a real example, by reviewing the starting prices of the models of Mercedes-Benz cars sold in Hungary. The price of the first item (Mercedes-Benz Citan Kombi) expressed in dollars was $22,745. The basic price of the most expensive model (S-class Cabriolet) was $148,015. The offerings included 29 models. The following figure shows a graphical presentation of the offerings.

It is clearly visible from the graph that the company largely used premium pricing for its last six models, because these prices do not fit the line formed by the prices of the first 22 models. It is therefore advisable to separate the offering and do the calculation for the first 22 models only.

The following data are available for the formula:

P_{max} = $59 127 (this is the real price of model 22)

P_{min} = $22 745

n= 22

First the value of **k** was calculated as follows:

log k = 1/(22 - 1) (log 59127 - log 22745),

log k = 1/21 (4.771786 – 4.356886),

log k = 0.019757,

k = 1.0465

Having the value of k allows us to calculate the price of the models situated between the two ends and to compare them with the actual prices offered by the car dealer (Table 9.1.).

EXHIBIT 9.1 THE HIGHEST AND LOWEST PRICE POINTS OF MERCEDES AND KIA BRANDS

The real strategic question is how to fix the prices of the two poles (namely the pricing of the cheapest and the most expensive members of the product line). These are the two points which draw the most attention of consumers, which are most likely compared with the competitors, and which are mostly recalled. *And these two poles can also serve as an indication to which market segment the given company is competing in.* Let's take for example the lowest and highest price points of Mercedes Benz and Kia in Hungary. According to the information available in January 2017 the list price of the cheapest product by Mercedes calculated at central rates on 1st January amounted to $22,745 compared to the $8,884 price of the cheapest model by Kia, while the difference between the prices of the top models was $148,015 as opposed to $43,071 as shown below.

The lowest and highest price points of Mercedes Benz and Kia cars (in dollars, January 2017).

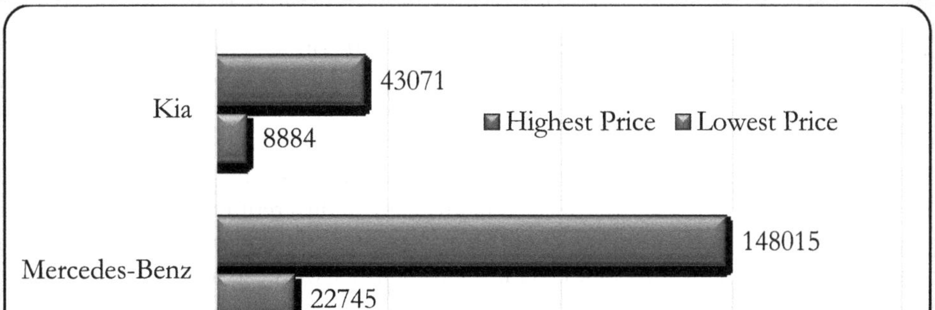

Source: list prices available on the Hungarian homepages of Mercedes and Kia companies on 1st January, 2017.

The comparison of the minimum and maximum prices leads us to the conclusion that Mercedes-Benz and Kia are not direct competitors.

Derivated from File: Mercedes Benz Logo 11.jpg,
Public Domain, https://commons.wikimedia.org/w/index.php?curid=30702375
By Kia, Public Domain, https://commons.wikimedia.org/w/index.php?curid=47193597

Figure 9.3 The prices of Mercedes products (in dollars, January 2017)

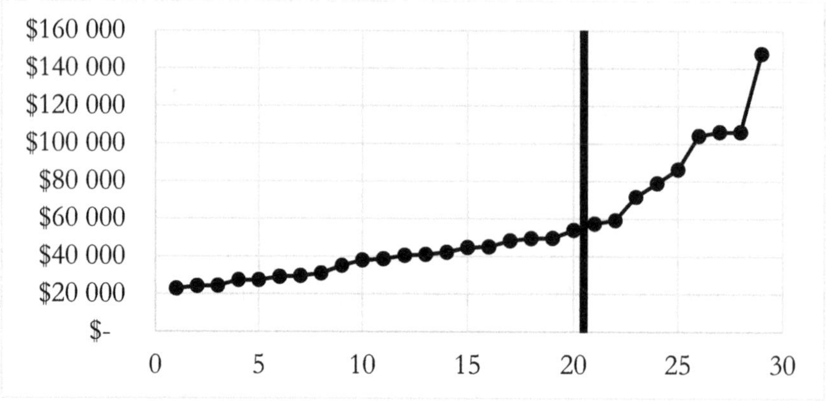

Let us summarise the method for determining price differences within the product line.

1. The products belonging to a product line should be ranked according to the benefits they offer by starting with the product with the fewest benefits to the one with the most.
2. The price of the cheapest member of the product line needs to be determined.
3. The price of the most expensive member of the product line needs to be determined.
4. The value of **k** needs to be calculated using the formula:

$$\log k = \frac{1}{n-1}(\log P_{max} - \log P_{min})$$

5. Knowledge of **k** allows calculating the price of the product ranked **j** using the formula:

$$\mathbf{P_j = (P_{min})k^{j-1}}.$$

6. The values obtained can only function as a tool, the theoretical value of each member of the product line can be modified according the pricing and marketing policy of the offerer.

9.2. The depth of the product line and the prices

Product line depth refers to the number of varieties of products offered in the same product item (brand). In the case of cars, these varieties can manifest in the different engine size, performance or different equipment. The special features of different varieties of packaged food items can include different pack sizes or different flavours. Deciding on the price of these individual product varieties is not easy.

Staying with the offer by Mercedes-Benz in Hungary, let's review the different characteristics of the depth of the passenger car product line (Figure 9.4.). We have selected five basic models (class A-B-C-E-S) out of the 29 cars listed in table 9.1 to be included in the figure. It can be seen that the company has offered a total of 77 varieties of these 5 models in January 2017 (excluding options). A very reasonable consideration lies behind such a deep assortment of varieties: customer service can be more personalised, the offerings can better meet different needs. Different consumer groups tend to value different things, and there are even consumers who would rather pay for higher performance in the price of a smaller car than buy a larger car. The price of the different product varieties can overlap.

Table 9.1 The real and calculated prices of the Ford car product line

No.	Model	The prices of Pappas Car Dealer ($)	Calculated price ($)	Difference ($)	Difference (%)
1	CITAN KOMBI	22 745	22745	0	0
2	B-CLASS	24 043	23 802	-241	-1%
3	A-CLASS	24 338	24 909	571	2%
4	GLA	27 260	26 067	-1 193	-4%
5	C-LIMUZIN	27 291	27 279	-12	0%
6	CLA COUPÉ	28 996	28 548	-448	-2%
7	CLA SHOOTING BRAKE	29 572	29 875	303	1%
8	C-CLASS T MODEL	30 846	31 265	418	1%
9	C-CLASS COUPÉ	34 967	32 718	-2 248	-6%
10	SLC	37 844	34 240	-3 604	-10%
11	SPRINTER COMBI	38 636	35 832	-2 804	-7%
12	E LIMUZIN	40 477	37 498	-2 979	-7%
13	V-CLASS	40 963	39 242	-1 721	-4%
14	C-CLASS CABRIOLET	42 095	41 067	-1 028	-2%
15	E-CLASS COUPÉ	44 685	42 976	-1 708	-4%
16	GLC	45 036	44 975	-61	0%
17	E-CLASS T M	48 181	47 066	-1 115	-2%
18	E-CLASS CABRIO	49 421	49 255	-166	0%
19	GLC COUPÉ	49 694	51 545	1 851	4%
20	GLE	53 810	53 942	132	0%
21	GLS COUPÉ	57 263	56 450	-813	-1%
22	GLS SHOOTING BRAKE	59 127	59 127	0	0
23	GLE COUPÉ	71 653			
24	GLS	79 071			
25	S-LIMUZIN	86 347			
26	SL	104 243			
27	G-CLASS	106 196			
28	S-CLASS COUPÉ	106 288			
29	S-CLASS CABRIOLET	148 015			

Source: Par Jakub "Flyz1" Maciejewski — Travail personnel, CC BY-SA 4.0, https://commons.wikimedia.org/w/index.php?curid=48136464
Note: The biggest difference (10%) occurs in the case of Mercedes SLC shown in the above picture. Here the real price is 10% higher than the calculated price. It is no doubt due to the fact that the model is new (2016-os) and offers several benefits which justify the higher price.

As can be seen in Figure 9.4, some of the top varieties in class C are offered at a higher price than those in the higher ranked class E. The products and prices belonging to the same product line should be built reasonably upon each other. Pricing in the depth of the product line is similar on the small

scale as the pricing of the whole of the product line, as the principles governing this type of pricing are the same as those governing the pricing of the product line.

Figure 9.4 The different varieties of the Mercedes-Benz passenger car product line (in 2017, in thousands of dollars)

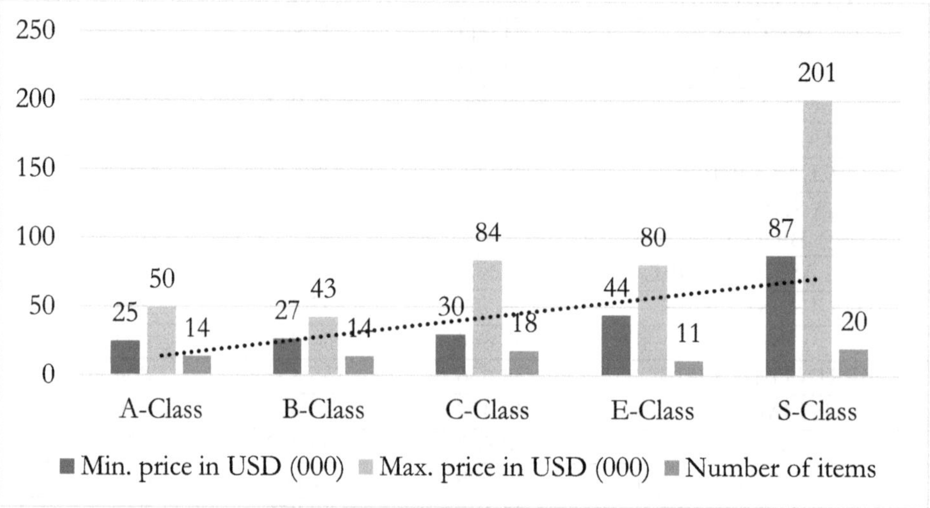

1. The price of each variety should be determined by being compared to the other in such a way that the difference in the prices reflect the differences offered by the product and perceived by the consumers.
2. It is particularly important to determine the two limit values within the different varieties of the same product. The lowest and the highest prices most influence consumers' value perception.
3. Pricing the assortment may lead to overlaps among the different items of a product line due the different benefits offered. Attention must be paid to the planning of overlaps, so that they don't interfere with customers' value perception. The prices of the product line and the pricing of the assortment should follow the logic of starting from the lowest price and progressing towards the higher price (see the trend line in the figure).

9.3. Pricing issues with regard to product line stretching

Modern planning of company offers gives priority to product line. This requires the development of basic competences which determine the identity and the image of the product line in the long term, and lay the basis for a coherent market positioning. An important issue in the management of the product line is its stretching by adding one or more new items. Stretching can happen in four directions. The move in any direction has different price and market related consequences. Figure 9.5. presents these possible directions.

The four ways of stretching a product line can be narrowed down to two typical problem areas with regard to prices and consumers' value perception:

9.3.1. Pricing in case of product line filling

Filling simply means that the company extends its product line with new products which match the existing ones in order to satisfy the market needs in a differentiated way. The limit values of the

product line remain the same, and the identity and the market position of the product line does not change either. It is, however, a basic requirement that the prices of the new items in the product line should fit the line of existing products. The pricing methods of the product line, the determination of the price differentials can provide guidance for this. An example of filling was when Toyota launched the Auris, a more youthful variety of its very successful brand Corolla onto the market. The base price of the two cars was nearly the same.

The market position of the product line changes in all the other three cases of stretching. The lower, the top or both limit values of the product line change. It also modifies how consumers evaluate the product line as a whole because, according to research results, consumers judge the whole product line on the basis of its limit values. It is referred to as a trading-up or trading-down strategy in the literature. These movements may carry several market policy concepts which can have an impact on the prices to be set and the branding policy to be applied.

Figure 9.5. The possible directions of stretching the product line.

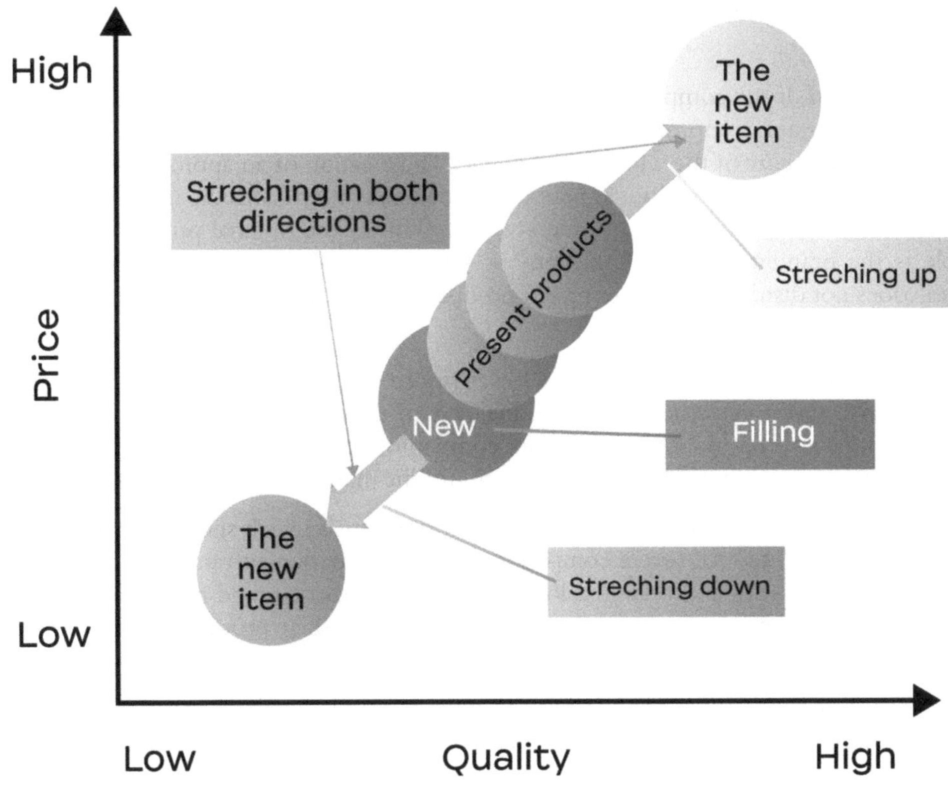

9.3.2. Pricing of product lines in the case of downward stretching

Downward stretching means that the original product line is extended by adding a lower priced product. One of the most well-known examples in international marketing literature is the introduction of the Saturn by General Motors.

This car was designed with the explicit aim of creating competition to the cheap but good quality cars imported from Japan. The starting price of the car manufactured in the brand new factory was 10 thousand dollars (for a detailed description see the article entitled "Success at a price", published in

By Reedred - A feltöltő saját munkája, CC BY-SA 3.0, https://commons.wikimedia.org/w/index.php?curid=7722105

the *The Economist* No. 323, 6/27:92), and which enjoyed great market success during the two years following its introduction, mainly due to its low price. Sales surged and its quality was also considered to be very good by the consumers. However, many problems occurred which allow for the generalisation of some of the problem areas related to downward stretching:

- If the company does not want to harm the image of the whole product line with the introduction of a new, low-priced item, there is a risk that the product will not be profitable on its own. (One of the main problems with Saturn was that it did not generate profit for GM, even after two years.) There are cases when companies consciously take this risk. They create loss leader products which are used to 'give a boost' to the turnover of the product line.

- On the other hand, if the company wants to create the new product to be profitable, it will have to make certain compromises with quality. This may have repercussions on the perception of the quality of the whole product line. The creation of an appropriate branding policy can provide protection in this situation. The company may distribute the new product under a new brand name which consumers will not link to the original product line. One example is the branding policy of the famous Japanese watch manufacturer Seiko. The company does not distribute its lower priced products under the brand Seiko, but under the brand name Alba.

- The introduction of a new item, especially a lower-priced one, in the product line can always entail the risk of *product cannibalisation.* If the majority of the turnover generated by the new product is not taken from the brands of other competitors but from the other items on the product line, the introduction of the new product into the market will not reach its objective.

As a result of the difficult market situation following the economic crisis which started in 2008, many so-called brand producers had to face severe competition from new market entrants, mostly coming from the large emerging countries and selling at lower prices. What can a brand producer do if the competitor companies, which pursue an imitation strategy, distribute their products at significantly lower (sometimes 50–60% lower) prices?

It can choose either not to react or to lower its prices itself. Both could be risky. The company might not be able to afford a significant price reduction because of its costs, while not reacting may result in the loss of market share. A third possible way is for the brand producer to introduce a lower positioned product as well. This strategy is often referred to as the 'two-product strategy against low-price competition' (Hilleke–Butscher, 1997). The positioning of these so-called second products can be illustrated as shown in Figure 9.6.

How should the price of such a product be determined? The answer to this question can only be given in view of the brand policy and quality. If the quality of the product is similar and the brand name is the same, it is not advisable to price the new item lower than 10–15%, otherwise the image of the original product line might suffer. If the brand name is different, the quality is lower and the

distribution channels used are different, the difference in price could be larger and the price might even be 30–35% lower in certain cases.

Figure 9.6. Positioning of the so-called second brand.

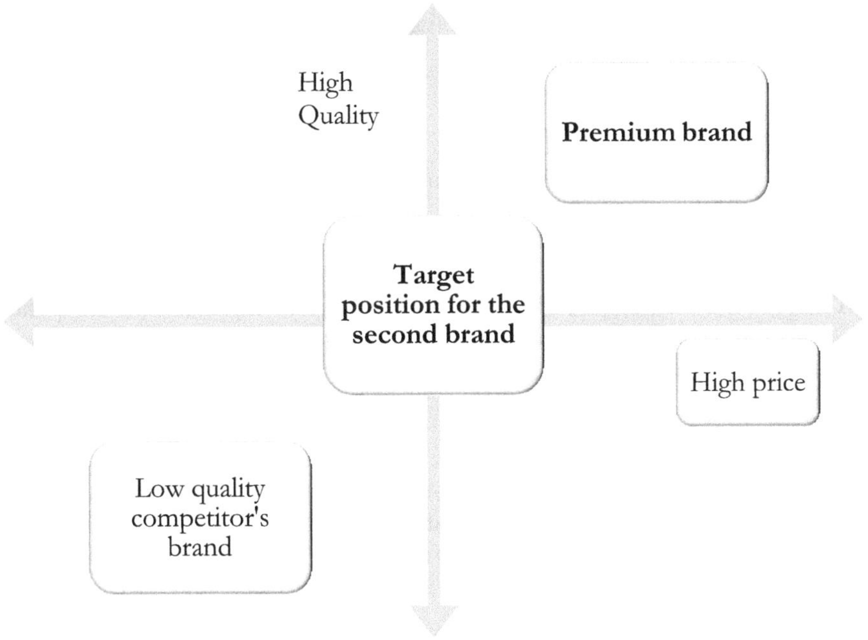

> A distributor of computers recounted that the company's purchaser had regularly bought the computers with the second best performance, even though the first one would have better met the needs of the company.
>
> When they asked him the reason, he simply replied that his superiors would have never agreed to him purchasing the most expensive item of a product line. The introduction of a higher priced product can solve such a problem too.

9.3.3. Pricing of product lines in the case of upward stretching

Upward stretching may lead to similar problems, although with opposite effects:

- The downside of a higher price is that the product may not be profitable on its own, because it cannot generate enough turnover. There are many companies that consciously take that risk. They do it because it allows them, for example, to increase the reference price of the other items in the product line. The most expensive product may seem more attractive to consumers than before if a new, more expensive variety appears on the market.
- Moving up in quality and price can be hindered by the relatively low image of established products. Product line management can protect against this by gradually pushing each product upward, which can take a long time, sometimes decades. For example, it took Audi almost one and a half decades to be acknowledged as one of the leaders.
- The new product may be distributed under a different brand name, using different

distribution channels and different marketing support than the earlier, established items in the product line. One of the most well-known examples for this strategy is the introduction of Lexus by Toyota.

Source: Mytho88 (original photo) - Mytho88's file: Image: MEGAWEB 09.jpg CC BY-SA 3.0CC BY-SA 3.0

The risk of product cannibalisation is generally very low in the case of upward stretching. If this risk appears, it may have a favourable impact on the company's results.

EXHIBIT 9.2 IS IT DAMAGING FOR PREMIUM BRANDS TO INTRODUCE CHEAPER PRODUCTS?

When in 2012-2013 Apple developed cheaper iPhone models to cope with the competition of Samsung the British Campaign Magazine put the question to marketing experts whether these cheaper products would damage the image of the premium brands. The answers were not unanimous:

- **Kristof Fahy**, Chief Marketing Officer, William Hill, said "no" and argued, "More people being able to afford an iPhone won't damage the brand, and could improve the iPhone apps eco-system by bringing greater distribution opportunities for developers. Brands should be able to stretch their offer, as long as they remain true to what is at their core."
- **Daryl Fielding**, Director, Daryl Fielding Consulting (formerly of Kraft Foods Europe) said "maybe", arguing "Companies can damage brands in the pursuit of volume in three ways. Undermining the brand's fundamental values, delivering poor quality to hit a particular price point, and by becoming ubiquitous."
- **Tracey Follows**, Chief Strategy Officer and Executive Partner, JWT London said "no" because, "In the telecommunications sector, innovation moves so quickly that a significant distance can be maintained, so that the high end always stays high end, and that will probably be the case for the extended Apple portfolio."
- **Ed Hayes,** Planning Director, Bloom said "maybe" and explained, "The A-Class is an ongoing success for Mercedes because its perceived quality is the same as its other models. It's cheaper because it's smaller, making it convenient for urban driving, and it doesn't feel like the poor man's choice. If Apple prioritises benefit over price, then the cheaper iPhone will make it appeal to a wider audience, but not erode brand value. The launch will have to be handled carefully. Using a sub-brand both to differentiate and get across the lead benefit would help."

Source: http://www.campaignlive.co.uk/article/1167582/damaging-premium-brands-introduce-cheaper-types-products-marketing-society-forum#fM0XUkTKbAhJUeQB.99 (02.01.2017)

9.4. The pricing of complementary products

By complementary products we mean that the sale of one product (say the 'main' product) triggers the sale of another product (let's call it a 'complementary' product). Many examples could be listed from practice. The most obvious ones include the correlation between the demand for razors and

razor blades, printers and cartridges, computers and operation programs etc. Pricing complementary products becomes problematic for a producer only if both products are manufactured by them. But the issue of pricing complementary products requires careful decisions in the commercial and in service sectors as well. Let's take mobile phones from the service sector and the sales generated by them, or any other similar examples.

Figure 9.7. Marketing the higher quality product line member.

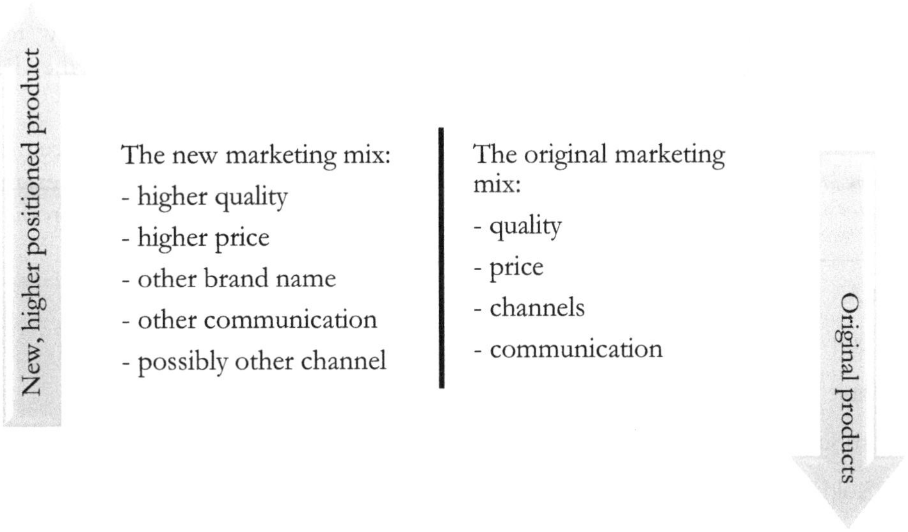

EXHIBIT 9.3. THE PREMIUM PRICE STRATEGY OF GILLETTE

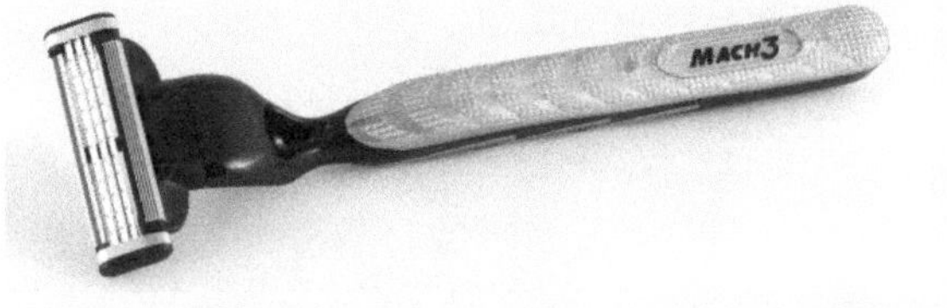

The pricing strategy of Gillette is clearly premium pricing. However, the quality of its products is accordingly very high as well. Products like Gillette's Mach 3 and now Gillette Mach 5 have taken the world by storm. The price level of Gillette shaving foam and gel is much more than its competitors but still Gillette has been able to maintain its customers' loyalty by its worth as well as marketing policies. Consumers are not afraid to pay the extra money in order to associate themselves with such an irreplaceable brand. Nowadays it is not easy to sway a customer's loyalty by a genuine price hike. The company is asking its consumers to place more value on emotions than on the cost price. The policy of Gillette is to encourage the customer to try its product at least once. The company is confident that after using this high quality product it will be difficult for the consumer to switch to other substandard items. Once the buyer is happy with the product, its high price does not matter.

Source: By Hitesh Bhasin Marketing mix of Gillette – Gillette marketing mix
November 29, 2016 http://www.marketing91.com/marketing-mix-of-gillette/
Photo by Crisco 1492 - Own work, CC BY-SA 4.0, https://commons.wikimedia.org/w/index.php?curid=42110706

In order for a company to be able to determine the prices of complementary products in an optimal way, it should be able to answer the following questions:

If both products are manufactured by the same company, what is the relationship between the manufacturing of the two products from a cost point of view?

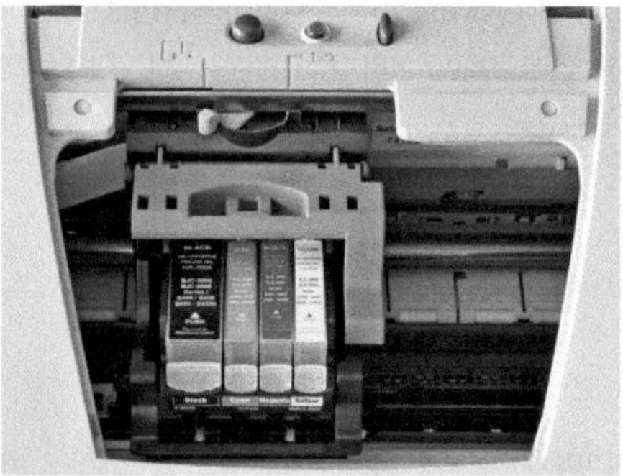

Canon S520 ink jet printer - opened.jpg
This file is licensed under the Creative Commons Attribution-Share Alike 2.5 Generic licence

- What is the price elasticity of the main product?
- How are the sales of the main and complementary products related?

In theory, complementary products can be priced independently (in isolation), or by taking into account the relationship between the demand for them.

Let's illustrate the difference between these two approaches through a hypothetical example. Let's assume that we want to sell a main product (A) and a complementary product (B).

Product A

Price: $1000

Unit variable cost: $600

Unit contribution: $400

Amount sold: 3000 pieces

Price elasticity of product demand: - 2.5

The sale of one product A induces the sale of 1.2 pieces from product B.

Product B

Price: $400

Unit variable cost: $200

Unit contribution: $200

Amount sold: 3,600 pieces

According to the two pricing methods, if the demand for the main product is elastic, it is advisable to price the main product low, because the induced extra sales of the complementary product can generate better gains (margin) for the company. In our example the 10% reduction in the price of the main product resulted in a 5.5% increase in the overall contribution of the two products (Table 9.2).

There are so-called main products, which can induce a much higher turnover for complementary products than their own (for example, mobile phones). In such cases the company can sell the main product below the level of variable costs, at a loss, or even for free, because these losses suffered will be sufficiently offset by the profit generated by the complementary product. Mobile phone service providers typically offer modern devices at a half or a quarter of the price if the consumer signs a one-year or two-year user agreement with them.

Companies producing and distributing complementary products should not base the setting of the prices on the costs (margins) calculated separately for each product, but rather on the joint contribution, or better to say on the profit per consumer.

Table 9.2 The result of decreasing the price of the main product by 10% when using complementary pricing ($).

Item	Isolated pricing		Complementary pricing	
	Product A	Product B	Product A	Product B
Price	1 000	400	900	400
Variable cost	600	200	600	200
Unit contribution	400	200	300	200
Sales (pc)	3 000	3 600	3 750	4 500
Total contribution	1 200 000	720 000	1 125 000	900 000
Total margin of the two products	1 920 000		2 025 000	

9.5. The pricing of spare parts and after sales services

The manufacturer of the products generally assumes the obligation to supply spare parts, repair and maintenance for production assets, especially for high value technological goods, but for consumer goods less frequently. These aftersales business activities account for a large proportion of the total sales in the different sectors, and an even larger proportion in the profit (margin) generating capacity of the sectors (Figure 9.8).

Figure 9.8. The importance of the after sales sector (%).

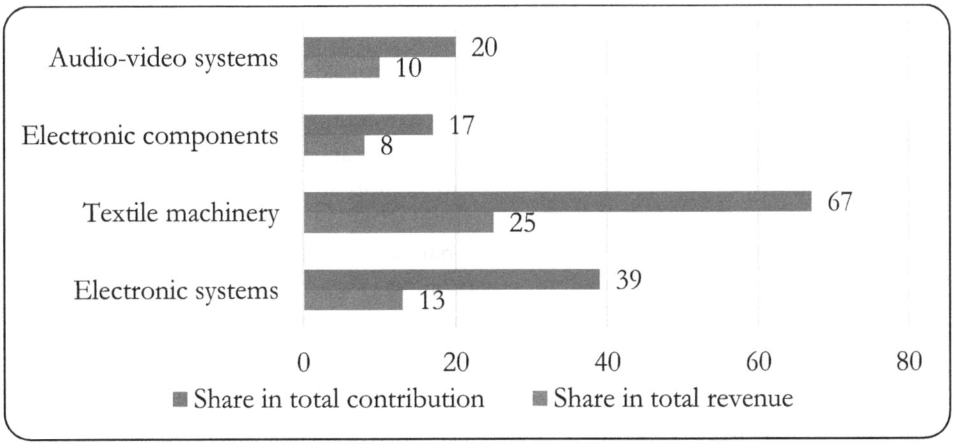

Source: From Knecht–Leszinsky–Weber, 1993: 80.

The pricing of these products and services is very similar to that of complementary products. The manufacturer of the original product is in a favourable position in supplying the spare parts necessary for the use of the product and repair and maintenance services following sales. The users of higher value products prefer, in most cases, to purchase original and replacement parts, as well as repair and maintenance services, from the original supplier who is the most skilled in the product. It is particularly true for industrial machinery, which plays a pivotal role in the buyer's production processes. Any stoppage due to a possible failure can cause huge additional costs and damage. Take, for instance, the process control computers used in chemical plants or in power plants, the parts of

aeroplanes, the maintenance of transport vehicles, etc. In these cases, the supplier will only be liable for damage arising from any breakdowns or failures if the user purchases the after sales services from the same supplier.

The original supplier of the product has a huge competitive advantage compared to other suppliers in providing spare parts, repair and maintenance services. The extent of the competitive advantage largely depends on the availability of interchangeable substitute products (spare parts), the size of the costs of switching the original product, as well as on how big an emphasis the company places on delivering fast and reliable service to its customers in the period following the sale of the original product. Knecht, Leszinsky and Weber conducted a survey about consumer preferences in the field of electronics spare parts and services. Their conclusions are summarized in Figure 9.9.

It can be concluded from the above that the supplier of the original product acts correctly if it bases the prices of spare parts and related services on the value offered to the customers rather than on the production costs. The value provided to customers depends on three factors:

- What other alternatives are available for consumers? The offering can be exhaustive and reliable, but there might not be any other alternative, or it might be difficult to gain access to it.
- What damage could the failure of the product or the lack of related services cause to the customer during the use of the original product? The damage can range from minor to high-value.
- The value offered to customers also depends on how customer-oriented the operation of the spare parts supply and service is. The company Caterpillar, for example, delivers the necessary spare parts within 48 hours anywhere in the world.

Figure 9.9. Consumer preferences in the electronics spare part supply and service.

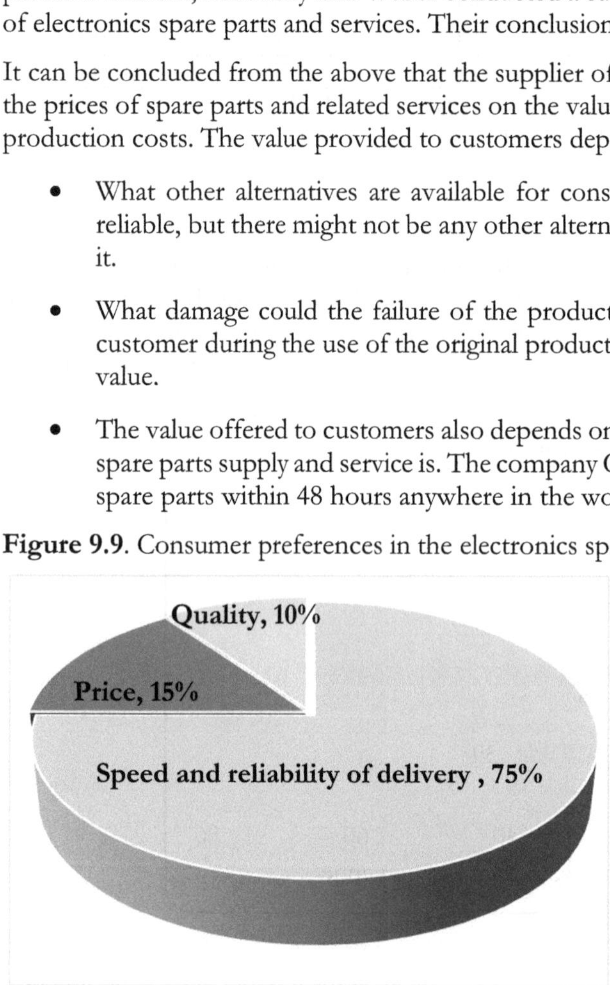

If customer value is outstanding, the supplier can achieve a high level of satisfaction among its customers even if it applies higher than usual prices. (This is what big brand car manufacturers do for example: the price of spare parts is several times higher than their production cost or their purchase price. Many have already concluded that if we were to purchase a car, part by part, it would cost 5-10 times more than the price of the car.) In the aftersales services sector the manufacturer even has the opportunity to differentiate higher prices compared to the original according to, for example, the speed of service. (A relatively high price for immediate services or availability within 24 hours, and lower price for service within a week, etc.)

CHAPTER 10. PRICE BUNDLING

OBJECTIVE 1 To establish what price bundling means and how product bundles can be priced in order allow bundle prices to generate higher turnover than pricing the products individually.

OBJECTIVE 2 To show the different attitudes of customers in case of pure and mixed bundles and to illustrate what unbundling means.

OBJECTIVE 3 To ascertain how bundling products may sometimes impact on competition law and may have adverse ethical considerations in the eyes of customers.

10.1 Introduction

In dealing with product line pricing we have discussed how a company with multiple products could determine the prices of products belonging to the same product line. The underlying assumption of the argument has been that every product has its price and consumers can buy these individual products separately. However, there is an increasingly popular business practice in which the different products and/or services are bundled, and consumers are offered these bundles.

It is not easy to distinguish between individual products or services and the bundles, because the individual products are composed of several components and they can even be complemented by different services; so many of the products can be considered as bundles in themselves. There is an endless list of other examples some of which are shown in Exhibit 10.1. Looking at the products and services offered to us, we can see that the number of products and services offered in a bundle is on the increase.

EXHIBIT 10.1. A FEW PRACTICAL EXAMPLES

Let's take a lawn mower as an example. The different parts of the machine can certainly be purchased individually and a very skilful person could assemble the machine at home. The lawn mower is therefore a bundle of the necessary parts. However, it is not considered to be a product or service bundle, because the different parts are necessarily related, and can only satisfy the given need (capability of cutting grass) together, in an assembled state.

Ham and eggs is also a bundle, because the ham and the eggs can be purchased separately. However, it cannot be considered as a bundle in the sense discussed here, because prepared together the ham and eggs can mean a type of food.

Letting a hotel room can also be thought of as a bundle, as the services of most hotels include the complimentary breakfast as well. However, it is not considered as a real bundle because providing breakfast has become an expected part of hotel services.

A daily paper or a scientific magazine is a bundle too: The Financial Times or the Harvard

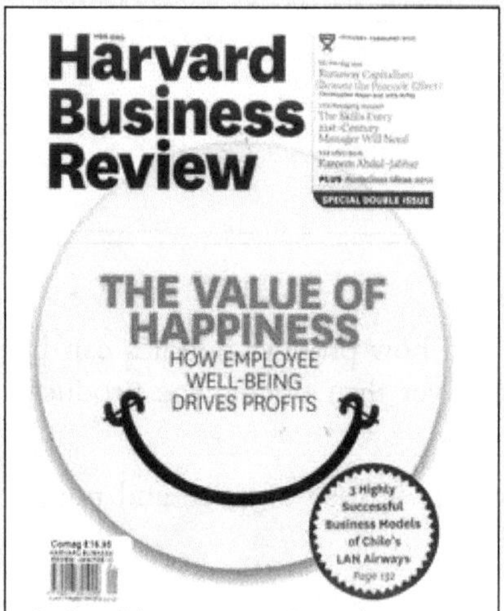

By http://www.newsstand.co.uk/196-Business-and-Finance-Magazines/3255-Subscribe-to-HARVARD-BUSINESS-REVIEW-Magazine-Subscription.aspx, https://en.wikipedia.org/w/index.php?curid=36418883

Business Review brings together, in each issue, news and features the vast majority of which represent value on their own and can be marketed, especially as a result of the services offered by the Internet. Perhaps they cannot be considered as a real 'bundle'.

However, the subscription to these journals can clearly qualify as a bundle, because those who subscribe get home delivery and obligatorily purchase the issues that they would never purchase otherwise. In the furniture industry a bundle is when furniture is sold in sets, and bundling is when a computer is sold together with a screen, a keyboard and a printer.

Also the practice of selling a computer with pre-installed software is definitely a bundle. Bundling certain elements of the offerings is widely spread in car distribution.

In the winter of 2014 Vauxhall offered a Winter Pack for its Corsa cars for 220 pounds, which included:

- Electrically heated front seats,

- Electrically heated leather-covered steering wheel.

(http://www.vauxhall.co.uk/bypass/download/gb/CorsaPriceGuide.pdf)

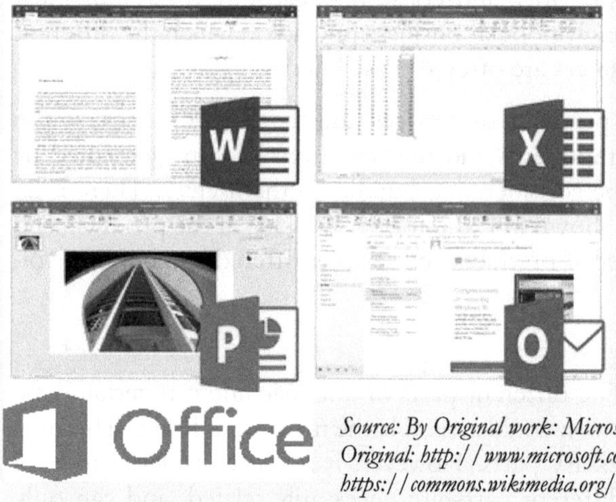

The majority of the offerings of travel agencies are also considered as bundles, as the packages include travel, hotel accom-modation, sightseeing, programs, as well as meals, etc. Most soft-ware comes in bundles too.

Microsoft Office includes the word pro-cessor program Word, the spreadsheet creator Excel and the editor program Power Point and Outlook (the pro-fessional version inc-ludes some other prog-rams as well).

Source: By Original work: Microsoft Corporation This SVG version: AxG at English Wikipedia - Original: http://www.microsoft.com/office/preview/This SVG version: Own work, Public Domain, https://commons.wikimedia.org/w/index.php?curid=20368968

10.2. The theory of price bundling

The majority of available literature presents the theory of bundling and pricing in a relatively homogenous way (Pepels, 1998; Simon and Fassnacht, 2008; Veres, 2009; Cao et al. 2015), with the only difference being that they all take a different product as an example. We are going to take the example of a bookstore specialized for selling management books to present why the use of bundle prices can lead to a potential increase in revenues for the supplier.

Let's take a simplified example of the book store selling a *Marketing Management Monography* (MMM) and a *Marketing Communication Monography* (MCM) – *charging $50 for the MMM and $40 for the MCM.* Let's have 5 consumers and assume we know the reservation prices of these consumers with regard

to both books, i.e. the maximum price they are willing to pay for MMM and MCM. The maximum price also serves as an indicator of how valuable the consumer considers the given product. Table 10.1 includes the maximum price paid by the consumers and the price of the bundle. (The bundle price is the sum of the reservation prices of consumers.)

It can be concluded from the table that consumers can be divided into 4 segments according to prices:

- Consumer 1 buys only MMM,
- Consumer 2 buys only MCM,
- Consumer 3 buys both books,
- Consumers 4 and 5 do not buy either book.

Figure 10.1. The case of individual prices - four segments

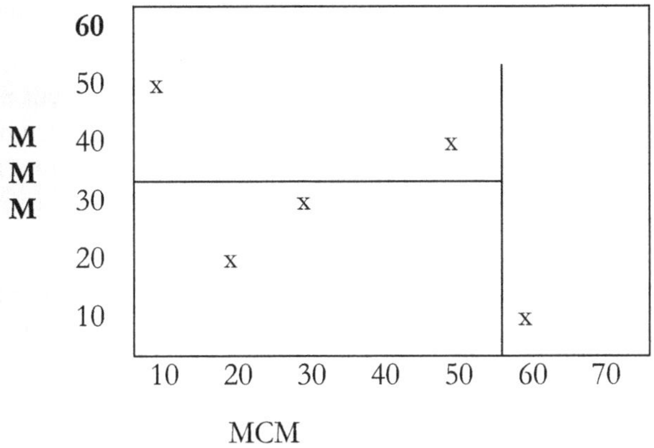

Table 10.1. Reservation prices of consumers

Consumer	Reservation prices of consumers ($)		Present prices of the bookstore ($)	
	MMM	MCM	MMM	MCM
1	60	10	50	40
2	20	50	50	40
3	50	40	50	40
4	30	25	50	40
5	24	18	50	40

The total sales will include two units of MMM and two units of MCM. The sales revenue will amount to 2x50 + 2x40, altogether $180.

If the bookstore decides, as a result, to sell the MMM and MCM only in a bundle and not as separate volumes, the price of the bundle should be determined according to the graph in Figure 10.2.

The optimum bundle price (the one generating the highest turnover) will be $55, that is $\mathbf{P_{MMM} + P_{MCM} = 55}$.

With this step, the earlier four segments of the market narrowed down to two segments:

- those who buy the bundle, and
- those who do not buy the bundle.

Figure 10.2. The case of bundling - two segments

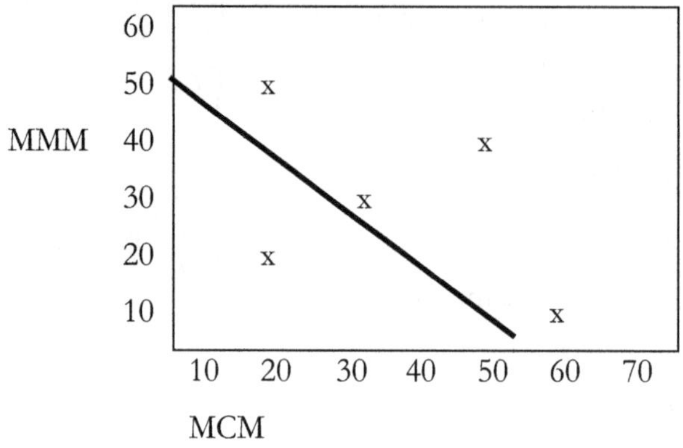

Consumers 1, 2, 3 and 4 belong to the first segment, while the second segment includes consumer 5, who is reluctant to buy the bundle. The total sales revenue is (4x55) = $220, which is higher by $40 than the turnover reached with individual prices. (In order to convince consumer 5, the bundle price would have to be decreased to $42, however, this price would generate less turnover, because 42x5 = $210.)

The result is surprising, as the optimum bundle price is actually lower than the sum of the optional individual prices ($50 + $40 = $90). What is behind this surprising result is referred to as the skimming of the consumer surplus in the literature. Based on Table 10.2, let us examine how much consumers spend in the case of individual prices and in the case of bundle prices. The difference between the two (last column) is the consumer surplus, which is skimmed by the company using a bundle price.

Table 10.2 Skimming consumer surplus

Consumer	Spending in the case of individual prices ($)	Spending in the case of bundle price ($)	Consumer surplus ($)
1	50	55	+ 5
2	40	55	+ 15
3	90	55	- 35
4	0	55	+ 55
5	0	0	0
Total:	180	220	+ 40

10.2. The conditions and methods of using bundled pricing

The use of price bundling as a strategic tool is spreading quickly in today's markets. Its rapid advance is especially palpable in the service sector, particularly in telecommunications and in restaurants and catering, etc. The question arises, which products are the most suitable to be offered in a package deal? We can agree with Murphy (1998) according to whom the products and services most suitable for bundling price strategy are the ones where:

The marginal costs of production are low. In other words, where the variable costs represent only a small percentage of the price. Varian (1999) highlights two sectors: Telecommunications and information services. As their services are based on modern technology, these sectors are characterized by the relatively high level of fixed costs and so-called shared costs (shared costs meaning that the tools of the productions are shared for the production of different end products and services) and very low, close to zero level of variable (marginal) costs.

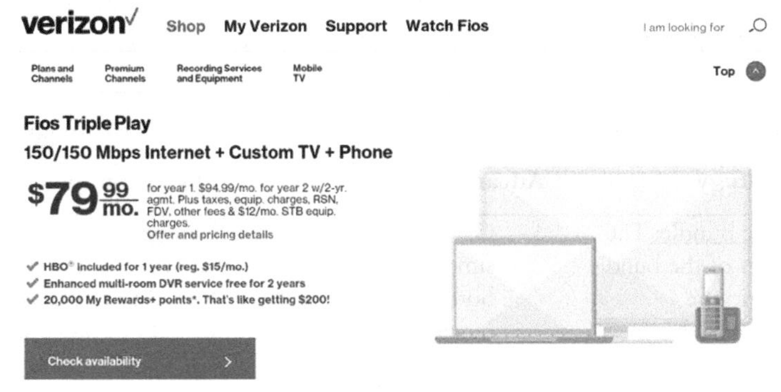

Source: http://www.verizon.com/home/fiostv/

- The correlation of the products and services included in the bundle is not too high. Offering interdependent products and services together does not lead to any special advantages.

- Consumers' willingness to purchase individual elements of the bundle varies, but can be compared separately. Bundling can become an effective strategy (as has been proved through the example of the two books), because the seller can compile its offering on the basis of the average willingness of purchasing, and is not forced to sell and price the products for which the willingness to buy is low separately.

A typical bundle in telecommunication, Fios Triple Play: Internet, TV and Phone

There are two known types of bundled pricing strategies: *compulsory bundling*, often called *pure* bundling, and *mixed bundling*. Today, with the liberalization of public services, a third type of bundling appeared in addition to these two, which offers the products typically sold in bundles separately (unbundling). These three strategies are reviewed in Table 10.3.

The extensive literature of bundling economics differentiate two types of advantages of organising the company offer into bundles:

- Cost related advantages. They argue that bundles can reduce the cost of production, distribution and transactions. They refer to the "economies of scope", which means that, in many industries, combining the production of different product lines will save costs compared to producing them separately. The same is true for marketing, especially for distribution, personal selling and communication costs.

- The second set of advantages are demand related gains, meaning that customers can be sorted into segments according to their reservation prices as seen in our book example and the supplier may skim larger amount of costumer surplus.

Some types of business offerings represent a transition between bundle prices and the other forms of price differentiation or promotion. They include:

- The linking of so-called main and ancillary products (captive pricing, tie-in sales) (this topic has been dealt with when discussing the pricing of complementary products). The supplier of the main product includes all the materials, spare parts and services that are necessary for

the operation of the product in the bundle. An example of price bundling is when the buyer of a printer compulsorily buys the paper and toner from the same supplier. Another typical example is the supply of mobile phones, where the phone company bundles the sale of the phone set with the communication services. Alternatively, when the seller of a car includes the restriction that the customer must have the car serviced with them in the bundle.

Table 10.3 Bundle price strategies – advantages and disadvantages for customers

Strategy	Advantages	Disadvantages	Examples
Pure bundle: The parts of the bundle cannot be purchased separately; the items are offered only in a bundle for a fixed price.	1. Offers a relatively simple choice for both the seller and the buyer. 2. The bundles can be differentiated and positioned according to consumer segments.	Can decrease customer choice, consumers can feel forced to buy things they would not buy otherwise.	- Cable television - Furniture sets - Windows - internet browser - etc.
Individual sales ('unbundled package'): The items normally sold in a bundle can only be purchased separately at individual prices.	1. Offers a big choice for the consumer. 2. Does not feel the 'constraint'. 3. Can easily be explained.	1. Consumers need to make more decisions, more psychological appropriation. 2. The supplier loses the synergies arising from joint marketing. 3. Individual prices can generate less turnover than bundle prices based on average price.	- Phone company operating in a non-competition market. - Microsoft's Office package. - etc.
Mixed bundle: The elements of the package can be purchased as part of a bundle or individually.	1. Maximum flexibility in serving consumers. 2. Greater variation of prices.	1. Makes offerings very complicated and chaotic. 2. The purchase decision requires serious comparison.	- The pre-set menus and a la carte offers of restaurants. - Car sales: packaged bundle and individual options. - etc.

- Bundles of co-branded goods, such as "Toyota cars with Panasonic audio equipment", represent a growing class of product combinations. "Such bundles arise out of firms' motivation to emphasize their core competencies and forge alliances with synergistic partners. Co-branded bundles represent a coming together of two or more firms" (Venkatesh, R. and Vijay Mahajan 2009, p 21).

- The case of sales rebate. A more favourable price or discount offered for larger volumes of purchases, which can also be considered as a bundle, or a form of non-linear pricing.
- The same way season tickets and subscription fees can function as a bundle price and a discount at the same time. Those who buy season tickets to the theatre purchase a package of performances; those who buy a swim pass or a bus pass can get the same service at a cheaper price in the interest of regular use as part of non-linear pricing.
- The so-called cross coupons are also a kind of bundle offer.
- It is a mix of bundle price and price promotion when consumers are offered a complimentary package much cheaper than the list price when purchasing a car.
- Another example for the mixing of price promotion and bundle price is when banks offer a travel insurance in addition to any credit cards purchased.

10.2.1. Pure bundling

Compulsory or pure bundling means that the products and services of a bundle are not sold separately, and consumers can only obtain them by purchasing the whole package. The main reason behind offering products or services in bundles is to provide increased sales opportunities for the seller. Bundles usually include products and services for which the willingness of purchase is different: as a result, the seller can make the bundle attractive by always including an appealing component. This leading component will make the package very attractive for consumers.

The underlying reason behind bundling is increased competition. Sellers try to position their bundles and make them attractive to different consumer segments. The deregulation of communication and banks has proved that, as soon as competition occurs in a given field, the suppliers immediately want to differentiate their offers; one of the tools is developing bundles and bundle prices. The dilemmas for product and price policy include:

- How many items should the bundle include?
- What should be the relationship between the individual components, that is, should they be substitutes or complementary items?
- What should be the price of the bundle, what discount should it offer to consumers?
- How should the individual prices of the individual items of different packages correlate with each other?

Herrmann, Huber and Coulter (1997: 99–107) have reported their findings in the field of car sales and repair bundles. They studied four factors with regard to willingness to purchase: (1) choice between pure and mixed bundles, (2) impact of price discount, (3) impact of the functional complementary between the items in the bundle, and (4) the impact of the size of bundle (number of items) on consumers' willingness. They concluded that:

- Consumers preferred pure bundles to mixed bundles. They thought that pure bundles offered more benefits to them than the mixed bundles (in this case the price of the individual items functions as the reference price of the bundle).
- A higher discount stimulates willingness to purchase.

- Willingness to purchase was the highest in the case of bundles containing 5 items: it was higher than in the case of bundles of 3 or 7 items.
- Consumers preferred bundles in which the items were closely related, and were less keen on the ones in which there was no or very little functional relation between the items of the bundle.

EXHIBIT 10.2. BANKS CAN INCREASE CUSTOMERS' TRUST, THEIR CUSTOMER POOL AND PROFIT BY SMART BUNDLING

Offering packages for individuals or SMEs can reduce customers' uncertainty about banking services. However, it requires careful planning to create the package structure. They should understand the preferences of their target market and they should build the package around a 'must have' service. Proper pricing of the bundles is of utmost importance. Since banks are competing to attract new customers, they should know their competitors' offers. Since switching banks is perceived as a complicated and costly procedure bundles can also help to maintain the customer base. Here you can see how NATWEST (National Westminster Bank) has divided its business customers and one of its offered packages for a new start-up.

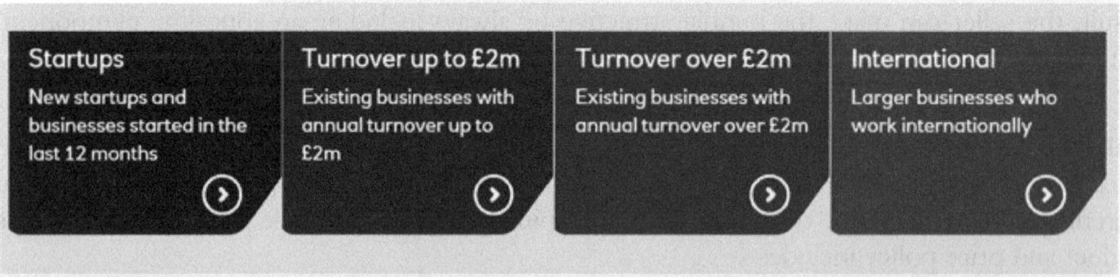

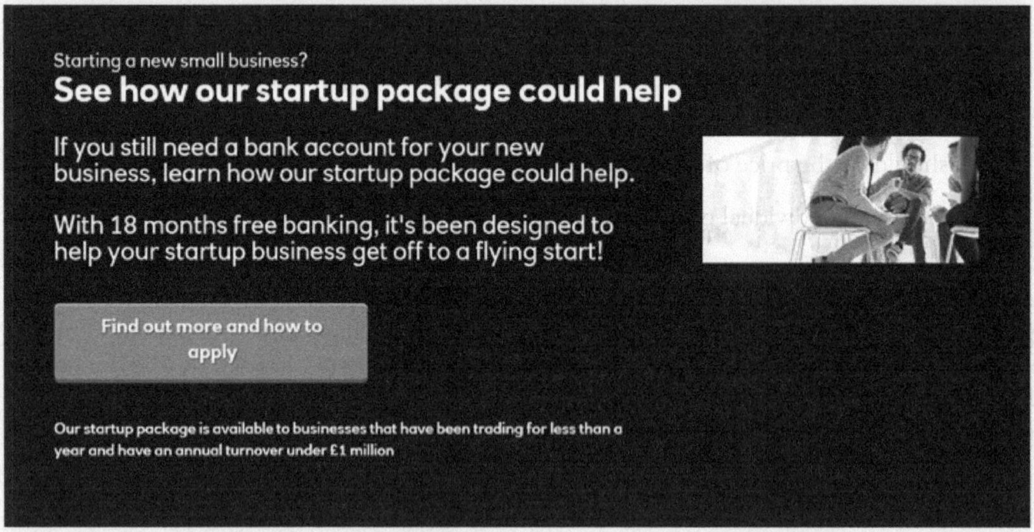

Source: http://www.business.natwest.com/business.html

10.2.2. Mixed bundling

In the case of mixed bundling the consumer has the option to purchase the elements of a bundle either individually or in a bundle. (The price of the bundle is generally lower than the total price of its individual elements.) This strategy can be advantageous for the seller, because he/she can count on consumers who are not interested in buying the bundle. Offering the individual items of a bundle separately can mean that the individual prices will function as reference prices making the package price more attractive. This strategy is used by restaurants offering pre-set menus. (A good example is the combo menus offered by McDonald's, or Burger King, which are composed of exactly the same food items you can buy separately.) The same strategy is used by Microsoft in selling the software included in the Office package. The price of the Office package is attractive for those who use the price of the individual items as a starting point.

The mixed-bundling strategy can also prove to be confusing for consumers, especially in telecommunications and information services, where the strategy of price bundling is very advanced. The rapid technological progress in these sectors goes hand in hand with the appearance of more and more new services. Phone companies in the most developed countries can offer as many as 40-50 different services in an endless combination. Consumers very often are unable to understand all the options. If they order one or the other service, they are unable to monitor the use and the billing; as a result those who opt for the so-called one-step (bundle) purchase resulting in one bill can get rid of the psychological burden.

The disadvantage of bundles is that consumers can feel pressured to buy products or services that they do not need. It is not necessarily true in these modern sectors. The marginal cost is practically zero, so companies can offer very attractive prices for their bundles.

10.2.3. Unbundling of the package

Unbundling means that the supplier does not prepare bundles. It only makes sense if the offerings are typically bundled. With the liberalization of public services, electricity providers were required to split the costs of the electricity and the network, allowing other service providers to use the established network.

10.3. Bundled pricing and the restriction of competition

The problems perceived in the often mentioned field of telephony and information technology in America highlight that the strategy of bundled pricing can sometimes be unethical and in conflict with the provisions of competition law. The lessons of the following two American cases are important because we may encounter similar problems sooner or later in other fields as well.

1. *The case of Microsoft.* The company Microsoft included its own internet browser as a compulsory component in its Windows 98 operating system. According to competitors and the American competition laws this step restricted the freedom of competition. The software giant was taken to court at the end of 1998 under the Anti-Cartel Bill. Microsoft argued that making bundles was nothing more than a common marketing tool, which offered many advantages to the users.

2. The Antitrust Law concerning the bundles used by the operators of telecommunication networks. The deregulation of telecommunication assumes that new competitors will appear on the market. These competitors, however, can only work effectively if they have access to the local networks, which have been operated by the telecommunication companies in a monopolistic position until that time, at a reasonable price. That is why a revolutionary

telecommunications act was introduced in 1996 in the USA. The act envisions ensuring free competition in all telecommunications market. It provides that the local exchange carriers should unbundle their packages and make all the network elements available to the new entrants for a reasonable price (Economides, 1997).

EXHIBIT 10.3. STATUS REVIEW ON THE IMPLEMENTATION OF DISTRIBUTION SYSTEM OPERATORS' UNBUNDLING PROVISIONS OF THE THIRD ENERGY PACKAGE (EU)

This CEER (Council of European Energy Regulators) document (C15-LTF-43-03) presents a Status Review on the Implementation of Distribution System Operators' Unbundling Provisions of the 3rd Energy Package.

The CEER Status Review provides an overview of the status of implementation of the unbundling provisions set out in the Directives of the 3rd Energy Package. Under this package the energy networks are subject to unbundling requirements which oblige member states to ensure the separation of vertically integrated energy companies, resulting in the separation of the various stages of energy supply (generation, distribution, transmission and supply).

This status review, together with the corresponding Status Review on the Implementation of Transmission System Operators' Unbundling Provisions of the 3rd Energy Package, aims to assess the status of DSO and TSO unbundling. Topics explored included related issues such as Branding; Financial inde-pendence in terms of staff and resources; Compliance programme and officer; Investments, Joint-venture TSOs and Joint undertakings.

Source: CEER Status Review Ref: C15-LTF-43-03 1 April 2016, Council of European Energy Regulators asbl Cours Saint-Michel 30a, Box F – 1040 Brussels, Belgium Arrondissement judiciaire de Bruxelles – RPM 0861.035.445, http://www.ceer.eu/portal/ page/ portal/EER_HOME/EER_PUBLICATIONS/ CEER_PAPERS/Cross-Sectoral/2016/C15-LTF-43-03_DSO-Unbundling_Status_Review-1-Apr-2016.pdf

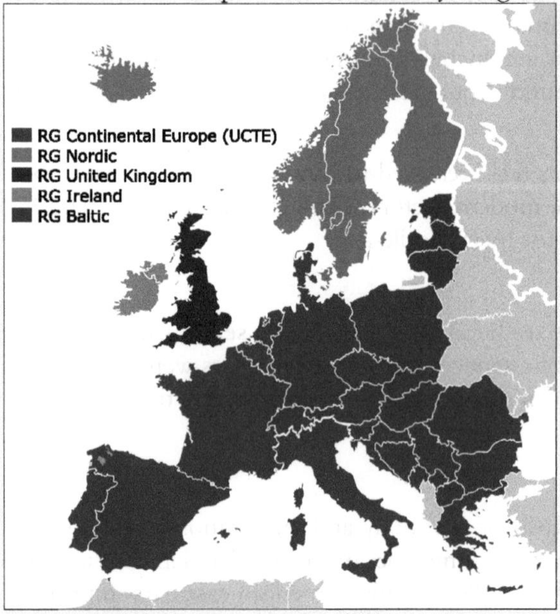

The synchronous grids of the European Union
Source: CC BY-SA 3.0, https://commons.wikimedia.org/w/index.php?curid=1387849

EXHIBIT 10.4. WHEN 2+2 DOES NOT EQUAL 3+1

Hamilton and Srivastava published an interesting study in the *Journal of Marketing Research* in 2008. In this study the authors examined what influence the splitting of the price (the 'unbundling' of the package) had on consumer preferences. They concluded that consumers assessed the utility individually in this case. If consumers are less sensitive to the price of the item in the package with the highest utility value, they prefer the splitting of the price, because in this way they can be sure to pay less for the items, which offer lower utility. The following figure presents the consumer preferences with regard to the displaying of spare parts and wages, and spare parts and shipping costs in the field of car repair. It shows that customers want to see how much they are paying as work fees, but they are less interested in the costs of shipping spare parts.

Presentation of consumer preferences

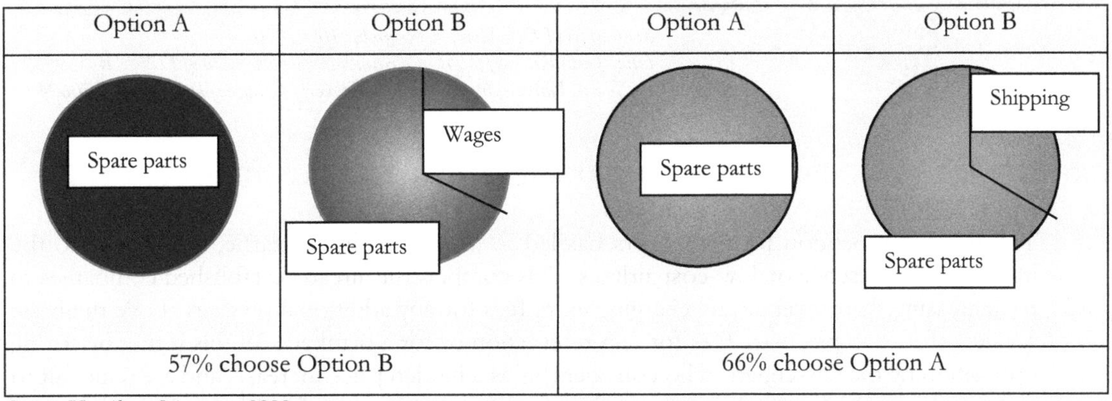

Source: Hamilton–Srivastava, 2008

EXHIBIT 10.5. THE OUTCOME OF THE MICROSOFT CASE

The United States contra Microsoft Corp. lawsuit was filed in 1998 and was not won by the company. As a result, the annual report of the company for 2008 included the following sentence:

"Lawsuits brought by the U.S. Department of Justice, 18 States, and the District of Columbia in two separate actions were resolved through a so-called "consent decree" (a decision taken by common agreement, in which the defendant promises to abandon the activity, which is the subject of the lawsuit, considered to be unlawful to reach a favourable final outcome – the author) that took effect in 2001. The final judgement was entered in 2002. These proceedings imposed various constraints on our Windows operating system businesses. ….. We believe we are in full compliance with these rules. However, if we fail to comply with them, additional restrictions could be imposed on us that would adversely affect our business."

Source: http://en.wikipedia.org/wiki/United_States_v._Microsoft (October 12, 2010)

EXHIBIT 10.6. AIRLINES INTEND TO CHARGE FOR PREVIOUSLY FREE SERVICES

Airlines barely recovering from the financial crisis are trying to increase and to charge for previously free services. The American airlines already charge a fee for each piece of luggage including cabin baggage and handbags. The transportation of these – up to a certain weight limit – used to be included in the fare price, but nowadays airlines charge between 20 and 90 dollars for this service. The largest European low-cost airline, the Irish carrier, Ryanair has already considered installing additional seats – practically stools – to increase the number of passengers. Passengers would use these seats at take-off and landing, but would stand during the rest of the flight so they would not block the way.

RYANAIR

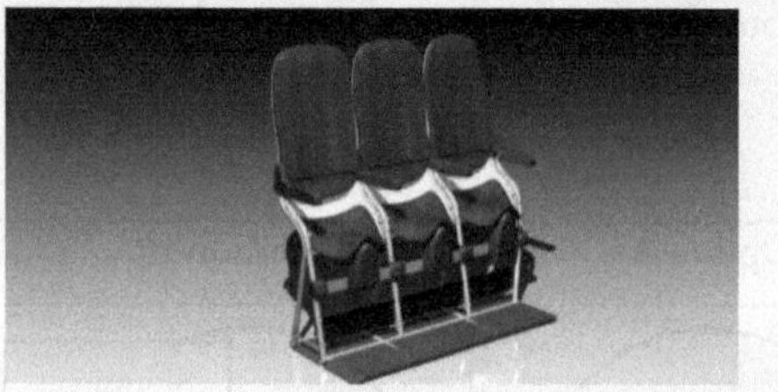

Sources: MTI Déli Monitor, November 10th, 2010
http://newatlas.com/future-of-air-travel-comfortable-seating/17751/#p129309
By Source, Fair use, https://en.wikipedia.org/w/index.php?curid=50650604

EXHIBIT 10.7. "UNBUNDLING THE PACKAGE" AND "SMART REBOUNDING" WITH THE TRADITIONAL AIRLINES

The fierce competition for passengers has led to low prices in air traffic, mainly due to the international presence of low-cost airlines. This compels the already established companies to try increasing their revenues by charging extra fees for any additional services above the basic services (for example, extra fees for seat reservation or for a blanket). All this is met by strong opposition by the passengers, who consider this as a hidden price increase, and are reluctant to make decisions during the flight about whether to pay extra money for the simplest of services.

Instead of using this approach, traditional airlines should look for a more promising strategy: a smarter way of "rebundling" the service package, which provides the opportunity to differentiate the offerings of the company from others, and which can restore shattered goodwill and increase profitability. The first step of smart unbundling is analysing the product, breaking it up to its elements and conducting a cost analysis of these elements, followed by an investigation into how much the different consumer groups are willing to pay for them. The packages should then be bundled again in a creative way to meet the needs and value expectations of the given consumer segments. Businesspersons travelling on international flights are more likely to prefer an express corridor at security check, while passengers of short flights are probably not interested in using the waiting lounge and would be satisfied with a voucher for which they could get a coffee in the airport café.

To be able to implement this new 'rebundling approach' airlines should challenge the traditional interpretation of their 'product'. They have already struggled with this task, but the solution cannot be postponed for long.

Source: excerpts from the article by Ringbeck et al. (2010: 5)

PART 3. INTERMEDIARY PRICING

CHAPTER 11. PRICING ACROSS THE MARKETING CHANNELS

OBJECTIVE 1 To show how manufacturers of goods and services can manage the prices of their offers across the distribution channels and to what extent they are able to control the prices that impact on the end user.

OBJECTIVE 2 To explore the pricing policies pursued by intermediaries acting in the distribution channel – wholesalers, retailers – and the internal (business economics related) and external (market and demand related) factors that determine the limits of the price policy.

OBJECTIVE 3 To examine the pricing methods, strategies or tactics applied by companies in contact with the ultimate buyer or consumer.

OBJECTIVE 4 To establish and evaluate the different forms and methods of discount and allowance policies adopted by producers to promote the sale of their goods.

11.1 Introduction

In this Chapter, we follow the logical process of business practice, examining how the distribution system, whose main function is to ensure that products and services reach the ultimate consumer or user, modifies manufacturers' prices and turn producers' prices into consumers' prices. In the previous chapters, we focused on price-related issues such as economic theories, external and internal factors influencing prices, strategic issues, and the different methods of price setting. We typically approached these issues from the viewpoint of manufacturers and with the intention of presenting the ways in which manufacturers and service providers should make decisions on the prices of their products.

Let us firstly examine the structure of the distribution system and the decisions concerning the marketing channels.

11.2. The system of distribution: movement of goods from producers to final users

The main role of the distribution system is to keep goods moving from the manufacturer to the user. The distribution system operates efficiently if its participants constitute a coherent system and co-operate in harmony, providing the services at the level expected by the target market.

Under the conditions that characterize the beginning of our century it is becoming increasingly self-evident that there is a lot more to market competition than simple rivalry between individual products and services. Today the market is the scene in which complete systems and networks – called supply chains - consisting of producers and traders and even suppliers compete. Most of the time the goods and related services reach the buyers through the distribution channel. This channel, however, is not

a passive catalyst of the process, but an active participant and adds value to the product, or – if its performance is not sufficiently good – detracts from it.

When a customer - say in the London Tesco Superstore - makes up his mind to buy a Phillips vacuum cleaner, his decision is motivated not only by the quality, shape and other features of the product, or the image of the manufacturer, but also by the following considerations:

- how much extra cost does distribution add to the factory price, i.e.
- what is the retailer's margin?
- in what kind of environment does the seller offer the product?
- how polite are the shop assistants and what kind of additional services do they offer? (e.g. home delivery and paying by instalments)
- how do they advertise locally, and what sales promotion tools do they use?

The complete system built by Phillips rivals other systems like those built by Sanyo, Toshiba or Siemens.

The role of the distribution channel is of vital importance for the market success of the products and their price-acceptance by the customers. Now we are going to review the most typical channels of distribution, the decisions that *manufacturers* must make when they choose the channel and the factors motivating these decisions.

The choice of channel is motivated by the following factors:

- *The capital required for the establishment or use of a distribution channel.* The biggest investment is needed if the company chooses direct distribution, i.e. decides to develop a distribution network of its own. This was the case, for example, when Citi and HSBC banks decided to introduce retail services for the population. They had to implement serious investments – both financially and in human resources - to create a national retail network for their services. Should a company decide against having a network of its own, it may still have to make certain investments? It is a basic requirement to have a return on investment and this has an impact on the price policy implemented by the channels.

- *Running costs of operating the distribution channel.* These costs take the form of commissions, margins, or other contributions (e.g. promotion) that arise in the course of operation. Their amount has an impact on the efficiency of operation and therefore affects the final price as well.

- *The possibility to control.* From a marketing point of view one of the most important questions is to what extent a manufacturer can make the members of the distribution channel accept and implement his own pricing ideas or, in other words, the extent to which he is able to control prices in different levels of the channel.

- *What is the degree to which the channel can reach the market segment targeted by the manufacturer?* After all, the manufacturer's main goal is to achieve an adequate turnover (or market share) in the target market or one of its segments. The distribution channel will meet the requirements only if it has everything that is indispensable for reaching the segment (shop network, properly trained staff, depositories in the given areas, warehouses, etc.).

- *Does its character (quality level) come up to the firm's price policy and quality expectations* related to the product in question? The distribution channel cannot function as a coherent system unless the firms participating in it can offer services of the same (or at least similar) quality. It would be a mistake to sell high quality luxury goods in discount shops and it would be a similarly big mistake to sell low quality commodities in exclusive luxury stores like Harrods (see the photo).

Harrods, one of the world's most famous luxury warehouses (London).

Source: By Diliff - Own work, CC BY-SA 3.0, https://commons.wikimedia.org/w/index.php?curid=22523059

Figure 11.1. Consumer marketing channels

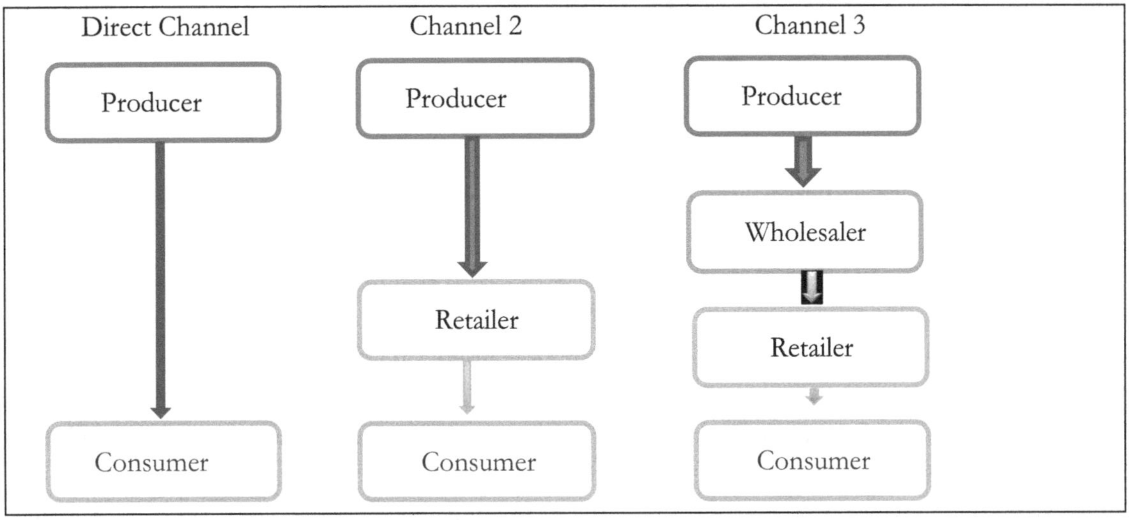

Figure 11.2. Business marketing channels

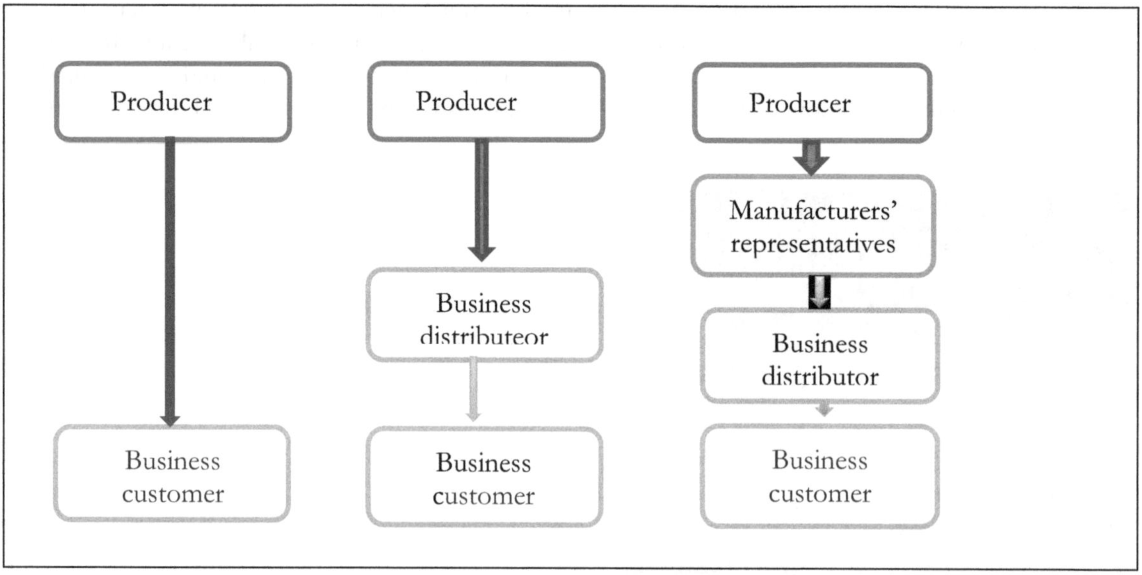

Sometimes retailers also may play role in the B2B channel. These so called hardware stores usually sell household hardware for home improvement, and they also serve mainly the SME-s (Small and Medium Sized Enterprises) with the supplies they need for their daily operations. In the photo you can see a DIY (Do It Yourself) shop in France.

By Myrabella - Own work, CC BY-SA 3.0, https://commons.wikimedia.org/w/index.php?curid=8007434

11.2. Interrelationships between decisions related to the distribution channels and price policy objectives

There are three important decisions to be made about distribution channels:

A decision should be made about *the length* of the distribution channels the firm intends to run. The length of the channel depends on how many times the goods change owners before they reach the ultimate buyer (in the Figure you can see 1-, 2-, 3-tier channels).

A channel of consumer goods is typically longer; we often find channels with two or more tiers, while industrial goods and their related services have a shorter route to the final user. The shortest route is

the one where the commodity is sold directly to the consumer (direct marketing). This solution is more frequently used for industrial goods and services but very rarely for consumer goods. A channel is considered long if goods change owners more than twice. Figure 11.3 shows the interrelationship between the length of the channel and the degree of the manufacturer's ability to control prices.

Figure 11.3. The length of the distribution channels and the degree of price control

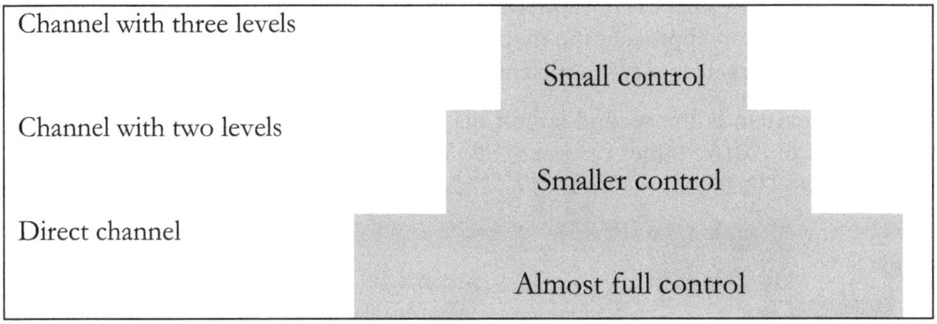

The second group of decisions is related to the *width of the channel.* This term refers to the number of intermediaries the firms work with at a given level of the distribution route. If, at a certain level of distribution (in the retail trade, for example), the firm contacts several intermediaries of different types, the distribution channel widens and commodities are spread more intensively. (The possible commodity distribution strategies will be discussed in the next exhibit.) The modes of distribution and the extent to which prices can be controlled are shown in Figure 11.4.

Figure 11.4. Interrelation between the width of the channel and the level of price control

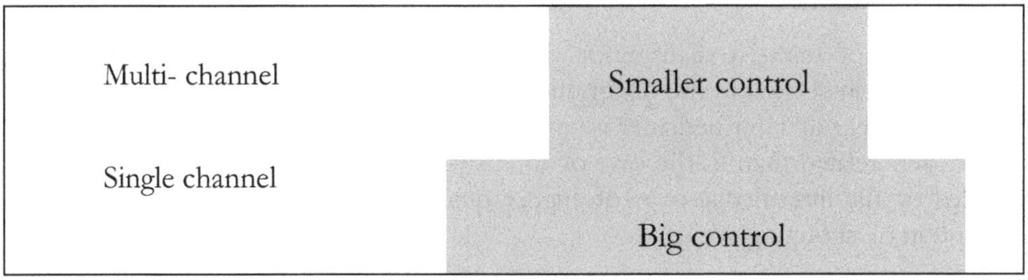

Figure 11.5. The intensity of distribution and the level of price control

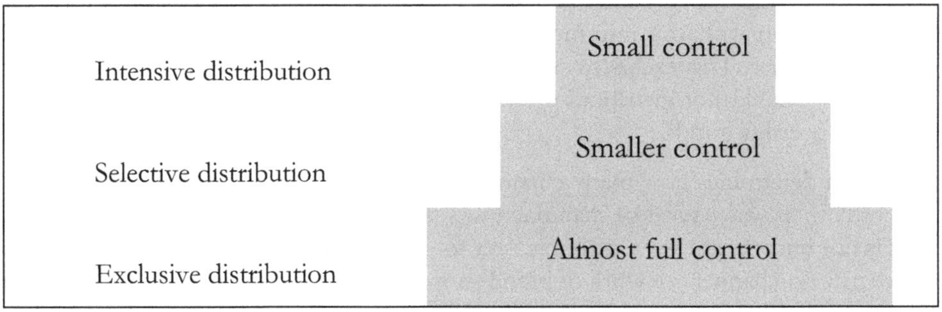

EXHIBIT 11.1. COMMODITY DISTRIBUTING STRATEGIES

Intensive distribution

The intensive distribution strategy means that the producer makes his/her products easily accessible for customers and sells them in as many places as possible. The number of intermediaries involved is quite large, but their relationship to the manufacturer is weaker. This form of distribution suits mainly convenience goods (e.g. fuel, tobacco, toothpaste, etc.) In an intensive distribution approach, the marketer relies on chain stores (like Target in the photo) to reach broad markets in a cost-efficient manner.

Target Corporation is the second-largest discount store retailer in the United States, behind Walmart. As of 2016, Target operated 1,803 locations throughout the United States. Their retail formats include the discount store Target, the hypermarket SuperTarget, and 'flexible format' stores previously named CityTarget and TargetExpress before being consolidated under the Target branding.

An older Target outlet within the Northgate Shopping Centre, Glenorchy, a northern suburb of Hobart.
Source: (https://en.wikipedia.org/wiki/Target_Corporation)

Selective distribution

In the course of selective distribution the manufacturer doesn't work together with all the intermediaries interested in the distribution of his product, instead he selects some of them. Since the number of intermediaries is smaller, the manufacturer and the intermediaries can be more closely related than in the case of intensive distribution. At the same time, the service provided by the intermediaries is of higher quality. This strategy is applied mainly for the distribution of shopping goods.

Exclusive distribution

An exclusive distribution strategy means that the manufacturer strictly limits the number of intermediaries, (most of the time to a single company or shop). The purpose is to develop a close relationship with the intermediary and have strict control over marketing activities, including the price. This exclusive strategy often goes together with the requirement that the intermediary should not distribute products by other manufacturers. The strategy is mostly applied to speciality goods.

The third decision determines how many channels the manufacturer intends to operate to reach his customers. Formerly it was typical of manufacturers to use only one channel to sell their products. Nowadays it is not uncommon for a manufacturer to operate or use several channels. They may, for example, have a direct channel (network of brand shops), but may also make use of the opportunities offered by intermediaries (wholesalers, retailers). This multi-channel distribution is often referred to as multi-marketing.

11.3. Prices and margins in the distribution channels

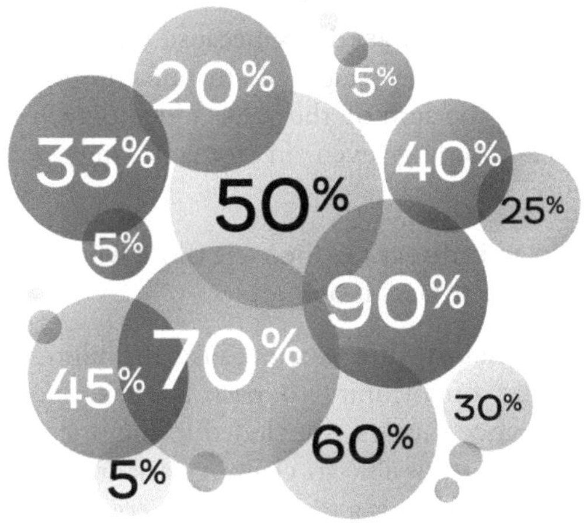

Participants in the distribution channel are independent business organizations. Their activity is profit-oriented and every one of them expects to gain a big enough part of the difference between the consumer price and the manufacturing costs to cover, on the one hand, the operating costs and, on the other, generate an acceptable profit. With a view to familiarizing ourselves with the price structure of the distribution channel, let us review first of all what kind of additional sums are added to the producer's price in the sales channel. As an example, let us take a commodity with a variable cost of $ 400 to make and which is sold at $ 1,000 in the retail trade (Figure 11.6).

Figure 11.6. Prices and costs and markups at the various levels of the distribution channel

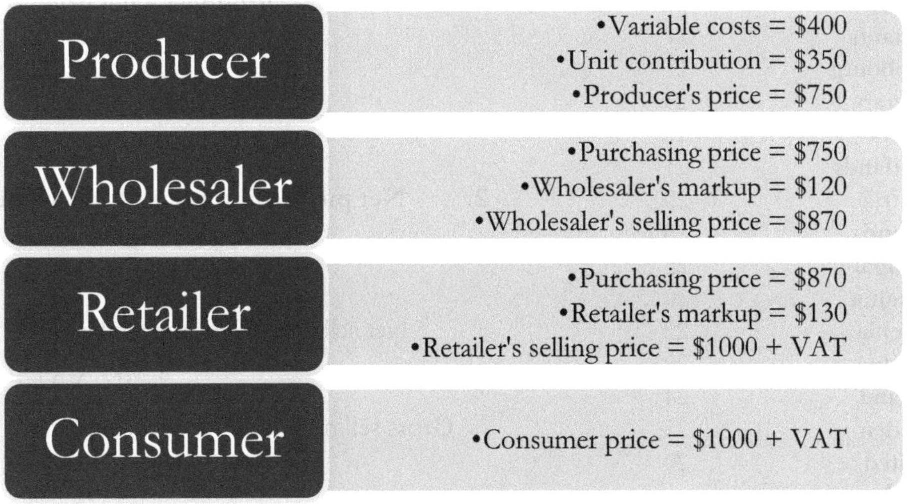

EXHIBIT 11.2. THE ROLE OF VAT (VALUE ADDED TAX)

In our previous example – as in all parts of this book – we have ignored the impact of VAT. We have done so (and continue to do so in the remaining part as well), because we believe that the measure of VAT is an issue that relates to policy that scientific books concerned with prices are not qualified to discuss. (The standard values of VAT valid in the member states of the EU in 2017 are shown in the table.). Experts, who read this book or university students who use it as a textbook are supposed to know how VAT should be used to change the calculations. For the sake of completeness, we will give a brief overview of the topic and then present the same example again, this time with the VAT included.

The characteristics of VAT

- It is an **all-phase tax**, because it must be calculated for all phases of manufacturing and

selling.

Member states of EU	Standard Rate of VAT (%) as of 01.01. 2017
Belgium	21
Bulgaria	20
Czech Republic	21
Denmark	25
Germany	19
Estonia	20
Ireland	23
Greece	24
Spain	21
France	20
Croatia	25
Italy	22
Cyprus	19
Latvia	21
Lithuania	21
Luxembourg	17
Hungary	27
Malta	18
Netherlands	21
Austria	20
Poland	23
Portugal	23
Romania	20
Slovenia	22
Slovakia	20
Finland	24
Sweden	25
United Kingdom	20

- It is a **net value-based tax** because the base of the tax payable in every stage of manufacturing or distribution equals the sum of the value added (which is reflected in its wording even in foreign languages: Mehrwertsteuer).
- It is also an **indirect tax**, because those who must pay it have a chance to pass it on.
- It is a **consumption tax** because the ultimate consumer has no opportunity to pass the tax on to somebody else. Since this tax is included in the price of the product, it is not possible to claim it back from the IRS, and so, all in all, VAT is a tax payable by consumers.

Having clarified these points let us return to the example in Figure 11.6, assuming a VAT of 20% as in the UK:

1. **Producer's net price = $750.00**

   + 20% VAT = $150.00

   Producer's gross price = $900.00

2. **Net purchasing price of the wholesaler = $750.00**

   + wholesaler's mark-up = $120.00

   Net selling price of the wholesaler = $870.00

   + 20% VAT = $174.00

   Gross selling price of the wholesaler = $1 044.00

3. **Net purchasing price of the retailer = $870.00**

   + retailer's mark-up = $130.00

   Net selling price of the retailer = $1 000.00

   + 20% VAT = $200.00

4. **Consumer price = $1 200.00**

The original example makes it clear that the organizations participating in the distribution channel (and the state) divide the gap between variable costs ($400) and the consumer price ($1,200) among themselves.

The charges added to the costs of manufacturing and due to be paid for the activity of the various participants can be presented as follows:

- The difference between the selling price and the direct variable costs arising at the manufacturer is called *unit contribution*. Its role is to cover the unit fixed costs and the unit profit of the producer. Sometimes the manufacturer takes the total costs to begin with and simply adds the profits to them. The profits added are usually expressed in percentages and are often referred to as *profit margin*. The total sum of the profits generated from the sale of all products sold is called the firm's profit before taxation. The ratio of the total gains to the sales revenue is the *profit ratio* or *profit margin*.

- Trading firms (both wholesalers and retailers) are interested in the difference between the purchase price and the selling price. In our example this difference is $ 120 for the wholesaler and $130 for the retailer in the case of the product in question. What is important here is not the actual amount (after all when a car is sold at $50 000 the mark-up will certainly be different), but the relative ratio, expressed as a percentage. The difference between the sale and purchase price is known as a mark-up both in the wholesale and retail trades. The value of the total mark-up and its share in the total revenue are important indicators of how well the trading companies are doing. The amount of the total mark-up covers the operating costs and the profit of the trading companies. In 2014 the world's ten largest commercial firms had an average net profit margin of 1.9%.

- When discussing either the contribution and profit of manufacturers or the mark-up of commercial firms we emphasized that percentage ratio is important. The question then arises as to what the basis of comparison is when the percentage of contribution or mark-up is calculated. No generally accepted answer has been offered either by international literature or business practice: the dilemma is whether the calculation should be made from the bottom up, starting from the costs, or purchase price, or top-to bottom, starting from the selling price. The two methods differ fundamentally: to demonstrate that let us employ an example in which the purchasing price is 60 and the selling price 100 units. In this case the mark-up is 66.67% (40/60) when calculated upwards, and only 40% (40/100) when calculated downwards.

- *In international practice, the most widely accepted method is to use the selling price as the basis of the profit or mark-up percentage.* In this current book, we also give priority to internationally accepted terminologies and methods. To those who still prefer the bottom-up method we have a good advice: if you want to avoid ambiguity, always make it very clear what you have used as a point of reference.

The conversion between the two forms is not very complicated: you can use the following formulae:

1. Conversion of the percentage calculated from the selling price base to the cost base:

$$Mark\ up\ \%\ on\ costs = \frac{\text{Mark up \% of selling price}}{100\% - \text{Mark up \% of selling price}}$$

$$\frac{40\ \%}{100\ \% - 40\ \%} = 66.67\ \%$$

2. Conversion of the percentage calculated on the cost base to selling price base:

$$Mark\ up\ \%\ of\ selling\ price = \frac{\text{Mark up \% on costs}}{100\% - \text{Mark up \% on costs}}$$

$$\frac{66.67\ \%}{100\ \% + 66.67\ \%} = 40.00\ \%$$

Coming back now to our product of $1 000 (+ VAT) we can describe the mark-ups arising at both the manufacturer and two other members of the distribution channel with the following percentages calculated with two methods.

EXHIBIT 11.3. CLASSIC GUIDELINES BY OXENFELDT FOR DEVELOPING PRICING STRATEGIES THAT INCORPORATE CHANNEL CONSIDERATIONS

"Oxenfeldt offers a set of classic guidelines for developing pricing strategies that incorporate channel considerations. These guidelines help those involved in pricing decisions to focus more clearly on the channel implications of their pricing decisions. The guidelines also offer some general prescriptions on how to formulate pricing strategies that will help to promote channel member cooperation and minimize conflict. Obviously, there is no guarantee that even scrupulous adherence to these guidelines will ensure this result. In fact, there are sure to be many particular circumstances and situations where some of these guidelines will not apply or will be irrelevant. Nevertheless, they are worthy of careful study because they do provide a basic framework and benchmark for pricing decisions that incorporate channel considerations. The guidelines are as follows:

1. Each efficient reseller must obtain unit profit margins in excess of unit operating costs.
2. Each class of reseller margins should vary in rough proportion to the cost of the functions the reseller performs.
3. At all points in the vertical chain (channel levels), prices charged must be in line with those charged for comparable rival brands.
4. Special distribution arrangements – variations in functions performed or departures from the usual flow of merchandise – should be accompanied by corresponding variations in financial arrangements.
5. Margins allowed to any type of reseller must conform to the conventional percentage norms unless a very strong case can be made for departing from the norms.
6. Variations in margins on individual models and styles of a line are permissible and expected. They must, however, vary around the conventional margin for the trade.
7. A price structure should contain offerings at the chief price points, where such price points exist.
8. A manufacturer's price structure must reflect variations in the attractiveness of individual product offerings."

Source: Alfred R. Oxenfeld, Pricing Strategies (New York, AMACON, 1975: 140). Cited by Rosenbloom, 1999: 349-350

Table 11.2. Values of contribution and mark-up percentages according to the different base

Item	Base data in $	Calculated on cost base %	Calculated on price base %
Manufacturer's unit variable cost	400		
Unit contribution	350	87.50%	46.67%
Selling price	750		
Wholesaler's purchase price	750		
mark-up	120	16.00%	13.79%
selling price	870		
Retailer's purchase price	870		
mark-up	130	14.94%	13.00%
selling price	1000		

11.4. Price control in the distribution channel

Manufacturers who also pursue marketing activities strive to be the ones who have the greatest influence on deciding the price that the ultimate buyer will pay for his product. This aspiration is quite understandable considering that the volume of turnover will also depend on this price, just as the image that customers will have about the product and the manufacturer. At the same time, manufacturers must also bear in mind, during their efforts to define the ultimate price, that the other participants of the distribution channel should also be interested in selling the product. Similarly, some larger intermediaries can also have the political ambition to define prices.

However understandable the intention of both parties may be to control prices, it is not easy to put into practice. What is more, revealing the final price by manufacturer to the retailer is against the law in nearly every country.

Which member is capable of controlling its own ultimate prices or significantly influencing its modifications depends on the power structure of the given industry.

There are several forms of controlling prices. We have summarized them in Table 11.3.

11.4.1. Relationship of equal standing between the manufacturer and the trader

It is the manufacturer of the product who defines the producer price but, since he has no influence over the intermediaries he has no direct influence on setting the final (consumer) price either. This is typical of situations in which the members of the distribution channel have more or less equal economic power, i.e. none of the parties are able to assert their will vis-a-vis the others. A bakery, for example, compiles the price list of the breads and other bakery products and sells its products to various food retailers at the prices listed there. The top two lines of Table 11.3 show that, in this equal relationship, price setting has two versions:

- If trading firms apply an automatic mark-up policy, the manufacturer will be able to influence the final price indirectly through producer prices. If the manufacturer builds on the assumption that the trading firm will automatically apply the purchase price+mark-up of an identical percentage formula (which is simply the commercial version of the cost+profit pricing method), he can indirectly affect consumer prices by changing the manufacturing costs. The most important tools of this indirect influence, i.e. flexibly changing manufacturer' prices, are various discounts and special offers by the manufacturers. These will be discussed separately.

- If commercial firms apply their own, so-called autonomous mark-up policy, the manufacturer's influence on the final prices is smaller. Consequently, it may be that goods sold at the same manufacturer price appear in the offer of the same merchant at various prices, but the difference can be quite significant between various merchants. Since manufacturers have no direct influence on consumer prices, the final prices depend on the commercial mark-ups and this solution may lead to a difference of as much as 30-40% in consumer prices.

Table 11.3. Versions of influencers of consumer prices

The relationship between the manufacturer and the trader	The main influencer of		
	The producer's prices	The trader's mark-ups	Consumer prices
Equal position	The manufacturer	The trader (using an automatic mark-up policy	Indirectly the manufacturer
Equal position	The manufacturer	The trader (using an autonomous mark-up policy	The trader
Cooperative position	Together	Together	Together
The manufacturer has a dominant position	The manufacturer	The manufacturer	The manufacturer
The trader has a dominant position	The trader	The trader	The trader

11.4.2. Co-operation between manufacturers and traders

Parties mutually cooperate with each other in setting producer price. The purpose of co-operation, both for the producer and the trader, can be to maximize profit (or perhaps market share). In a competitive situation, the starting point for price setting is an ultimate (consumer or retail) price that buyers may qualify as acceptable. Counting backwards from it they define mark-ups: their own and those of the other members of the distribution channel (in a way that is acceptable for the others as well) and the producer's price. What the parties actually do is to divide among themselves the difference between the consumer price as well as between the manufacturing and distribution costs as shown in Figure 11.3.

EXHIBIT11.4. THE JOINT BUSINESS PLAN OF WALMART AND P&G

https://commons.wikimedia.org/w/index.php?curid=7697697 Public Domain

WalMart Stores Inc. is working every day with around 20,000 suppliers; although maybe the largest is Procter & Gamble.

This relationship has had its peaks and valleys, according to Jeff Schomburger, president of the Walmart Global Consumer team at P&G: "I have worked with Walmart for the past 25 years and have the grey hair to prove it," he said.

In that time, he said P&G has grown its Walmart business from $400 million to $10 billion, moving in step with the retailer along the way – and even making together a few wrong turns.

Schomburger and Duncan Mac Naughton, chief merchandising officer at Walmart U.S., recently shared how the two firms in 2011 laid down their angst and rolled up their sleeves to get their business relationship back on track. The executives spoke on the relevance of joint business planning during the retail conference in Fayetteville at the University of Arkansas on Oct. 30.

JOINT BUSINESS PLAN

When I joined Walmart (in 2009) we were a bit contentious with our supplier partners. We made some strategic decisions about five years ago to go a different way. The strategy was well founded but at the end of the day there were some severe unintended consequences, like the alienation of our supplier partnerships, and we became misaligned on our mission to deliver to our customers."… "We had to try and create a model of transparency and trust with our suppliers that could help us build our businesses together," Mac Naughton said.

Public Domain : https://commons.wikimedia. org/w/index.php?curid=11887955

In these meetings, he said the teams work on shared goals that help both businesses grow sales and market share. In a year's time, Mac Naughton said between 200 and 300 suppliers conduct joint business planning meetings with Walmart U.S.

Latest news on this cooperation:

On 14th of June 2016 The Wall Street Journal reported that **Walmart and P&G's $10 billion marriage was under strain,** as both companies face stalling growth, the big-box retailer challenged the consumer-products giant with more store brands, lower prices and less shelf space, and Walmart Stores Inc. stocked a European competitor right next to the company's iconic Tide detergent. It was a barb for the consumer-products giant, which has long considered Walmart's shelves to be its most valuable retail real estate.

Source: TBP November 6, 2013 http://talkbusiness.net/2013/11/wal-mart-pg-discuss-joint-business-planning/ By SARAH NASSAUER and SHARON TERLEP Updated June 14, 2016 7:57 p.m. EThttp://www.wsj.com/articles/wal-mart-and-p-g-a-10-billion-marriage-under-strain-1465948431

Such cooperation is only conceivable between larger firms (or more precisely partners of similar size) that have confidence in each other (like, for example, Procter & Gamble and Walmart: their co-operation has been going on for more than 25 years, growing from a $400 business to one of 10 billion).

Figure 11.7. The zone of profit sharing between producer and traders

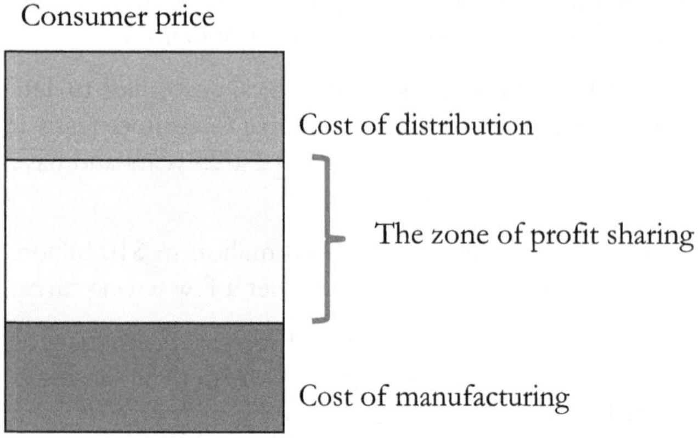

11.4.3. Manufacturer's dominance

Producers of well-known branded products and services make efforts to have control over their prices at all levels of the distribution channel. What they consider vitally important is to see ultimate consumer prices take shape in agreement with their own market policy. It is, however, against the law to fix prices vertically (and horizontally as well), therefore the producer's price definition can only take the form of recommended price. The producers' price control can be strong only if the large manufacturers are faced with a relatively fragmented commercial sector. This situation is best illustrated with the Japanese distribution system.

11.4.4. Traders' dominance

The first two decades of the 21st century have been characterized by the strong concentration of trade in most parts of the world. Mergers and acquisitions lead to the establishment of huge commercial conglomerates in Western Europe and North America that, as a result of their global policy, now play a determining role at the FMCG markets – not only in Western Europe or North America, but in other parts of the world as well (Table 11.4).

These huge ventures are suitable as price setters both on manufacturers' and consumers' sides. They are even capable of making them pay an extra fee for having their products displayed on the shelves (shelf-fee). Manufacturers may often find their relations with the larger commercial firms advantageous because this allows them to deliver large quantities of goods to one or just a few traders. Consequently, co-operation with these large or 'mass retailers' can lead to a rapid increase in the turnover of the suppliers.

Increase in turnover, however, does not always go together with profit growth. Meeting the price and other conditions set by financially strong traders exercises a kind of pressure on the manufacturers' unit contribution margin. Bolen and Davis (1997:40-53) reported that, although the suppliers of mass retailers in the United States enjoyed a faster increase in turnover than other manufacturers, the increase in their profits was considerably slower. Even giant corporations like Procter & Gamble, Unilever, or Kraft, which are in a serious bargaining position, are looking for new methods, with a view to supplying their large customers in a profitable way.

Supplying mass retailers may lead to conflicts in the case of those producers who also sell to other (let's call them traditional) channels. In the case that these producers do not meet the price

expectations of the mass retailer than they may be omitted from the list of suppliers. If they do then it may hurt their traditional channels. The producers are compelled to maintain a careful balance between the low prices of the mass retailer and the higher prices of the traditional channels. According to the opinion of retailer experts, the customers of the traditional channels accept, for the higher service value, 10-15% higher prices. Producers are compelled to implement a pricing strategy which does not increase price differences.

Table 11.4. Worldwide Top Ten Retailers

Rank	Name	Country of origin	Revenue in 2014 (US $ Billion)	Profit margin	2009-2014 CARG*	No of countries of operations	% of revenue from foreign operations
1	Walmart Stores Inc.	US	485.7	3.5%	3.5%	28	28.3
2	Costco Wholesale Corp.	US	112.6	1.9%	9.5%	10	18.6
3	The Kroger Co.	US	108.4	1.6%	7.2%	1	0.0
4	Schwarz (Lidl)	Germany	102.7	n/a	7.7%	26	59.2
5	Tesco PLC	UK	99.7	-13.0%	1.8%	13	30.0
6	Carrefour S.A.	France	98.5	1.9%	-2.8%	34	52.7
7	Aldi	Germany	86.5	n/a	6.8%	17	57.1
8	Metro AG	Germany	85.6	0.3%	-0.8	32	59.3
9	The Home Depot Inc.	US	83.2	7.6%	4.7%	4	10.2
10	Walgreen	US	76.4	2.7%	3.8%	2	1.5

**CARG = Compound annual growth rate*
Source: Deloitte (2016) Global Powers of Retailing 2016 - Navigating the new digital divide pp 23

EXHIBIT 11.5. PRODUCER-CONTROLLED DISTRIBUTION CHANNELS IN JAPAN

One particular feature of the Japanese distribution system is that the manager of the marketing channel ('channel captain') is typically the producer in the case of the well-known large brands. In North-America and Western Europe the large and strong retail networks dominate a lot of areas in the distribution channel (they are closer to the consumers, they determine what is needed, they control prices, etc.). In Japan the strong manufacturers, most of the time in an oligopoly situation, face a fragmented set of commercial firms and in this context the manufacturers' basic marketing strategy is to coordinate the distribution channels and keep them under control. The distribution channel functions as a vertical marketing system, operated by the manufacturer and, in several cases, the other member organizations of the channel depending on their size (and often due to their participation as well). The tools of non-administrative control are quite varied and efficient. Some of them are important elements of the Japanese business practice, such as:

- The system of (recommended) consumer prices set by the manufacturer. Manufacturers in their oligopoly position loathe fighting price wars with each other. In the oligopoly

market a price competition always has the potential of becoming a double-edged weapon. Therefore, they would rather prescribe prices to the vulnerable traders in the form of 'recommended consumer prices'. Traders consider these recommendations compulsory for themselves, since their survival depends on the manufacturers' goodwill.

- At the same time, the manufacturer performs the functions of marketing promotion (nationwide advertising, local sales promotion, etc.) and provides the services related to the product (guarantee, replacement, product information, etc.).
- In Japan, the possibility of the producers taking back obsolete goods is an important element of commercial practice. It means that salesman returns the goods to the manufacturer even if they weren't sold in consignee. This practice (together with the recommended prices) means security for the salesmen and guarantees their ability to produce their margin. Manufacturers also prefer to take back the products than apply price reductions. (Perhaps the goods can be sold somewhere else and, in this way, they do not harm the quality image of the brand.)
- At the same time, Japanese manufacturers apply a range of benefits (rabats, ribeito) to ensure the loyalty of the traders. The purpose of this solution is to prevent outside competitors from entering the channel.

Source: Rekettye, 1994: 266–268

EXHIBIT 11.6. THE RELATIONSHIP BETWEEN SUPERMARKETS AND SUPPLIERS: WHAT ARE THE IMPLICATIONS FOR CONSUMERS?

The buyer power of these multinational retailers enables them to control their suppliers. The imbalance of bargaining power is especially true in the case of agricultural products. In any national market only a handful of supermarket gatekeepers stand between thousands of suppliers and millions of consumers. As a result, suppliers have access to fewer alternative large buyers and therefore considerably less bargaining power. Here is the UK example (See the infographic below).

The imbalance of bargaining power allows retailers to carry on abusive buying practices and this has been documented across the EU and in other developed economies. The abuses are financial in nature and/or create uncertainty for suppliers. Examples of abusive practice are shown here:

- Listing fees
- De-listing/threat of de-listing
- Slotting fees
- Demanding extra or unforeseen discounts or payments from suppliers
- Demanding retrospective payments, extra discounts, and after-sale rebates
- Return of unsold goods to supplier
- Late payments
- Retrospective changes to agreed terms

- Below cost selling
- Influencing product availability to, or raising the costs of, other retailers
- Promotion of retailers' own brands (own brands).

In spite of this high bargaining power and low buying prices, consumer prices still remain high: a great share of margin is taken by the distributors and retailers. The above figure shows the percentage shares of the participants of a Costa Rican pineapple supply chain.

Source: The relationship between supermarkets and suppliers: What are the implications for consumers? Summary of the main report, (2012) Consumers International (CI) Organisation Infographics Tania Hurt-Newton. http://www.consumersinternational.org/news-and-media/resource-zone/the-relationship-between-supermarkets-and-suppliers-summary/

11.5. Discounts, benefits and refunds provided by manufacturers

Manufacturers have various methods, like discounts, benefits of refunds flexibly to change or modify prices in the distribution channel. In this part of the chapter we are going to focus on the tools that manufacturers (and wholesalers) most frequently use to make their prices more attractive, to win over and motivate their commercial partners. The impact of the discounts is very similar to the method of price differentiation. The main difference is that, in the course of price differentiation, it is the declared price (list price) itself that is changed, whereas in the case of discounts the declared price does not change; what does change is the sales revenue realized by the seller, just as in the case of price differentiation. In this respect, the price discounts are more flexible tools of managing prices than price differentiation.

Price discounts are divided in literature into the following groups:

- quantitative discounts,
- commercial and functional discounts,
- seasonal discounts,
- promotional discounts,
- discounts tied to payments.

11.5.1. Quantitative price discounts

Quantitative discounts are the best-known form of price discounts. Their purpose is to motivate buyers (resellers) to place ever-growing orders. There are, however, considerations of cost rationalization underlying these discounts: with larger quantities ordered, the seller will have smaller unit distribution costs, even if we disregard manufacturing costs (decreased inventory, storage, invoicing, occasional packaging and transportation costs). We must not forget either that quantitative discounts are traditional tools of the trade that have been with us and widely accepted for centuries.

The discount has several types, which can be distinguished by:

- the quantity of the commodities sold (tons, pieces, litres, etc.) or
- the value of commodities sold (in this case perhaps it is not correct to speak about quantitative discount, we had better call it 'value discount').

Firms (primarily manufacturers) which sell only a small number of easy to distinguish products mainly use the first type. Discount based on value (which is more typical of wholesale) is used by firms that are present at the market with a wide range of goods. Tables 11.5 and 11.6 give examples for these two types of discount.

Table 11.5. Discount given for the quantity of a one-time purchase

Quiantity of one time purchase (tons)	Discount given from the invoice (in %)
1 — 5	0,0
6 — 10	3,0
11 — 20	4,0
Over 21	5,0

Table 11.6. Discount given for the value of a one-time purchase

Value of one-time purchase (in USD)	Discount given from the invoice (in%)
Under 50 000	0.0
50 001 — 100 000	3.0
100 001 — 500 000	4.0
Over 500 000	5.0

Another way of distinguishing quantitative discounts is possible depending on whether they are linked to:

- individual purchases (non-cumulative discount), or
- the total of purchases realized in a period of time (e.g. a year), or
- to an action (temporary discount).

The purpose of the non-cumulative discount is to motivate customers to buy a larger quantity on one occasion. This is in the seller's interest mainly for cost-efficiency consideration. Cumulative discount motivates customers to keep on buying from the same firm; because they can count on significant discounts in this way. This solution not only encourages the purchase of larger quantities but also helps keep customers' loyalty. The impact of bonus-type refunds is very similar to that of cumulative discounts. Traders get bonus points for the turnover realized in a certain period of time (e.g. a year)

and when this period is over, the manufacturer gives them a refund according to the conditions agreed earlier.

There are, however, some decisions that the seller must make anyway, namely:

- what is the minimum quantity or value that triggers the discount,
- what grades or steps should be included in the structure of the discounts parallel with the increase of the quantity or value,
- how much is the discount that should go together with the individual grades,
- whether discounts should be given separately at each grade, or
- only in a total for the whole order (the differences between the latter two methods are shown in Table 11.7).

Table 11.7. The differences between the discounts given gradually and the discounts granted for the order as a whole.

Grades of the discount by the magnitude of the turnover					
From the amount (USD)	to the amount (USD)	Discount %	Turnover	The amount of total discount in case of gradual discount policy (USD)	The total amount of discount calculated for the whole order (USD)
0	50000	0%	40000	0	0
50000	100000	5%	80000	1500	4000
100000	250000	7%	160000	6700	11200
250000	500000	9%	320000	19300	28800
500000	and above	12%	640000	46300	76800

11.5.2. Commercial and functional discounts

Manufacturers grant commercial and functional discounts to resellers for the functions and services they provide at various levels of the distribution channel. This may sound a little strange at first because, so far, we have simplified the process, saying the traders purchase the goods; add their mark-up to the purchase price and then sell the product. Manufacturers, who wish to keep control over the retail price of the well-known brands they produce, often define their list prices as consumer prices. From this list price, they then give discounts of various amounts to the retailers, depending on which level of the distribution channel they operate (whether they are wholesalers or retailers). To facilitate the understanding of the commercial or functional discounts let us examine how the $1,000 consumer price shown in the example at the beginning of this chapter changes in the system of discounts.

There are manufacturers who insist on including even the discount given to the customers in the invoice. Table 11.9 by Rosenbloom (1995:378), presents the price anatomy of a 10-dollar guitar string.

Table 11.8. Commercial and functional discounts.

List price	**$1 000**	Consumer price	$1000+ VAT
Discount to wholesaler	**25%**	Wholesaler's purchase price	1000 · 0.75 = $750
Discount to retailer	**13%**	Retailer's purchase price	1000 · 0.87 = $870

Table 11.9. The price anatomy of a 10 -dollar guitar string in the distribution channel

List price	10 $
Wholesaler's discount	66%
Wholesaler's purchase price	3,40 $
Retailer's discount	50%
Retailer's purchase price	5,00 $
Discount to consumer	25%
Purchase price of ultimate buyer	7,50$

One problem with commercial and functional discounts is that these days the distinction between wholesalers and retailers is not as clear-cut as it used to be. The large commercial chains perform both functions; consequently, it is not easy to decide to which type of discount they are entitled. This is the reason why discounts and benefits depending on the quantity or value of the purchase are becoming more and more widespread.

11.5.3. Seasonal discounts

There are a large number of goods that are produced and consumed in different seasons. Either their production (e.g. agricultural produce) or their consumption (e.g. air conditioners, heaters, holidays, etc.) is limited to a certain period. The producers' fundamental business interest is to make consumption more even, and bring it closer to the pace of production. This is why they have developed the kind of discounts which are meant to motivate resellers to buy these products and services outside the peak season as well, thus reducing the costs arising from storage of the goods. Seasonal discounts can sometimes reach considerable proportions. The measure of the discount depends on the difference between the time of purchase, and the peak consumption period.

11.5.3. Promotional discounts

Discounts, benefits and refunds applied for promotional purposes can take several forms:

- The classical promotional discounts are granted by manufacturers to the reseller with the expectation that they should perform the tasks of local sales promotion in return for it. Manufacturers of big, national or even global brands organize the national or international campaigns themselves. However, these are not always sufficient to raise the interest of the local customers; there is a need for local action too, which is typically organized by the retailers distributing the product locally.

- Supporting local sales promotion can be realized with a discount of a certain percentage, but other solutions are also possible, such as a refund: if a certain turnover is realized the manufacturer reimburses a part of the advertising costs incurred by the trader.
- Quite frequently the price promotion campaign is initiated by the manufacturer: for a certain period, the manufacturer gives a discount to the trader with a view to transferring it to customers.
- The exercise when the reseller is given a certain quantity of goods after the purchase of a given quantity of products has an effect similar to that of the price discount. On the whole he will obtain the product more cheaply and can resell it at a better price.

11.5.4. Other discounts and benefits

Promotional discount has a specific form, called 'push money'. In order to increase sales, manufacturers (and sometimes wholesalers) decide to motivate retail personnel directly. The benefit (also promoted as a prize sometimes) given after the sale of a product is called push money in literature.

Discounts linked to the time of payment

It is a typical business practice that the seller of the products and services offers a discount to the customers who pay their bills before the due date. The discount given in the case of immediate payment is called skonto in international trade. The amount of the discount is influenced by the traditions dominant on the market concerned and the prevailing interest rate. The person who offers the discount should define:

- the length of time agreed for the validity of the discount,
- the measure of the discount and
- the interval within which the customer must pay without discount (beyond that date he will be penalised).

It is considered covert discount if the seller significantly increases the deadline for payment generally accepted in the business, without threat of price rise or any other disadvantages. Large commercial chains often impose such covert price discounts on their suppliers and this is the reason why they have an advantage over the traditional channels.

11.6. List price, discounts and pocket price

So far, we have reviewed the various types of discounts, benefits and refunds. It must be noted, however, that items reducing the list price can appear not only one by one, but also altogether, added up. The large number of discounts often makes actual prices inextricable for the companies. List prices are usually decided at the level of top management, on the basis of market trends, cost forecasts, expected competition, inflation forecasts, etc. Discounts are defined at lower levels of the organization's hierarchy (such as the commercial department). Promotional tools are the responsibility of the product or brand manager. This explains why it is such a complex task to co-ordinate actions.

Marn and Rosiello (1992:84-93) named the price that companies actually receive for their products the 'pocket price' and pointed out in their study that proper monitoring and management of the various discounts is an important part of price management. They drew attention to two phenomena:

- one is called *pocket price waterfall.* Companies can waste a significant part of their profit by letting various units of their organization give discounts – most of the time without co-ordination – to their customers. They observed the pricing activities of a linoleum seller and found that the received price was almost 23% lower than the list price.

- The other phenomenon is called price band (See exhibit 11.6). It refers to the situation when the same commodity is offered on the market at strikingly different prices in consequence of the various discounts, and this does not always serve the manufacturer's interest. The notion of price bands used in the context of retail prices is analyzed in detail by Davey, Childs and Carlotti (1998:116-127). Exhibit 11.8 presents the way in which agents of some leading pop music stars do business: instead of using fixed prices they prefer price bands.

EXHIBIT 11.7. AN EXAMPLE FOR THE PRICE BAND

One of the students of the author made a quick personal survey in the shops near the university to check the price band of the local cooking oil brand Vénusz in Pécs Hungary. She found that the price band's width was 38% with the cheapest price in Tesco, and the highest in a neighbourhood convenience shop.

EXHIBIT 11.8. HOW MUCH DOES IT COST TO BOOK YOUR FAVOURITE BAND?

The question was put by Andrea Seikaly in Variety as follows: "How much does it cost to have Justin Timberlake play in your back yard? Booking agency Degy Entertainment has got you covered.

The company has released a list of the approximate per-show rates suggested by some artists' agents, ranging from $1,000 to over $100,000. Taylor Swift, Madonna, Justin Timberlake, Justin Bieber, James Taylor, Dave Matthews, Bruce Springsteen, and Bon Jovi each stand to bank over $1 million per performance, while acts like the Black Eyed Peas, Kanye West and Maroon 5 cash in upwards of $400,000.

While these numbers are only rough figures - actual prices can be negotiated and are dependent upon other factors - the list serves as a gauge of how much you'd have to shell out to book your favourite band."

Justin Timberlake at a Concert in St Paul, Minnesota

Source: http://variety.com/2014/music/news/degy-entertainment-breaks-down-artist-booking-fees-1201189498/

CHAPTER 12. RETAIL AND WHOLESALE PRICING

OBJECTIVE 1 To examine current developments in wholesale and retail trade and to ascertain how these new circumstances influence pricing attitudes.

OBJECTIVE 2 To discuss the role psychology is playing in retail businesses in setting consumer prices and to illustrate the different tactics used by retailers to secure their customer base.

OBJECTIVE 3 To examine the competition between large retail chains and the role private labels play in that competition.

OBJECTIVE 4 To review the development of online retail, and to examine pricing policies of online retailers.

12.1 Introduction

In this chapter, we examine the elbow room traders have in price policy, their possible pricing strategies and all the price related actions that traders (mainly retailers) are prepared to perform in order to attract customers

12.2. Reshuffle of retail and wholesale functions

Traditionally, the trading function is divided into two roles: wholesaling and retailing. Trade has the task of bridging those temporal, spatial, assortment-related and other differences that separate the manufacturers of products and services from the ultimate consumer or user.

Customers of wholesalers are typically retailers, and/or direct business and organizational users. Wholesale has the following functions:

- Buying large quantities and breaking them down into smaller parts, i.e. prepare commodities for the retail trade.
- Storage and stockpiling.
- Transportation.
- Financing and risk taking.
- Selling and wholesale promotion.
- Collection and transfer of market information.
- Services and counselling for direct buyers.

The functions of a retailer are determined by the fact that they are the one who meet the ultimate buyers and connects directly with customers; consequently, their efforts should be focused on the quality of the service they provide to customers.

To perform these tasks, retailers also buy and store goods, keep stocks, collect information, act as middlemen, finance, take risks, decide on assortments, take care of the shopping environment, sell (of course), and apply the direct tools of promotion. As you can see, the two functions are fundamentally quite similar. It follows from this fact that we often witness the merger of these two functions within the same business organization, since wholesale as a separate organization or unit is gradually losing importance. This does not mean to say that the wholesale function is going to disappear or lose all importance, but it has been observed that its existing and important tasks are often taken over by the manufacturers or retailers:

- Manufacturers can decide to employ agents of their own, establish depots for wholesale and manage services to retailers within their own organization. In this case the manufacturer will keep the wholesale mark-up to himself, or - better to say - he can sell his product to the retailer at a higher price.
- What happens even more frequently is that larger commercial chains (originally retailers) decide not to buy from the wholesaler any longer, but establish a unit within their organization to perform the wholesale function (these are called 'distribution centres' most of the time), which supply their retail units.
- Smaller retailers can also establish an association for buying and this will take over the wholesale function.

EXHIBIT 12.1. LIDL'S WHOLESALE LOGISTIC SYSTEM IN HUNGARY

Lidl - often described as a 'hard discount' retailer – opened its first store in Hungary on November 18, 2004 and, at present (2017), the number of its stores in this country is 164. The firm's global purchasing strategy is strongly determined by the Procurement Department in Germany. Lidl's core activity is food retailing supplemented with selling detergents, household electronic appliances, and clothing.

As far as Hungarian logistics is concerned, Lidl has divided the country into two parts with centres in Székesfehérvár and Hejőkürt, which supply the areas assigned to them. Each store is assigned to one of the centres; the centres receive the goods and supply the stores. For economic reasons, certain products or brands are available only in one of the centres and sold in the stores that belong to that centre.

12.3. Price strategies in trade

Both the wholesale and retail trades have a number of types. Their description can be found in marketing textbooks (Schoell-Guiltinan, 1995; Bradley, 1995; Bauer-Berács, 2006; Kotler-Keller, 2006; Agárdi 2010).

Traders are usually grouped according to the commodities they sell, their targeted clientele, the range and depth of supply, the quality and price level applied, but for retail shops some other criteria are used, such as the size of the store, the method of serving shoppers, and the geographical location of

the store. The scope of this book does not allow us to give a detailed description of the various types. From the viewpoint of their price policy, the following categories are to be distinguished:

- very aggressive price policy, with the view of having the most favourable supply as far as prices are concerned,
- aggressive price policy, focusing on - besides the products of average price - the supply of products at bargain price as well, gaining, in this way, a head-start on the competition,
- average level price policy, with not very striking, rather weak bargain prices,
- services and strong awareness of image (special shops, boutiques), high prices,
- high prices, supply meant to fill niches, services (shops with special offers),
- high price level, shops selling innovative products (industrial design, design centre).

The key decision that commercial firms make concerning price policy is actually the determination of the position they intend to occupy as far as price and quality are concerned. This decision is inseparable from the firms' product and assortment policies. The decision that commercial firms make in this respect is more complex than that of the manufacturing companies because it concerns not only the position of the goods traded, but also the quality and value increasing effect of the services provided by the traders. It is also not easy achieve the requested perception from retail consumers. Reading the following by McKinsey experts it becomes clear that the price perception of consumers is dependent not on the whole assortment offered by the shop, rather on some product categories and some items - called by them Key Value Categories and Key Value Items.

EXHIBIT 12.2. Key Value Categories

New methodologies, powered by big data and advanced analytics, can help retailers attract value-conscious consumers without sacrificing margins.

As retail executives know all too well, most pricing decisions require a trade-off between margin and price perception. To avoid a "race to the bottom" - the self-defeating exercise of trying to beat every competitor's price on every item - retailers must hone their ability to make smart pricing investments. Indeed, the savviest retailers identify key value categories (**KVCs**) and key value items (KVIs) - those product categories and SKUs whose prices consumers tend to notice and remember. If a retailer can do this accurately, it can price those specific products competitively while charging higher prices on other items.

Yet, despite the importance of KVC and KVI identification, many retailers still lack a systematic, fact-based process for doing it. Some retailers rely almost entirely on the commercial intuition of experienced category managers. To be fair, a number of retailers do use data to try to isolate KVCs and KVIs: for example, they might benchmark their assortment and prices against those of discounters, on the assumption that price-sensitive consumers use discounters as a baseline for comparison shopping. Some retailers apply a simple heuristic - they use a combination of weighted criteria such as purchase frequency and brand perception to select KVIs.

But in today's data-rich business environment, retailers can - and certainly should - go beyond these basic techniques. To accurately identify KVCs and KVIs, leading retailers tap into the treasure trove of transaction data, loyalty-card data, and online research available to them. They use sophisticated methodologies that require the ability to analyze billions of transactions and hundreds of gigabytes of data. Harnessing the power of advanced analytics to improve price perception can have significant impact: a margin boost of one to two percentage points, with steady or even increasing sales volume.

Which categories and items affect consumer price perception?

Broadly speaking, products can be classified into two groups: frequently bought items (purchased twice a month or more often) and infrequently bought items. Most grocery items fall into the former classification, but grocery retailers - particularly hypermarkets, which have higher shares of nonfood products - also carry infrequently bought items. By contrast, the assortment of home-improvement retailers consists mainly of infrequently bought items such as power tools and home appliances. Our recommended methodology for identifying KVIs and KVCs differs slightly for each of these two product groups.

Ideally, KVIs will account for 15 to 25 percent of sales in the category. Other products in the assortment are classified as either "foreground" or "background" items (exhibit).

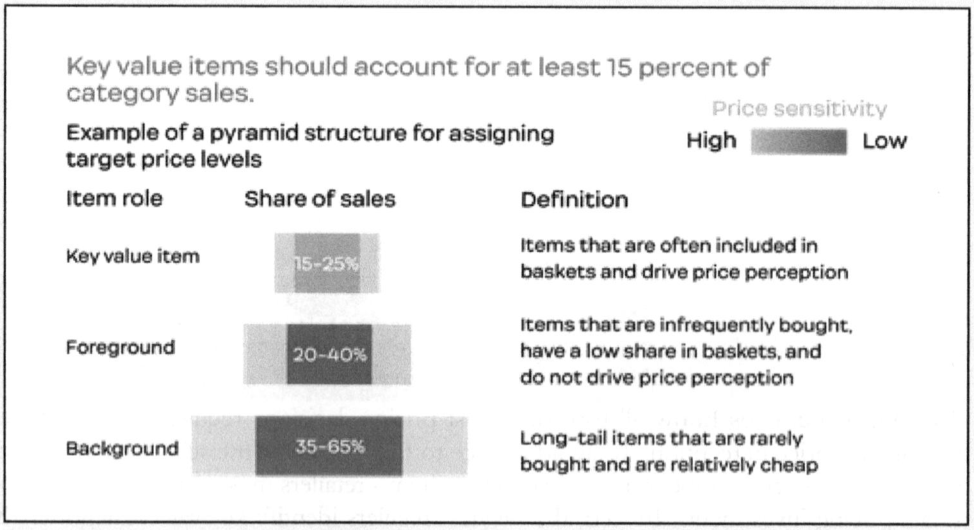

Identifying KVCs and KVIs among frequently purchased products

For frequently bought items, retailers can select KVCs by calculating a normalized score for each category based on three criteria: frequency of purchase (weighted at 40 percent), customer reach (40 percent), and promotional share (20 percent). Then, to identify KVIs, retailers can take four sequential steps, each of which involves the use of big data and advanced analytical models and calculations.

First, identify SKUs that are a 'good deal' or represent good value for money. These SKUs are either cheap relative to the category or have a low per-unit price. A two-liter bottle of soda, for example, might qualify as a good deal whereas a half-liter bottle might not, since the two-liter bottle's price per liter is much lower. These calculations should be done for every item for every week of data, to correct for any temporary price changes and promotions. (An item on sale might be a good deal that week, but not during other weeks when it is sold at full price.)

Next, identify customers who buy mostly good-value-for-money SKUs, on the assumption that these are price-sensitive customers who are likely to remember the prices of the products they buy. The analysis can only be done with loyalty-card data. Retailers without loyalty-card data can identify price-sensitive baskets instead of customers, using transaction data.

Third, assess the relative importance of items purchased by price-sensitive customers. This step requires the retailer to answer two questions about each item: What percentage of price-sensitive customers buy the item? And what percentage of all the customers who buy the item are price-sensitive customers? Those two metrics are then combined and averaged into a price-awareness score.

Finally, rank the SKUs, according to price-awareness scores, within their categories. The top-ranked SKUs are KVIs.

A methodology for infrequently bought products

For retailers whose assortment consists primarily of infrequently bought items, we recommend a slightly different methodology that combines three sets of analytics, again using big data. Each set of analytics helps the retailer determine which product categories meet the following criteria:

- **Frequently researched online and purchased fairly regularly** (perhaps once every two to three months). The assumption is that consumers tend to remember the prices of items in such categories. The data on online pre-purchase research is typically sourced from web-analytics providers such as Google Analytics, whereas the data on actual purchases is from the retailer's own transactional data.

- **Expensive or purchased fairly regularly**. To perform this analysis for a category, the retailer needs to calculate average ticket price and frequency of purchase.

- **Often found in price-sensitive baskets.** By analyzing transaction or loyalty-card data, retailers can determine which products often appear in baskets alongside other price-sensitive items (that is, those that meet the first two criteria).

Triangulating the three sets of results yields a comprehensive list of KVCs. The retailer can then calculate a price-awareness score - based on frequency of purchase and share of category sales - for each item in the KVCs. The highest-scoring items are the KVIs.

Practical advice for implementation

In each case, the results of the analyses should be commercially validated - that is, category managers and the commercial team should review and approve the results. Typically, they would evaluate the KVC list using several lenses. For example, does the category play a strategic role for the retailer? Is the category a traffic driver or one that typically triggers additional purchases? (The purchase of a can of paint, for instance, is likely to trigger purchases of paintbrushes, a ladder, drop cloths, paint thinner, and so on.) Does the category have one or more highly visible brands? We've found that the most accurate KVC and KVI lists result from a blend of art and science: category managers' commercial knowledge and experience, combined with the rigor of big data analytics.

Implementing these methodologies doesn't require expensive new systems or an army of data analysts. We've found that many retailers need just one person with analytical skills to learn how to run the algorithms and codes. That person can then train the commercial team to interpret and use the results.

These methodologies have yielded impact across different types and sizes of retailers in both small and large markets. An Eastern European grocery chain, for instance, had been trying to beat all of its main competitors' prices on almost every item. Since shifting to a KVC- and KVI-focused pricing strategy, its margins have risen two percentage points. Similarly, a Western European specialty retailer used these methodologies to revamp its pricing architecture and achieved a margin increase of 1.5 percentage points.

Source: McKinsey&Company, November 2016
Reprinted with the permission of McKinsey&Company

In the very concentrated retail market there are also quality tiers, as in all markets, with hard discount shops at the low end and the luxury warehouses and haute couture at the high end. A typical Lidl store stands at the lower end of the retail market. Products are stacked on removable pallets for easy re-stocking.

Source: iBy Besjollen - Own work, CC BY-SA 3.0, https://commons.wikimedia.org/w/index.php?curid=26159658

Passage Pommeraye, an ultra-upscale shopping hall in Nantes, UNESCO World Heritage site (the shops here belong to the high end of the market).

Source: By Original uploader was Shadows44 at fr.wikipedia - Transferred from fr.wikipedia; transferred to Commons by User:Bloody-libu using CommonsHelper., CC BY-SA 1.0, https://commons. wikimedia. org/w/index. php? curid=19207419

The quality tiers differentiate themselves with the quality and prices of the goods they carry and the value of services they offer to their clients (Figure 12.1).

Figure 12.1. Possible positioning of trade

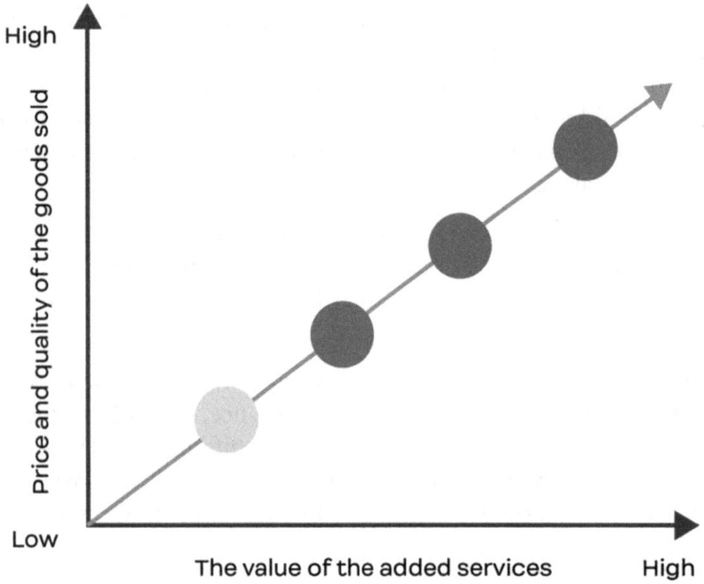

The price level of a trading company depends on the purchase prices and the mark-ups applied. Mark-up is to cover the costs arising from the distribution of the products and the unit profit. All in all, the level of mark-up depends on the costs incurred by the firm (the level of the services provided by trade) and its profit expectations. No trader can pretend to be independent from the mark-up level established in the business, i.e. the competitors.

Table 12.1. Average gross mark-ups and net profit levels (in % of the sale) in some selected branches in the third quarter of 2016

Branches	Gross mark-up %	Net profit (%)
Apparel retail	39	4.72
Internet and mail order	32	1.84
Department and discount stores	28	2.81
Drug retail	76	5.29
Grocery retail	22	2.86
Home Improvement retail	34	3.88
Specialty retail (in 1st quarter of 2017)	53	9.28
Technology retail	15	1.58
Automotive aftermarket	17	2.43
Wholesale	14	2.05

Source: The data of CSIMarket company (csimarket.com)

The price policy of the trading companies is realized through the differentiated application of the mark-ups. Different mark-ups are used by the different traders and shops and there can be significant

variations in the percentage used even within the same company or store for products of different quality or different brands, etc.

Wholesalers usually work with list prices. From this price they give various discounts, benefits or refunds to their customers. The types of discounts, benefits and refunds are the same as those granted by the manufacturers. Therefore we are not going to discuss them now, but will instead turn our attention to retail prices, and the price policy, pricing methods practised by retailers.

EXHIBIT 12.3. RETAIL MARK-UPS AND THE POWER OF AMAZON

Everyone knows bricks-and-mortar retailers have lots of overheads, the result of buildings and shelf space and inventory and sales people to help you find what you're looking for.

It's not cheap to be a retailer - we got that much. But how much does it cost the consumer, really? What sort of mark-up do retailers add to the wholesale cost so they can cover their overheads and squeeze out a decent profit as well?

The answer might surprise you. The range of mark-ups is quite wide indeed.

And while mark-ups are of interest to consumers (they're paying the bill, after all), they're also important to investors in retail stocks. As a general rule, retailers who impose large mark-ups are more vulnerable to competition from low-overhead online retailers than are retailers with modest mark-ups.

Amazon's average mark-up, for example, is 15%. Critics of Amazon say the collection of sales tax (and the cost of shipping for non-Prime members) mitigates Amazon's advantage over traditional retailers. But they don't understand just how wide the gulf really is. (Think Grand Canyon and you're close.)

How much do retailers add to wholesale cost?

At the low end of the continuum is Costco where the average mark-up is 10%. Such a low mark-up puts them in an enviable competitive position - an unassailable position, really - against all comers, and that includes low-overhead online retailers.

In the middle of the continuum are biggies Wal-Mart avg. 32% mark-up and Target (46%). While these retailers are noticing incremental pressure from online vendors, they're also fighting back, demanding help from suppliers via exclusives and differentiation of product, among other things. This, combined with the fact that they sell a lot of perishables and low-priced items (which are not practical to ship), make them less vulnerable to online competition.

Also in the middle are specialty retailers, such as Staples (avg. 41% mark-up) and Dick's Sporting Goods (50%). Investors should avoid getting involved in the stocks of hard goods retailers like these, as they're clearly in the gun sight of online retail. Given their overhead burden (much of which is fixed), Staples and Dick's will never be able to match (or even come close to) Amazon's mark-up.

At the high end of the continuum mark-ups approach and exceed 80% - which is the average mark-up at Macy's, for example. Macy's shoppers have to be a bit surprised by the large average mark-up, given the retailer's heavy use of promotions and coupons. By way of comparison, high-end competitor Nordstrom averages a 67% mark-up, and Nieman Marcus, 65%. These apparel-centric retailers are thriving in the current environment, but they'll be subjected to plenty of pressure in the years to come. With a huge mark-up advantage (15% compared to

65-80%), it's no wonder Amazon CEO Jeff Bezos recently called the apparel opportunity "very exciting."

Another retailer at the high end of the continuum, Bed, Bath & Beyond has an average mark-up of 81%, and sits squarely in the path of Amazon's unrelenting Price Efficiency Revolution. With Amazon's ability to sell just about everything Bed, Bath sells, with a hundred-fold broader selection and at a tiny fraction of Bed, Bath's mark-up, it's only a matter of time before their margins suffer considerable pressure.

What's the future look like for retail?

Bricks-and-mortar stores are never going away - rest assured, shoppers! - but how they'll look and who will survive is anybody's guess. An entirely new type of shopping model might emerge, such as a low-overhead, low-mark-up 'showroom'. It's also conceivable that conventional shopping malls will evolve into something resembling today's outlet mall, where brands deal direct with consumers, for the simple reason that it's more efficient.

As it stands today, Nike marks up a product by 50%, then sells it to Big Box Retailer, who marks it up - let's be conservative - by another 50% before selling it to the consumer. As consumer empowerment grows in the coming years, it's going to get tougher and tougher to justify that second mark-up.

Source: http://blogs.marketwatch.com/great-columnist/2012/10/15/retail-markups-and-the-power-of-amazon/ Written by Arne Alsin.

12.4. Setting the ultimate (retail, consumer) price

When the retail price policy is put into practice, specific prices are defined with so-called price multipliers (in other words: mark-up multipliers). Their use is very simple. All you do is multiply the purchase price with the multiplier calculated well beforehand and you get the selling price. This is the commercial application of the formula: 'cost + profit', which has now become 'purchase price + mark-up'. This, however, does not work everywhere and certainly not in the same way. The use of price multipliers is just a *technique*, but traders can also take as a starting point the prices that consumers deem acceptable and count backwards, using the purchase prices to produce the price multiplier that employees will be requested to use during the practical implementation of pricing.

The price calculated with the multiplier is not necessarily the ultimate selling price, because it can undergo certain changes with regard to various criteria. (For example, if the price multiplier produces a unit price of $200 the firm may decide to change it to $199 following the so-called odd pricing rule.)

Retail shops can have many different forms (Figure 12.2). A typical fact about these shops is that they sell many unrelated products. The price policy applied by the firm does not focus on the individual products, but on the shop or firm as a whole. Within this system an important role can be played by the various mark-ups used to set the prices of certain product categories and product families. The pricing of the various product categories and product groups is related within the shop by the goal profitably to sell the assortment as a whole and this can be achieved even if occasionally a product is sold without profit or at a loss.

Retail (consumer) prices are considered very important because these are the ones that buyers encounter and they can seriously influence their decision to shop. Consumer prices also play a part in promotion and influence the decision to buy with price psychology tools as well.

Figure 12.2. Retail shop types

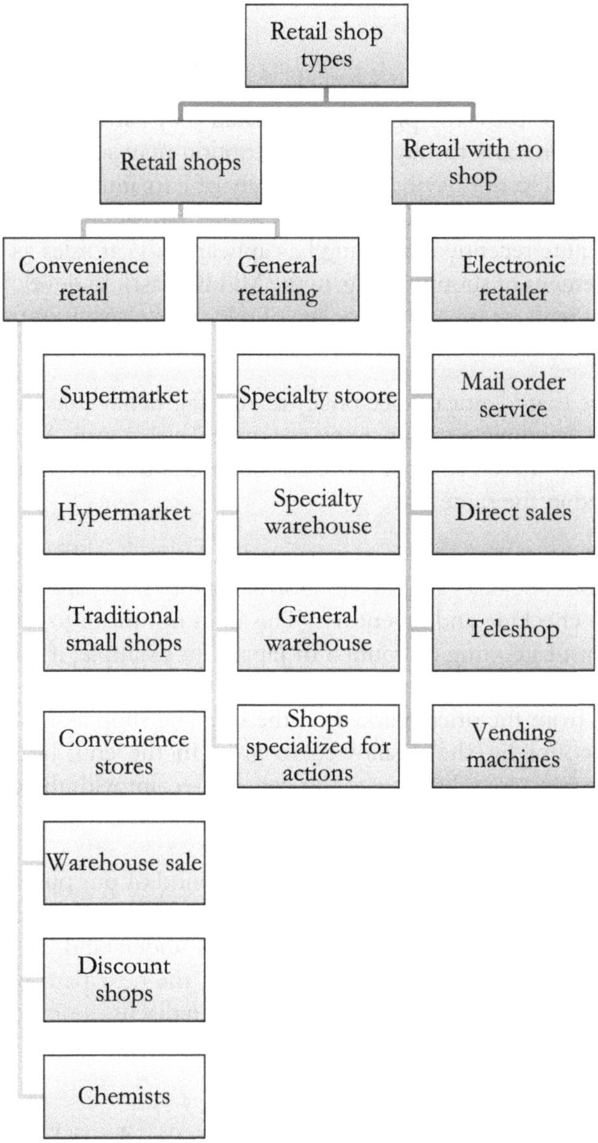

(Source: Agárdi, 2010:51)

Summarizing what has been said so far, we can conclude that retail pricing is a complex activity. Technically the task is relatively simple: multiply the purchase price of the individual products with the mark-ups - the complication comes from the need to take into consideration the price elasticity of demand of various products, the expected trends in demand in the market as well as competitors' prices. The sum of the mark-ups applied to the goods sold constitutes the total amount of mark-ups (contribution) that has the function to cover the fixed costs of the trading firms and, in addition,

generate profit as well for the firms. The differentiated application of the mark-ups can help to achieve the goals set by the business policy

12.4.1. Fixed prices or price bargaining

One of the fundamental price policy decisions that retail shops must make is whether they should charge the same price to all buyers for the same product, or should they allow bargaining, i.e. make prices dependent on customers' willingness to buy. This latter option may sound a little strange in many countries, since people are used to not having the possibility of bargaining in the shops. There are exceptions, though. We can find markets and businesses where bargaining is allowed: a good example is the market place, but quite recently bargaining has appeared in car sales as well. In some countries bargaining is a natural element of shopping (e.g. in the Middle East). In developing countries the possibility of bargaining is on the decrease and the policy of one price prevails in trade. There are basically two reasons for that:

- Most of the buyers believe that identical price policy is truly fair behaviour on the part of the shop, because it does not discriminate against any consumer in this way. A lot of customers are averse to bargaining and therefore have more confidence and would much rather shop where everybody is treated in the same way.

- Allowing bargains makes the work of price management a lot more difficult: an important part of price decisions should be delegated to the shop assistants' level, and this increases the time and energy spent on checking and inventory. (This does not mean to say that the shop assistants abuse their right of granting discounts. In Japan, for example, if you go to a retail shop to buy a watch it is quite usual that you bargain with the shop assistant. You may end up with a 30% reduction from the price marked on the tag. The shop assistant is instructed about the maximum discount he/she is allowed to give. In the end, he/she enters the discount price in the cash register and the customer gets the receipt with the discount price.)

12.5. The role of price psychology in setting consumer prices

Consumer price, the stimulus that is always detectable in the background of our purchases, is closely related to psychology. There are, however, some pricing methods that literature discusses under the heading of 'price psychology', others under 'promotion'. We must understand, however, that all pricing tactics have both psychological and promotional aspects. In the next part, we are going to present some specific areas where price psychology is applied and then discuss so-called promotional pricing, always bearing in mind the significant overlap between these two categories.

12.5.1. Odd pricing — the 9 ending

If you have a good look at the prices that surround us, for example leafing through the price list of a catalogue or glance at the price tags of the goods displayed in a shop, you will hardly ever find prices in round numbers. Prices ending in odd numbers - especially 9 - seem to be extremely popular in retailing in spite of the fact that – in contrast with round numbers – they mean extra work in the records, and for the cashier as well. Looking for an explanation to this phenomenon we end up in the field of psychology.

Psychologists have found that people prefer odd numbers. Today we cannot be satisfied with this statement, because nowadays the setting of consumer prices is dominated not only by odd numbers, but even numbers close to round ones also have a significant presence (e.g. 48 $, 98 $) and, in countries where it makes sense, fractions close to the whole are also very frequent ($2.99, £0,78, etc.).

However, 9 is undoubtedly the most popular ending. This is why this method is also called pricing 9. Surveys have found that 9 is followed by 5 in the order of frequency

In Monroe's view those who prefer odd pricing assume that the demand curve – since its shape depends on price endings - will follow the pattern of the teeth of a saw (see Figure 12.3). The demand curve will slope down as usual, but within this decreasing trend it rises a little around the numbers 4 and 9, perhaps due to the beneficial effect of 5 and 9. Extensive use of the terminal digit 'nine' – like in the case of this fan petrol station – suggests that psychological pricing is at play

By Manecke - Own work, CC BY-SA 3.0, https://commons.wikimedia.org/w/index.php?curid=1986162

If this is true, the trader responsible for setting the price will take the right course of action if - instead of rounding the price figures produced by the price multiplier according to the well-known rules - he changes the prices between 100 and 110 to 109 and those between 111-120 to 119.

Several research projects have been conducted to find out whether there is any practical evidence for the advantages of pricing 9. The research findings are contradictory, and do not prove the hypothesis of this pricing. Some opinions are overtly opposed to it. Monroe quotes, e.g. Schindler and Kibarian, who concluded that the odd prices definitely conjure up the image of low prices and low quality. In 1996, however, the same two authors performed an experiment, which proved the advantages of pricing 9, in contrast with their previous statements (See next Exhibit.)

Figure 12.3. The assumed demand curve of odd pricing (Based on Monroe, 1990, 49).

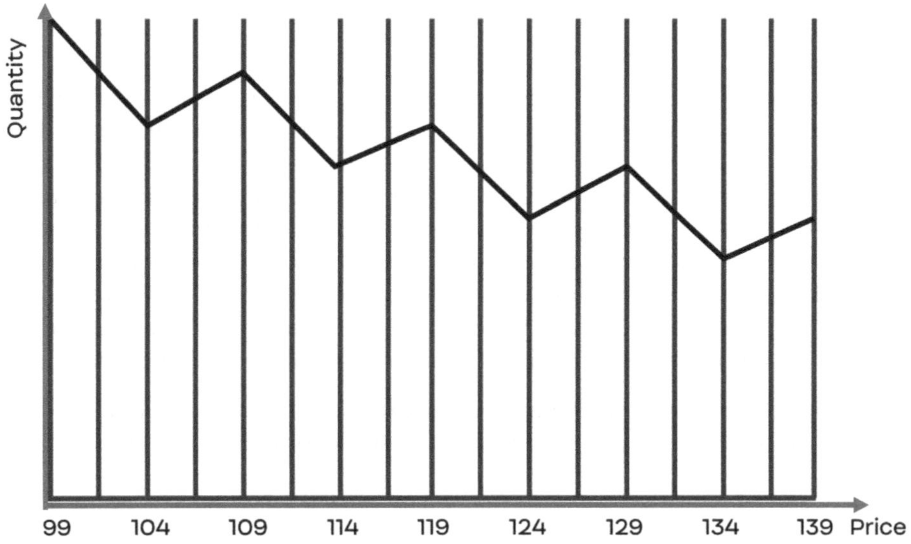

EXHIBIT 12. 4. THE EXPERIMENT PERFORMED BY SCHINDLER AND KIBARIAN

The two researchers agreed with a retailer selling ladies wear to perform an experiment studying the effect of pricing 9. The retailer did his business mainly by sending out catalogues. They agreed that, for the sake of the experiment, they would print the catalogue in three versions. In the first, prices ended in 99 cents. In the second, all prices were rounded, to end in 00. At the retailer's recommendation a third version was also printed in agreement with the previous method, i.e. most of the prices ended in 88. (As a result, the same product cost $ 17,99 in the first catalogue, $ 18.00 in the second and $ 17,88 in the third.)

Thirty thousand copies of each version of the 24-page black and white catalogue containing 169 items was sent out to 90 000 clients. In the period after mailing the turnover generated by the three catalogues was measured. The result proved the advantage of pricing 9. Although the 1 cent cheaper price meant a mere 0.03% advantage for the customers, the turnover generated by the price ending in 9 was 8% higher than the turnover of the catalogue with prices ending in round numbers. Prices ending 88 generated approximately the same turnover as the round numbers.

A detailed description of the experiment was published by the authors under the title: 'Increased consumer sales response through use of 99-ending prices' in 1996.

12.5.2. Price lines

It is a widespread practice in the clothes departments of West-European and North American stores to arrange commodities into price lines (the practice is spreading to other departments as well) and try to fit each product into one of the families. This is called price lining. Let us suppose, for example, that one of London's department stores sells men's suits in four price lines: those in the first cost £90, the ones in the second cost £120; the price of suits in the third is £150 and in the fourth £200. Those who choose this kind of practice seem to believe that the majority of the customers expect men's suits to cost between £90 and £200. They also seem to believe that within the same category, for example between £120 and £150, customers would not consider the actual price differences of the price line to be very serious. It means that the differences within the category are below the threshold value defined in Weber's law.

Arranging goods in price lines is based on the psychological principle of categorization, which facilitates consumer decision making. The shop groups the commodities for the customers in their interest, saving them the trouble of having to choose between too many goods with different price points and qualities. More than fifty years ago the owner of the Filene store declared that, regardless of the product, three categories: good, better and best are more than enough to inform the customers (Hanna-Dodge, 1997:144). Traders do not use more than three to four groups. It takes careful deliberation on the part of the trader to decide how many price categories they want to have, at what price level and with what price difference between the categories. Familiarity with the clientele and the practical solutions used by the competitors can be of great help in making these decisions.

With price lines, the periodical rearrangement and maintenance of the commodities within the same groups allow the stores to keep their prices (i.e. their price lines) stable for quite a long time.

12.5.3. "It was" prices

At the time of price reduction, the retailer has two methods to choose from: either he marks the original price, or writes only the new, reduced price. Findings of price research and price psychology

suggest that it is more advantageous to mark the old price, because it can function in the minds of the customers as a kind of external reference price. The only problem that can arise is the two big differences between the two, because in this case the reference price will have no credibility for the customer, and he/she will seek new information. Using fake older prices is against the law.

12.5.4. Premium pricing or luxury pricing

In Veblen's view a part of our consumption is so-called conspicuous or prestige consumption, aimed not so much at meeting real needs, but rather to show off our riches (lifestyle, taste, etc.). In this case, the high prices do play a part in ensuring that the prestige product comes up to the level of prestige consumption. If a retailer sells goods of this kind, he will certainly use a high mark-up and the services he offers together with the goods will be varied and of a high quality.

12.6. Price promotions in the retail trade

12.6.1. Loss leader pricing

In the course of loss leader pricing the retail unit chooses one or more products whose price is set to be - for a longer time or temporarily - lower than usual (it may also be a loss maker) in order to raise customers' interest in the product line or the shop concerned.

The causes and purposes of loss leader pricing are the following:

- To lure customers into the shop and thereby increase turnover. The price setter's idea is that customers will buy not only the loss leader product but others as well, consequently he can obtain compensation for the lower income generated by the loss leaders or the loss suffered thanks to the increased turnover of other products.
- To increase sales of the product in question. (Of course, this goal will only be achievable if the price of the product is not so low as to make a loss.) The increased turnover generated by the low-priced product may contribute to the increase in the shop's profits despite the lower mark-up.
- It is also possible that the loss leader product is a complementary product, therefore an increase in its sales entails an increase in the sales of other products as well. This explains why the careful selection of low-priced products is an important part of loss leader pricing. The following recommendations are found in literature:
    - o the product chosen should be well known, something people buy frequently,
    - o it should be a (preferably branded) product with whose usual price customers are relatively familiar,
    - o it should be a relatively cheap /low-priced product,
    - o It should have a high price elasticity of demand,
    - o it should be easy to compare with similar products sold in other shops,
    - o it should be carefully separated from other similar goods sold in the same shop, otherwise there will be the risk of product cannibalism.

When using loss leader pricing, retail shops have two methods to choose from:

- They can choose some products, suited for the purpose. It is advisable to coordinate with the suppliers, because some suppliers may find it detrimental to their image if their product is sold at such a low price. On the other hand, there may be suppliers who are happy about such an increase in their turnover.

- In larger retail units (e.g. in supermarkets) a whole section can be chosen for this purpose. The supermarket can decide, for example, to make the dairy products the section of low prices. This will attract customers who will walk through the whole store: after all it is a good idea to arrange such sections deep in the store and hopefully they will buy other products as well.

Loss leader pricing may have disadvantages too:

- customers will buy only the low-priced product in the shop and nothing else;

- the shop may create the impression that it is not of very good quality;

- competitors may launch actions against it that may lead to a price war.

12.6.2. Discounts, rebates - price cuts

A discount is any form of reduction in price

Source: By Henning Schlottmann (User:H-stt) - Own work, CC BY 4.0,

Discounts or temporary price cuts are frequently used sales promotion methods in the price policy of retail trade. They appear under different names, like discounts, special actions, sales, which may have slightly different meanings.

End of season sale. When the season is drawing to its end retailers often reduce the price of seasonal products in the hope of getting rid of them in this way, and clearing the shelves for the new season's goods. In clothes shops, for example, you can expect to find lower prices for summer clothes as early as the end of July or early August, to make room for the new styles of autumn.

Discount for procurement mistakes. It happens sometimes that the retailer does not estimate the turnover of certain products well and is not able to sell the quantity ordered at the regular price. In order to get rid of his stock he reduces the price of the product, hoping to attract more customers to buy it at a lower price.

Price cut before the end of shelf life. When the shelf life of the product is nearing its end, the retailer usually chooses to reduce the price of these products and sell them during their shelf life. (Later he will not be able to do that, because it is against the rules.)

Sales of obsolete products. Shops frequently pile up commodities that are not defective or seasonal, but the launch of new products has made them obsolete. The best way of getting rid of these products is, again, price cuts.

https://commons.wikimedia.org/wiki/File:British_Home_Stores_closing_down_sale_Wood_Green,_London_3_August_2016_06.jpg

Closing-down sale/sellout. A campaign of price reductions preceding the close-down of a shop is called a closing-down sale. The author was present in a town in the USA when plans were made for the closingdown of a store. As the date of the final close-down was approaching, the price cuts became bigger and bigger: Three weeks before the given date all commodities were sold at a 40% discount, and this changed to 60% two-weeks before the close-down, then to 70%, 80% and finally goods were sold at a discount of 90%.

12.6.3. Pricing actions and business policy

This form of promotional pricing (discount) is not connected with any of the reasons mentioned above. The purpose of such actions is to revitalize the business and attract new customers (see description of loss leader pricing). In this case, the commodities are faultless, and popular, and they are sold at a discount price only temporarily, as illustrated in Figure 12.4.

Figure 12.4. Questions of price promotion actions

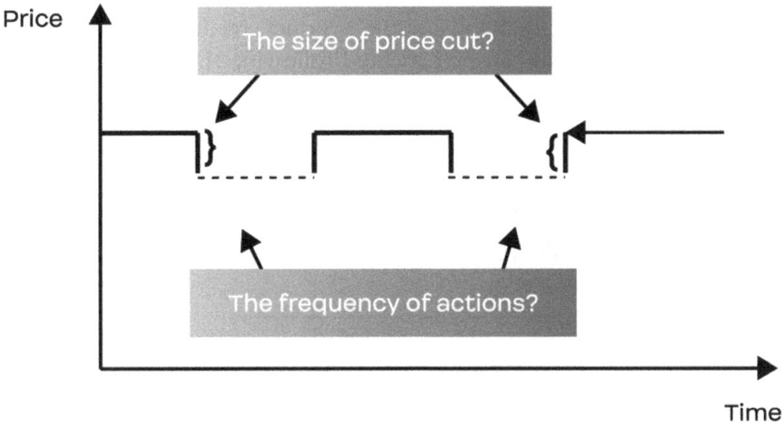

The main questions that arise in this context concern the time, frequency and measure of the discounts. There is no universal answer to any of these questions because customers react to prices and even more to price actions differently, depending on the country or region in which they live, the consumer group they belong to and by product category and brand name.

When deciding on the frequency of price actions, traders should study the reference prices and how frequently the product group is bought.

- Firms are interested in keeping the reference prices at a high level if possible. At the time of the price action the former, regular price is used for reference. If, however, price actions are too frequent, customers may perceive reference prices to be lower than they actually are. If the price cuts are not regular and very frequent, the reference price remains unchanged and the customer feels he/she has made a particularly good deal with the lower price.

- In the case of products bought less frequently, regular price cuts seem unjustified. Before deciding the frequency of action, you are recommended to take the practice that has developed during the time the product has been marketed into consideration, and the activities of the competitors as well.

The strategy usually denoted with the acronym EDLP (Everyday Low Price) is very different from the ones presented here. This strategy is typically used in the case of price sensitive, easy to replace products. It is usually initiated by the manufacturer, who agrees with the retailer to keep the price low at least for a month, but if necessary for a whole year (instead of the usual one to two-week actions) to achieve a quick growth of turnover.

No recipes are available for the degree of price cut either. The discount used in the actions depends on the character of the product, the price elasticity of demand and the strength of the brand, too. Davey, Childs and Carlotti, Jr published an interesting study on this topic in 1998, based on the study of price related data of 30 products. They call the difference between the regular price and the discount price a price band, and in the title of the study ("Why your price band is wider than it should be?") they already refer to the fact that the price cuts given by the retailers are often higher and consequently price bands are wider than justified.

The degree of the discount or the success of the action depends on several factors:

- The most important is the price elasticity of demand for the product. In the case of product categories where a general increase in demand can be expected following the price cut, bigger discounts can also be justified.

- The strength of the brand is also important. Stronger brands typically have higher prices at the market, consequently their action zone in price policy is also larger. It is not very practical to give big discounts, because it can harm the image of the brand.

Figure 12.5. The result of price actions by the degree of the result and the type of marketing support

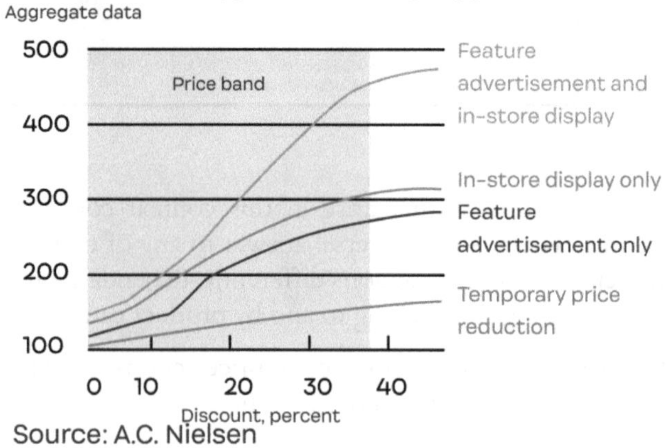

Source: A.C. Nielsen

The success of the actions also depends on the marketing support they get: promoting the action within the shop and special advertisements are very important. The survey made by the authors quoted is presented in Figure 12.5.

The figure makes it clear that the marketing support considerably increases the result. The growth of the sales index is the biggest in the band

between 10-20% and the curves flatten around the price-cut of 35%, which means that a bigger price cut will not produce additional results.

EXHIBIT 12.5. BEYOND THE TRADITIONAL DEMOGRAPHY

Booz & Co (Egol et al 2010) concluded from a survey that the new segments which differ from firms' traditional demographic segmentation are with us already. They distinguish six segments in their study:

1. *Shoppers* 2.0. From a technological point of view, this is the most highly developed segment. Its members have the willingness to buy on-line. They are price sensitive, often make use of discounts and show limited loyalty to brands or shops.

2. *Deal Hunters.* They are extremely price sensitive, use vouchers and they have the least loyalty to brands or shops. In contrast with the segment 2.0 shoppers, they do not buy online, but use the online search facilities to find the cheapest offers in the shops.

3. *Online Window-Shoppers.* They also conduct intensive searches before shopping but are less price sensitive and have more loyalty than the previous two segments.

4. *Channel Surfers.* They are the most likely to change the shops they frequent to find the place where their favourite brands are available at the cheapest price. For a good deal, they are prepared to give up comfort.

5. *Loyalists.* They are the least willing to change brands or shops for the sake of a better price. They insist on keeping their brand preferences.

6. *Laggards.* These show the least willingness to change their habits. They do little online searching, use few vouchers and do not change much.

The study of the buying habits has shown that since the onset of the global economic depression a serious transformation has been going on in consumer behaviour that stays with us even after the depression has ceased.

The key components of this new consumer behaviour can be summarized as follows:

- Customers will become more *price sensitive.*
- Customers' readiness to make compromises about quality will also increase. For the sake of a better price they are ready to reduce their value preferences (i.e. their expectations of benefits that the product should provide).
- In order to have a better price they are willing *to change brands and shop*s more quickly.
- Online opportunities will be used more efficiently. This means partly the *comparison* of prices, but *online buying* also appears as an increasingly serious competition for the so-called 'bricks and mortar' - i.e. physically present - retailers.

12.7. (Price) competition among the retail chains

In the previous chapter we have already referred to the global trend of increasing concentration that is going on in the field of wholesale and retail businesses. The few large global chains that have emerged from the multitude of traders have already been competing with one another for some time, but under pressure from the economic depression starting in 2008 the competition became fiercer in order to win over customers and increase market share (Krafft–Mantrala, 2010). If businesses want

to hold their own in the competition they should become aware of the changes in customer habits, and modify their assortment and pricing policy accordingly.

In the competition among the commercial chains a key role is played and is going to be played in the future too by (low) prices. In this fierce competition the chains put a lot of pressure on their suppliers with respect to their prices, as we have already remarked on in the previous chapter. In addition to what has been said so far, price competition has three more, important characteristics to highlight:

- Private brands gain ground over manufacturers' brands, because they are cheaper;
- Flexible use of the price actions (HiLo – High-Low) and EDLP (Every Day Low Price) policy and its effective communication;
- Responses to online prices and price comparisons.

12.7.1. Private labels gain ground

We are now living in the age of the third generation of private (store, own) brands (Rekettye, 2009). The main feature of this age is the transformation of own brands into *real brands:* large mass retailers - bearing in mind the rules of brand building - develop their own brands, differentiate them according to consumer expectations and also engage in serious advertising. With the arrival of the third generation of own brands, internationalization and globalization begins. Some authors now openly write about the manufacturers' brands being overshadowed. Thomassen, Lincoln and Aconis (2006) shared the view that manufacturers' brands have fallen into a multiple trap. They are pushed by the customers, retailers, the media and their own brand products so badly that many of them are simply fighting for survival. "The world's largest resellers are much bigger today than manufacturers producing the world's great brands; therefore there can be no doubt where the power lines run in reality. As long as a few commercial chains own 75 % of the market, not even the largest brands can call more than a few % their own," they write in the introduction. A change of paradigm is going on in the world of brands and nowadays we must learn from the traders how a brand can be made successful. To describe this process the authors coined a new notion that is also the title of their book: Retailization.

EXHIBIT12.6. PRIVATE LABEL BRANDS IN TESCO

In order fully to understand the process it is worth reviewing Tesco's brand policy First they introduced their own brand under the name **Tesco** with about 3,000 products. After that, Tesco stretched the quality range both downwards and upwards. Downwards (using the name: **Tesco-Value**) trying to compete with the Lidl or Aldi chains, both belonging to a lower category; upwards against Spar, which is considered to have better quality (bearing the name **TESCO-Finest**). This was followed by the launch of brands meeting special needs: **Tesco-Colourful, Tesco-Fitt, Tesco-Organic**. Besides differentiation, we can observe diversification also appearing in the assortment and brand strategy as well. In the spring of 2008 Tesco introduced two new brand lines in clothing: **Cherokee and F&F**, challenging C&A's and Marks & Spencer's own brands, while the brand called **Technika** was launched to brand electronic appliances.

Besides the strong concentration of trade, we can observe its differentiation as well. A s a result, the war of the brands has not remained the rivalry of manufacturers and traders but has expanded into the *fight of commercial brands against one another.*

12.7.2. Spread of private labels in the world

At this point private brands have obtained a determining role all over the world, but their share varies dramatically around various continents and countries. A survey conducted by AC Nielsen in 2014 found that the average dollar proportion of own labels is 16.5%. Figure 12.6 shows the national and regional differences in the prevalence of private labels. The unquestionable leading role that Europe has can be attributed to the fact that the concentration of retail business took place here most quickly.

A KPMG study found that commercial brands are 25% cheaper to produce and distribute than manufacturer's products. The lower cost is not due to the use of poor quality raw material and packaging, but to the lower share of fixed costs, less sales costs, cheaper marketing and distribution (Table 12.2).

Table 12.2. Example for the cost components of manufacturers and store brands (in %)

Cost components	Manufacturers' brands	Private labels
Raw materials	35	35
Packaging	12	12
Manufacturing costs		
Variable	9	9
Fixed	5	-
Research and Development	3	-
Sales staff	4	-
Advertising, promotion	9	5
Transportation and delivery	5	2
Other costs	10	10
Operational costs	8	2
Consumer price	100	75

Source: OXIRM on the basis of manufacturer annual reports and company accounts. In: Customer Loyalty & Private Label Products, KPMG, 2004.:11

12.7.3. Price actions vs everyday low price

Example of an "Everyday Low Price" advertisement at Walmart. Source: By LateNameGuys - Own work, CC BY-SA 3.0, https://commons.wikimedia.org/w/index.php?curid=32022004

The price race seems to divide traders into two easily distinguishable groups as far as the price policy applied is concerned (Johnson, 2003). EDLP is applied by a lot of successful firms (it started in Wal-Mart), but the number of those applying promotional prices has also increased. Seasonal discounts start earlier and earlier every year, and the quantity of the commodities involved in the price cuts (actions) also shows a two-digit growth every year. Traders keep looking for the best solutions, but they know very little about which method will produce the best result in any particular case.

Figure 12.6. National and regional differences in the prevalence of private labels

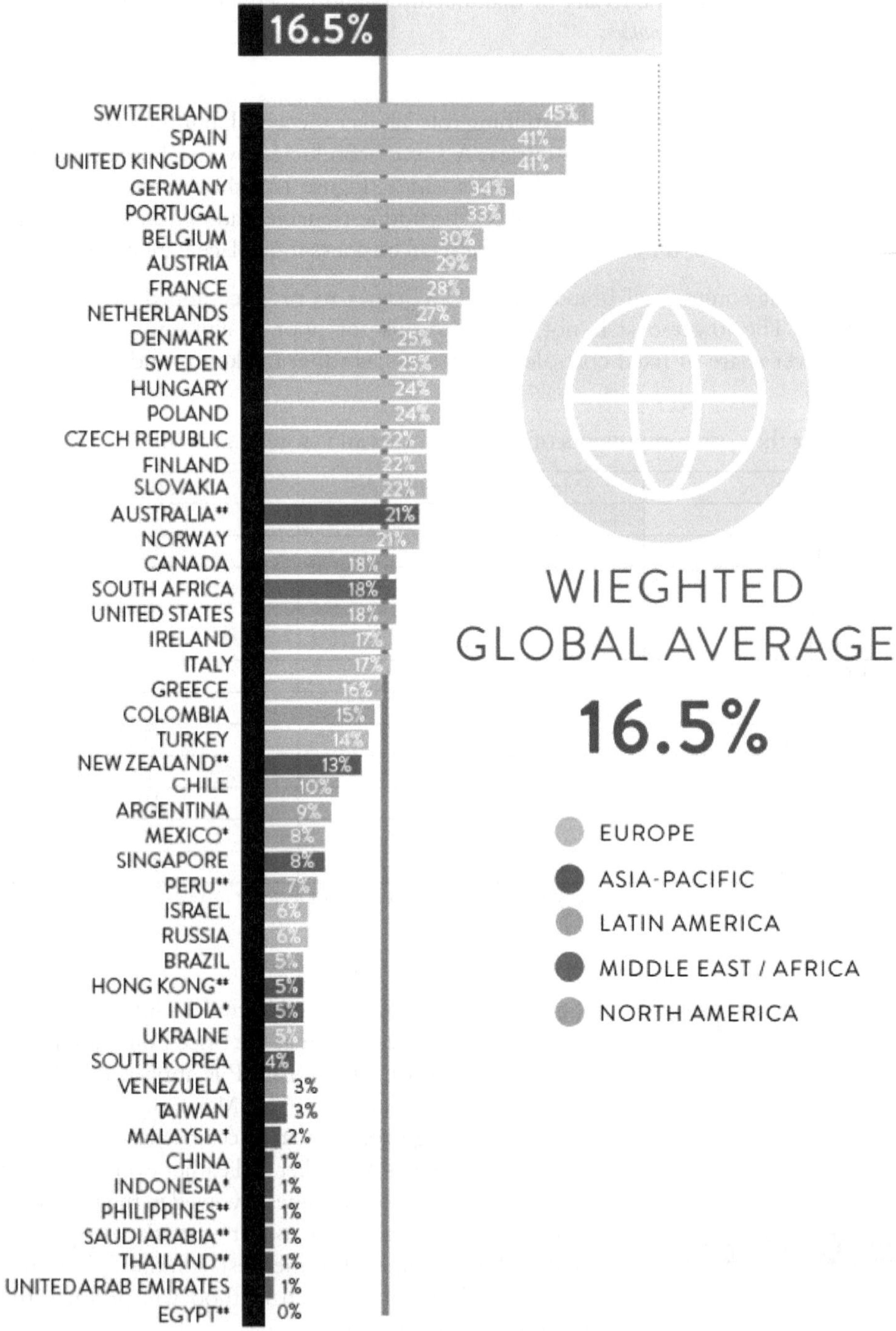

*Source: Nielsen; 2013 for most countries; * Indicates 2014 YTD; ** Indicates 2014 MAT; Note: For a consistent cross-country view, all categories are weighted; equally to produce an average private-label share. Individual country reporting may vary due reporting differences. (The state of private label around the world, 2014, The Nielsen Company, p. 5.)*

EXHIBIT 12.7. INVESTIGATION BY SEIDERS AND VOSS

Two American marketing researchers, Kathleen Seiders and Glenn B. Voss, spent 15 months investigating the price policy behaviour of 38 American retailing units operating in 11 different product categories. First, they assessed the firms in three dimensions:

- by the extent they change prices (from those applying EDLP with practically no change to those who frequently apply promotional prices),
- by the measure advertising support is given to price promotion,
- by the extent of price cuts.

On the basis of the measures found for the above three dimensions they created the general index of price promotion and ranked the firms.

This was followed by the evaluation of the firms by the following two criteria:

- What is the overlap in the assortment they offer like, i.e. what is the degree of similarity among the assortment they offer?
- How long is the life cycle of the assortment for sale, i.e. how quickly do the usually offered products become obsolete?

We are convinced that efficiency of price promotion in retailing mainly depends on the extent to which the price strategy applied matches these two factors. From the two dimensions, a matrix of four parts can be created in the following way:

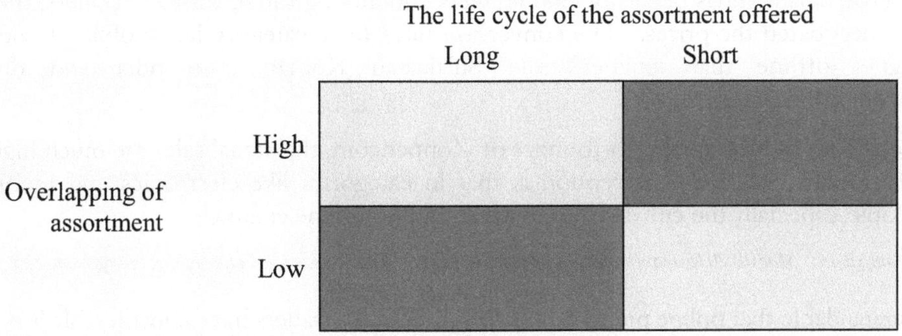

Their conclusion is that promotional pricing (HiLo) is more efficient in firms that fall in the two darker boxes compared with the EDLP pricing strategy. In the consumer electronics or the car business, for example, traders sell products with considerable overlap and relatively short life cycle. They have good reason to rely on promotion based on significant price changes in contrast with the other two categories where the HiLo (always low or high) pricing strategy will be more efficient. Stores or supermarkets that, due to the wide range of products they have to offer, may fall into several boxes and are considered hybrids.

The Researchers conclude that the right procedure is for the trader to define his position in the given system first and decide on the price policy to follow afterwards.

Source: A detailed report on the research written by Johnson (2003:10-11) appeared in MT Sloan Management Review.

Some of the large international chains (Tesco, Interspar, Cora, Auchan) can probably be classified as hybrids, and apply a hybrid price policy accordingly, i.e. besides advertising their everyday low prices they have significant price actions and other incentives, which they use - together with their communication strategies - to strengthen or improve their competitiveness.

12.8. Online trade

Online trade is on the increase all over the world. A new commercial channel has been created, to rival retail shops, mainly the dominant multinational chains. The expansion of online trade is closely connected with the spread of the internet.

12.8.1. Pricing in online retailing

If we examine the most popular product groups in online trade (CD, DVD, books, etc.), we can see right away that online prices are typically lower than shop prices. The best way to compare online and offline prices is to put the same product up for sale in both channels. If you have a look at the website of the Hungarian Academic Publisher (http://akademiai.hu/), you will find that the publisher (which sells only its own editions) offers a 15 to 25% discount from the price of the books ordered online (and if your order is over HUF 9,000 i.e. around $30, you get free delivery). The same books can be found in the range offered by the web stores but the discount is a little less.

EXHIBIT 12.8. COMPARE ONLINE AND OFFLINE PRICES SITTING AT HOME

Some of the price comparison portals and marketplace players are incorporating the product and price details of nearby retailers as well of e-commerce sites. Price comparison portal MySmartPrice has started listing the price quotes and product details of mobile phone retailers in Hyderabad. It has details of 300 retailers and among them, with 75 retailers, the company has negotiated the prices. "The conversion rates for a category like mobile phone are much higher offline than online," said Sulakshan Kumar, co-founder and director of MySmartPrice.com

According to Neeraj Jain, co-founder of Zopper.com, the actual sales are much higher offline than online, while the perception is that in categories like electronics and mobile phones people, especially the city dwellers, have shifted to online channels.

Source: By Sangeetha G. Mar 08 2015 http://www.mydigitalfc.com/news/compare-online-and-offline-prices-sitting-home-383

It is understandable that online prices can be lower, because traders have considerably less costs than shopkeepers. The initial unit cost begins with the purchase price of the product. How much this is depending on from where the online retailer buys his stock: the manufacturer or the wholesaler. Then the costs of online trading are added. These can be considerably smaller per unit and are composed basically from the following items:

1. Costs arising from the logistics of the product, because the good must be available and, in the case of an order, transportation should also be arranged by the retailer.
2. Appearing online also involves costs. There are many different ways - both cheaper and more expensive - to maintain the webstore page. Sometimes the fee should be paid in a lump sum, in other cases the payment depends on the success of the page. In the latter case, the so-called conversion rate (the ratio of the number of clicking and the deals completed) should also be taken into account. We are not very far from the truth if we presume that only a very small percent of the clicks (1-5 %) will end in actual buying.

3. In addition to the above, other costs will arise as well, e.g. wages.

Since these total costs are well below the costs of offline trade, online retailers can manage with smaller mark-ups as well. The question is how much this mark-up should be. Well, Beye et al, (2007:5) recommend the use of a model starting from *price sensitivity* to define the mark-ups.

Information about price sensitivity is given by price elasticity. Price elasticity of demand - as has already been discussed in detail in Chapter 2 - is the ratio of the percentage change in demand and the percentage change in price. Online retailers can prove that with experiments.

EXHIBIT 12.9. THE PIXMANIA EXPERIMENT TO MEASURE PRICE SENSITIVITY OF CUSTOMERS

Pixmania is a large European e-trader: it has understood the importance of price experiments. Pixmania sells more than 10.000 items of consumer electronics. It uses Kelkoo's site (http://www, kelkoo.co.uk) to lure potential buyers on his website. The Tungsten T3 PDA (a personal digital assistant) product was used to perform the experiment. The price was changed 11 times in a period of 14 days in the price range of £268 and £283 and then the quantity of sales was measured. Pixmania performed several experiments of this kind to explore price sensitivity.

Source: Beye et al. (2007: 6-7)

The mark-up model, based on price sensitivity (price elasticity of demand) recommends online retailers to define optimal price in the following way:

optimal price = product unit costs multiplied with the optimal mark-up multiplier

The optimal mark-up multiplier can be calculated from the price elasticity of demand for the product, as follows:

$$Optimal\ mark-up\ multiplier\ = \frac{E_d}{1-E_d}$$

Where E_d is the price elasticity of demand for the product.

If the price elasticity of demand is -.4 (i.e. there is a price cut of 1%), it will entail a 4% rise of demand and the optimal price multiplier is 1.33. If price elasticity is -10 the mark-up multiplier becomes 1.11.

It can be concluded that the higher the price elasticity, (i.e. price sensibility), the lower the mark-up percentage that online retailers have to work with.

The overview of online commerce shows that the price policy used here is more *product-centred* than offline trade, which is rather assortment centred. It is because customers want the product in the first place and not the seller or the shop. Considering that all they can see online is the picture of the product - in contrast with the retail shop where their opinion on the product is influenced also by the shop's atmosphere and the behaviour of the shop assistants - customers become a lot more price-centred. Consequently, online traders can only be more successful if they focus on niche markets and

specialize in meeting their needs. What is more, their price policy can be characterized with *frequent price changes*. Since, in online trade, competition is practically restricted to price, competitors keep watching one another. If that is the case, frequent price changes can embarrass competitors. It is an important argument against frequent price changes that it may disturb potential buyers as well. It is sometimes called 'hit and run' pricing in literature: find the cheapest price then quickly apply a higher one and frequently alternate this method.

EXHIBIT 12.10. THE IMPACT OF THE INTERNET ON PRICE POLICY

The fundamental impact of the internet on price policy is most obvious in the transparency of prices. Customers have access to information on prices and this allows them to have a clear picture of the sellers' real costs. This is an advantage for the wallets of customers, but makes it more difficult for sellers to develop a good price policy:

- The increasing amount of information customers have about mark-ups and its forces sellers to reduce mark-ups.
- It promotes commodization i.e. the process, when products and services become mass commodities.
- It is detrimental to loyalty (especially when buyers do not think the mark-up applied is fair enough).
- It makes customers question the correctness of sellers' prices.

Source: Levens, 2010: 144

12.8.2. Comparability of prices on the internet

We have already mentioned that online commerce significantly increases price transparency. This trend is intensified by web pages created explicitly for comparing prices. There are also independent pages, which compare information collected from every accessible source. This can be general, or focusing on individual sectors, international or concerned with certain countries, or smaller areas. If you search Google for American price comparing web-sites you will end up with lists of several dozen or even several hundred such sites.

Every piece of price information can be used as a reference. This is the case with the prices of online commerce as well, and especially with price-comparing information. Consumers' access to offline price information is often restricted by physical barriers, while chances of obtaining online information have practically no limitations thanks to increasingly sophisticated technical solutions. This leads to the conclusion that online price comparisons play a very serious role in shaping people's internal reference prices (Lii-Lee, 2006).

A GMA (Grocery Manufacturers' Association) research project investigating the purchase processes of CPG products (Consumer Packed Goods) found that only 41% of the products (brands) that people intend to buy are chosen before a visit to the shop, and about 59% of the final decision is made in the shop. This finding can be a relief for offline retailers.

On the other hand, information and communication technology develop rapidly. In the middle of the last decade, we witnessed the appearance of mobile phones that have internet connection and can solve the problem of giving online information about the prices of competing products at the site of the purchase (Broeckelmann- Groeppel-Klein, 2008). By now it is possible to upload an application

on the phone which reads the barcode of a product in practically no time and the customer immediately receives information about the prices of all the competitors in the neighbourhood.

EXHIBIT 12.11. HIDE AND SEEK IN PRICING

With the rapid development of information and communication technology a game of hide and seek in pricing has developed. Sellers want to hide the real prices, buyers want to discover them.

Some of the developments of this game are favourable. For example, the increasing possibility of consumers to learn and understand almost everything about the product will force sellers to provide authentic information in their marketing communications (Rekettye, Jr., 2016). It is also true that it has some disadvantages. While companies try to customize their prices, the privacy of their customer pool will undoubtable be hurt. Online shopping, filling out surveys, using different cards, participating in loyalty programs, etc. provide lots of information to the sellers, enabling them to prepare a customized product and price offer for their customers. One can agree with Andrew Odlyzko, Director of Minnesota University's Digital Technology Center, who states: "The result is likely to be that price discrimination will grow, but in a concealed form. Stress will be on tactics such as bundling and loyalty programs, which tend to disguise the actual price that is charged…On the other hand, there will be continued pressure to erode privacy in order to find out just what the willingness to pay is, as well as to control how products and services are used. Thus privacy will continue to erode" (Odlyzko 2003, 4). The game is ongoing between sellers and buyers of the consumer markets. Sellers want to disguise their real prices to hinder price comparison, which usually increases the price elasticity of demand. Buyers, on the other hand, try their best to secure the most favourable prices. In spite of the fact that buyers have more and more instruments to discover prices in the 'hide and seek pricing' game, sellers seem to have a better position.

Source: Rekettye and Liu (2018)

CHAPTER 13. PRICING IN INTERNATIONAL MARKETS

OBJECTIVE 1 To examine the differences between domestic and international pricing, and to illustrate the different pricing strategies used for entering foreign markets.

OBJECTIVE 2 To outline the relationship between domestic and foreign prices and to investigate the escalation of domestic prices due to the different cost factors appearing in international transactions.

OBJECTIVE 3 To ascertain the role transfer pricing plays in international supply chains.

OBJECTIVE 4 To examine how prices used in international tranactions are influenced by different modes of transportation and methods of international payment.

13.1 Introduction

International pricing policy operates with the same concepts as domestic pricing policy: demand-supply, price elasticity of demand, the price and value perception of consumers, costs, competition and profit. The difference is that the importance of these factors can vary according to the nature of foreign markets, the legal and the ethical requirements thereof, and the objectives of the company with regard to the given market.

As a matter of fact, we can talk about *two different prices* in connection with the goods intended for foreign markets:

- the 'domestic' or export price of the product, at which the product leaves the factory; this price has a decisive role in export marketing,
- the other and more important price is the one the foreign consumer has to pay for the product.

There may be huge differences (100%, 200% or even higher) between these two prices due to additional costs (shipping, duty, insurance, etc.) and the mark-ups (importer, wholesaler, retailer, etc.). Which price is more important for the seller depends on how he/she is present on the foreign market, how much and how long he/she is able to keep the prices under his/her control.

For example, the Apple Company will determine the consumer prices of products sold in Apple stores even if the store is located at the other end of the world.

The price of Pick salami (see on the photo), however, can be controlled by the Pick producer up to the point the international importer has taken over the good, but the exporter will have difficulty in controlling the prices charged for the salami by retailers in the Netherlands or in Japan.

The famous Hungarian Pick Salami
Source of photo: Creative Commons

The two prices are naturally interrelated. Starting from the domestic price and using the so-called progressive calculation, the minimum sales price in the foreign market can be calculated by estimating the additional costs. This calculation can be performed backwards (retrograde calculation) as well: in this case the market price considered realistic is used to calculate backwards how much the ex-works price should be to allow the product to be successful on the market.

13.2. Global and local prices

One of the fundamental questions in international marketing is how similar or different the marketing tools applied on the market are. It requires the company, when developing its pricing strategy, to decide whether it wants to sell its products at the same prices in foreign markets, or at separate prices. Accordingly, we can distinguish between a **global** (standard or geocentric) pricing policy and a **differentiated** (local or polycentric) pricing policy. The decision will primarily be influenced by the characteristics of the target markets and the company's internal factors Table 13.1.

EXHIBIT13.1. THE GLOBAL PRICES OF CISCO

The giant corporation CISCO, which manufactures active elements for information networks, can serve as a good example for the application of global prices. Comparing their price list, valid in the United States, with their prices applied in Hungary, we can see that the prices are similar. The name of the price list applied in Hungary, MEA – Middle-East Europe, Africa, also implies this global nature. The price of the CISCO PIX 535 type gadget is $59,000 both in the USA and in the MEA region as well.

Cisco logo Source: Wikimedia

13.2.1. Global prices

Companies working with one (usually domestic) production basis apply the **one price policy** in most cases. The popularity of global behaviour lies in its simplicity for setting prices. The company publishes a written price list each year, allowing it to give quotations very quickly in markets of all

kinds. According to Keegan, companies with **ethnocentric** price behaviour apply the same prices in all their markets, including the domestic market.

Table 13.1. Factors influencing the use of global or differential pricing policy

Factors favouring the use of global prices	**INTERNAL FACTORS**	**Factors favouring the use of differentiated prices**
Global ←	COMPANY OBJECTIVES	→ Multi-local
Centralized ←	COMPANY CONTROL	→ Decentralized
Long term ←	COMMITMENT TO FOREIGN MARKET	→ Short term
High ←	DEGREE OF INTERNATIONALIZATION	→ Low
	EXTERNAL (MARKET) FACTORS	
Weak ←	COMPETITION	→ Strong
Stable ←	LEVEL OF DEMAND	→ Variable
Strong ←	LEGAL AND GOVERNMENT CONSTRAINTS	→ Weak
Healthy ←	GENERAL ECONOMIC SITUATION	→ Weak
Adequate ←	FOREIGN EXCHANGE SUPPLY	→ Bad

Source: Based on Samli–Still–Hill (1993, 360.)

When the calculation is based on domestic prices, the *escalation* of prices should be taken into account, that is, a lot of extra costs are added to the domestic (producer) prices in international trade before the product reaches the final consumers. Let us take a hypothetical example for price escalation (Table 13.2).

It is due to the price escalation that, in reality, the prices for export tend to be lower than domestic prices:

- for exporters to succeed in the target market against competitors, they must compensate for additional costs resulting from the longer transportation and potential duties with lower prices;
- the net export prices are not subject to the costs of domestic sales and marketing;
- export commodities are the result of **excess** production in many companies, so using a calculation which takes into account only additional costs can also be justified;

- although the rules of international trade prohibit government subsidies in many cases, especially in the case of agricultural goods, these government subsidies allow the use of export prices that are lower than domestic prices.

Table 13.2. The escalation of prices in international trade

Item	Domestic channel	Foreign channel (the wholesaler imports)	Foreign channel (involving a separate importer)
Producer price	1 000	1 000	1 000
Shipping (CIF)	-	200	200
Duty (20% of CIF)	-	240	240
Purchase price of importer	-	-	1 440
Importer's margin (on a cost basis 20%)	-	-	288
Purchase price of wholesaler	1 000	1 440	1 728
Wholesaler's margin (on a cost basis 20%)	200	288	346
Purchase price of retailer	1 200	1 728	2 074
Retailer's margin (on a cost basis 40%)	480	691	830
Domestic/foreign consumer price	1 680	2 419	2 904

Companies, however, should be very careful when using a policy of very low export pricing, because price regulations in most countries include the tools for protecting domestic producers against **dumping prices**. Reference is often made to the WTO (World Trade Organization) in the case of dumping prices. According to the WTO definition we talk about dumping prices when a good is exported at less than its normal price. It can mean that the price of the good sold in the importing market is lower than in the domestic market or in a third market, or that the good is sold below its production costs.

The disadvantage of the 'one price' policy is that it is very inflexible. Companies applying such policy usually use the 'cost + margin' calculation, and the price obtained this way can be lower than the prices prevailing in certain markets, while they can be too high in other markets. (In the first case, the company will lose its extra profits, and its extra turnover in the second case.)

13.2.2. Localized prices

A differentiated price policy, that is, the setting of different export prices for different markets allows more flexible price behaviour. This kind of price policy, however, requires a thorough knowledge of the market that only a very few companies have; these are mostly multinational companies which have their own marketing and/or production organisation in the target markets. The company's marketing units can decide independently on the prices that best suit the given market.

The disadvantage of differentiated prices is that if the prices are very different from one market to another, it will cause arbitrage i.e. a flow of the product which cannot be controlled by the company, from countries with lower price levels to countries with higher levels.

Dual pricing represents a transition between global and differentiated pricing policies. Here pricing is based on the **marginal cost of production for export.** According to this method the fixed costs are levied only on production for the domestic market, while the marginal costs of export only include the direct costs related to export sales (Cateora Graham, 2001).

This kind of pricing is generally used by companies, which manufacture primarily for the domestic market and use their excess capacity to sell in foreign markets. The export price determined with the dual pricing method is usually lower than the domestic producer price. Companies should be careful however, because they can very easily be accused of dumping.

EXHIBIT 13.2. EXAMPLES OF ARBITRAGE

American pharmaceutical companies sold certain medications at cheaper prices in several developing countries knowing the purchasing power of the local population, but then were surprised to find out that the local distributor re-exported these goods to a richer country where the pharmaceutical company applied higher prices due to the higher GDP per capita. The fluctuations in exchange rate also give the opportunity for such transactions. Import quotas and high tariffs have similar consequences. The most extreme example is that many Japanese made products are cheaper in other countries than in Japan, due to the very high Japanese consumer price levels. For example, Panasonic mobile phone costs 152 dollars in Tokyo, while the same product is only 58.95 dollars in the USA, or a Sony walkman which costs 165 dollars in Tokyo and only 89 dollars in the USA (Cateora, Graham 2001). A similar phenomenon can be observed in the European car market, but the introduction of the euro has decreased the possibilities of parallel import to a great extent.

The decision between global and differentiated pricing strategies also depends on in which stage of globalization the company is. The evolution of the pricing strategy shows a kind of development path, which can be divided into three stages.

1. **In the first stage,** companies have just stepped into the international market. These companies are present only in a limited number of markets and their main goal is to captivate the consumers with their products. They apply a selective segmentation strategy and local prices. As these companies are present only in a relatively few markets at this stage, they can reach their goals with a relatively careful strategy and avoid uncertain markets.

2. **In the second stage,** companies seek to increase the importance of the local markets and to boost their international sales. Companies have to face a number of difficulties in this phase. Some of their markets are stable, while others are less so. They try to apply unified prices in the case of similar consumer needs in stable markets, and use differentiated strategy in the less stable ones. This stage requires more attention and several actions from the companies.

3. The companies in the **third stage** are heading in the direction of a globalized company. They focus on expanding their global operations, rationalizing, and decreasing their costs. These companies need to take into account not only the changes in the different markets but the interactions between the markets as well. Their marketing strategy should be flexible enough to allow them to respond to the challenges presented by the different markets. Reaction time is also an important consideration. Companies that are able to adapt to environmental changes more rapidly will enjoy an advantage. In theory, companies apply global prices in this stage, but the characteristics of some foreign markets may require localization.

It is believed that the price policies of many companies will continue to be characterized by the use of local prices for a long time, even in markets such as the European Union. The reasons are the following:

- The inequality of income between the richest and poorest countries of the European Union will prevail for a long time and may never disappear. As a result, companies must face varying degrees of purchasing power in different regions.
- Cultural differences between the regions will not disappear from one day to the next either; and willingness to purchase is largely influenced by the culture of the consumers.

13.3. The level of prices

What the initial price level should be when the product enters different markets is an important price policy decision for a company having a global or localized price policy. This decision is closely related to the product policy decision of what quality level the products represent: high, medium or low quality price level.

The decision is determined by how well the company and its products are known and their level of quality. High price level is chosen by exporters only if the image of the company and the quality of the products meet the same level as that of competitors belonging to the highest category. A medium price level can and should be applied in markets where the proportion of middle class people is high and this kind of price positioning promises the highest sales as a result. Low price levels are usually characterized by large volumes and go hand in hand with fierce competition. This is because the majority of the developing countries are trying to enter the markets in this way. Their attempt forces the other competitors to upgrade. If the upgrading fails, the moderately developed manufacturers may be forced to withdraw from the market. The competitive structure and the effects on the price structure must be analysed before making the decision.

13.3.1. The relationship between export prices and domestic prices

When exporters are planning the price level of their products, they usually want to fit their own prices into the price structure of the target market, should it be a consumer or industrial market. To do so, they must understand the relationship between the export price and the final price. The main question is how the final price is calculated from the exporter's producer price, what factors will influence it and what additional costs are added to it. Government regulations in the target market may divert the prices from the course of their normal, market evolution.

The companies involved in distributing the products in the target market also have margins and costs. The knowledge of these allows the exporter to deduce, from the observed consumer and user prices, the possible export price with relative certainty.

Besides the rarely used direct price regulations, the state has the opportunity to influence the evolution of the prices with different parafiscal charges, even in market economies. For the exporter, the most important are the import duties.

Import duties are paid by the importer ad valorem i.e. based on the value the goods, so they can influence the pricing of imported goods in a direct way. In addition to import duties the goods imported can be subject to other charges, and taxes that are levied on this type of product (e.g. consumption tax, or VAT etc.).

The process of backwards calculation from the consumer price observed in an overseas country is the following (Figure 13.1).

To avoid complicated calculations many exporters apply a so-called constant coefficient established empirically.

For example, the European manufacturer of canned products displayed in shop windows in Tokyo can use a 0.25 coefficient to deduce its own export price adapted to this price. The reciprocal of the coeffiecient works as well: by multiplying his price by 4 the producer can fit his price into the consumer price structure in Tokyo.

Figure 13.1. The process of backwards calculation of the factory price

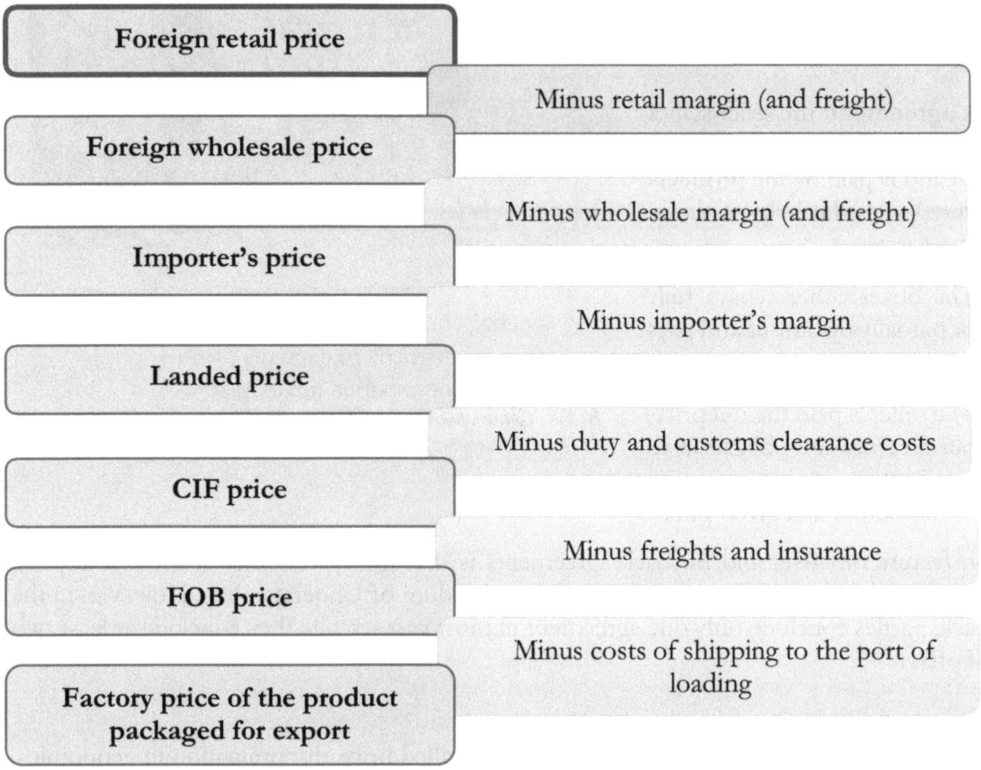

13.4. Special foreign trade transactions and prices

A very special area of international pricing is the so-called pricing in special foreign trade transactions. Countertrade is the oldest form of trade, and its significance started to increase in the 1980s. Today 10-15% of international trade is carried out this way. Countertrade has several forms. Here are some of them:

- In the case of **barter** (exchange without the use of cash) the goods are directly exchanged between two parties without the involvement of a third party. One of its important features is that goods are expressed in natural units and not in monetary ones. The two deliveries offset each other completely; no prices are set, but if they are, they have no practical significance.
- **Compensation trade** is similar to barter. The main difference is that the monetary value of the counter product is also determined. In the case of compensation in whole there is no monetary flow, however if the compensation is only partial the seller is paid partly in cash and partly in goods, that is why the price must be determined.

- **Offset or counter-trade:** the seller is paid in cash but is obliged to spend a part of the money in the country of the buyer within a given period of time. The value of countertrade can exceed the sales price. When Hungary purchased the Gripen fighter aircrafts, the agreement was concluded for 100% offset.
- **Buyback agreement:** the seller sells a site, a procedure or some technical equipment and is paid by the products manufactured with the help of these. It takes two forms:
    - The buyer either repays fully or partially by output and pays the rest in cash.
    - The seller is paid the full price, but assumes the obligation to buy back a certain percentage of the output at a given price.

An 1874 newspaper illustration from Harper's Weekly, showing a man engaging in barter: offering chickens in exchange for his yearly newspaper subscription.
By F.S. Church, published in Harper's Weekly, January 17, 1874, p. 61. https://commons.wikimedia.org/w/index.php?curid=5273657

The common feature of offset and buyback agreements is that the agreements of the two reverse transactions are linked with a third agreement or a Memorandum of Understanding. However, in the case of buyback, parties conclude only one agreement in most cases, while they conclude at least two in the case of offset.

13.5. Dynamic pricing – flexible prices in international transactions

Using different prices for the same products or services is called price discrimination in economics. It may also happen in international trade. The terms 'dynamic pricing' and 'flexible prices' were used in the heading instead of 'price discrimination' because some of the price changes discussed here are initiated by the exporter and, theoretically, do not really belong to the group of discriminatory changes.

The exporter can alter its prices a) by time, b) by markets, c) by buyers and d) according to quantity and the size of the order.

13.5.1. Altering the price by time

The most obvious forms of price changes may happen by time. For example:

- **When a new product is introduced:** should the exporter opt for either penetration or a skimming price strategy, he will change the initial price in both cases by time, usually deliberately. He will increase the initially low prices later and then will decrease the high price. The international market for colour televisions and mobile phones can be mentioned as typical examples for price decrease.

- **Foreign trade of fashion articles** is also a typical example for using flexible prices by time. Fashion often gives such high value to cheap and easily imitable goods that the general rules of pricing fail; the high starting prices are not the consequences of high production costs or high value, but the high price, which is independent from production costs, can give the impression that the product is valuable.

- **If the delivery is faster than usual in international trade** the exporter can generally charge a higher sales price. The higher sales price can only be considered real price discrimination if the difference exceeds the cost increase arising from faster delivery.

- **A change in the market situation** may also result in modified prices. An economic downturn can force exporters to decrease their prices; however an improvement in the market situation will allow them to increase prices.

13.5.2. Using different prices by markets (spatial differentiation)

The seller is faced with different market conditions in different export markets, which not only differ from each other but, to a great extent, from the conditions which prevail in the exporter's domestic market. As a result of differing market conditions it often occurs that a given export product is sold at different prices in different markets in international trading, even if the sales conditions are the same. This kind of price discrimination can be attributed to the recognition of the exporter, the closeness of the relationships and other factors.

13.5.3. Adjusting prices to consumers

Price discrimination by buyers used to be an evident component of the seller's pricing. Today, the buyer's role in the setting of export prices is not very important, although it cannot be neglected in certain product groups. The place the buyer occupies in the market hierarchy, however, can be interesting from two aspects: 1) Where is the buyer located in the export distribution channel (= vertical price discrimination)? 2) What is the buyer's reputation, where is his place in the business hierarchy (= horizontal price discrimination)?

The need to apply **vertical price differences** occurs primarily in the export of consumer goods. These products are typically sold through multiple channels, which means that the exporter sells the same type of product simultaneously to several buyers located at different points in the distribution channel of the same market. The parallel nature of the distribution paths requires the export prices to be properly differentiated. The disadvantage is that the application of the 'same market - same goods - same price' principle can prove to be a risky automatism by which the exporter creates his own competition.

Horizontal price discrimination happens when the exporter sells the goods at different prices to traders situated at the same point of the distribution channel (that is, he differentiates-discriminates between wholesale buyers or between retail buyers in a given market). The buyers' different creditworthiness, goodwill, places in the hierarchy of traders in the importing country, their standards, the closeness of their business relationships, business traditions, etc. all allow the exporter to charge different prices to the same type of resellers. Considering and using horizontal price discrimination occasionally may also contribute to increasing revenues from export.

13.5.4. Quantity price discrimination

Quantity price discrimination is usually attained by providing quantity discounts. It is evident that those buying larger quantities can achieve more favourable prices. What 'larger quantities' means can

naturally vary from country to country and from market to market. Technically, there are many solutions to quantity price discrimination, which can be studied in more detail in the textbooks dealing with international trade techniques.

13.6. Transfer pricing in international marketing

Transfer prices are those used in the trade between the different business units of multinational companies, which is why they are often referred to as 'intracompany prices'. The concept of the profit centre is becoming more and more widespread among companies working in an international context. Decentralized profit centres can be ideal for companies to measure performance and efficiency. In addition, the motivation of the profit centre's management is also an asset. For the concept of the profit centre to function efficiently it is essential to have a sensibly developed system of transfer prices.

Well-chosen transfer prices may contribute to improving profits in three areas:

- reducing duty paid by delivering components, spare part, structures (and sometimes end products) to countries where the level of duties is high,
- reducing profit tax by exporting the above products to high-tax countries at higher prices than would otherwise be realistic,
- repatriating dividend may become cheaper if the company concentrates its profits where repatriation is easiest and cheapest.

A multinational company thinks intelligently if it considers **not only the profit improving** impacts of transfer prices but their impact on the company's full resource allocation as well, and tries to find out how - and to what extent - this solution can contribute to meeting the following objectives:

- increasing international competitiveness,
- decreasing the amount of taxes and duties payable,
- cash-flow management,
- minimizing exchange rate risks,
- avoiding conflicts with domestic and target country governments,
- internal company objectives, for example ensuring the harmonization of company objectives and motivating managers of subsidiaries.

As a result of the above objectives, transfer pricing poses a problem for the top management of the company as well. According to international literature there are several methods of setting transfer prices, from which we will highlight the following (Kazainé–Reszegi 2010):

1. cost-plus method: the transfer price is set on the basis of direct costs and additional costs on top of that,
2. market-rate method: the transfer price is derived from the final market price,
3. price comparison method: the transfer price is the same as the price the independent parties would have achieved in the market.

EXHIBIT 13.3. OECD TRANSFER PRICING GUIDELINES

On June 27, 1995 the first draft of the OECD Transfer Pricing Guidelines for Multinational Enterprises and Tax Administrations ("OECD Guidelines") was published. These Guidelines are a revision of the *OECD Report Transfer Pricing and Multinational Enterprises* that was published in 1979. Since then, the OECD Guidelines have been continually developed and updated which resulted in the current OECD Guidelines. They have been approved for publication by both the Committee of Fiscal Affairs and the OECD Council on July 22, 2010.

The OECD Guidelines provide guidance on the application of the "arm's length principle" for the valuation, for tax purposes, of crossborder transactions between associated enterprises. In a global economy where multinational enterprises ("MNEs") play a prominent role, governments need to ensure that the taxable profits of MNEs are not artificially shifted out of their jurisdiction and that the tax base reported by MNEs in their country reflects the economic activity undertaken therein. For taxpayers, it is essential to limit the risks of economic double taxation that may result from a dispute between two countries on the determination of the arm's length remuneration for their crossborder transactions with associated enterprises.

Source: http://www.oecd-ilibrary.org/taxation/oecd-transfer-pricing-guidelines-for-multinational-enterprises-and-tax-administrations-2010_tpg-2010-en

13.7. Certain factors affecting pricing in international trade

Corporate price policy is manifested in the prices of specific transactions. As a consequence, price policy considerations should also include factors influencing the setting of the price which occur during the negotiation of the contractual terms of the transaction, in addition to the strict manufacturing and distribution costs, and marketing expenses. We will discuss two such contractual conditions: the terms of **shipping** and the terms of **payment**.

13.7.1. The terms of shipping – Incoterms 2010

One of the most important points of the sales agreement concerns how the parties should share the transport related risks and costs. It is possible - and happens quite often - that the parties involved find solutions that best reflect both of their business interests. However, the business partners are often not aware of the differences between the commercial practices of their countries. The risk of real or deliberate misunderstanding is quite high in such cases.

ICC
International Chamber of Commerce
The world business organization

By Source, Fair use, https://en.wikipedia.org/w/index.php?curid=45076908

In recognition of this, the Paris based International Chamber of Commerce compiled the rules, containing the most frequently used solutions and the ones that proved most effective in practice, which were first published in 1936. These conventions are commonly referred to as Incoterms (International Commercial Terms). The contents of Incoterms were amended several times during the past decades (in 1953, 1967, 1980, 1990 and 2000)

and the latest set of terms, *Incoterms 2010*, came into force on 1st January 2011. The latest modifications were necessitated primarily by the expansion of international commerce, the development of technology, the prominence of safety requirements and the growing importance of electronic communication. (The ICC has begun consultations on a new revision of Incoterms, to be called *Incoterms 2020*).

Incoterms are not law; their application is not obligatory unless the sales agreement between the parties expressly states that one of the clauses of Incoterms 2010 should be used.

The importance and widespread use of Incoterms is most certainly explained by the following:

- it clearly specifies *the share of the risks* and the geographical point where *the risk is transferred*,
- it clearly specifies the *allocation of costs* related to the transportation of goods between the seller and buyer, and determines the geographical point at which the costs are transferred,
- it defines any other obligations relating to the fulfilment of the contract (documents, notification obligation, etc.),
- the so-called conformity clause (included in every Incoterms clause) specifies that the seller is obligated to deliver the goods according to the provisions of the sales agreement and to certify this with the appropriate documents.

It was approved during the amendment in 2000 that electronic data exchange may be used in addition to or instead of the traditional documents, which can make the fulfilment process between the parties run more smoothly.

The next part (and Table 2.3) presents the clauses of Incoterms 2010 in the increasing order of the seller's obligation. (The 3-letter formats of the terms are given together with their full name and a brief commentary on the content of the parities.)

According to the modes of transportation, commercial practice distinguishes between clauses related to transportation by land, by sea and multimodal transport (complex, involving more than one mode of transport). We can also talk about single-point (when the transfer point of risks and costs are the same) and double-point (when these two points are not the same) parities. Unlike previously, Incoterms 2010 are divided according to the different modes of transportation. A part of the clauses (EXW, FCA, CPT, CIP, DAT, DAP, DDP) can apply to all modes of transportation – by land, by air, and by sea – as well as for multimodal transport. These are advantageous, especially for the transportation of containers. The other group includes the parities to be applied in the case of transportation by sea or inland waterways, when the goods are destined for a given port (FAS, FOB, CFR, CIF).

The following clauses can be used for transportation by sea and any other transportation mode, as well as for intermodal transport.

EXW (ex works)

All the costs and risks related to the transportation of the goods and the acquisition of the documents (except export licence) are **borne by the buyer**. The sales price is to be paid upon the receipt of the goods unless otherwise agreed by the parties.

FCA (free carrier)

The obligations relating to the costs and risks are transferred from the seller to the buyer when the seller has handed over the goods into the charge of the carrier named by the buyer at the named place. This parity is suitable in all cases where a carrier is involved in the transportation of the goods (as is most often the case), or when, in the case of transportation by sea, it is the obligation of the seller to place the goods in a warehouse before the arrival of the ship. The seller must bear the risks and the costs even if he has no control over the processes.

CPT (carriage and freight paid to…)

The underlying principle of this clause is the same as that of CFR (see later), but it must be added that the mechanism of contracting is different for the different modes of transport making the actual solutions different, e.g. with regard to reception of goods or responsibility. **The risks arising during the transport are borne by the importer, while the costs are borne by the exporter.**

CIP (carriage, insurance and freight paid to …)

It works on the same principles as CIF (see below). **The seller bears the costs,** including the costs of freight and insurance **up to the point of destination. The risks are transferred to the buyer** after the first carrier has taken charge of the goods.

DAT (delivered at terminal)

This term is a one-point clause independent from the mode of transport, which can be applied in multimodal transport as well. In the case of DAT **the seller delivers** when the goods, having been unloaded from the transport equipment after arrival, **have been placed at the port specified by the buyer or at the named terminal (port, warehouse, or other destination).** The seller is responsible for arranging the export licences, but is not responsible for obtaining the import licences, to pay duty and to clear the goods for import. DAT is mainly advantageous when shipping containers.

DAP (delivered at place)

Under DAP terms **the seller is responsible for bearing all the costs and risks** related to getting the goods to the named place of destination, with the exception of costs related to clearing the goods for import. According to DAP the seller delivers when the goods are placed at the disposal of the buyer at the named place of destination, ready for unloading from the means of transport. The seller must arrange for the export licence, but is not responsible for obtaining the import licences, for paying duty or import and customs clearance.

DDP (delivered duty paid … named place of destination in the country of importation)

The seller's obligation is to bear all the risks and costs, including duties, costs of customs clearance and taxes that may have to be paid in the country of destination, and to forward the required documents to the buyer. **The buyer's obligation is to take over the goods at the agreed place and to pay the agreed price for the goods.**

Clauses applicable for transportation by sea and inland waterways

The following part will cover all the terms that Incoterms 2010 defined for transportation by sea and inland waterways.

FAS (free alongside ship)

The seller is responsible for placing the goods alongside the ship ready to be loaded in accordance with port requirements or in lighters if the ship is berthed further away from the quay,

also for notifying the buyer. It includes the clearance of the goods for export. **Buyer is responsible for supplying a vessel and notifying the seller thereof, and bearing the costs and risks once the goods have been placed on the quay.**

The container ship *Nyk Aphrodite* carrying up to 6500 containers

Source: By AlfvanBeem - Own work, CC0, https://commons.wikimedia.org/w/index.php?curid=19499332

FOB (free on board)

This is the most frequently used term in overseas trade. FOB has so far meant that the point where the risks and costs shift from the seller to the buyer is when the goods pass the ship's rail in the port of departure. One of the novelties in Incomterms 2010 is that the notion of 'shiprail' is no longer used. The seller has practically fulfilled his obligations when the goods have been loaded onto the ship and a so-called clean Bill of Lading has been provided to the buyer. The seller and the buyer must agree when the goods are considered to be 'loaded on board' depending on the means of transport and the type of goods. It is the responsibility of the buyer to reserve or rent a space in a ship and notify the seller about it, as well as to bear the risks from the moment the goods have been loaded onto the ship as agreed.

CFR (cost and freight, also often abbreviated as C&F or C+F)

The risks are transferred to the buyer at the port of shipment over the ship's rail, but all the costs arising during the transportation are borne by the seller. As the risks arising during transportation are borne by the buyer, it is particularly important that the required notifications are done in time, and that the seller forwards the transport documents to the buyer as soon as possible. The transport document used in sea transport, the Bill of Lading, is a document of title, that is, it represents full ownership of the goods. Possessing the B/L makes it possible for the buyer, now the owner, to dispose of the goods on board the ship (use them as cover for insurance, sell them, etc).

CIF (cost, insurance and freight)

This covers practically the same ground as C&F with one very important exception. In this case the Incoterms explicitly obligate the seller to take out insurance against the buyer's risks under at least the minimum cover, which should be a minimum of 110% of their value. The buyer's rights of ownership are enforced and strengthened by another negotiable instrument, the insurance policy.

You may have already noticed in connection with CFR, and it is all the more striking in this case, that the seller does not fulfil his obligations by delivering the goods to the buyer as under other previous terms, but by handing over the documents of title to the goods. In fact, the sale doesn't concern the goods, but the instruments (Bill of Lading; insurance policy) representing ownership of the goods and

the rights to compensation with regard to the goods. The buyer, therefore, is obliged to pay the price of the goods **against the appropriate documents**. Consequently, the goods and the documents do not follow the same path; for example, the seller may request payment against the documents, even if the goods have perished in the meantime.

DES (delivered ex ship)

The risks and costs are transferred at the place of destination, on board the ship. Shipping companies often include the costs of unloading in the liner terms, and the seller must provide compensation in the price or in other ways.

Table 13.3. The clauses Incoterms 2010 in the increasing order of the seller's responsibilities

INCOTERMS 2010 SHARE OF RESPONSIBILITIES ACCORDING TO THE DIFFERENT CLAUSES											
Cost, charges	Any transportation method		Transportation by sea and inland waterways				Any transportation method				
	EXW	FCA	FAS	FOB	CFR	CIF	CPT	CIP	DAT	DAP	DDP
Packaging	Seller v. buyer	Seller	Seller	Seller	Seller	Seller	Seller	Seller	Seller	Seller	Seller
Costs of loading	Buyer	Seller	Seller	Seller	Seller	Seller	Seller	Seller	Seller	Seller	Seller
Delivery at port or place	Buyer	Seller	Seller	Seller	Seller	Seller	Seller	Seller	Seller	Seller	Seller
Export duties and taxes	Buyer	Seller	Seller	Seller	Seller	Seller	Seller	Seller	Seller	Seller	Seller
Costs of departure terminal	Buyer	Buyer	Seller	Seller	Seller	Seller	Seller	Seller	Seller	Seller	Seller
Loading onto carrier	Buyer	Buyer	Seller	Seller	Seller	Seller	Seller	Seller	Seller	Seller	Seller
Costs of vehicle	Buyer	Buyer	Buyer	Buyer	Seller	Seller	Seller	Seller	Seller	Seller	Seller
Insurance						Seller		Seller			
Costs of arrival terminal	Buyer	Buyer	Buyer	Buyer	Buyer	Buyer	Seller	Seller	Seller	Seller	Seller
Delivery to final destination	Buyer	Buyer	Buyer	Buyer	Buyer	Buyer	Buyer	Buyer	Buyer	Seller	Seller
Import duties and taxes	Buyer	Buyer	Buyer	Buyer	Buyer	Buyer	Buyer	Buyer	Buyer	Buyer	Seller

Multimodal parities that can be used for each method of transportation

DEQ (delivered ex quay)

These terms contain the most costs and risks in transportation by sea. According to this parity the seller has fulfilled his obligation when he has made the goods available to the buyer on the quay at

the named destination. Incoterms distinguish two versions of this parity. Duty and the related costs are borne by the buyer.

Figure 13.2. "Map of Incoterms" (countries where the application of Incoterms is accepted)

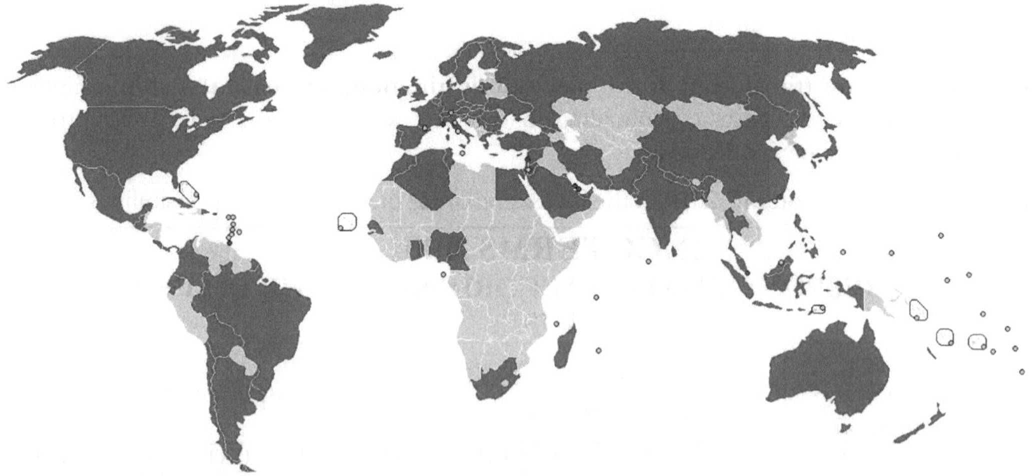

Source: Wikimedia Commons

13.7.2. A few criteria relating to choosing the best Incoterm parity

There is a completely clear relationship between the parity and the selling price: the more the costs and risks are borne by the seller, the higher the selling price and, vice versa, the more costs and risks are borne by the buyer, the lower the price he is willing to pay.

We can say that, in general, contracting with the longest parity seems to be the most advantageous for both the buyer and the seller. In practice, it means that the exporter should sell CFR or CIF, while the importer should buy FOB. This general consideration, however, does not necessarily mean the best solution, because the Incoterm chosen, and the contract price can be influenced by several other factors in any given business transaction.

One of the important factors may be the currency of the contract and the currency in which the costs of the transport and the insurance have to be paid. A similarly interesting and important issue concerns the changes in the exchange rate of the currency of the contract.

The relationship with the carriers can also play an important role. It can be very advantageous to export CIF and charge the listed freight rate if the exporter benefits from a discount from the shipping company. The choice of parity can also be influenced by the situation of the freight market. If there is a good supply of carriage and the rates are relatively low, one should try to sign an agreement for a longer parity, while in the reverse case it is recommended to leave the task of handling the freight market difficulties to the partner.

Naturally the partner also tries to enforce all of the above, which means that the market powers between the partners will have a considerable impact on the choice of parity too.

In addition, many countries have national standards and/or established market practices with regard to parity selection which the parties cannot ignore, no matter how much they would like to.

13.7.3. The terms of payment

The terms of payment, in addition to the terms of shipping, may be equally important for the partners from both foreign trade technique and marketing points of view. The term of payment is a price factor, on the one hand (and this is the role we wish to highlight) and is a market influencing factor, on the other. By appropriately selecting the term of payment exporters may be able to create additional demand for their products (if, for example, they sell on credit in a market poor in capital, they may increase their turnover or market share).

Payment represents the area with the highest risks, and the selection of the payment terms reflects the partners' efforts to decrease and share those risks. During negotiations the exporter and the importer both seek to reach the most favourable payment position possible. The primary interest of the sellers is to receive payment for the goods as soon as possible, preferably in parallel with delivery. The importers, however, would like to receive the goods for their money according to the conditions of the sales agreement.

The balance of power between the partners, the exporter's level of capitalization and goodwill, as well as the importer's credit standing, all play an important role in the setting of payment terms. The general economic situation, the product's position in the market, and the dominant payment practices cannot be disregarded either. The general strategy of the partners with regard to payment and the tactic to be used is also limited by the different government regulations in force.

In reality there are two decisions to be made when setting the terms of payment: the means of payment and the method of payment.

13.7.3. The means of payment

When deciding about the means of payment the partners should agree whether the buyer will pay the counter-value of the goods in the local currency, in foreign currency or in goods. Paying in local currency is not a standard procedure in today's trade practice; paying in goods can be used in the case of certain special transactions, so the typical means of payment in international trade is foreign currency. The three basic cases of payment in foreign currency are: bank transfer, the use of bill of exchange or cheque.

Bank transfer

Bank transfer is the simplest form of payment in foreign currency. A certain amount of money is credited to the account of the seller in the sales transaction (beneficiary) on behalf of the buyer in a foreign trade transaction by a bank, or by several banks, from the bank account of the buyer in most cases. The bank transfer becomes payment if the beneficiary (implicitly or explicitly) accepts it. The bank transfer in international trade is generally effected through interbank relations.

Bill of exchange

This is an ipso jure negotiable instrument with strict formal requirements representing an order to pay or a promise to pay. The 'order to pay' type is referred to as a bill of exchange and the 'promise to pay' type is known as a promissory note. The rules relating to the strict formal requirements were specified by the Geneva Convention in 1930.

The Geneva type bill of exchange must include the following formal elements (which distinguish the Geneva type of bill exchange from the Anglo-Saxon type):

1. the term 'bill of exchange' inserted in the body of the instrument in the language used to draw up the instrument,
2. an unconditional payment order for a specific amount of money (an unconditional promise in the case of promissory notes),
3. the name of the drawee (the person ordered to pay, or the maker in the case of a promissory note),
4. a statement of the time of payment. There are four ways to specify the time of payment: (1) on a named date, (2) at a fixed period after the the date of issue, (3) at sight, (4) at a fixed period after sight. If the time of payment is not specified, the bill of exchange is deemed to be payable at sight,
5. a statement of the place (if the place of the payment is not named, the place of payment of the bill of exchange is deemed to be the premises of the drawee),
6. the name of the person to whom or to the order of whom the payment must be made,
7. the place and date of issue of the bill (issue),
8. the signature of the issuer of the bill (drawer).

The Bankers Trust Building on Wall Street

Wall Street is one of the hubs of the financial world and is home to many banks. Payments are always closely linked with banks; indeed, international trade would be impossible without them.

Photo: Wikimedia Commons

A 1939 bill of exchange from India

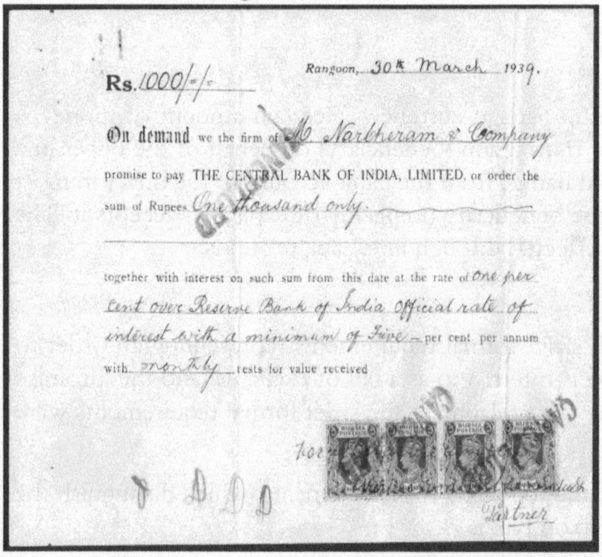

Rs. 1000/-/-

Rangoon, 30th March 1939.

On demand we the firm of M. Narltheram & Company promise to pay THE CENTRAL BANK OF INDIA, LIMITED, or order the sum of Rupees One thousand only.

together with interest on such sum from this date at the rate of One per cent over Reserve Bank of India Official rate of interest with a minimum of Five – per cent. per annum with monthly rests for value received

Partner

Source: Rs 1000 bill of exchange from Rangoon, 1939 – Wikimedia Commons

Cheque It is similar to a bill of exchange in many ways, but there are some important differences. A bill of exchange is primarily a lending instrument, while a cheque is considered to be a cash equivalent payment instrument. The issue of a bill of exchange represents only the beginning of the payment process, which ends when the bill is drawn.

Sample of a cheque from Canada:

MR. JOHN JONES
1645 DUNDAS ST. W, APT. 27
TORONTO, ON M6K 1V2

243

DATE 20061201
Y Y Y Y M M D D

PAY TO THE ORDER OF Wikimedia Foundation $ 100.55

One Hundred Dollars and 55/100 DOLLARS

Security features included - Details on back

FIRST BANK OF WIKI
Victoria Main Branch
1425 James St., P.O. Box 4001
Victoria (B.C.) V8X 3X4

MEMO Donation

John Jones MP

⑈243⑈ ⑆00005⑉123⑆ 123⑉456⑉7⑈

Source: Wikimedia Commons

A cheque is an order to the bank, which is based on the cheque agreement signed between the client and the bank. In the cheque agreement, the bank undertakes to cash the cheque drawn to its name if:

- the cheques are valid,
- there are sufficient funds to back them,
- they meet all the formal requirements, and
- the signature of the drawer matches the specimen signature on the cheque agreement.

Cheques are very frequently used payment instruments in international trade, despite the fact that their use is mostly advantageous for buyers. The bank will only pay the amount of the cheque to the account of the buyer when the cheque is presented for payment. Another advantage is that banks do not charge a commission on them.

13.7.4. The methods of payment

In addition to the balance of power between partners, the choice of payment method is motivated by the efforts to avoid title risk, although there is no method of payment which is completely safe.

Open account. One of the simplest and safest methods of payment for the buyer, but the one representing the highest risks for the seller, is the *open account.* It means that the seller ships the goods to the address and to the availability of the buyer, and buyer pays only at a later date.

Cash in advance. Advance payment is the safest form of payment for the seller, but an incredibly risky one for the buyer. The name already suggests that the seller is willing to deliver only after the

payment has been made. Advance payment seems to be a version of this payment method but, in reality, advance payment can be made in any method of payment.

The next part will deal with the payment methods which can be referenced by the International Chamber of Commerce.

Cash against documents (CAD). This belongs to the methods of payment where the security of payment is increased by the involvement of a trustee. The trustee can be either the forwarding agent on the goods side, or a bank on the finance side. The main characteristic of this payment method (as the name suggests) is that the payment is made upon the presentation of the documents and not the receipt of the goods.

The basic case of cash against documents (which requires the involvement of only one trustee - the bank) is called the **clean collection.** The seller ships the goods to the buyer and entrusts his bank to collect the payment from the buyer against the documents which evidence the delivery. Considering that the buyer takes over the goods, clean collection carries the same risks as open account trade. The fact that the buyer is instructed by a bank to make the payment lowers these risks to a certain extent.

The documentary collection has two forms, which can further decrease the seller's risks:

- **Documents against acceptance means** the seller ships the goods to the address of a forwarding agent (usually situated close to the buyer) with the instruction that the goods can be released to the buyer if the buyer can evidence that the payment has been made. The seller forwards the set of documents related to the export to his bank and instructs it to collect the debt from the buyer. When the payment has been made the buyer can claim the goods from the forwarding agent's warehouse by presenting the payment confirmation from the bank. The most frequently used type is the **banker's draft.** The seller ships the goods to the international forwarder's address and to the order of a named bank. When the payment has been made the bank instructs the forwarding agent to release the goods to the buyer.

- In the second case the seller ships the goods to the address and to the order of the bank. The bank releases the goods or the document representing title to the goods once the payment has been made.

Documentary Credit (D/C). The International Chamber of Commerce has developed the rules of documentary credit as well. (The Uniform Customs and Practice for Documentary Credits, 1993 Revision, ICC Publication No. 600). The current version has been in force since 1st July 2007. Documentary credit is the most frequently required payment method in international sales agreements, despite its quite complicated nature.

It can be costly for the importer, but it provides the highest security to the partners, all things considered. Documentary credit is an independent legal transaction, a contract the fulfilment of which is separate from the goods. Documentary credit means that the financial fulfilment is done according to the rules of documentary credit, strictly against the documents. The abstract nature of documentary credit can also mean that the beneficiary is not paid due to formal errors, even if the sales transaction has been completed in accordance with the sales agreement, or the payment can be made even if the conditions of the sales agreement have not been met, but those of the documentary credit have.

The use of documentary credit offers additional security, as it is not the importer that promises to pay, but a bank (the issuing bank) entrusted by the buyer. The issuing bank undertakes,

- to make a payment to or to the order of the beneficiary immediately or at a later date or to accept and pay bill(s) of exchange issued by the beneficiary,
- to authorize another bank to make such payment or to accept and pay such bill(s) of exchange,
- to authorize another bank to negotiate against the documents

if the terms and conditions of the credit have been met.

The use of documentary credit is advisable in all cases where the partners hardly know each other, when there is little mutual confidence between them, or if the risks of the exporter are enhanced by the insecure political and economic situation of the buyer's country.

Documentary credit protects both parties against title risk. As it is an international convention, it provides a uniform interpretation of the payment terms, which is advantageous for both contracting parties.

The special advantage for the exporter is that he will be paid the price of the goods at the moment when the documents are approved.

It can be advantageous for the importer, since using the letter of credit as a recognized secure payment method may be associated with better trade conditions (e.g. lower price). At the same time it can also be disadvantageous for the buyer that the fulfilment of the terms of the credit may not necessarily mean the fulfilment of the sales agreement, because the documentary credit transaction is separate from the goods transaction.

The process of documentary credit begins by the applicant (the buyer in the sales transaction) asking the issuing bank (it is almost always his own account managing bank) to set up a line of credit (the line of credit being the documentary credit itself) in favour of the named beneficiary (the seller in the sales transaction). The issuing bank promises to pay, or to accept a bill of exchange, or if the beneficiary forwards the documents requested in the documentary credit by the given date and informs the beneficiary about all this by letter or by any other way of post. The obligation of the issuing bank can be revocable or irrevocable. The applicant is obligated to transfer the funds providing cover for the documentary credit to the issuing bank.

The advising bank (the seller's bank or another bank involved) can have the following functions in documentary credit:

- Advising the bank to forward documents. In this case, the beneficiary is notified about the opening of documentary credit through another bank.
- The confirming bank confirms the obligations of the issuing bank as its own. The bank will have the same obligations as the issuing bank. Banks are not obliged to accept the request for confirmation, but must notify the issuing bank about this. It is perfectly conceivable that the commitment to fulfil by the seller's own bank reassures and puts the beneficiary into a comfortable position.
- The paying bank acquires the documents specified by the documentary on behalf of and under the cover of the issuing bank. If, however, the paying bank accepts documents that do not meet the requirements of the documentary credit, the issuing bank can reclaim the payment which may have already been made.

- The negotiating bank purchases (advances) the sets of documents at its own cost and at its own risk. The difference is that the purchasing is done at the request and on behalf of the issuing bank, i.e. officially, while the advancing is done upon the request of the seller.

Special knowledge is required with regard to documentary credit. Payment credit promising immediate payment can be regarded as the basic version of documentary credit, nevertheless the type of credit must be mentioned in all documentary credit.

The main areas requiring special knowledge concern the documents and the verification of the documents. According to the scheme, the obligation of the bank to make the payment depends on whether the beneficiary has presented all the necessary documents by the given deadline and according to the terms of the documentary credit.

As regards the origin of the documents it is best to quote Article 20.b of The Uniform Customs and Practice for Documentary Credits, which provides that:

"Unless otherwise stipulated in the credit, banks will also accept as an original document(s) a document(s) produced or appear to have been produced:

1. by reprographic, automated or computerized system,
2. as carbon copies provided that it is marked as original and, where necessary, appears to be signed.

A document may be signed by handwriting, by facsimile signature, by perforated signature, by stamp, by symbol, or by any other mechanical or electronic method of authentication."

The most important documents with regard to the exporter's fulfilment are the transport documents, in particular the bill of lading, because of the special risks related to the transportation by sea and because it is a document of title.

The authentication of the document means that the bank compares the documents presented by the beneficiary with the specifications of the credit, the rules of documentary credit and with each other. It is essential in this regard that the banks are obligated to perform a thorough examination of all the documents required by the credit, and to make sure that they comply with the formal requirements and the conditions of the credit. The issuing bank has only two options: to make the payment or to deny payment.

The letter of credit. Several types of documentary credit were developed in commercial practice. The most widely used type is freely negotiable documentary credit, better known as **the commercial letter of credit** (Letter of Credit, L/C). The bank issuing a commercial letter of credit makes a commitment to accept a draft drawn on its name (issuing bank) in favour of any of the bona fide holders, on the presentation of the compliant documents and the letter of credit itself, by the deadline. The commercial letter of credit is primarily popular in the trade practices of Anglo-Saxon partners, and rightly so. There are several significant differences between the commercial letter of credit (L/C) and the so-called documentary credit (D/C).

- A D/C has only one beneficiary. A documentary credit is negotiable, but only once. An L/C also has a named beneficiary; however, the issuing bank can pay to or to the order of any bona fide holders. The "bona fide holder" clause must be inserted in the letter of credit. The letter of credit actually becomes freely negotiable and freely and securely transferable as a

result of this. The aim of this solution is to ensure that the beneficiary is paid as soon as possible, and the method is very advantageous for the banks willing to negotiate.

- The letter of credit is also accompanied by a draft. It is, however, not a compulsory element of documentary credit.
- The standard documentary credit is a bank payment order, while the letter of credit itself represents the credit, and that is why the letter of credit must be enclosed in the stock? of other documents.

Figure 13.3 shows how the risks increase for the buyer (importer) and the seller (importer) with the use of the different payment methods.

Figure 13.3. The increase in risk according to the different methods of payment for the exporter and the importer

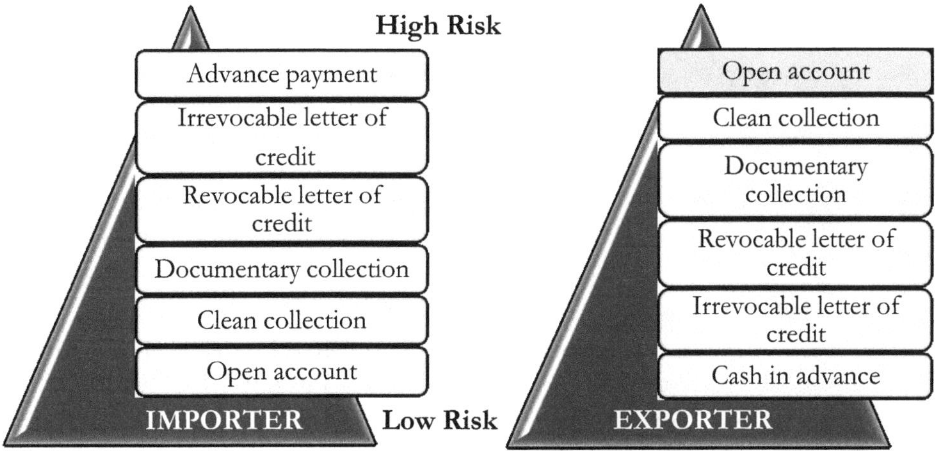

Case Exhibit: Blackthorn Foods
OUR STORY

Our aim is to make the best fudge around

Blackthorn Foods specialises solely in the manufacture of a quality handmade fudge. Blackthorn Foods is a family business based in Belfast, Northern Ireland and is run by three sisters Cathy, Jenny and Dorothy.

Blackthorn Foods is a family business specialising in award-winning gourmet handmade fudge produced in the artisan way, in a range of natural flavours. Established in 2004 by three sisters, the company now employs a further six people. Having started exporting in 2013, Blackthorn already sells to the Netherlands, Denmark, Sweden, Germany, the United Arab Emirates and Spain. Exports are now 25 per cent of all sales for the company. Dorothy Bittles, co-founder and partner, shares her experience of how to set pricing in new markets.

HOW YOU DO DECIDE ON A PRICING MODEL FOR YOUR EXPORT BUSINESS?

People always try to force your prices down, on account of transport costs. Our export business is all about volume orders, because the fudge is being shipped out per pallet. When

we initially started exporting, we tried to build our transport costs into our price, but it varies so much by country that we now just quote prices ex works. Some large companies might have good carriage infrastructures in their countries and it's cheaper for them to collect the product themselves.

It also means that if you're at a trade show and someone from Spain, for example, asks about your pricing, it's much easier to quote an ex works price. Some countries do have a sugar goods tax so there are other things to consider, too. They might pay an extra heavy VAT on it.

IF YOUR PRODUCTION COSTS ARE FIXED, IN WHAT WAYS CAN YOU BE FLEXIBLE TO ENSURE YOUR EXPORTS ARE SUFFICIENTLY PROFITABLE?

As opposed to offering a discount on the price, if shopkeepers in a particular country say they don't really know fudge very well, we would offer more point of sale material and support of the brand, as opposed to lowering our price. In a case of 32 bars, we would offer three or four wrapped differently, so that the shopkeepers can sample it, and we include information about the product's unique selling points. We have a shelf-ready case and we would get a sticker made in the appropriate language, telling the customer about the product.

WHAT ADVICE DO YOU HAVE ABOUT PRICING A PRODUCT CORRECTLY IN A NEW MARKET?

Ours is such an artisan product that we can't sell it cheaply even if we wanted to: we would just be busy fools. We have a cost and we're not going to make it for less than that, so we're quite rigid on our pricing. We don't discount.

As an exporting company, you do need to support the brand, and there is a cost involved – but it doesn't have to be on the product. There are advertising costs, but it's so the product can continue to sell at the price you've set. What we have done in some countries, where they weren't familiar with fudge, if a retailer doesn't want to commit to a full pallet, for the initial order, we contribute to the transport costs and reduce the amount on a full pallet, and that is a good enticement.

Source: http://exportstartguide.com/how-to-export/set-pricing-export-markets/ www.blackthornfoods.co.uk)
Printed with the permission of Blackthorn Food Company.

CHAPTER 14. SUCCESSFUL PRICE NEGOTIATIONS

OBJECTIVE 1 To understand the impact of price negotiations on the supply chain and other parts of the marketing and distribution channels.

OBJECTIVE 2 To facilitate an awareness and understanding of the role of culture in the case of international negotiations or where dealings are cross-border and may involve parties from different national cultures. As world trade has become increasingly important, understanding the partner's culture is of the utmost importance in negotiating terms of agreement.

OBJECTIVE 3 To explore the processes of price negotiation to develop strategies and tactical plans to facilitate planning and managing those processes.

14.1 Introduction

This chapter explores the negotiation process and investigates the importance of taking a strategic view of negotiating. The chapter commences by looking at the consumer and questions whether the consumer can actual bargain. At a time when world trade is becoming more important as markets become globalised the art of negotiating can impact on the profitability and survival of the company.

14.2. Can the consumer bargain?

In shops you are usually not supposed to bargain about the prices marked on the tags; shops, supermarkets, insurance companies, banks, utilities, theatres, work according to a fixed price list. Even if they are prepared to give a discount, it is linked to well specified conditions and not open to negotiations. At first sight, ordinary people may have the impression that prices - in most cases - cannot be subject to bargaining. Perhaps the only exceptions are fruit and vegetable markets or flea markets.

This may be more or less true for modern societies. To what extent consumer (retail) prices can be negotiated varies from country to country. There are some in which culture and tradition allow more opportunities for a mutual agreement on prices. Those who have visited Arabic or Near East countries have certainly experienced bargaining as an integral part of the shopping procedure; what is more, sellers take it as an insult if the buyer fails to start haggling. It may sound surprising but even in a highly developed country like Japan buyers

can bargain about the price of valuable goods (e.g. furniture, television, etc.) in most shops (perhaps with the exception of large department stores).

Stores inside Istanbul's Grand Bazaar where bargaining is a must

Source: By Dmgultekin - Own work, CC BY-SA 3.0, https://commons.wikimedia.org/w/index.php?curid=13251723

The fixed prices prevailing in Central and Eastern Europe during the decades of socialism made consumers (and often business people as well) lose the habit of negotiating prices. People feel ashamed to bargain, although those who initiate a bargain as buyers are determined to try to assert their interests vis a vis the seller and the interest declared in their prices. Nowadays some bargaining has become possible even in the retail trade of these former socialist countries. When someone buys a flat, furniture, a car or other consumer goods of great value, even a few percent discount can result in considerable economies. A price negotiation of this kind can also be in the interests of the seller. He may get a better deal by giving a discount of a few percent and selling the product to the customer than by letting the customer leave without buying anything.

14.3. The importance of price negotiation in the supply chain

However, the role of negotiating prices is really important in other parts of the supply chain and other levels of the distribution channel. Producers fight tooth and nail with their suppliers and sub-contractors, wholesalers with manufacturers and retailers do the same with wholesalers and/or manufacturers. Bargaining is a process of negotiation, which can be either simple or complicated, depending on what the subject of the bargaining is, or who the negotiating parties are. International trade is inconceivable without price negotiation. These talks are, however, more difficult if the parties involved come from different cultural environments, respect different traditions and speak different languages. The next exhibit gives you an insight into the problems a businessman may have to face

in China, a country that is becoming more and more important internationally, if he is not familiar with the local culture of negotiation.

EXHIBIT 14.1. SAVE FACE! -i.e. THE GUANXI AND THE CHARACTERISTICS OF WESTERN-CHINESE BUSINESS RELATIONS

There is a fundamental difference in their way of thinking, which makes the development of relations rather difficult between China and the Western world. In terms of Hofstede's dimensions, the United States of America qualify as individualistic beyond doubt while the Chinese society can be described as collectivist.

In collectivist societies, like China, people would much rather work in teams, because collective action helps maximize the gains the individual can realize and thereby achieve his personal goals as well.

Information is shared indirectly and before getting down to the facts they start the negotiations with explanations, while the Americans prefer direct, to-the-point style negotiations. In contrast with their American counterparts, partners on the Chinese side never have full decision-making power. During the talks, the Chinese tend to ask more questions and they find the negotiating techniques of their Western partners quite aggressive.

Negotiators preparing for their meetings in China are given advice like: “don't forget always to have plenty of business cards with you”, “take your own interpreter”, “use short sentences,”, ”be dressed in a conservative way.” These pieces of advice may be enough to start the negotiations but certainly not for long-term business success.

Partners often leave the negotiating table dissatisfied: the Americans think the negotiation was too long and had little efficiency, they consider the administration too slow and the management simply incompetent.

Guanxi (the Chinese network of relations) is deeply rooted in the philosophy of Confucius. Confucianism defines five basic relations and the moral values that belong to them: (Lin 2011).

Five basic relations	Moral value of relations
father – son	love, affection
monarch – subject	respect
Husband - wife	acceptance of roles
old – young	proper order
friend – friend	loyalty

The individual's rights and obligations are not universal in China; they vary depending on the relationships in which they are involved. Chinese society accepts inequality in connections. Guanxi is the science of establishing and managing relations, the root of the Chinese social system and economic build-up.

In the next part in addition to the theory of guanxi we are also going to present the findings of 7 in-depth interviews studying Sino-Hungarian business relations. (The interviewees all had at least 5 years' experience in the field of Chinese relations).

Guanxi or Guanshi	
Traditional Chinese	關係
Simplified Chinese	关系

The Chinese word **guanxi** consists of two characters: *guan* meaning 'gate', and '*xi* 'meaning 'relation'. Guanxi means social relations among those who have 'entered through' the gate.

Guanxi permeates private life, politics and business as well. It includes family relations but reaches beyond them, joining the members of the clan into one community, those who have the same family names, come from the same village, have the same religion, went to the same school, or shared any kind of common experience in the past. Those who are within the circle can experience being 'one of us' while those left outside the circle can feel excluded, or strangers. The guanxi circles are exclusive, and it is extremely difficult to get inside either in the business or social dimension.

The interviewees all emphasized the importance of guanxi for anyone intending to enter the Chinese market. In their opinion, it is mainly at the beginning of a business relationship that guanxi is very important. "*Without guanxi it is extremely difficult or even impossible to do business in China.*". At the same time several respondents, who had been active in the market for a longer period of time, referred to a decrease in the importance of guanxi over the last 10 years. They attributed this change to the widespread use of written contracts applied and required by multinational companies that operate in China in increasing numbers, the slow but steady adjustment of the legal system to international standards, different attitudes of the new generation in the age group of 30-40 years and the impact of the Internet.

Most members of the 'new' generation in leading positions had studied abroad. Managers who returned to work in the large cities of China do not consider losing face such a serious personal matter and accept more readily the style of negotiation and emotional reaction that characterize their European partners. The assistance provided by the Internet is becoming more and more helpful in collecting information about the partners and mapping their relations. However, the interviewees also pointed out, that these changes could only be observed in large cities.

While in relationship marketing we speak of a relationship network, the Chinese guanxi could be compared to a structure composed of **concentric** circles. Guanxi is usually presented as three concentric circles: the inner circle representing the needs, the middle circle the emotions and the outer circle rationality.

Every circle represents different rights and obligations. The nature of the relationships is also different: in the innermost circle, they are strong and pronounced, in the middle circle they are mixed and, in the outer circle, cooperating. Family relations and close friendships constitute the innermost circle. Here belong duties towards family members, like taking care of and looking after the elderly, unquestionable duties and rights that cannot be ignored under any circumstances. The more remote relatives and looser friendly relations belong in the middle circle. Acquaintances are located in the outer circle. The differences also appear in the allocation of resources: in the innermost circle everybody has access to resources according to their needs, and responsibility for family members overrules individual interests. In the middle

circle, emotions and love for the others also play a part. The external circle is completely free from emotions; it is governed by rational considerations and is built on an effort to achieve mutual interests. The latter is the area of business relations.

Guanxi has **three main dimensions**: emotion or empathy, mutuality, and face. The higher the level of **empathy,** the easier it is to build relations. In order to avoid open conflicts or refusal, the Chinese never express their desires or objectives openly, therefore what remains untold is always more important than what is said. Without a high degree of empathy and emotional openness it is not possible to get to know your partner's purposes.

'Emotional dimension' also means the human effort made by individuals to maintain lasting relations for emotional reasons. It encompasses family members, teacher-student relationships in China and close friends. Chinese people distinguish two levels of friendship. In a close friendship, parties are prepared even to make financial sacrifices for each other while, in a loose friendship, they focus on financial equilibrium, which can be mutually advantageous. Our interviewees were not able to interpret the dimension of emotions in their business relations; they could approach it only at the rational level. Good personal relations lend a kind of positive, apparently emotional but rather rational content to successful transactions. Respondents preferred to call this emotional factor 'trust'. Using the term 'empathy; instead of 'emotion' helped them think back on several experiences.

"They are very friendly, and this may mislead the Hungarian partner. They have good observation skills and can read the partner's mental and health condition from his face and turn this information into power that they can use during the negotiation."

In a personal relationship one party does the other a favour in the hope of seeing it returned at a later date. The party who was given the favour feels obliged to return the service as soon as he has the opportunity. There is no time limit for this and it needn't be immediate.

The notion of reciprocity is well known in Western societies as well, but there it means offering short-term help symmetrically that is not big enough to overturn the balance. In China reciprocity also means symmetric assistance in the long run, and several years can pass without people returning the favour. Partners remember the services rendered to each other though and reciprocity is a very strong social norm. Not keeping it is inconceivable in Chinese society. Those who fail to keep it are excluded from the circle; they disgrace themselves, their families and all those who belong to the same guanxi circle. The interviews emphasized the importance of mutual favours and the respondents admitted using them in their business relations within ethical and lawful limits. In answer to the question how long their business partners remembered the favours, the Chinese partners said: *"Forever". "to the end of time". "They remember and speak about it for a very long time". "They learn how to keep these things in their minds since childhood".* Every Chinese person has a computer in his head which manages the favours given and done.

Giving presents, which is a way of maintaining relations, especially in the long run, was also listed together with mutual favours Two respondents linked it with corruption, especially in cases where cash was the gift, which is customary in Chinese culture. This kind of present, they say, is refused by Hungarians – amid uneasy explanations of company policy. However, one respondent revealed that refusing a small amount - offered as a kind of pocket money - can actually ruin a relationship. "*There is nothing wrong with handing over money in an envelope. This is not corruption, not even a bonus, but simply a present.*"

The idea of corruption arises only when gifts of great value or larger amounts of money are given, but small presents are considered indispensable for maintaining the relationship. When asked about their favourite presents, all respondents mentioned personalized gifts or objects typical of the country, region or a product of local craftsmanship. However, large Chinese firms about to enter the multinational scene tend to consider giving presents less important. One of the respondents had the experience with their partner, a multinational Chinese firm, that the buyer was forbidden to accept any present.

"On one occasion, the middle manager, to whom I handed over my present, a bottle of 25-year-old-Scotch when a colleague of his was present, dropped it to the floor right away saying that company policy does not allow them to accept presents. Then, as if to prove that he was serious, he sent the bag under the table with a kick. Later he sent me a note, saying the whisky was great and he appreciated the present. He had to save face both to his colleagues and to me."

The importance of **saving face** can only be interpreted in a social context. It means the image that others have created about the individual in the course of interactions. Although it is present in most societies, the concept behind the term is interpreted differently in Western cultures and China.

Wang Jianlin, Chairman and President, Dalian Wanda Group, speaks during the Success versus Survival in a Global Downturn session at The World Economic Forum Annual Meeting of the New Champions in Dalian, China 10-12 September 2009. Wang Jianlin was the richest businessman in Chine in 1916 according the Forbes

This file is licensed under the Creative Commons Attribution-Share Alike 2.0 Generic license.
(https://www.forbes.com/china-billionaires/#5b55b31ae431

In Western cultures, the face is considered an element of personal identity; in China, however, it is a kind of positive social value, that the individual can obtain in the course of social interactions performed with others. The face also means the individual's image and his/her status within the social structure. Its social importance is vital, because saving it is in the interest not only of the individual, but his/her business partners and relatives as well, while losing it has an impact on their life too. Losing face means bringing shame on the whole family and all those who belong to the same guanxi circle. In the USA one either has a face or not, it does not make a big difference; in China, however, its measure or value can be determined, as in the case of money. You can collect it, give it, lose it, or take it from somebody. A person loses face if he/she provokes an open conflict, shows his/her anger in the presence of others, behaves in an aggressive or arrogant way, directly and openly criticizes others or does not treat the status of others properly. Cardon and Scott (2003) identified five strategies for saving face:

- Avoid informality, which means primarily the avoidance of conflict situations. Should it become impossible, they switch to a certain formality in verbal communication, and say things like: "There are certain difficulties...."
- In conflict situations they employ intermediaries who have strong features and are usually highly respected.

- Praise the partner's status, competences and position, taking care to do so when others are present and can hear it.
- Ask openly for a specific service, which is meant to express the strength of the relationship between the partners and, if the other partner refuses to provide the service, the first has reason to believe that he was not given due respect. The strategy of humiliation is applied in cases when somebody breaks the rules of behaviour connected with the face.

Every respondent mentioned as a general problem the fact that Hungarians are impatient, and at times negotiate in an aggressive way, sticking too much to the point. The expression of anger, frustration or aggression at the negotiating table is followed by loss of face, therefore these forms of behaviour should be avoided.

Two of the interviewees summarized their experiences as follows: "The Chinese partner's face does not betray any feelings, and only a very experienced sinologue can recognize anything on it". " The Hungarian partner reacted in an aggressive way, and this informed the Chinese that we had lost mental control and this meant victory in their reading".

During interviews, the notion of modesty was brought up in connection with the face. Three of the interviewees pointed it out without any question being asked about it in the interview. "T*he Chinese have great respect for modesty in a person, but modesty also has its tactical function. There was a shooting competition and my business partner said that he was very bad at shooting in spite of the fact that he was a sharp shooter." "He said he did not speak the language very well, and then continued in English without accent".*

The interviewees listed the duality of the **written contracts and verbal agreements** among the significant problems. In the case of a good guanxi the verbal agreements work without difficulty, consequently the written contracts are merely considered as a formal framework. The Hungarian partners had the most difficulty with the verbal promises and the way they were kept, as well as getting the written contracts delivered. "*It was no use writing the contract if he had something else in his mind or had a different interpretation of the lines and what mattered for him was the ideas in his mind and not what was written in the contract". "We signed the contract one day and the Hungarian partner sat back happily, thinking they had achieved something at last, and we did not understand why the next day the Chinese started the whole negotiation from the very beginning".*

"It is not always the contract that governs. If the relationship is good, it is worth a lot more than any written contract. And however excellent a written contract may be, it will not be delivered if the relationship goes wrong".

"The contract is simply the confidence put in writing. And not the declaration of the terms of the contract. It is just a framework that keeps changing as the personal interests change". "What is put down in a contract is just a small part of the verbal agreement. If there is mutual confidence the verbal agreement works perfectly."

Dinners, as important venues for reaching agreements and creating guanxi, were also studied in the interviews. One of the respondents found himself in a most unpleasant situation during a dinner given by his partner because the promises made there were considered by the partner as an agreement overruling the written contract. This misunderstanding caused him significant difficulties. For a Hungarian firm only an agreement written on paper can be a binding contract

and primary evidence.

However, there was one point our respondents agreed on, namely that globalization and the expansion of multinational firms gradually increases the importance of written agreements.

Source: Berend (2012)

14.4. The objectives of price negotiations

Now we turn our attention to the *seller* and examine the price negotiation from his point of view.

During the preparation for price negotiation it is important for the seller to bear in mind at least two points:

- What does he expect to achieve and why?
- What does the buyer expect to achieve and why?

In order to answer these questions, it is necessary to collect data both from within and outside the company. The seller must be familiar with all information concerning the product such as costs, capacities, quality, stocks, transportation, etc. He should also be aware of the interests that have an impact on his own negotiating position. He must know the limitations which restrict his zone of activity and be equally conversant with the market situation, the supply and conditions of competitors as well as anticipated influencing factors. This, however, is only one aspect of the problem. If he wants to be truly successful during negotiations, he should also collect information about the negotiating partner.

He should estimate what the partner hopes to achieve, what his interests, his limitations and his arguments are. Negotiating is both science and art. The scientific aspect includes the preparation, and the availability of information, while the artistic side depends on the partners' abilities, style and attitudes.

> This quote, allegedly from Abraham Lincoln, explains how he prepared himself for negotiation: "I spend one-third of my time thinking what I am going to say and two-thirds thinking about the other and what he is expected to say."

The subject of price negotiation is price itself. It must be made clear, however, that price cannot be interpreted in a vacuum. When we speak about price, we inevitably imply the product, and a host of other factors that also have an impact on price. The quantity of the commodity, the delivery time. and manner, scheduling, transportation costs, warranty, guarantee, repair services, spare parts, instructions for use, training before sale, the required technical accessories, installation, services before, during or after sale, discounts (quantitative, financial, functional) related products and options, replacement policy, waiver from the contract or its modification, defective products, compensations, etc.).

Negotiating team members put the visiting cards of the others down at the table to be able to distinguish them and call them by name.

14.5. The process of negotiation

The process of price negotiation including the period required for preparation is illustrated in Figure 14.1.

Figure 14.1. The process of price negotiation

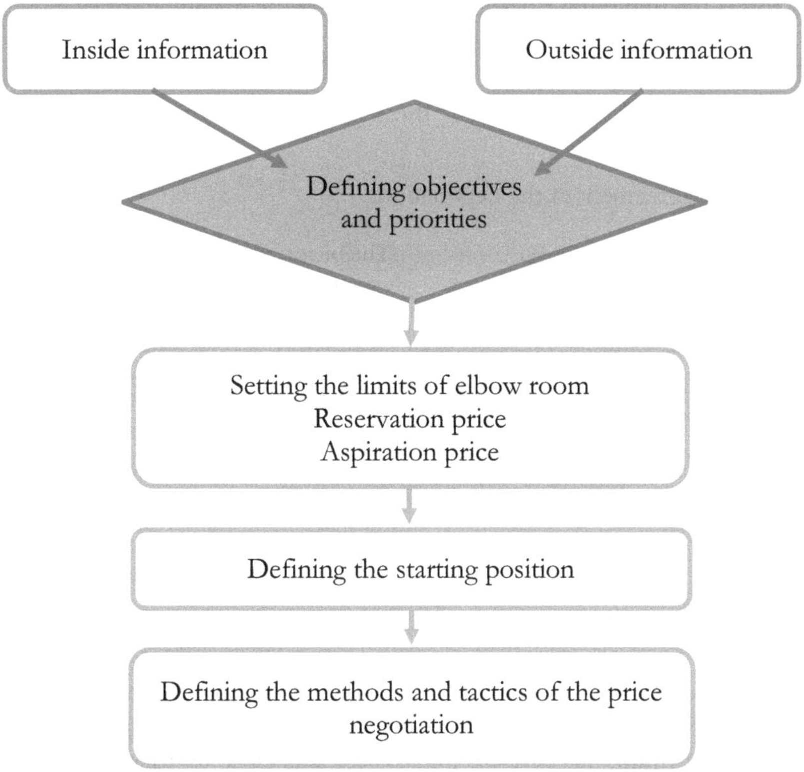

14.5.1. The initial offer and the zone of potential agreement

To facilitate clarification of the topic we have included here an example that is frequently quoted in the literature.

Mr Smith and Mr Tailor are negotiating the sale of a car. Smith, the seller, is ready to accept any price over $10,000 for his second-hand car. Tailor, the potential buyer, is willing to pay at most $15,000 for it. Both of them know their own so-called reservation prices and the price at which they lose interest, but they are uncertain about the partner's intentions. Consequently they do not know that every $10 000 and $15 000 price is better than not having a deal at all. Tailor asks Smith to make an offer. Smith thinks that Tailor is prepared to pay at least $13 000 but will lose interest at $17 000. He does not want to offend Tailor with a very high offer therefore he decides to set the price of $16,000 for the car. Before making the first offer, Tailor did not try make out at what price Smith would lose interest. The offer is $1 000 more than he had expected. He believes that the minimum price Smith sets is at least $15 000. For a second it comes to his mind that the deal cannot be done. Feeling a little uncertain, he offers $13 500. They continue bargaining: Smith says 15 000 and Tailor offers 14 000.

Then Smith suggests that they halve the difference and let the price be $14,500. Tailor happily accepts, because he has bought the car at a cheaper price than what he originally meant to pay.

What happened during the negotiation process? Why was the final price close to Tailor's reservation price, and why was Smith able to pocket the larger part of the profit? Before answering these questions let us first review the related notions (Figure 14.2).

- *Reservation price* is the ultimate price at which the seller or the buyer is still willing to close a deal; for the seller this is the minimum price and for the buyer the maximum price.
- *Aspiration level*: the price that the partners strive to reach.
- *Zone of Possible Agreement:* limited on one side by the seller's, and on the other side by the buyer's reservation price.

Figure 14.2. The zone of possible agreement at the negotiation.

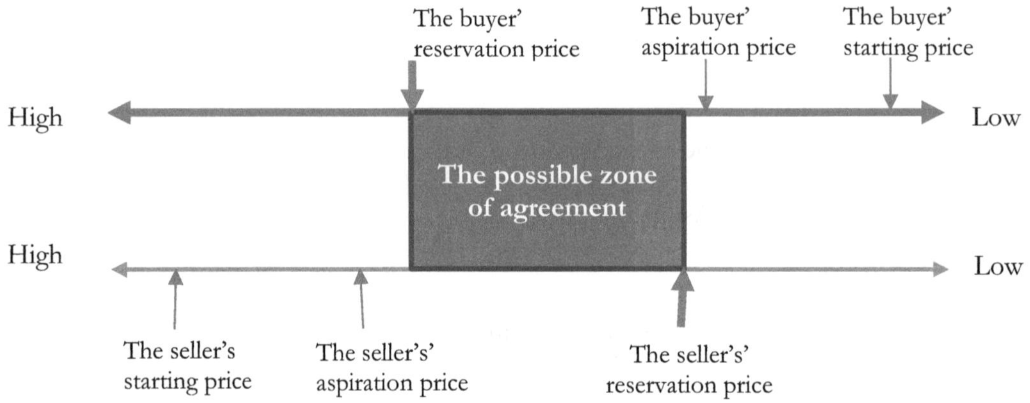

Source: Morris and Morris, 1992, p 78

The price became unfavourable for Smith, because his initial offer was close to Tailor's reservation price. The *initial offer* is always extremely important, because in this situation we can observe the psychological phenomenon called 'anchor' in literature (Wu, 1996c). Every further offer is related to that. The anchor is something like the reference price that we have already mentioned in the chapter on consumer behaviour. Similarly, to reference price, an anchor can be an external, or even an irrelevant price. WU (1996b) illustrates the latter with the following experiment:

The Japanese interpreter – who was, by the way, very hard to understand, seemed to have said: the firm would accept a price of $12 (and $32 for the control group). When somebody asked him about it again, he said he had never mentioned prices. What is more, the Japanese explicitly request the partner to give their price quotation the next day. Consequently, the price of $12 (or 32 $ for the control group) was irrelevant, because the Japanese never mentioned it. In spite of that, the next day the group whose members seemed to have heard $12, offered $19.50 on average, and finally those who had heard 32 dollars, offered $27.78.

The first offer is always important during the management of the negotiation. This is a starting point, depending on how realistic or how unrealistic the initial offers are. It also depends on the reliability of the information available to the bidders on the true intention of the bidders. The negotiating partner strives to reach the so-called aspiration price. It is important to define this price beforehand because its absence can make the negotiators become uncertain during the process of negotiation.

14.5.2. The psychological trap of price negotiation, the definition of the situation

The initial price was the first trap. The second was a psychological trap (Wu, 1996a) the definition, description and presentation of the situation, called framing in English. There is a well-known story about the shoe export business and two market researchers who are sent into an African country. The report that the first writes says there is no market for shoes there at all, because "everybody walks barefoot". The second researcher speaks about extraordinary opportunities, saying "everybody here walks barefoot". It is used to explain that people may have a different understanding of the same phenomenon. Let us take another example: there is a one-litre bottle with half-a litre of drink in it. Some say: the bottle is "half full", others may say the bottle is "half empty". The description is different in meaning and in connotation.

During bargaining, the practising negotiator always chooses a description that will make the given situation, his offer, or the discount he has just offered look more attractive for his partner. Let us suppose, for example, that the price of a house worth 200,000 dollars is being discussed and at this point the difference between the seller's and the buyer's offer is only 10 000 $. The buyer, or his agent, can sum up the situation as follows: "The difference is a mere 5% and this small amount will certainly not prevent you from buying the house of your dreams". Or, if he uses a trickier approach, the buyer or his agent can say, "This amount is hardly more than the price of a daily glass of beer that I could save in the next ten years by not drinking". In contrast with this, the buyer may see the same situation differently, thinking, "This amount will be just enough to buy some new furniture".

When describing the offer, or formulating a newly granted discount, the negotiating parties will frame the event in such a way that:

(1) the wording should significantly emphasize its value (or its worthlessness, as the case may be),

(2) the other party is granted some kind of justification for accepting the offer or a similar discount,

(3) a fair opportunity is given for sharing the benefits gained during the negotiation.

There are some useful rules to observe in the course of the wording:

- *Gain-loss.* Psychological studies have proved that a loss always seems to be bigger than a gain i.e. people make more effort to avoid losses. Losing x dollars causes more pain than the pleasure found in gaining the same amount. Whether a certain price is regarded as a loss or a gain is merely a matter of judgement. Thinking about prices, people do not use absolute sums most of the time but compare them with reference prices. Therefore the negotiating partner should find the references that make the outcome of the negotiation look like a gain.

- *Short-term, long-term.* Our judgement of the result of the negotiation largely depends on whether it is related to the long or short term. People often fail seriously to face the fact that small daily expenses can pile up to quite large amounts if calculated for a longer period (in California, for example, smoking a packet of Marlboro cigarettes a day costs more than 2,5 thousand dollars annually at 2017 prices). Consequently, the time factor chosen for the definition of the situation may play an important role in persuading the partner.

- *Addition – subtraction.* It is a very effective element of negotiating technique to contract certain elements of the supply and present it to the buyer in this form. A 300 dollar CD player for the car may seem expensive for the buyer, but if it is compared to the car that costs 25,000 dollars and offered as part of a package, its cost is, in fact, hardly more than1.2% of the price. In other situations, the road to success is the other way round; it happens quite frequently

that the price of industrial equipment is much higher than the competitive product. The negotiator can present it cleverly, removing the additional functions one by one and prove to the buyer that the basic function is actually cheaper than that of the competitors.

- *Emphasizing the ultimate usefulness.* There are products which represent relatively little value, but, as parts of a larger system, they have an important role in the operation of the whole system (for example, the role that car tyres play in the safety of the car, or computers in the control of a nuclear power plant). The best way to present these products is to emphasize their ultimate usefulness.

The technique of presentation called 'framing' is always present at price negotiations. Since this technique can be manipulative, the partners in the negotiation should be prepared for it. They should go through the process in their minds and try to imagine the various wordings and the ways in which these can be reframed and put into different, more favourable forms. (Such a reframing happened, for example, when the buyer of the 200,000-dollar- house came up with a different interpretation of the $10,000. The unprepared negotiator often adopts the approach used by his partner (thereby falling into the trap) he cannot produce a new approach, because he will be able to continue his efforts only in the direction set by his partner).

14.5.3. Price negotiations and consumer types

The seller should be fully aware of the type of buyer he is dealing with when choosing the right approach. In the case of industrial goods, for example, purchasing is often highly centralized, performed by so-called buying centres. The staff members of the buying centres responsible for the centre's various functions are listed in literature as follows: initiators, users, buyers, gatekeepers and deciders. Each type should be approached differently for business negotiations.

Buyers of consumer goods can also be grouped (Harmer-matrix); there are price sensitive buyers, loyal buyers, value-oriented buyers and buyers for whom convenience is a priority.

The different buyer types require different approaches during price negotiations, because they differ in their interests, and also in their opinion of the products, or values and prices of the other businesses.

14.5.4. Sources of mutual gain

Business partners engage in negotiation because they are convinced that in the end they will be able to close down the negotiations with a benefit, or gain. The gains, however, cannot be realized unless they understand what the source of the advantage is. Negotiating partners are typically very different, have conflicting interests and opinions of the topic in question. But, strangely enough, it is precisely these differences that can become the source of mutual advantage. Mutual gain can be obtained, for example, when both parties get something valuable in return for another thing that they do not consider as valuable. (Wu, 1996c). It is conceivable, for example, that postponing a payment is more important for a retailer than low price. At the same time, the manufacturer is more interested in the price and if he can reach the price he expects to, he accepts a postponement of, say, two months on the part of the retailer. Here again mutual gain is based on the difference, namely the two parties have different judgements of the cash flow.

14.5.5. Some technical and tactical proposals for price negotiation

Negotiation is a science and art at the same time; this is the reason why we cannot find any eternal rules or recipes for its technique and tactics. Certain experiences and customs can, however, assist the less experienced negotiator to become familiar with this extraordinary genre.

Every personal negotiation can be divided into stages. The first is called *opening*. It immediately follows the introductions, and it is in this part that the partners mutually agree on:

- the topics they are going to discuss,
- the agenda of the negotiation, i.e. the order in which the topics are discussed,
- the time frame or schedule of the negotiation, and - depending on the time available - the speed of the negotiation. It is also in this stage that all participants are introduced to one another.

EXHIBIT 14.2. ONE EXAMPLE FOR NEGOTIATING THE AMOUNT OF ROYALTY.

Let us construct a hypothetical experiment to find out how it is possible to resolve differences between two parties in the hope of mutual gain. I sincerely hope that the publisher of this book will not be insulted if I use him as an example.

Let us assume that the author and the editor have significantly different opinions about the expected success of the book. The publisher believes that at most 10 000 copies of it can be sold. With this possibility in mind he offers the author a royalty of $5,000 (lump sum). The author believes (as do all authors) that the book will be a great success, and as many as 50 000 copies can be sold. Therefore, he expects to be paid at least $8,000.

Both parties seem to be adamant; there is no hope of an agreement. For the sake of simplicity, let us assume that there are only two possible outcomes: either 10,000 copies or 50,000 copies are sold. The publisher gives a chance of 80% to the smaller number and only 20% to the larger number. In contrast with this standpoint, the author predicts 80 % for the 50 000 copies sold and 20% for the lower number.

The conflict can be solved if they make a conditional agreement, like this:

- The publisher can offer a lump sum of $3,000 and an additional sum of $8,000 to be paid when 40,000 more copies have been sold.
- In this case the publisher will probably incur the following costs: (0.80 × 3 000) + (0.20 × 10 000) = $4 400, which is lower than his original offer.
- The author will probably have the following income: (0.20 × 3 000) + (0.80 × 10 000) = $8 600, which exceeds the minimum he has envisaged..
- Both parties finish the negotiation with a gain over the original expectation. The deal can be concluded.

Both parties have exchanged something they find less valuable, for another thing they value greatly. For the publisher it is not too much to promise $8,000 more, because in his opinion the probability of the realization is not more than 20%. At the same time, the author received real value, because it is nearly certain that his version will come true.

The opening stage should be spent in the hope of reaching an agreement. An important issue that may even influence the outcome of the negotiation is, who should chair it? It is usually the host who assumes the task of launching the talks. After that the parties should have about the same length of time to state their points if they are to have a well-balanced discussion. Participants are highly recommended to use the dialogue form, with short questions and answers.

The opening is followed by the stage of *exploration.* The purpose is to get to know the standpoints of the parties. If the negotiation is of a larger scale, both parties first present their views. These introductory speeches are still independent from each other, both parties focus on their own viewpoints. At this stage, the participants do not react to the other's comments. The presentation of the initial standpoint should touch upon the following points:

- what is our approach to the topic in question?;
- which are the areas that should be discussed during negotiations?;
- what are our interests?;
- what do we seek to achieve?;
- what are our priorities, which do we consider the most important issue?;
- declaration of our commitment and contribution to making the negotiation a success;
- results of earlier dealings with the partner, the conclusions, the related worries and hopes.

The introduction should be brief; at this stage the statements are not very detailed. The negotiation is lateral rather than vertical (going deep in the discussion of a point). During this time, the other partner is supposed to listen attentively (and not waste his time looking for counter-arguments). If there is anything he does not understand he should ask questions and offer feedback at the end, making sure he has understood the point.

After the exploration both parties have a chance to modify the negotiating strategy they have planned beforehand.

After the exploration *an offer is made.* The guiding principle in this situation should always be to start with the highest possible bid that can be justified, for the following reasons:

- the initial price sets a limit that we cannot exceed later on;
- the initial price influences the partner's value judgement;
- it gives possibility for manoeuvre in later stages of the negotiation and, thanks to all of these,
- it can influence the outcome of the negotiation.

You must take care not to let the bid be too unrealistic, because this will give the impression that you are not very serious. When the time comes to make the offer, the bidder should appear determined, be able to express himself clearly, avoid making excuses, or giving explanations. He is also advised to focus not only on the price i.e. make the bid well founded, including all the related conditions.

The bidding stage is followed by *bargaining.* In order to be successful in this stage it is necessary to:

- Gain a clear picture of the partner's standpoint. This requires the careful study of every point of the bid. We must be able to find the points in which he is flexible and those where he is rigid. Always ask the reason why.
- Assess the differences in the actual situation, the views, opinions on the various points and interests.

- Analyse the location of the borderlines of the possible zone of agreement, the partner's requirements, whether they are more determined and to what extent, etc.

It should also be decided whether we accept the offer or not, whether we need a new offer, or prefer to make a counter-bid. We can also decide to put the whole negotiation into a different context or propose an agreement that is completely different from the original (e.g. co-operation instead of selling, etc.).

The golf club is one of the favourite places where businesspeople can meet for informal discussions.

Source: https://www.quora.com/Business/Who-are-some-of-the-successful-but-not-well-known-Indian-businessmen?page_id=14#!n=54

There are some tactical knacks that you may want to use in the course of bargaining:

- You might consider the ding-dong fight. For this purpose, you should review all the topics that might be brought up, identify the points where you can give in, and also decide what you would like to get in return.
- If you choose the tactics of discounts, you should bear in mind the following:
  1. to withhold the discounts until the moment you really need them,
  2. ask and receive discounts in return for discounts,
  3. discounts should be granted at a similar pace,
  4. you should get your partner to believe that every discount we give is of great importance.
- It is a useful knack to direct attention to things that are not very important for us, but are very important for the partner, and can be used to make the partner feel successful.
- If the talks get stuck, we can always apply techniques that help to move on, for example:

- "it is beyond my competence" (it gives you a chance to withdraw, ask for instructions, consider the next step, etc.).
- Ask for a break or suggest having one. The break is a good opportunity to reconsider the situation and prepare for further negotiation.
- Set a deadline: if the parties agree on a specific time when they intend to close down the negotiation, this may have a stimulating effect on concentration.
- "What if..." tactics: bringing up new approaches.
- Suggesting full openness: (will only work if it is mutual): for example, speak sincerely about restricting factors, etc.

There are, of course, several other knacks you can use (bluffing, entertainment, including some sport, etc.). Which of these you want to use should be carefully deliberated, with due regard to the circumstances.

Most importantly: do not forget negotiation is science and art at the same time.

The purpose is for the parties to feel satisfied when they leave

BIBLIOGRAPHY

Agárdi I., (2010). *Kereskedelmi marketing és menedzsment (Sales and Marketing Management)*, Akadémiai Kiadó, Budapest

Aggarwal - Cha (1998). Asymmetric price competition and store vs national brand choice, *Journal of Product and Brand Management*, Vol.7. No.3., pp. 244-253

Alavi, H., (2016). Mitigating the Risk of Fraud in Documentary Letters of Credit, *Baltic Journal of European Studies*, Vol. 6. Issue 1. Published Online: 2016-02-16

Allenby, G.M. and Rossi, P.E. (1991). Quality Perceptions and Symmetric Swithching between Brands, *Marketing Science*, Vol. 10, No. 3. Summer, 1991, pp. 185-204

Anthony, S. (2016). Kodak's Downfall Wasn't About Technology, July 15, 2016, *Harvard Business Review* (https://hbr.org/2016/07/kodaks-downfall-wasnt-about-technology)

Armstrong, M. (2006). Price Discrimination, University College London, Working paper

Baker, R.J. (2006). *Pricing on Purpose*, John Wiley & Sons, Inc., Hoboken, New Jersey

Bakos, Y. - Brynjolfsson, E. (1998). Bundling Information Goods: Pricing, Profits and Efficiency *Working Paper Series, MIT Sloan School of Management*, April, 1998.

Barancsuk, J (2008). *Mikrogazdaságtan (Micro Economics)*, PTE, KTK Kiadó, Pécs

Barua, A., Gruner, D. and Bandyopadhyay, S. (2015). Global value chains: More a development strategy than a mere process, In: *Global Economic Outlook 4th Quarter 2015*, Deloitt University Press

Berend, D., Á. (2012). *A Guanxi szerepe a nemzetközi kapcsolati marketingben, (The role of guanxi in the international relationship marketing)* NKE KTK, Budapest

Black, J. (2003). Sharper Tools for Discriminatory Pricing, July31, 2003, *Business Week*

Blattberg - Wisniewski (1989). Price-Induced Patterns of Competition, *Marketing Science* 8, pp. 291-301

Bolen - Davis (1997). Overreaching for mass retailers, *The McKinsey Quarterly*, No. 4. pp. 40-53

Bradley, Frank (1995). *Marketing Management - Providing, communicating and delivering value.* Prentice Hall

Broeckelmann, Ph. and Groeppel-Klein, A (2008). Usage of mobile price comparison sites at the point of sale and its influence on consumers' shopping behavior, *The International Review of Retail, Distribution and Consumer Research*, Vol. 18, No. 2, May 2008, 149–166

Bush, P.S. - Houston, M.J. (1985). *Marketing*, Strategic Foundation, Irwin, Homewood, Illinois

Cavero and Cebollada (1999). Loyalty and Price Elasticity. A segmentation Analysis, *Marketing and Research Today*, February, pp. 15-21

CEER (2016). Status Review Ref: C15-LTF-43-03 1 April 2016, Council of European Energy Regulators asbl Cours Saint-Michel 30a, Box F – 1040 Brussels, Belgium Arrondissement judiciaire de Bruxelles – RPM 0861.035.445,

Chernev, A. (2003). Reverse Pricing and Online Price Elicitation, Strategies in Consumer Choice, *Journal of Consumer Psychology, 13*(1&2), 51–62

Cooper, Robin (1994). Sony Corporation: The Walkman Line, *Harvard Business School*, 9-195-076, pp 1-9

Corey, Raymond E. (1982). Note on Pricing Strategies for Industrial Products, *Harvard Business School*, 9-582-124, pp 1-15

Coulter, K., S. And Coulter, R., A. (2007). Distortion of Price Discount Perceptions: The Right Digit Effect, *Journal of Consumer Research* Vol. 34 August 2007

Davey- Childs- Carlotti (1998). Why your price band is wider than it should be? *The McKinsey Quarterly*, No. 3. pp. 116-127

David W. Gillen, D.,W., Morrison, W.,G., and Stewart, C. (2006). *Air Travel Demand Elasticities: Concepts, Issues And Measurement, Final Report*, http://www.fin.gc.ca/consultresp/Airtravel/airtravStdy_-eng.asp

Dean, Joel (1976). Pricing Policies for New Products, *Harvard Business Review*, Nov.-Dec. pp. 1-12

Deloitte (2016). Global Powers of Retailing 2016 - Navigating the new digital divide.

Diller, Hermann (1999). Entwicklungslinien in Preistheorie und –management, *Marketing*, 21. Jahrgang, No. 1. pp. 39-61

Ding, M., Ross Jr., W.,T.and. Rao, V., R. (2010). Price as an Indicator of Quality: Implications for Utility and Demand Functions, *Journal of Retailing*, Vol. 86, Issue 1, pp 69-84

Dolan, Robert ,J. (1984). Basic Quantitative Analysis for Marketing, *Harvard Business School* (584-149)

Dolan, Robert ,J. (1984). Pricing Policy, *Harvard Business School* (9-585-044)

Dolan, Robert ,J. (1995). How Do You Know When the Price is Right, *Harvard Business Review*, Sept-Oct. 1995

Economides, N. (1997). The Telecommunications Act of 1996 and its Impact, Presented at the Annual Telecommunications Policy Conference, Tokyo, Japan, December 4, 1997.

Emmons, Willis (1993). Note on Pricing and Public Policy, *Harvard Business School* 9-794-027 1-15 pp.
Estelami, H. (1999). The Computational Effect of Price Ending sin Multidimentional Price Advertising, *Journal of Product and Brand Management*, Vol, 8, no 3, pp 244-56
Estelami, H. (2008). Reflection and Emerging Perspectives on the Strategic Implications of a Multi-dimentional Pricing Environment, In: Rothenberg and Siems (eds): *Pricing Perspectives*, Palgrave MacMillan, New York, pp 58-75
Fabiani, S., Druant, M., Hernando, I., Kwapil, C., Landau, B., Loupias, C., Martins, F., Mathä, T. Y., (2005). The Pricing Behavior of Firms In The Euro Area, *European Central Bank Working Paper Series*, No. 535 / October 2005
Fishburn, Odlyzko, Siders (1999). Fixed versus unit pricing for information goods: competition, equilibria, and price wars, First Moday, Internet
Forbis, J.L. and Mehta, N.T. (1981). Value-based strategies for industrial products, *Business Horizons*, Vol. 24, May-June, pp. 32-42
Gabor and Granger (1964). Price Sensitivity of the Consumer, *Journal of Advertising Research*, 4 /Dec. 1964/ 40-44 pp.
Gabor and Granger (1966). Price as Indicator of Quality: Report on an Inquiry, *Economica*, Vol. 33. No 12. Pp. 43-70
Gabor, André (1988). *Pricing - Concepts and Methods for Effective Marketing*, Gower
Gady, F-S., (2016). Sri Lanka Mulls Purchase of New Fighter Aircraft August 14, 2016, *The Diplomat* (http://thediplomat.com/2016/08/sri-lanka-mulls-purchase-of-new-fighter-aircraft/);
Garda and Marn (1993). Price War, *The McKinsey Quarterly*, No. 3. pp. 87-100
Gerardi, K., S., and Shapiro, A., S. (2009). Does Competition Reduce Price Dispersion? New Evidence from the Airline Industry, *Journal of Political Economy*, 2009, vol. 117, no. 1
Ghemawat, P. (1985). Building Strategy on the Experience Curve, HBR From the March 1985 Issue
Gittins, P. and Luke, S. (2012). Impact of the recession on household spending, Office for National Statistics, 21 February 2012, http://webarchive.nationalarchives.gov.uk/20160105160709/ http://www.ons.gov.uk /ons/dcp171766_256980.pdf
GMA, SheSpeaks and Booz & Co (2009). Shopper Marketing 3.0: Unleashing the Next Wave of Value, the Grocery Manufacturers Association (GMA),
Goodman, Sam R. (1970). *Techniques of Profitability Analysis*, Wiley, New York
Gunatilleke, N. (2016). Cabinet nod to purchase multirole fighters, Thursday, August 11, 2016 - Daily News;
Hamilton, R. and Srivatava, J. (2008). Slicing and Dicing Your Pricing, *Harvard Business Review*, Nov, 2008
Hanna, N and Dodge, H.R. (1997). *Pricing - Policies and Procedures*, Macmillan Business
Heinrich, O., Mussa, A., Zerbi S. (2016). *How retailers can improve price perception — profitability*, McKinsey & Company, November 2016
Herrmann, Huber, Coulter (1997). Product and service bundling decisions and their effects on purchase intention, *Pricing Strategy & Practice*, Vol. 5., No. 3, pp 99-107
Hibbert, E.P. and Liu, J (1996). *International Market Research - a financial perspective*, Blackwell, Business
Hollander and Rassuli (1999). Shopping with Other People's Money: The Marketing Management Implication of Surrogate-Mediated Consumer Decision Making, *Journal of Marketing*, Vol. 63. No.2, pp. 102-119.
Hollensen, S. (2011). *Global Marketing, Fifth Edition*, Prentice Hall, Europe
Holmes, George (1995). To tender or to negotiate: the buyer's dilemma, *Journal of Marketing Practice: Applied Marketing Science*, Vol. 1., No. 3. pp. 7-17.
Hooley - Saunders (1993). *Competitive Positioning*, Prentice Hall
Howard, D. J, & Kerin, R. A. (2006). Broadening the Scope of Reference Price Advertising Research: A Field Study of Consumer Shopping Involvement, *Journal of Marketing*, Vol. 70 (October 2006), 185–204
Isler, Karl (2009). GDS capabilities, OD control and dynamic pricing, *Journal of Revenue and Pricing Management,* Vol. 8, 2/3, 255–266
Ismael P. Soler and Germán Gémar (2016). The impact of family business strategies on hotel room prices, *European Journal of Family Business* (2016) 6, 54-61 Available online 13 July 2016
Johnson, L., K. (2003). Duelling Pricing Strategies, *MIT Sloan Management Review*, Spring 2003
Kalyanaram, G and Winer R.S., (1995). Empirical Generalizations from Reference Price Research, *Marketing Science*, Vol. 14, No. 3 Supplement, Summer 1995, pp. 161-169
Karasiewicz, Grzegorz (1997). *Marketingowe strategie cen Polskie Wydawnictwo Ekonomiczne*, Warsawa
Kell, J. (2016). Adidas Is Once Again No. 2 in America, Oct 25, 2016, *The Fortune* (http://fortune.com/ 2016/10/25/adidas-under-armour-nike/)
Kimes, S.E. and Wirtz, J. (2003). Has Revenue Management Become Acceptable? *Journal of Service Research*, Vol 6. No.2 125-135
Kluge, Jürgen (1997). Reducing the cost of goods sold: Role of complexity, design, relationship *The McKinsey Quarterly*, No. 2. pp. 212-215
Knecht, Leszinsky, Weber (1993). Making profits after the sale, *The McKinsey Quarterly*, No. 4. pp. 79-86

Koku, Paul Sergius (1995). Price Signalling: does it ever work? *Journal of Consumer Marketing*, Vol. 12. 1. Pp. 45-49.
Kotler, P., & Keller, K. L. (2003). *Marketing Management: international edition.* Printice Hall. New Jersey.
Kotler, Philip (1994). *Marketing Management, Eighth Edition*, Prentice-Hall
Krafft, M. and Mantrala, M., K. (2010). *Retailing in the 21 st Century*, Springer, Heidelberg
Krämer, A., Jung, M., & Burgartz, B. (2016). A Small Step from Price Competition to Price War: Understanding Causes, Effects and Possible Countermeasures, *International Business Research*; Vol. 9, No. 3; 2016, pp. 1-13
Kranz, G. (2000). *Failure Is Not an Option: Mission Control From Mercury to Apollo 13 and Beyond*, Simon & Schuster, Paperbacks, New York
Leszinsky and Marn (1997). Setting value, not price, *The McKinsey Quarterly*, No. 1. pp. 98-115
Levens, M. (2010). *Marketing - defined, explained, applied*, Pearson, Boston.
Lichtenstein, Ridgeway, Netemeyer (1993). Price Perceptions and Consumer Shopping Behavior, *Journal of Marketing*, Vol. XXX. 234-245 pp.
Lii, D. Y. S., & Lee, M. (2006). Online advertised reference pricing: consumers' perceptions and responses. *Journal of Global Competitiveness*, 14(1), p37-50.
Lovelock Christopher and Jochen Wirtz (2007). *Services Marketing: People, Technology, Strategy*, 6th ed. Upper Saddle River, New Jersey: Prentice Hall.
Marn and Rosiello (1993). Managing Price, Gaining Profit, *Harvard Business Review*, Sept.-Oct. pp. 83-93
Marn, M., V., Roegner, E., V. and Zawada, C., C. (2004). *The Price Advantage*, Hoboken, NJ: John Wiley & Sons
Marshall, Arthur (1979). *More Profitable Pricing*, McGraw-Hill
Mazumdar, T., Raj, S.P. & Sinha I. (2005). Reference Price Research: Review and Propositions, *Journal of Marketing* Vol. 69 (October 2005), 84–102
McConnell, C., Brue, S., and Flynn (2008). *Economics*, McGraw-Hill Economics
McEachern, William A. (1988). *Economics*, South-Western Publishing Co., Cincinnati, Ohio
Meffert, H. and Bruhn, M. (1995). *Dienstleistungsmarketing*, Gabler, Wiesbaden
Meffert, H. (1998). *Marketing, 8. Auflage*, Wiesbaden, 1998
Mohan, B., Buell, R. W. and John, L. K., (2016). Lifting the Veil: The Benefits of Cost Transparency, *Harvard Business School Technology & Operations Mgt. Unit Working Paper* No. 15-017.Available at SSRN: https://ssrn.com/abstract=2498174 or http://dx.doi.org/10.2139/ssrn.2498174
Monroe, Kent B. (1990). *Pricing - Making Profitable Decisions*, McGraw-Hill International Editions
Morris, H. and Morris, G. (1990). *Market Oriented Pricing - Strategies for Management*, NTC Business Books, Lincolnwood, IL.
Mudie, Peter (1997). *Marketing - an analytical perspective*, Prentice Hall
Murphy, Terry (1998). *Service Bundling: a Profitable Strategy for Today's Market*, Medalist, Internet
Nagle and Holden (1995). *The Strategy and Tactics of Pricing - A Guide to Profitable Decision Making, Second Edition*, Prentice Hall
Niepmann F., Schmidt-Eisenlohr T. (2016). Trade finance around the world. http://voxeu.org/article/trade-finance-around-world, published on 11 June 2016
Nishikawa, Clare and Perrin, Jane, (2005). The Power of Private Label 2005, Executive News Report from ACNielsen Global Services, September 2005
Odlyzko, A. M. (2003). ICEC 2003: Privacy, Economics, and Price Discrimination on the Internet. Proceedings of the 5th International Conference on Electronic Commerce Pittsburgh, Pennsylvania; New York, NY: ACM, pp. 355–366.
Oxenfeld A., R., (1975). *Pricing Strategies*, AMACON, New York
Popescu, I., & Wu, Y. (2007). Dynamic pricing strategies with reference effects. *Operations Research*, 55(3), 413-429.
PWC: The World in 2050 Will the shift in global economic power continue? PWC 2015, February https://www.pwc.com/gx/en/issues/the-economy/assets/world-in-2050-february-2015.pdf
Rajendran, K. and Tellis, G (1994). Contextual and temporal components of reference price, *Journal of Marketing*, Vol. 58, pp. 22-34
Rekettye G. and Orosdy (1999). *A villamosenergia-szolgáltatással való fogyasztói elégedettség 1998 (Customer Satisfaction with the Electricity Supply – Summary of the research)* JPTE, KTK, Pécs,
Rekettye G. and Rekettye G., Jr. (2013). Global trends and their influence on future business performance, *International Journal of Business Performance Management* (IJBPM) 14: (1) pp. 95-110. (2013)
Rekettye, G and Liu J. (2001). Segmenting the Hungarian automobile market brand using perceptual and value mapping, *Journal of Targeting, Measurement and Analysis for Marketing* 9:(3) pp. 241-253.
Rekettye, G and Liu J. (2017). The Present State of the Game Hide and Seek in Pricing, *International Journal of Business Performance Management* (IJBPM), Vol. 19. No.2. pp 158-168.
Rekettye, G. (1999). *Értékteremtés a marketingben, (Value Creation in Marketing)* KJK., Budapest
Rekettye, G. (2011). *Multidimenzionális árazás (Multidimensional Pricing)* Akadémiai Kiadó Budapest
Rekettye, G. (2017). Hotel Makár Sport and Wellness, In: Deli-Gray, *Case Studies in Tourism*, Akadémiai Kiadó Budapest

Rekettye, G. (2009). A kereskedelmi márkák szerepe a versenyben (The Role of Private Brands in the Competition), *Magyar Tudomány* – Vol. 170. No 6.
Ringbeck, J. Starr, R. and Manning, C. (2010). The Airlines' Global Dilemma, Strategy + Business, 25 October, (http://www.strategy-business.com/article/00047?pg=all)
Rosenbloom, Bert (1995). *Marketing Channels (Fifth Edition)* The Dryden Press
Schindler and Rogulic (1998). Vom Preiskampf zur Steuerung des Preisimages, Absatzwirtschaft, *Zeitschrift für Marketing*, 12/98, pp. 68-72
Schindler- Kibarian (1996). Increased consumer sales response through use of 99-ending prices, *Journal of Retailing*, Summer 1996 v72 n2 p187(13).
Schindler, R., M. (2006). The 99 price ending as a signal of a low-price appeal, *Journal of Retailing* 82 (1, 2006) 71–77
Seiders, K. and G. B. Voss (2004). "From Price to Purchase," *Marketing Management*, Nov./Dec., 38-43.
Shapiro and Jackson (1978). Industrial Pricing to Meet Customer Needs, *Harvard Business Review*, Nov.-Dec. pp. 1-10
Shapiro, Benson P (1987). Variety Versus Value: Two Generic Approaches to Product Policy, *Harvard Business School*, 9-587-119, pp 1-16
Shapiro, Benson P (1998). Precision Pricing for Profit in the New World Order, *Harvard Business School*, 9-999-003, pp 1-24
Sherman, N. (2015). Unilever to close last Md. Factory, *The Baltimore Sun*, May 12, 2015,
Silva, W. (2016). Govt. Mulls International Fighter Jet Tender, May 1, 2016, Sunday Leader (http://www.thesundayleader.lk/2016/05/01/govt-mulls-international-fighter-jet-tender/)
Simon, Hermann (1995). *Preismanagement Kompakt*, Gabler, Wiesbaden
Sinha, P., K. & Prasad P. V. R. (2004) Reference Price: Impact of Shopper's Behaviour at the Store, *Decision,* Vol. 31, No. 1, January - June, 2004, pp 19-50
Sivakumar and Raj (1995). Quality-Tier Competition: Impacts of the 'Whether' Decisions and the Direction of Price Change, *Marketing Science Institute*, pp. 95-106
Sivakumar and Raj (1997). Quality Tier Competition: How Price Change Influences Brand Choice and Category Choice, *Journal of Marketing*, Vol. 61. No.3, pp. 71-85.
Slaughter and May (2010). An overview of the EU competition rules. Available at: http://www.slaughterandmay.com/media/64569/an-overview-of-the-eu-competition-rules-dec-2010.pdf
Stiglitz, J.E. and Walsh C.E. (2002). *Principles of Microeconomics, 3rd Edition*, New York: Norton,
Team T. (2015). Analysis of the Kraft-Heinz Merger, *The Forbes*, Mar 30, 2015
The state of private label around the world (2014). The Nielsen Company
Thomas J. and Morvitz, V, (2005). "Holistic Versus Digital Models of Multi-Digit Numerical Comparison" *Advances in Consumer Research* (Volume 32) pp 446-448
Thomassen, K., Lincoln, A. and Aconis, L. (2006). *Retailization - Brand Survival in the Age of Retailer Power*, Kogan Page Ltd.
Thompson, K.N. and Coe, B. J. (1997). Gaining sustainable competitive advantage through strategic pricing: selecting a perceived value price, *Pricing Strategy & Practice* Vol.5. 2, pp. 70-79.
Turpin, Dominique, V. (1995). Japanese Approaches to Customer Satisfaction: Some Best Practices, *Long Range Planning*, Vol. 28., No. 3. pp 84-90
Urbany, J. E., Dickson, P. R., & Kalapurakal, R. (1996). Price search in the retail grocery market. *The Journal of Marketing*, 60(2): 91-104.
Valentiny Pál (2004). Árprés és felfaló árazás, (Price press and predatory pricing) *Közgazdasági Szemle*, LI. évf., 2004. január (24–45. o)
Vanhuele M., and Drèze, X. (2002). Measuring the Price Knowledge Shoppers Bring to the Store, *Journal of Marketing*, Vol. 66, No. 4, October 2002, 72–85
Vanhuele, M., Gilles, L., Dreze, X. and Kenesei, Zs. (2005). How Do We Memorize Prices? A Numerical Cognition Perspective, *Advances in Consumer Research*, Volume 32, pp 445-449
Varian, Hal R. (1999) Differential Pricing and Efficiency, *First Monday*, Internet
Venkatesh, R. and Vijay Mahajan (2009). Design and Pricing of Product Bundles: A Review of Normative Guidelines and Practical Approaches, pp. 232-257, In: *Handbook of Pricing Research in Marketing*, Vithala R. Rao (editor). Northampton, MA: Edward Elgar Publishing Company.
Veres Z, (2009). *A szolgáltatásmarketing alapkönyve (The Basics of Service's Marketing)*, Akadémiai Kiadó, Budapest
Wallop, H. (2016). Supermarket price wars: are they real or phoney? 144 Mar 2014 *The Daily Telegraph* http://www.telegraph.co.uk/finance/newsbysector/retailandconsumer/10698008/Supermarket-price-wars-are-they-real-or-phoney.html
Wheatley and Chiu (1977). The Effects of Price, Store Image, and Product and Respondent Characteristics on Perception of Quality, *Journal of Marketing Research*, Vol. XIV. 181-186 pp.
Wilson, Robert B. (1993). Nonlinear Pricing, Oxford University Press

Wirtz, J. and Kimes, S.E. (2007). The Moderating Role of Familiarity in Fairness Perceptions of Revenue Management Pricing, *Journal of Service Research*, Vol 9. No.32, 229-240
Wu, George (1996a). Two Psychological Traps in Negotiation, *Harvard Business School*, 9-897-036, pp. 1-8
Wu, George (1996b). Exercises in Negotiation Analysis, *Harvard Business School*, 9-897-037, pp. 1-7
Wu, George (1996c). Sources of Joint Gains in Negotiation, *Harvard Business School*, 9-396-241, pp. 1-9
Xiaomeng Guo and Baojun Jiang (2016). Signalling Through Price and Quality to Consumers with Fairness Concerns. *Journal of Marketing Research,* Vol. 53, No. 6, pp. 988-1000.
Yoon, E and V. Kijewski (1997). Dynamics of the Relationship between Product Features, Quality Evaluation, and Pricing, *Pricing Strategy & Practice* Vol.5. 2, pp. 45-60.

INTERNET REFERENCES:

http://appleinsider.com/articles/13/04/16/price-war-breaks-out-between-apple-and-samsung-in-india
http://bbj.hu/economy/hungarian-car-fuel-sales-up-63-in-jan-sep_123343
http://blogs.marketwatch.com/great-columnist/2012/10/15/retail-markups-and-the-power-of-amazon/
http://ec.europa.eu/eurostat/statistics-explained/index.php/File:Price_level_index_for_4_groups_of_goods_and_services,_2015,_EU-28%3D100C1.png
http://ec.europa.eu/eurostat/statistics-explained/index.php/Population_structure_and_ageing
http://en.wikipedia.org/wiki/United_States_v._Microsoft
http://europa.eu/rapid/press-release_IP-08-1877_en.htm?locale=en)
http://exportstartguide.com/how-to-export/set-pricing-export-markets/ www.blackthornfoods.co.uk)
http://newatlas.com/future-of-air-travel-comfortable-seating/17751/#p129309
http://pcworld.hu/diszkriminativ-itunes-arak-20070404.html)
http://talkbusiness.net/2013/11/wal-mart-pg-discuss-joint-business-planning/
http://thenextweb.com/apple/2016/01/18/apple-raising-the-price-of-apps-in-7-countries-within-72-hours-due-to-exchange-rages/
http://variety.com/2014/music/news/degy-entertainment-breaks-down-artist-booking-fees-1201189498/
http://www.business.natwest.com/business.html
http://www.campaignlive.co.uk/article/1167582/damaging-premium-brands-introduce-cheaper-types-products-marketing-society-forum#fM0XUkTKbAhJUeQB.99
http://www.consumersinternational.org/news-and-media/resource-zone/the-relationship-between-supermarkets-and-suppliers-summary/
http://www.fin.gc.ca/consultresp/Airtravel/airtravStdy_1-eng.asp#1
http://www.gartner.com/newsroom/id/3323017
http://www.intel.com/content/www/us/en/silicon-innovations/moores-law-technology.html
http://www.moderntiredealer.com/news/719480/michelin-adds-new-uhp-tire-to-pilot-line
http://www.mydigitalfc.com/news/compare-online-and-offline-prices-sitting-home-383
http://www.oecd.org/competition/abuse/2375661.pdf
http://www.oecd-ilibrary.org/taxation/oecd-transfer-pricing-guidelines-for-multinational-enterprises-and-tax-administrations-2010_tpg-2010-en
http://www.priceintelligently.com/blog/all
http://www.sas.com/resources/whitepaper/wp_5073.pdf (22 September, 2010
http://www.unum.co.uk/hr/the-worlds-oldest-brands-and-the-secrets-to-their-longlives
http://www.verizon.com/home/fiostv
http://www.wsj.com/articles/wal-mart-and-p-g-a-10-billion-marriage-under-strain-1465948431
https://en.wikipedia.org/wiki/Electronics_(magazine)
https://pogue.blogs.nytimes.com/2007/09/06/the-iphone-price-drop/comment-page-3/
https://www.ftc.gov/tips-advice/competition-guidance/guide-antitrust-laws/price-discrimination-robinson-patman
https://www.macstories.net/stories/the-great-disparity-in-global-itunes-prices/
https://www.westminster.gov.uk/parking-zones-and-prices
www.ceer.eu/portal/page/portal/EER_HOME/EER_PUBLICATIONS/CEER_PAPERS/Cross-Sectoral/2016/C15-LTF-43-03_DSO-Unbundling_Status_Review-1-Apr-2016.pdf.

INDEX